Via tazzoli 3
outlet round
caner

DESIGNER BARGAINS IN ITALY

From

The first English language guide to 'Made in Italy'
brand names now in its 5th edition!

co so
como

Editoriale Shopping Italia

Lo ScopriOccasioni   2005   8th edition   ISBN 88-86132-12-3
Designer Bargains in Italy   2005   5th edition   ISBN 88-86132-13-1

Published by:
Editoriale Shopping Italia srl
Via Santa Valeria, 4
20123 Milano - MI
Italy   Tel. 02 72008068
For information:
Tel/Fax 034486176
E-mail: info@scprioccasioni.it
www.scprioccasioni.it
ISBN 88-86132-13-1

Publisher   Theodora van Meurs
Graphics   Jenneke terHorst
Layout   Zincograf - Farigliano - CN
Printer   Milanostampa - A.G.G. Farigliano - CN

Advertising ISR@libero.it

CONTENTS

Italy, as the world's no.1 producer of luxury goods, remains a bargain hunters paradise. In this guide, the 5th edition, over 1100 of the best factory outlets have been carefully selected, reviewed and updated, with all the big designer names well represented, a veritable Who's Who of 'Made in Italy' brand names. To this heady mixture we added some big city bargain basements known for their designer clothing at competitive prices, vintage shops, regional lists of amusing antique/brocante fairs or local markets and some highly specialized artisans who truly represent the backbone of Italian fashion.

The maps on the inside of the bookcover show where to find a high concentration of silk or cashmere manufacturers or the areas that are best for shoes, handbags, clothing, jewelry or designer kitchenware. The English/Italian dictionary on page 6 and the size charts on page 10 will make your shopping a breeze.

All the outlets in this guide have been visited to ensure that the detailed information is correct and up to date. Our website www.scprioccasioni.it will post any unforeseen changes, closures or major new addresses. We have tried to give a straightforward account of the merchandise for sale and do not carry endorsements. Our reader's comments and shopping experiences are highly valued by us and we would appreciate hearing from you either by e-mail at info@scprioccasioni.it or by sending a fax to 0039034486176.

Visiting some of the industrial zones away from the usual tourist cities like Florence, Venice or Rome will show you a different, hard working country that is the unseen sight of the Italian peninsula. We, your shopping scouts, Sally, Lucia, Laura Jane, Valentina & Theodora hope you have as much fun discovering this hidden world of high quality workmanship and innovative design as we did in finding these factory outlets for you!

The guide has been arranged from North to South:

Aosta, Piedmont, Lombardy, Veneto etc. to finish with Sardinia then alphabetically by province, by town and by subject

Region: Piedmont,
province: Alessandria
town: Casale
subject: Clothing

*see also the geographical index on page 312 and the list of provinces on page 320.

All prices are quoted in Euro € and rounded. All sizes are Italian.

*see size converter chart on page 10).

Bargain Shopping Tips
Opening hours:

- Italian opening hours are subject to sudden change. Call first if you plan to make a special trip.
- On Monday morning only food stores and local markets are open.
- In August most factory outlets are closed the 2nd and 3rd week of the month, some the whole month.
- Especially in the central and southern part of Italy in summer some shops open later in the afternoon and stay open later.

Shopping tips:

- Buying a lot, showing this guide and paying in cash is still the strongest incentive for an additional price cut.
- The American Express credit card is not widely accepted by factory outlets in Italy.
- Check merchandise for possible defects, missing buttons, mismatched sizes.
- Be prepared to carry your purchases and keep an eye on your handbag at all times.
- Bear in mind that not every outlet has changing rooms but always try everything on anyway.

Good morning, I am looking for...

Good Morning/Good afternoon	Buongiorno
Good evening	Buonasera
Goodbye (formal)	ArrivederLa
Goodbye (informal)	Arrivederci
Bye (Informal)	Ciao
Mrs.	Signora,
Miss	Signorina
Mr.	Signor
Please	Per favore, prego
Thank you	Grazie
It's a nice day	È una bella giornata
I am cold	Ho freddo/a
I am too hot	Ho troppo caldo/a
I am looking for	Sto cercando
Can you please show me	Mi puo far vedere per favore
Can I try this on?	Posso provarlo?
Can you tell me the price?	Quanto costa, per favore?
Do you have a smaller/bigger size?	C'e una misura più piccola/più grande?
Thank you, I'll take this	Grazie, lo prendo
Do you accept credit cards?	Posso pagare con una carta di credito?
I don't like it	Non mi piace
It is too expensive	Il prezzo è troppo alto
Do you have something at a lower price?	Cerco qualcosa ad un prezzo più basso
I would like to have a discount	Mi concede uno sconto?
Do you know a nice restaurant nearby?	Mi puo suggerire un ristorante vicino?

Clothing

A coat	Un cappotto
A jacket	Una giacca
A suit for men	Un completo
A suit for women	Un tailleur
A pair of pants	Un paio di pantaloni
Jeans	Un paio di jeans
Bermuda shorts	Un bermuda
A T-shirt	Un T-shirt
A top	Una maglietta
A heavy sweater	Un maglione
A sweatshirt	Una felpa
A cardigan	Un cardigan
A shirt	Una camicia
A blouse	Una camicetta
A skirt	Una gonna
A dress	Un abito

Accessories

English	Italiano
Gloves	Guanti
Hat	Cappello
Scarf	Foulard

Tie	Cravatta
Lingerie/underwear	Biancheria intima
Shoes	Un paio di scarpe
Sandals	Sandali
High heels/low heels	Tacchi alti/bassi
Socks/stockings	Calze/collant
Belt	Cintura
Wallet	Portafoglio
Handbag	Borsa
Evening bag	Borsetta
Travel bag	Borsa da viaggio
Necklace	Collana
Earrings	Orecchini
Bracelets	Braccialetto
Watch	Orologio da polso

Household goods

Cutlery	Posateria
Dinner set	Servizio da tavola
Cups	Tazze
Plates	Piatti
Coffeepot	Caffettiere
Pressure cooker	Pentola a pressione
Pasta pan	Pentola per la pasta

Food

Wine, red/white	Vino, rosso/bianco
X-virgin olive oil	Olio d'oliva X-Vergine
Honey	Miele
Balsamic vinegar	Aceto balsamico
Raw ham	Prosciutto crudo
Truffles	Tartufi
Sun dried tomatoes	Pomodori secchi

Sizes

Sizes	Misure
Small	Piccola
Medium	Media
Large	Grande
Xlarge	Molto grande
Too large/too small	Troppo grande/piccola
Half size	Mezza misura
Too narrow	Troppo stretto
Short sleeved	Manica corta
Long sleeved	Manica lunga
Collar size	Misura del collo

Styles

Sportive	Sportivo
Elegant	Elegante
Classical	Classico
Casual	Casual
Stylish	Stile
Sexy	Sexy
Fashionable	Molto moda
Subdued	Poco appariscente
Too old	Troppo vecchio
Too young	Troppo giovane
Just right	Perfetto

Colors

White	Bianco
Beige	Beige
Red	Rosso
Bordeaux	Bordeaux
Blue	Blu
Light blue	Azzurro
Yellow	Giallo
Green	Verde
Lilac	Viola
Pink	Rosa
Orange	Arancione
Brown	Marrone
Grey	Grigio
Black	Nero
Light brown	Marrone chiaro
Dark brown	Marrone scuro
Muted color	Colore neutro
Single color	Unicolore
Printed pattern	Fantasia
Plaids	A quadretti
Striped	Rigato
Embroidered	Lavorato
Flowery	A fiori

Quality

Sewn	Cucito
Machine made	Fatto a macchina
Hand made	Fatto a mano
A copy of	Una copia di
Fake	Imitazione
Alteration service	Servizio di sartoria
Made to measure	Su misura
To measure	Misurare

Fabrics

Wool	Lana
Acrylics	Acrilico
Cashmere	Cashmere
Cotton	Cotone
Silk	Seta
Linen	Lino
Rayon	Viscosa
Mixed	Misto
Lace	Pizzo
Jacquard	Jacquard
Leather	Pelle
Suede	Camoscio
Fur	Pellicce
Fake fur	Pellicce sintetico
Velvet	Velluto

On the road

City	Grande città
Town	Città
Village	Paese/villaggio
Motorway	Autostrada
Road	Strada
State road	Strada Statale - S.S.
Provincial road	Strada Provinciale S.P.
Bridge	Ponte
Harbour	Porto
Railway station	Stazione Ferroviario - S.F.
Hospital	Ospedale - H
Sports field	Campo Sportivo
Roundabout	Rotonda
Left	A sinistra
Right	A destra
Straight	Diritto
First street to the right	Prima a destra
Cross	Oltrepassare
Parallel	Parallela
Industrial Zone	Zona Industriale - Z.I.
Artisan Zone	Zona Artigianale - Z.A.

....
....
....
....
....
....

Sizing charts for clothes.
(This chart is for general reference only since sizes between different manufacturers vary)

Women
Dresses, coats, suits

	XS	S	M	L	XL
Italy	36	38-40	42-44	46-48	50-52
Europa	32	34-36	38-40	42-44	46-48
UK	28	30-32	34-36	38-40	42-44
USA	4	6-8	8-10	12	14-16

Knitwear

Italy	40-42	44	46	48	50-52
Europe	36-38	40	42	44	46-48
UK	34-34	36	38	40	42-44
USA	30-32	34	36	38	40-42

Shirts

Italy	38-40	42	44	46	48-50
Europe	36-38	40	42	44	46-48
UK/USA	30-32	34	36	38	40-42

Shoes

Italy/Europe	35-35.5	36-36.5	37-37.5	38-38.5	39-40
UK	2-2.5	3-3.5	4-4.5	5-5.5	6-7
USA	4-4.5	5-5.5	6-6.5	7-7.5	8-9

Men's sizes

Shirts

	S	M	L	XL
Italy/Europe	36-37	38-39-40	41-42	43-44
UK/USA	12-14	14.5-15-15.5	16-16.5	17-17.5

Knitwear, suits, coats

Italy/Europe	44-46	48-50-52	54-56	58-60
UK/USA	32-34	36-38-40	42-44	46-48

Socks

Italy/Europe	39-40	41	42	43	44	46
UK/USA	10	10.5	11	11.5	12	12.5

Shoes

Italy/Europe	39-40	41	42	43	44	45	46	47
UK/USA	6	7	8	9	10	11	12	13

Children

Shoes

Italy/Europe	19	20	21	22	23	24	25	26	27-28	29-30	30-3
UK/USA	3	4	5	6	7	8	9	10	11	12	13

Sizes	1 year	2/3 years	4 years	5/6 years	6/7 years
	18-20	21-23	24-26	27-29	30-32

NAME	DRESSES	SHIRTS	SKIRTS	SWEATERS	PANTS	JACKETS	SOCKS	SHOES

CUPBOARD	BED	CURTAIN	WINDOW	WALL PAPER	CHAIR	CARPET	SOFA	LIVING

Mc ArthurGlen Designer Outlet

Via della Moda, 1 - 15069 **Serravalle Scrivia** (AL) 0143 609000
10.00-20.00. October-May 10.00-21.00 C.C.:All Major

By car: From Genova or Milan take autostrada A7, exit Serravalle Scrivia. About 900 m. from the autostrada exit. From autostrada A26 take the exit at Novi Ligure at the connecting road between the A26 and the A7. The Designer outlet is about 7 minutes away.

The first major American style Designer outlet in Italy with more than 120 shops selling Versace, Etro, Byblos, 1°Classe Alviero Martini, Ck, Pal Zileri, Nike, Asics, Coccinelle, Mandarina Duck, Samsonite and many others discounted between 30% - 50%. Sales in January and July. Visiting this outlet center will take at least a morning, if not a day. There is something for everybody, a kiddy corner, bars, restaurants, parking and lots of good buys!

Vicolungo Outlets

Via Vicolungo - 28061 **Biandrate** (NO) 0321 835032
10.00-20.00. From Mon. to Thu. 10.00-19.00 C.C.:All Major

Autostrada A4, exit Biandrate, immediately after the intersection with the autostrada.

Recently opened 'open air' outlet center near the A4 from Turin to Milan. About 40 shops, mostly clothing and household linen, with all Italian brandnames like Mariella Burani, Vestebene, Zucchi, Gabel, Foppa Pedretti and many others. The outlet also offers cafés, children's play areas, large parking.

La Galleria Outlet Center

Via Tonale, 101 - 24061 **Albano S. Alessandro** (BG) 035 584611
10.00-21.00. Sunday closed C.C.:All Major

Autostrada A4, exit Seriate to S.S. 42, Sarnico/Lovere. Large parking.

A recently opened outlet center with about 30 indoor shops mostly selling clothing and lingerie. You'll find Playtex, Cacherel, Dim, Boggi, Vestebene, Coin, Golden Lady and many more. There is a bar on the first floor.

Franciacorta Outlet Village

Piazza Cascina Moie, 1 - 25050 **Rodengo Saiano** (BS) 030 6810181
10.00-20.00. Open on Sundays C.C.:All Major

Autostrada A4, exit Ospitaletto. Follow the directions for Moie and Franciacorta Outlet Village. It takes about 5 minutes to reach the outlet village from the autostrada.

Another fairly recent addition to the Italian outlet centers/villages, done in a rustic Lombard style, very pleasant, with bars, a restaurant, an icecream parlour, a gym and lots of parking. Mostly clothing shops and household linen by Bassetti, Bottega Verde, Benetton, Conte of Florence, Frette, Levi's, Mila Schon, Nike, O'Neill, Para, Pompea, Pupa, Stefanel, Swinger, Versace and others. Average savings between 10% and 30%.

Fashion District

Via Marco Biagi, Loc. Basse di Mezzo
46031 **Bagnolo S. Vito** (MN) 0376 25041
10.00-20.00 C.C.:All Major

Autostrada A22, exit Mantova Sud, the outlet center is right there.

Large, 35,000 sq.m., designed like a medieval village, with circa 60 shops representing more than 180 brand names: Mariella Burani, Just Cavalli, Gianfranco Ferré, Corneliani, Extè, Bassetti, Rosenthal, Villeroy & Boch. Also gourmet food, musical events, bars, restaurants and kindergarten. English spoken. There is another Fashion District outlet center at Valmontone near Rome.

Fidenza Village

Via S. Michele Campagna, Loc. Chiusa Fernanda
43036 Fidenza (PR)   0524 335511
10.00-19.00. Sat. & Sun. 10,00-20,00   C.C.:All Major

Autostrada A1, exit Fidenza, after 50 m on the left and well indicated. Large parking.

A fairly recent outlet center with an Egyptian theme. Circa 32 shops: Versace, Trussardi Jeans, Golden Lady (good deals), Bassetti, Stefanel, Samsonite, Reebock, Bodum, Mantellassi, Blunauta, Triumph, Bodum, a restaurant, bar, playground for kids, all very clean. Prices are circa 20 - 30 % lower.

San Marino Factory Outlet Center

Via III Settembre, 3 - **47031 Serravalle** (RSM)   0549 904014
9.00-19.00   C.C.:All Major

Autostrada A14, exit Rimini Sud to San Marino. After Dogana on the right, a bright balloon indicates the entrance to the outlet center.

A large outlet center full of tourists in the summer. There are 27 shops selling brand names like La Perla, Calvin Klein, Mariella Burani, Valentino, Superga, Vestebene, Ferré, Les Copains and others. All collections (last season or end of line) are discounted 50%, in July there are sales that last for at least 5 weeks.

The Mall - Gucci

Via Europa, 8 - **50060 Leccio Reggello** (FI)   055 8657775
10.00-19.00. Sunday 15.00-19.00   C.C.:All Major

Autostrada A1, exit Incisa in Val d'Arno, take the S.S. 69 Pontassieve/Firenze. After 6/7 km to the right after the Fina service station, follow directions. For info on the shuttle bus between Florence and the Mall tel. 055 8657775.

The Mall was opened on August 4, 2001 and now houses outlets by Bottega Veneta, Emanuel Ungaro, Ermenegildo Zegna, Giorgio Armani, Gucci, Tod's, Ferragamo, Loro Piana, Sergio Rossi, Yves Saint Laurent, Fendi, Valentino, La Perla, I Pinco Pallino e Marni. Large, luxurious, just like a store in the city, busy, busy, a lot of buses in the tourist season, very helpful personnel. There is a new coffeeshop and restaurant named Dot.Com on the premises.

McArthurGlen Outlet Center

Via Ponte di Piscina Cupa, 64
00128 Castel Romano (RM)   06 5050050
Sat. & Sun. 10.00-22.00   C.C.:All Major

From Rome: EUR Via C. Colombo-Via Pontina (SS148), exit Castel Romano
            EUR Via Laurentina-Via di Trigoria-Castel Romano
From the GRA, exit 26 - Via Pontina- dir. Pomezia-exit Castel Romano

This is the 2nd designer outlet center of McArthurGlen in Italy with more than 90 shops: Lagostina, O'Neill, Mariella Burani, Mandarina Duck, Moreschi, La Perla, D&G, Luca Barbieri, Stefanel, Viceversa, Rifle, North Sails, Golden Lady, Sutor Mantelassi, Etro and many others. The best brandnames in clothing, textiles, accessories, household goods, either first choice, stock, overproduction. Large parking, bars and restaurants and a play area for children.

Fashion District Valmontone

Loc. Pascolaro - **00038 Valmontone** (RM)   06 9599491
10.00-20.00   C.C.:All Major

From Rome, take the A1 south, exit Valmontone.

A fairly recent outlet center with around 100 shops, parking for 2000 cars, a bar and restaurant, a fast food, congress center and children's play area. There are both Italian and foreign brandnames: Mariella Burani, Just Cavalli, Gianfranco Ferré, Corneliani, Extè, Bassetti, Rosenthal, Villeroy & Boch and many others.

A O S T A   V A L L E Y

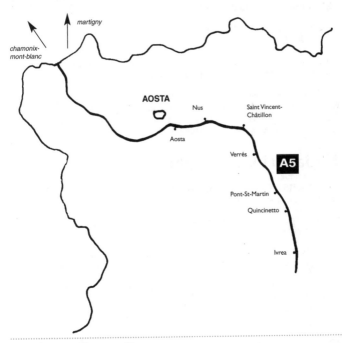

Maison Bertolin

Loc. Champagnolaz, 10 - 11020 Arnad (AO)
9.00-12.00/15.00-19.00 Open on Sundays

0125 966127
C.C.:All Major

Food, local products
GOOD PRICES

Autostrada A5, exit Pont S. Martin towards Aosta, circa 10 km. On the right, just before the village.

A famous local product is the 'Lardo di Arnad', a type of lard, unsmoked, rather sweet in taste and sliced very thinly. Other specialities are salami, speck, ham with juniper berries, game, goat cheese, herb cheese, local wines, apple vinegar and honey. This shop is a must for gourmet and gourmand, one can visit the premises and follow the preparation of all these delicacies. They speak English and French.

Guichardaz Outlet

Via Dent de Geant, 62 - 11013 Courmayeur - Verrand (AO)
9.30-12.30/15.30-19.30 Open on Sundays
Closed Wed., Thurs. morn. and October

0165 843019
C.C.:All Major

Clothing
DISCOUNTS

Just before Courmayeur, a major ski resort near the Mont Blanc tunnel. From Aosta and the provincial road S.S. 26 turn right to Verrand. The shop is on the right, after a small parking area.

The Guichardez shops in the center of Courmayeur sell all the best names in casual and ski clothes: Prada Sport, Aspesi, Tod's, Hogan, Fay, Ralph Lauren. In their outlet in Verrand last season's unsold items are reduced 50% and more. A cardigan with zip in cashmere for men € 345,00, a polo shirt in cotton by RL € 49,00, eiderdown jackets € 85,00.

Fifty Factory Store

Località Amerique, 125 - 11020 Quart (AO)
10.00-19.30. Monday 15.00-19.30

0165 775186
C.C.:All Major

Clothing, sportswear, casual, jeans
DISCOUNTS

Autostrada A5, exit Aosta Est. Follow the indications for Aosta Centre for about 600 meters, the Fifty Factory outlet is on the left, parking in front.

This large outlet has all the big brand names in casual like Nike, (a large space on the first floor), Marina Yachting, Invicta, Docks, Ragno, Pepper, Triumph, Company Corner. Prices are circa 30% less than normal shop price, and special offers abound. Layout is spacious with ample opportunity to browse, all sizes available.

Napapijri Geographic

Loc. Amerique, 75 - 11020 Quart (AO)
9.30-12.30/15.00-19.00. Saturday 10.00-19.00
Open on Sundays from 1/8-1/1

0165 773576
C.C.:All Major

Clothing, sportswear, casual
FACTORY OUTLET

Autostrada A5, exit Aosta Est towards the center, circa 500 meters. Look for a small shopping center on the left called L'Amerique, (Conbipel). Parking in front.

A very useful address for sharp, sporty dressers who like to hit the slopes in the latest of hightech gear. T-shirts, matching skipants, matching sweaters with or without slogans, colour coordinated, bags, socks, gloves, all at truly discounted prices. Sizes from S to XXL.

Ottoz Lorenzo

Loc. Saint Germain, 104 - 11020 Saint Christophe (AO)
9.00-20.00

0165 361148
C.C.:All Major

Wine, liqueurs
GOOD PRICES

Autostrada A5, exit Aosta Est for the center. Beyond Fifty Factory store on the left, look for the Ottoz sign. Ample parking.

Great choice in whiskey, you can find all the international brand names in various sizes and special packaging, at 'less than tax-free' prices. Also grappa, pastis, vermouth, wines plus local specialities like their own grappa 'Genepy'. Gift packs of 3-colour pasta, salami and whole hams. Free sampling of the Ottoz products.

[Map of Piedmont region showing cities and highways including BIELLA, NOVARA, VERCELLI, TORINO, ASTI, CUNEO, and various towns with autostrada markings A4/5, A5, A4, A21, A6, A26, A7]

L'Artigiano Torlasco
Via delle Rose, 6 - 15053 Castelnuovo Scrivia (AL)
8.00-12.00/14.00-18.00. Saturday closed

0131 826300
C.C.: All Major

Shoes
ARTISAN'S WORKSHOP

Autostrada A7, exit Castelnuovo Scrivia to the center, where we suggest to ask for directions.

In their factory outlet they sell men's shoes and small leather goods, also in croccodile and ostrich or other luxury materials. The style is classical, well made and elegant. They offer samples and showroom models at low prices. Their shop is in Via Gramsci, 43 where they also sell women's shoes, open only in the afternoon from 16.00-19.00.

Città della Moda
S.S.35bis dei Giovi Alessandria KM 19 - 15065 Frugarolo (AL)
9.00-12.30/15.30-19.30

0131 295301
C.C.: All Major

Clothing, household linen
GOOD PRICES

From Milan, Autostrada A7, exit Serravalle, circa 15 minutes towards Alessandria. From Turin take A21, exit Alessandria Est, 10 minutes towards Novi Ligure.

A large complex of 2.500mq offering medium quality clothing, lingerie, household linen, knitwear at more or less wholesale prices (an average saving of 30%). There are over sizes, showroom samples, special offers, a restaurant and a special play area for children.

Mc ArthurGlen Designer Outlet

Via della Moda, 1 - 15069 Serravalle Scrivia (AL)　　　　0143 609000
10.00-21.00　　　　　　　　　　　　　　　　　　　　　C.C.:All Major

Clothing, accessories
FACTORY OUTLET CENTER

By car: From Genova or Milan take autostrada A7, exit Serravalle Scrivia. The outlet is on road no. 35bis in the direction of Novi Ligure, about 900 meters from the autostrada exit. From autostrada A26 take the exit at Novi Ligure at the connecting road between the A26 and the A7. The Designer outlet is about 7 minutes away.

The first major American style Designer outlet in Italy with more than 120 shops selling Versace, Etro, Byblos, 1°Classe Alviero Martini, Ck, Pal Zileri, Nike, Asics, Coccinelle, Mandarina Duck, Samsonite and many others discounted between 30% - 50%. There is something for everybody, a kiddy corner, bars, restaurants, parking and lots of good buys!

Bquattro

S.S. 10 per Voghera, 93 - 15057 Tortona (AL)　　　　0131 881261
9.00-12.00/14.00-17.30. Saturday closed　　　　　　　C.C.:All Major

Lingerie, underwear
FACTORY OUTLET

Autostrada A7 or A21, exit Tortona. Take the provincial road to Voghera on the left, past 'Fiat' and the light-blue sign for 'Ditta Cantale'. The Bquattro factory is on the left immediately after Cantale.

Production of lingerie, bathing costumes, bikinis for various Italian or international brand names like Selene, Les Copains and Katherine Hamnett. In this large outlet they sell samples, remnants and seconds of last year's beachwear- and lingerie collection. All sizes from XS to XXL, also for bras and briefs. Bikinis go up to cup size 38d.

La Fabbrica dell'Oro

Via Circ. Ovest, 14 - 15048 Valenza (AL)　　　　0131 943195
9.00-12.30/15.00-19.00　　　　　　　　　　　　　C.C.:All Major

Jewelry, bijoux
ARTISAN'S WORKSHOP

Autostrada A26, exit Casale Monferrato Sud to the left, continue for 15 km. At the junction follow indications for Autostrada Alessandria and after the traffic light 'La Fabbrica D'Oro' is on the right. From Autoroute A7 exit at C. Scrivia.

Production of gold and silver jewelry: white and yellow gold 750 18kt, bracelets, necklaces in white gold, solid or hollow, earrings with clips or pierced. They also stock a large selection of watches. La Fabbrica dell'Oro has been around for more than 30 years. Valenza is a production center of gold jewelry.

Linclalor

S.S. 31km,18 - 15030 Villanova Monferrato (AL)　　　　0142 338411
9.30-13.30/15.00-19.00. Saturday 9.00-12.00/15.00-19.00　C.C.:All Major

Lingerie, underwear
FACTORY OUTLET

Autostrada 21, exit Casale Nord, turn right twice, continue for 1,5 km, the factory outlet is on the right inside the factory grounds. Or take S.S.31 km 17 Villanova Monferrato, main road Casale-Vercelli in front of the Shopping Center Monferrato.

A large factory outlet of practical underwear, pyamas, shirts and socks for the whole family. Styles tend to be of the wash and wear variety. Baskets full of samples offered at low prices, also many 2nd choice items. Lace briefs € 4,00, 5 pairs of stockings Filadora € 1,50, cotton chemises € 2,50 - € 6,00 (seconds).

Barbero Davide
Via Brofferio, 84 - 14100 Asti (AT)
8.00-12.00/14.00-18.00. Saturday & August closed

0141 594004
C.C.: All Major

Food, chocolate, coffee
FACTORY OUTLET

Autostrada A21, exit Asti Est to the center of Asti. The outlet is near the train station.

A must for chocomaniacs. They produce tons of chocolat but even more nougat (in Italian 'torrone'). White nougat, or covered in bitter chocolat, milk chocolat, nougat with hazelnuts, raisins, walnuts, all in excellent quality. They make up special baskets for Christmas and large chocolate eggs for Easter. Friendly, multilingual personel.

Spaccio John Peter
Via Caboto, 5 Z.I. (ang. Via Maggiora) - 14100 Asti (AT)
9.00-19.30

0141 440455
C.C.: All Major

Clothing, leatherwear
FACTORY OUTLET

Autostrada A21 Torino-Piacenza, exit Asti Est, follow the signs indicating the John Peter outlet to the right.

Two collections are for sale, one casual/classical medium quality in showroom size 44 for women and 50/52 for men. The second collection is tuned in to the latest styles with some snazzy designer names in showroom size 42 for women, for men 48/50. There is a good chance to find seconds and remainders at low prices.

Griffes Diffusion Revedi
Via Conte Nuvoli, 2/a - 14015 San Damiano d'Asti (AT)
9.00-12.30/15.00-19.30. Sunday 9.00-12.30. Closed Tuesday

0141 975903
C.C.: All Major

Clothing, shoes
FACTORY OUTLET

On the provincial road Asti-Canale, next to the local cemetry.

Large outlet of 400 sq.m. offering an even larger choice of dresses, jackets, trousers, shirts, blouses, ties, skirts, coats, handbags, shoes etc. Classical or sporty styles for M/W. Sizes either regular or special XXL sizes. They give 30% discount on current merchandise, more on samples and seconds.

Laifel
Strada Trossi, 8 - 13871 Benna (BI)
15.00-19.00. Saturday 9.00-12.30/15.00-19.00

015 5821241
C.C.: All Major

Clothing
FACTORY OUTLET

Autostrada A4, exit Carisio. You'll find Laifel after circa 10 km on the road to Biella. The entrance is on the right, look for a small staircase to the basement. Parking.

Elegant coats for the more mature in alpaca wool €180,00, Marco Testi suits € 145,00, dresses € 145,00 all sizes. The San Lorenzo showroom collection of beachwear is mostly in size 42, but there is a corner for XL ladies up to size 52. Racks of trousers in summer wool at € 27,00.

Chiorino Outlet Store

Strada Alla Fornace, 8 - 13900 Biella (BI)
9.00-12.30/14.30-19.00

015 8497404
C.C.:All Major

Handbags, leathergoods
FACTORY OUTLET

Take the road to Occhieppo/Mongrando, from Via Fratelli Rossetti on the left. Their show-room is close to the Liabel factory outlet.

End of series, showroom samples or the absolute latest styles in handbags by Rocco Barocco, La cage aux folles, Mandarina Duck and their own brandname Zani del Fra', all discounted. Professional bags for medical doctors in lovely leather, Kelly bags in canvas and leather in three colours € 175,00. Lovely golf bags in leather plus small leatherproducts like agenda's, belts.

Lanificio Angelico

Via Cottolengo, 28 - 13051 Biella (BI)
9.00-12.30/15.00-19.30. Closed Monday

015 8492664
C.C.:All Major

Clothing, fabrics
FACTORY OUTLET

Autostrada A4 Milano-Torino, exit Carisio, continue towards Biella. In front of the Aiazzone store turn left, continue to the next traffic light, turn right. After 500 m on the left.

For the over fifty crowd looking for men's suits in pure wool, € 115,00 - € 175,00, ideal for the office, all sizes available. For women a blazer in summer wool € 65,00, tailleurs € 115,00, trousers € 32,50. It's all super classical in styles that will last forever. Coupons in pure wool at € 10,00.

Lanificio F.lli Cerruti

Via Cernaia, 40 - 13900 Biella (BI)
9.00-13.00/15.00-19.00

015 351144
C.C.:All Major

Clothing
FACTORY OUTLET

From the center of Biella towards Cossato. The Cerruti factory can be seen from above taking Via Cernaia. After the traffic light and the descent, a little before the cross road at the end, turn right towards the factory. Parking outside the gate.

Industrial revolution atmosphere outside and modern salesrooms inside. Large choice in men's suits in summer wool € 230,00, polo shirts with Cerruti logo € 25,00. Windbreakers, shirts, bermuda's, trousers in classical, durable designs. Women's classy suits in crease-free gabardine € 175,00. Raincoats in tornado-proof quality, vests, pants, it's all very understated but elegant. All sizes available.

Liabel

Via Padre G. Greggio, 8/A - 13051 Biella (BI)
9.00-12.00/14.00-18.30

015 8487426
C.C.:All Major

Lingerie, underwear
FACTORY OUTLET

To find the Maglificio Biella take the road towards Occhieppo/Mongrando, from Via Fratelli Rosselli to the left. From Via Rigola it is the second on the left.

Woollen camisoles for adults and toddlers € 5,50 and up. Baskets full of second choice underwear plus good deals in woollen/acrylic sweaters at €12,00 circa. Brandnames Liabel, Blue Stone and Babycresci. Very busy and a worthwhile visit for large families.

River - Nouveau Né

Via Papa Giovanni XXIII, - 13882 Cerrione fraz. Vergnasca (BI)
10.00-19.00. Closed Monday & August

015 2583651
C.C.:All Major

Clothing
FACTORY OUTLET

Autostrada A4, exit Santhia direction Biella, S.S. 143 to Santhia and fraz. Vergnasco.

Large salesroom with an even larger choice of baby, toddler and kid's clothes (from 0 to 14 years old) by Nouveau Né. This is a luxurious and fashionable collection which can be found in the best stores in Milan. 50% off last year's, 20% off current year's collection, but prices are still a touch high. Nevertheles, a must for chic 'bambini'.

Rossignol

Via Cavour, 61 - 13052 Gaglianico (BI)
10.00-12.30/15.30-19.00. Sunday phone first

015 2547225
C.C.:All Major

Clothing, sportswear
FACTORY OUTLET

Autostrada A4, exit Carisio to Biella and the 'Strada Trossi', circa 10 minutes from the Autostrada exit to Gaglianico.

Sporty, high-tech clothing for skiing, all sizes available. Jackets, parka's, overalls and vests for men and women in the latest colours and styles, also accessories like gloves, hats and bags. Friendly, multilingual personnel.

Lanificio Lessona

Via 2 Giugno, 60 - 13866 Masserano San Giacomo di (BI)
10.00-19.00. Sun. open in Dec. Closed Monday

015 9871620
C.C.:All Major

Knitwear, cashmere
FACTORY OUTLET

Autostrada A4, exit Balocco for Masserano. Well indicated.

A new outlet selling all the things the Biella area is famous for: cashmere sweaters, twinsets in mixtures of silk and cashmere, large stoles € 70,00 and up, jackets and coats in double cashmere from € 500,00. There is a corner for home furnishings: plaids in cashmere € 200,00 and up, various beautiful throws in wool/cashmere, cushions in a cashmere cable knit.

Lanificio Guabello

Via Provinciale, 67 - 13888 Mongrando (BI)
9.00-13.00/15.00-19.00 - Saturday 10.00-19.00
Sunday open from 1/10-1/1

015 2564968
C.C.:All Major

Knitwear, cashmere
FACTORY OUTLET

Autostrada A4, exit Carisio towards Biella, to the left in the direction of Mongrando.

The outlet is situated in an old wool mill dating from 1815, in a large and luminous space. Knitwear, fabrics, clothing in 100% cashmere 'Soft Gold' Guabello, all first choice, there are no seconds or remnants. Shortsleeved sweaters € 60,00, a jacket made to measure in cashmere € 500,00 and up. All very luxurious.

Linificio R. Siletti

Via Q. Sella, 6/ang.V. Marconi 1 - 13899 Mongrando (BI)   015 666555/666253
9.00-12.00/15.00-18.30. Closed in August   C.C.:All Major

Household linen, various
FACTORY OUTLET

Autostrada A4, exit Carisio for Biella. From Biella direction Ivrea S.S.338 (approx. 7 km). Siletti is in the center near the church.

Ample choice and books full of samples in linen, linen/cotton for sheets € 22,00 per m, 2.70 wide, price depends on the weight but 40-50% below list price. Sheets can be made to measure and they ship. There is a corner with linen towels, in a fringed granny style € 15,00, their speciality, hand-finished linen handkerchiefs 3 for € 7,50. Also seconds and linen sold by weight.

Telerie F.lli Graziano

Via Martiri Libertà, 84 - 13888 Mongrando (BI)   015 666122
8.00-12.00/14.00-18.00   C.C.:All Major

Household linen, various
FACTORY OUTLET

S.S.338 Ivrea-Biella: from Ivrea on the left just before Mongrando.To enter ring "uffico" sign.

Linen teatowels by Valentino at € 9,00, damask napkins by GFFerré, fringed guest towels in white jacquard linen, charming gifts for the home in cotton and linen. Unbleached cotton for home furnishing at 2.70 m. wide, € 6,00 per meter. Some seconds in linen are sold per kilo. Also sheets, terrytowels, bathrobes and a nice assortment of material for petitpoint embroidery. Sales and they speak English and French.

F.lli Piacenza

Reg. Cisi - 13814 Pollone (BI)   015 6191733
10.00-19.00. Sunday from 1/10-1/1. Monday 14.00 - 18.00   C.C.:All Major

Clothing
FACTORY OUTLET

From Biella take S.S. 144 towards Oropa/Polone.The factory is at the beginning of the village.

The Fratelli Piacenza woollen mill produces luxury fabrics in cashmere, alpaca, vicuna, camel and mohair since 1733! At their large and pleasant outlet snap up blankets in vicuna/alpaca or in 100% cashmere. Cashmere coats are circa € 500,00, in classical, impeccable taste. The Piacenza outlet is also a good source for woollen challis, or flawless cashmere blazers with regimental buttons for men at € 275,00 circa. Sales from 1/1-1/3 and 1/7-1/9.

Lanificio di Pray

Via Cesare Battisti, 80 - 13876 Sandigliano (BI)   015 2494211
9.00-12.00/15.00-19.30. Saturday 9.00-12.00. Closed Monday   C.C.:None

Fabrics, knitwear
FACTORY OUTLET

Autostrada A4, exit Carisio towards Biella.Turn to the left for Sandigliano, the outlet is well indicated. Entrance inside the gate, parking.

A charming shop front just off the main road to Biella. Rolls of fabric in carded wool, summer wool, cashmere. Old sewing machines, spools and other industrial relics make this outlet fun to visit. Knitwear in cashmere/wool, coupons, tweeds, scarves, it's all there.

Zegna Outlet Store

Via C. Battisti, 99 - 13087 Sandigliano (BI)   015 2496199
9.00-19.00   C.C.: All Major

Clothing
FACTORY OUTLET

Autostrada A4, exit Carisio for Biella, circa 12 km. After the Verrone traffic light continue for 2.5 km. The oulet is on the left.

Last year's Ermenegildo Zegna and Zegna Sport collection; suits, jackets, trousers, shirts, elegant ties, accessories and office wear. The Zegna Sport line offers luxurious casuals, jeans, underwear, knitwear. There is a lot of choice in all sizes and savings are circa 30% compared to shop price. Some classical women's wear with the Agnona label is also for sale. They speak English and French.

Filatura di Tollegno Lana Gatto

Via Roma, 16 - 13818 Tollegno (BI)   015 2429228
9.00-12.00/14.00-19.00. In Dic. open on Sundays. Monday closed   C.C.: All Major

Knitting wool, fabrics, knitwear
FACTORY OUTLET

About 2.5 km from the center of Biella. Take a narrow road to the right just before Tollegno.

Two floors and a 500 mq. showroom stashed with unbeatable offers in knitwear, knitting wool by Lana Gatto, lovely woollen fabrics in flannel, super worsted, silk/wool, but also handknitted cardigans. Weekly offers galore, a corner with fabrics and knitting wool, either 2nd or 3rd choice at super low prices, it's all rather tempting! Sales in January/February and July.

Centro Zegna

Via Marconi, 44 - 13835 Trivero (BI)   015 756539
9.00-12.30/14.30-19.00. In Dec. open on Sundays   C.C.: All Major

Clothing
FACTORY OUTLET

Autostrada A4, exit Carisio towards S.S. 232 Cossato-Trivero. The road goes through the many small villages that make up Trivero, in the direction of the 'Panoramica Zegna' worth a detour. Turn to the right at the sign post 'Zegna' and a large parking.

This shop carries the complete Ermenegildo Zegna line, from cashmere jackets to raincoats at normal shop prices. A corner with special offers in knitwear, and end of line clothing at discounts of up to 50% make this a worthwhile trip. Sizes for men from 46/48 to 58. Their winter collection goes on sale at the end of July. They make to measure and speak English.

Luigi Botto Store

Via Q. Sella, 9 - 13855 Valdengo (BI)   015 881976
10.00-19.00. From Wednesday to Saturday   C.C.: All Major

Do it yourself
FACTORY OUTLET

Autostrada A4, exit Carisio towards Cossato, on the provincial road no.142 Cossato - Biella. A factory with a garden in the front. The outlet is on the left. Parking.

Knitting wool by Filatura di Crosa & Monterosa, fabrics by Luigi Botto. Coupons in wool € 7,00 for 80 cm., a good collection of yarns in wool, mohair, mixtures of silk and wool, cottons, cashmere/wool by Filatura di Crosa sold at 1/3 of shop price, simply because the paper label might be torn or the first strand of wool is a bit tangled. Recommended for embroidery and needlepoint too.

Lanificio Reda

Via Robiolo, 25 - 13825 Vallemosso (BI)   015 7049225
9.00-18.00. Closed Monday   C.C.:All Major

Clothing, fabrics
FACTORY OUTLET

From Biella or from the autostrada exit Carisio take the road to Cossato-Vallemosso. After Località Falcero turn left to Via Bacconengo and the center, before the center turn right in the direction of Parco Robiolo, Parco Reda.

This is an interesting collection because of the mixture of Italian and English styles, men's suits in superior quality, the type of clothing that is always fashionable in a quality that lasts. Sizes for jackets, suits, trousers, shirts start at 46 up till 58. They also make to measure.

Beta - Fred Perry

Via Antica Per Benna, 1 (ang. strada Trossi 13) - 13050 Verrone (BI)   015 2556411
9.00-12.30/15.00-18.45   C.C.:All Major

Clothing, sportswear, casual, jeans
FACTORY OUTLET

Autostrada A4 exit Carisio. After the crossing in Verrone, Beta is on the right, opposite the Grillo Hotel. Look for the Fred Perry/Gant/Watro sign. Parking.

The Fred Perry line of sportswear is sold at a 35% discount on normal list price. They stock the whole colour range in cotton polos, plus some baskets with end of line and discontinued colours. Attractive swimsuits by Ungaro beachwear in spring and summer at € 42,00, also Ungaro T-shirts and tops. For M The 'Gant' American sportwear: 'The Blazer', 'The Rugger' or 'The Parka', € 110,00. Last but not least: Watro raincoats for Anglophiles.

Fila Store

S. S. Trossi, 8 - 13871 Verrone (BI)   015 5821541
9.30-12.30/14.30-19.00. Saturday 9.00-19.00   C.C.:All Major

Clothing, sportswear, casual, jeans
FACTORY OUTLET

Autostrada A4, exit Carisio. On the busy strada Trossi on the left, well after the Verrone intersection.

Large, packed with sporty clothes, part normal collection and a small area dedicated to last years remainders, some 2nds and special offers: Fila boots in honey-coloured suede € 32,00 (sizes 40-46). Women's furlined one piece skisuits € 130,00, Ciesse Piumine down vest € 65,00, ski jacket Fila € 67,00, men's cotton polo's € 12,00.

Gruppo Fontanella

Strada Trossi, 13 - 13871 Verrone (BI)   015 5821880
9.30-12.30/15.00-19.00. Closed Monday   C.C.:All Major

Clothing
FACTORY OUTLET

From the autostrada A4 exit Carisio to Verrone. The outlet is in front of the Il Grillo restaurant and after Aiazzone Mobili Verrone.

Men's and women's suits made with their own fabrics in classical designs, in wool, wool and silk or summer wool. Sizes for women start at 42 - 48, for men 46 - 54, all sizes available. Their prices for the quality offered are excellent value.

Tessuti Angelo Bonino

Strada Trossi 19 - 13871 Verrone (BI)
8.30-12.00/14.30-19.00

015 5821829
C.C.: None

Fabrics
FACTORY OUTLET

Autostrada exit Carisio towards Biella. After the Verrone traffic light continue for 500 meters, on the right there are two white buildings with a sign 'Bonino Tessuto'.

Bonino specializes in woollen fabric for men's suits. They offer the finest 'super pettinato', woollen gabardines, summer wool, merinos wool and it is possible to buy remnants by weight or fabric per meter at really good prices.

Vestebene Factory Store

Via S.Margherita, 23 - 12051 Alba (CN)
9.30-19.30. Monday 15.30-19.30

0173 299311
C.C.:All Major

Clothing
FACTORY OUTLET

From the Superstrada head towards the center/Railway Station FS, then in the direction of Savona. Follow the signs.

The Vestebene Factory Store is very large and sells some well-known French brandnames: Daniel Hechter, Caractère, Moi-meme, C'est comme ça in sizes from 38 to 46, but also Krizia Poi, HDM and Elena Miro in over sizes up to 61. Racks and racks of clothing, sweaters, suits, cotton skirts and dresses are discounted from 30 to 50%. Good choice in large sizes.

Nike Factory Store

Via Cuneo, 72 - 12011 Borgo S. Dalmazzo (CN)
9.30-19.30. Sunday 9.30-19.30. Monday 14.00-19.30

0171 268022
C.C.:All Major

Clothing, sportswear, casual, jeans
FACTORY OUTLET

From Cuneo take the road for Borgo S. Dalmazzo, the outlet is near the Iper Standa.

800m2 of space selling the entire Nike collection. Casual wear, sporty goods, sneakers, track shoes with discounts of 20% to 50%. A fidelity card for extra discounts can be asked at the cashier. Special sales in April and October and sales in January and July. They speak English and French. There is another Nike outlet in S. Christophe - (Aosta).

Maglificio Chiemar

Via Mazzini, 1 - 12061 Carrù (CN)
8.30-12.30/15.30-19.30. Closed Monday and August

0173 750898
C.C.:All Major

Knitwear, cashmere
ARTISAN'S WORKSHOP

Autostrada A6, exit Carrù, approximately 2 km. On the main road in the center of Carrù, to the right, just before a service station.

Knitwear in classical and fashionable shapes and colours, all in pure wool/merinos, brandname Anneclaire and Chiemar. Matching tunics and skirts, jackets and trousers, for M/W and sizes from 40 to 54, plus some XXLsizes. Good quality that lasts, a cardigan starts at € 60,00, a multistriped woollen scarf was fun.

Tovagliari Stock

Via Fossano, 26 - 12040 Cervere (CN) 0172 474223
14.30-19.00 Saturday 8.30-12.30/14.30-19.00 C.C.:All Major

Shoes
BARGAIN BASEMENT

Autostrada A6, exit Marene for Fossano. Tovagliari Stock House is on the local road in the center of the village, on the right. Well indicated.

Two large rooms with famous brandname shoes for M/W. A pair of Prada sandals with stiletto heels € 90,00, Moschino € 100.00, Vivien Leigh, Parma, The Saddler, MiuMiu € 90.00, also snazzy shoes by Roberto Cavallini. Showroom sizes for women 36/37, for men 40/41. Especially recommended for men's shoes. Sales at 50%.

Cantina Sociale del Dolcetto

Fraz. Madonna d. Neve, 19 - 12060 Clavesana (CN) 0173 790451
8.00-12.00/14.00-18.00 C.C.:All Major

Wine, liqueurs
GOOD PRICES

On the road from Mondovi towards Farigliano, turn right for Clavesana, the Cantina is almost immediately on the right. Parking inside the gates.

Clavesana is famous for its Dolcetto wines. The Cantina Sociale is an excellent place to stock up on various types of local Dolcetto: from € 2,90 for a bottle or per liter, or € 3,60 for a 1.5 liter bottle and up. They sell other types of red and white wine: Dolcetto DOC di Dolgiani/Alba/Langhe Monregalesi, grappa di dolcetto and spumante.

Città Antiquaria

Frazione Loreto - 12045 Fossano (CN) 0172637121
10.00-18.30. Open 4th Sunday C.C.:All Major

Antiques
GOOD PRICES

Autostrada A6 Torino - Savona, exit Fossano. Follow the directions for Salmore, Città Antiquaria.

During the week this large covered wharehouse is very quiet and some shops will be closed, but on Friday/Saturday all 112 shops are open. One can find all kinds of antiques and brocante, classic 'Piemontese' furniture, French sofas and chairs, old cupboards from the nearby Liguria region but also more recent pieces from the fifties and sixties and original Scandinavian and North European furniture.

Gruppo Industrie Moda

Fraz. Cussanio, 11 - 12045 Fossano (CN) 0172 6532242
9.00-12.00/15.00-19.30. Monday closed C.C.:All Major

Clothing, sportswear, casual, jeans
FACTORY OUTLET

On the S.S. Fossano Genola, from Fossano on the right. A large factory building with parking in front.

A spacious, modern outlet selling jeans and sporty clothes for the whole family. Jeans by their own brandname Rica Lewis, Chinook € 27,00 and up. Quantities of sporty jackets, maxi skirts and trousers for daily use and large quantities of 2nd choice jeans in corduroy, brushed velvet and cotton, some with the Fila label at € 15,00, (but they need to be checked carefully).

Griffes Diffusion Revedi

Corso Principi di Piemonte, 65 - 12035 Racconigi (CN) 0172 813187
9.00-12.30/15.00-19.30. Monday 15.30-19.30 C.C.:All Major

Clothing, shoes
FACTORY OUTLET

From the Reggia di Racconigi follow the S.S. 20 to Cuneo. Next to the Dico Discount store.

Revedi is part of the Mariella Burani Group. Two piece suits for M/W by Revedi or trouser suits for W in practical styles for everyday use at € 130,00 circa. Also interesting were the men's shirts and ties, women's handbags and the special corners with festive suits and dresses by some major brandnames, all seconds, sizes from S to XXL at low prices. It needs a keen eye but bargains can be found.

Mabitex

Via S. Rocco, 18 - 12060 Roreto di Cherasco (CN) 0172 485411
16.00-19.00 Saturday 9.00-12.00/16.00-19.00. Closed in August C.C.:All Major

Clothing
FACTORY OUTLET

Autostrada A6, exit Marena/Bra, continue towards Fossano. After 'Edelarte' and before 'Trony' turn right. The outlet is at the back of the factory near Merula.

Mabitex's strong point is the production of casual pants (brandnames Vestium, Officina and Dunhill) for men in corduroy € 35,00, in linen, canvas or in light summer cotton € 25,00, great offers in 2nds (to be checked very carefully) 3 pairs for € 27.00. Jackets by Nick Name € 85,00. Coats for W, € 145,00, blousons in tweed, plus a large choice of knitwear made elsewhere.

Outlet Store Magazzini Montello

Via Bra, 113- 12062 Roreto di Cherasco - Bra (CN) 0172485650
8.30-12.30/15.30-19.30 C.C.: All Major

Clothing, shoes
BARGAIN BASEMENT

From Bra towards Fossano, on the right, a shopping center with a large parking.

A separate building next to the main shopping center. All the center's unsold items end up here and with a bit of patience one can find shoes, boots and sneakers by Clarks, Timberland, Stonehaven or Superga at € 16,00 - € 36,00. Also sportswear by Conte of Florence, Henry Cottons, El Campero, Sixty, Lacoste (sleeveles polo W for € 25,00) and others at sharply reduced prices.

Vicolungo Outlets

Via Vicolungo - 28061 Biandrate (NO) 0321 835032
10.00-20.00. from Monday to Thursday 10.00-19.00 C.C.: All Major

Clothing, household linen
OUTLET CENTER

Autostrada A4, exit Biandrate, immediately after the intersection with the autostrada.

Recently opened 'open air' outlet center near the A4 from Turin to Milan. About 40 shops, mostly clothing and household linen, with all Italian brandnames like Mariella Burani, Vestebene, Zucchi, Gabel, Foppa Pedretti and many others. The outlet also offers cafés, children's play areas, large parking.

Liolà Tex

Via Matteotti, 86 - 28021 Borgomanero (NO)   0322 833311
9.00-12.30/14.30-19.00 Saturday 8.30-12.30/14.00-17.30   C.C.: All Major

Clothing
FACTORY OUTLET

Autostrada A26 exit Borgomanero towards the center. Turn left after the railway bridge. After the second/third traffic light turn left, entrance immediately to the right. Large parking.

Jersey clothing for the more mature, sizes from 42 till 50/52 plus half sizes. Styles reflect a mixture of Chanel/Hermes and an Yves St. Laurent infusion of colour, flattering, in excellent quality wool. Recent collection: full price, last year 's -30%. 2nd choice -50%, which means dresses are circa € 125,00, suits € 175,00. Friendly & competent staff, customer friendly changing rooms.

Maglificio di Borgomanero

Via G.B. Curti, 7 - 28021 Borgomanero (NO)   0322 81612
9.00-12.00/14.30-18.30 Saturday 9.00-12.00   C.C.: All Major

Lingerie, underwear
FACTORY OUTLET

Autostrada A8, exit Arona. Take S.S. 229 towards Lago d'Orta. Via Curti is a crossroad of Corso Sempione, 50 m from the traffic light is number 7. The outlet is attached to the factory.

Lingerie and underwear for M/W of high quality. Chemises, T-shirts, slips, camisoles, boxer shorts, nightdresses and pyamas in classical styles and very good quality. There are special offers, end of line, 3 for 2, samples on offer all year round.

Sampa, La Cucina Infrangibile

Via Matteotti, 28 - 28021 Borgomanero (NO)   0322 845696
9.00-12.00/14.00-19.00. Saturday closed   C.C.: All Major

Household goods
FACTORY OUTLET

Autostrada A26, exit Borgomanero. From the center take the road for Romagnano. The outlet is near the new sports area or 'Campo Sportivo'.

They produce platters, plates and utensils in melamina, unbreakable, resistent to oven temperatures of over 130°, can be stored in the freezer, washed in the dishwasher, heat resistent, and antiscratch. Large plates € 4,40, mugs, platters, a special set for kids € 8,00. Also special offers of 3 for € 5.00.

Sicrimaglia

Via Casale Tabuloni, 24 - 28021 Borgomanero (NO)   0322 834777
10.30-12.30/13.30-19.00. Closed Monday and August   C.C.: All Major

Knitwear, cashmere
FACTORY OUTLET

Autostrada A26 exit Borgomanero towards the center. Turn left at the railway bridge. After the second/third traffic light take the narrow road in front and take the entrance immediately to the left. Parking.

An interesting outlet with some very fancy knitwear in fashionable colours and designs, very well made and original, often produced for the German & Japanese markets. Coordinated sets of long tunic/matching skirt, dress/matching coat, twinsets in cashmere, woollen bouclé, in summer silk, linen and viscose knits, brand name Carla Viariala. Medium price for a sweater € 80,00. There is a corner with fantastic offers and they speak English and German.

Sergio Tacchini Factory Outlet

Strada Statale 229, km 8 - 28010 Caltignaga (NO)　　0321 651800
10.00-12.00/15.00-19.00 Saturday 10.00-19.00　　　　C.C.:All Major

Clothing, sportswear, casual, jeans
FACTORY OUTLET

Autostrada A4 exit Novara Est, follow directions for Lago d'Orta. Before Caltignana on the left.

In their factory outlet you'll find baskets full of special offers in sweatshirts, tennis gear, sneakers, rows and rows of skiwear, track shoes, polo-shirts, windbreakers, anoraks and tracksuits. They also have a special area for 2nds, last years collection, 3 for the price of 2 for Sergio Tacchini Tennis, Fitness, Jogging shoes. They speak English.

Bossi

Via dei Martiri Partigiani, 48 - 28062 Cameri (NO)　　0321 518477
9.00-12.15/15.00-19.15. Closed in August　　　　　　C.C.:All Major

Fabrics, home furnishings, household linen
FACTORY OUTLET

Autostrada A4, exit Galliate, towards 'Laghi', the lakes. Via Partigiani is a crossroad to Via Galilei, east of the village.

Large, modern outlet. Lovely bedlinens, linea 'CasaBossi', Country' or 'San Gallen'. Linen fabric € 7,50 per meter 1.45 wide, sheets in scottish plaid motifs, bathrobes € 17,00 - € 36,00, all very classy. Seconds in table linen and sheets. Special offers & sales in February.

Spacci Bassetti

Via Mazzini, 1/a - 28066 Galliate (NO)　　　　　　0321 865285
9.30-13.00/14.00-18.30. Monday 14,30-18.30　　　　C.C.:None

Household linen, various
FACTORY OUTLET

Autostrada A4, exit Galliate towards the center, the acquaduct and continue to the sports hall.

Bargains in Gran Foulard material at € 10.00 per kilo, terrytowel material € 11.00 per kilo, linen napkins € 0,60, end of series in blankets, duvets, sheets & pillow cases, bathrobes, also various small items for gifts. Average savings 30 - 40%.

Casam Cravatte

Via Romagnano, 6/a - 28074 Ghemme (NO)　　　　0163 840220
9.00-12.00/14.00-19.00　　　　　　　　　　　　　　C.C.:None

Ties
ARTISAN'S WORKSHOP

Autostrada A4, exit Agognate, S.P. 299 towards Romagnano Sesia or continue to the A26, exit Ghemme. From Novara take the provincial road, turn left towards Ghemme center. The outlet is on the left after two small houses with turrets.

A pleasant showroom with a collection of classical ties from € 15,00 to € 25,00. These ties are made in heavy silk, handfinished and in classy designs. One can see them made on the premises. They also sell handkerchiefs in silk, silk scarves and chokers.

Emporio del Lino - Crespi 1797

Via Crespi, 14 - 28074 Ghemme (NO)　　　　　　　0163 844563
10.00-19.00. Closed on Monday　　　　　　　　　C.C.:All Major

Fabrics, home furnishings, household linen
FACTORY OUTLET

Autostrada A26, exit Ghemme. At the crossroad for Ghemme turn right, first street on the right, circa 200 mt. Look out for a sign 'Crespi'. Parking.

This is an interesting outlet for those who love linen, their speciality, but they also produce and sell cotton, wool and high-tech mixtures, either sold per meter, per weight or as remnants, all at unbeatable prices. They also sell clothing made of their fabrics for M/W in sizes starting at 40 up to 54 and men's shirts and accessories. Sales in July.

Herno

Via Sempione, 87 - 28040 Lesa (NO)　　　　　　　0322 76746
9.30-12.00/15.00-19.30. Sunday 10.00-19.00. Open in August　　C.C.:All Major

Clothing, raincoats
FACTORY OUTLET

Autostrada A8/A26 exit Arona towards Stresa S.S.33. A new outlet before Lesa on the right in front of the 'Cantieri Nautici'.

Very good quality classical dresses for the more mature, suits and raincoats, beautifully made summer dresses, showroom models € 80,00. A box with remnants at € 15,00. Great choice in raincoats for men. We suggest a visit during their sales period, telephone for the right dates in June!

Costa Alimentari

Corso Vercelli, 3 - 28100 Novara (NO)　　　　　　0321 450861
8.00-12.30/16.00-19.00. Closed Wed.aft.　　　　　C.C.:All Major

Food, milk products
FACTORY OUTLET

Autostrada A4, exit Novara Est to Vercelli. At the beginning of Corso Vercelli, next to the Banca Nazionale del Lavoro and in front of the Q8 service station.

Novara is well known as a center for the production of Gorgonzola cheese and Costa is the only outlet where one can try, buy and admire all the various types of Gorgonzola: with mascarpone, sweet, spicy, sold per 100 grams or per kilo. They also sell many other types of cheeses and the locally produced rice and home made ravioli.

Sipario Manifatture

Via Marie Curie, 6 - 28100 Novara (NO)　　　　　0321 399979
10.00-12.30/14.00-19.00　　　　　　　　　　　C.C.:None

Clothing, accessories
GOOD PRICES

Autostrada A4, exit Novara Ovest towards Novara then take the direction for Biandrate. An Industrial zone just outside of Novara after the Lancia dealer on the left.

Large collection of accessories: handbags, sunglasses, bijoux, belts, scarves, ties. Cute knitwear € 60,00 in cotton, a mini Kelly handbag € 55,00, belts from € 10,00. Rather smashing big straw hats, ideal for weddings € 20,00 and up, seconds. For men some classical good quality silk ties € 10,00.

Bolgheri

Via Novara, 71 - 28047 Oleggio (NO)   0321 922450
9.30-13.00/14.30-19.00 Saturday 9.30-19.00. Closed Tuesday   C.C.:All Major

Clothing, accessories
FACTORY OUTLET

Autostrada A4, exit Novara towards Arona for approximately 15 km. Autostrada A26, exit Castelletto Ticino, towards Novara for approximately 15 km. Parking in front of the factory.

Snazzy men's fashions in a large space. Jackets by Ermenegildo Zegna, Les Copains and Givenchy in summer wool or wool/cashmere € 175,00. Also rain-coats, windbreakers, anoraks. Ties by Aquascutum, Church's, Memphis € 20,00, 2nds € 10.00. Ties by Leonard de Paris € 36,00 regular, € 20,00 2nds. Lots of cashmere. Sales in January & July at 50%.

Spaccio F. Gagliardi

Via Sempione, 33 - 28047 Oleggio (NO)   0321 91441/97541
8.30-12.30/15.00-19.30. Open from 1/5-1/8 Closed Tuesday   C.C.:All Major

Clothing, beachwear
FACTORY OUTLET

Autostrada A4, exit Novara Est to S.S. 32 in the direction of Lago Maggiore. For the Gagliardi outlet take the third exit for Oleggio/Marano Ticino. To the right towards Oleggio, after the traffic light there is a large gate on the right. Parking inside.

Bikinis and bathing costumes in excellent quality by Yves St.Laurent € 40,00, Well-made bikinis € 13,00, or bathing costumes by Crystel. Equally tempting are the bermudas for men, € 10,00 in sizes up to XXL. Beach T-shirts by Yves St. Laurent € 35,00, men's Tshirt by Albatros € 10,00. Nice things for kids from € 5,00. All sizes available, also XL, their showroom size is a miserly 2a for W.

Mattel Toys

Via Vittorio Veneto, 119 - 28040 Oleggio Castello (NO)   0322 231311
9.30-12.30/15.00-19.00. Sunday 15.00-19.00 Monday closed   C.C.:All Major

Toys
FACTORY OUTLET

Autostrada A26, exit Arona. After the Stop to the right, after approximately 1 km the Mattel factory is on the right. To enter the outlet stop at the porter's gate.

All Mattel Toys are for sale at a discount of 15%. This outlet is of special inte-rest during the Christmas season when choice is larger and opening hours are extended. Just the place to find Barbie a discounted disco outfit.

Sambonet

S.S. 11, km 84 - 28060 Orfengo (NO)   0321 879711
9.30-12.30/14.30-19.00. Closed Monday   C.C.:None

Household goods
FACTORY OUTLET

From the Autostrada A4 take the A26 towards Alessandria until the exit for Vercelli Est. Take the local road no. 11 towards Novara.

Knives, forks, spoons 'seconds', sugarbowls, egg-cups, jam jars, ashtrays in stain-less steel € 2,50, alpaca dessert spoons € 3.00, (end of series). One can find the complete Cordon Bleu cooking range and the Arthur Krupp kitchen knives and implements at discounted prices. They speak English and French.

Almar Center Shop

Via per Borgomanero, 36 - 28040 Paruzzaro (NO)   0322 538612
9.00-19.30 Open in August   C.C.:All Major

Shoes
FACTORY OUTLET

Autostrada A8 then A26, exit Arona towards Borgomanero to the right. Parking.

900 sqm of selling space with shoes for everybody from toddlers to tired feet.
Tennis shoes with platform soles, ballerinas in various colours € 30,00 large leather bags € 45,00, men's loafers circa € 35,00, all in acceptable quality and a
really tremendous choice. They sell a lot of popular brandnames.

Lanificio Ing. Loro Piana

Via per Novara, 484 - 28078 Romagnano Sesia (NO)   0163 826875
10.00-19.00. Open on Sundays   C.C.:All Major

Clothing, fabrics
FACTORY OUTLET

Autostrada A26, exit Romagnano Sesia/Ghemme.

The Loro Piana showroom is very elegant and shows the complete collection of
fabrics, clothing and accessories. Cashmere scarves regular size or large stole type
scarves. Fabrics per meter, also some coupons. For a real fanatic, cashmere socks
in pale blue or a cashmere mantella, very elegant, € 500,00 and up. A corner with
special offers and seconds, but alas, prices are halved but still stratospheric.

Tecadue

Via S.Antonio da Padova, 7 - 28068 Romentino (NO)   0321 860101
8.30-12.30/14.30-19.00 Closed Monday   C.C.:None

Clothing, shirts
ARTISAN'S WORKSHOP

*Autostrada A4, exit Novara Est towards Galliate/Romentino. After the third roundabout
turn to Romentino and the traffic light, at the intersection turn to the right, after 50mt.
to the left.It's the last house at the end of the street.*

Men's shirts in a great variety of sizes, shapes and fabrics. A button-down shirt
in a nice stripe, made to measure, € 55,00, intials € 3,50 per letter extra. Sales
from June 1 - August 1 and November 1 - January 1.

Maglificio di Sozzago

Via Cerano, 16 - 28060 Sozzago (NO)   0321 70372
9.00-12.00/15.00-19.00. Sunday open in Dec.   C.C.:All Major

Knitwear, cashmere
FACTORY OUTLET

*Autostrada A4, exit Galliate towards Trecate, Cerano. The Maglificio di Sozzago is on
the road from Cerano on the left just before Sozzago. Entrance in the courtyard.*

Two large rooms with knitwear in a classical style in wool, merinos and cashmere
Loro Piana by Iucci Bellomi. Capes in wool € 65,00 or in cashmere € 300,00, twinsets € 130,00 circa. In summer silks and silk/viscosa, all very wearable, also XL sizes
but no sales and no seconds. Sales in february and september and they speak English.

Manifattura Pertusi

Corso Roma, 128 (interno) - 28069 Trecate (NO)　　　0321 71112
15.30-18-30. Saturday closed　　　C.C.: None

Shirts
FACTORY OUTLET

Autostrada A4, exit Galliate for Trecate or S.S. 11 Novara-Milano. At the entrance of the village follow the yellow arrows indicating 'Spaccio Pertusi'.

Men's shirts € 20,00 - € 45,00, with 2 initials stitched by hand € 5,00. Cotton blouses for W from € 20,00 - € 25,00. Handkerchiefs in cotton or linen/cotton, white or coloured with woven-in initials in presentation boxes € 3,00 - € 6,00 - €10,00. They also make shirts to measure and sell accessories like ties, ascots and scarves.

Spaccio Liontex

Via Parini, 2 - 28069 Trecate (NO)　　　0321 76211
9.00-12.00/15.00-19.30　　　C.C.:None

Clothing
FACTORY OUTLET

Autostrada A4, exit Galliate. Follow the indications for Trecate and Liontex. S.S.11, take Via Milano, straight to Via Gramsci, fourth street on the right.

A worthwhile outlet for XL ladies with a preference for classical, well-made clothes with luxury touches like fur collars and cashmere shawls. Showroom size 42, largest size 62. Winter coats in wool/mohair € 300,00, 3/4 jackets € 175,00, at discounts of 30% to 70%. Best time to visit: beginning of summer and winter season, April and October.

Can. Soc. Bricherasio

Via Vitt. Emanuele II, 2 - 10060 Bricherasio (TO)　　　0121 599052
8.00-12.00/15.00-19.00. Sun. 9.00-12.00　　　C.C.:All Major

Wine, liqueurs
GOOD PRICES

From Pinerolo to Bricherasio, at the beginning of the village at the roundabout to the right.

A well known winery that sells mostly red wines like Barbera, Bonarda, Freisa and some Rosé or a good Chardonnay. Price per bottle circa € 3,00 or bringing a demigiano one can buy a decent red wine at € 1,25-€ 1,50 per liter.

Tessitura Enzo Stella

Via Padana Inf. 48 - 10023 Chieri (TO)　　　011 9472997
8.00-12.30/14.00-19.00. Saturday 9.00-12.30. Closed in August　　　C.C.:All Major

Fabrics, home furnishings
FACTORY OUTLET

On the road from Chieri to Asti. Parking inside the gate.

A small outlet selling fabrics for soft furnishings at good prices but it is a bit difficult to see the collection since everything is on rolls covered in plastic. They produce quilted bedspreads in three different weights, or one can order a bedspread in matching material. The price per meter for cotton is € 8,00 up to € 12,00, curtains € 7,00 and up. Friendly service.

Tessitura Pertile

Via A. Gastaldi, 24 - 10023 Chieri (TO)   011 9472850
9.00-12.30/15.00-19.00. Sat. 9.00-12.00/15.00-18.00   C.C.:All Major

Fabrics, home furnishings, household linen
FACTORY OUTLET

Take the road to Chieri. After the Enel plant follow the signs for Pertile. Parking.

A large selling point, good choice, prices clearly visible. On the goundfloor household linens by Bassetti, Gran Foulards, towels plus underwear. In the basement curtain material of their own production at very competitive prices. This is also a good place to find bits of material for quilting and patchwork. They speak English and French.

Tessitura Piovano

Corso Torino, 4 - 10023 Chieri (TO)   011 9474711
8.30-12.30/14.00-18.00.   C.C.:None

Fabrics, home furnishings
FACTORY OUTLET

From Torino and Pino Torinese, before entering Chieri there is a sign on the left.

Beautiful material for interior decorating at prices that reflect this very high level of quality in a large showroom full of rolls of fabric, all covered with plastic and without a price tag. We suggest you look through the sample books first to get an idea of what is for sale since personnel is scarce or very busy.

Vay

Corso Matteotti, 81- 10023 Chieri (TO)   011 9413089
8.30-12.30/14.30-19.00. Monday closed   C.C.:All Major

Fabrics, home furnishings
FACTORY OUTLET

Take the ring road around Chieri in the direction of Villanova d'Asti. After the cemetery on the left. Large parking.

A small outlet, very busy in the morning. They sell their own production, fabrics for curtains, lace curtains, upholstery, sheets and bedspreads at very good prices. There are also some imported fabrics. You can browse around at leisure.

Vincenzo Quagliotti & Figli

Str. Cambiano, 58 - 10023 Chieri (TO)   011 9413720
8.30-11.30/14.00-18.00 Closed Saturday   C.C.: None

Household linen, various
FACTORY OUTLET

From Chieri take Via Diaz in the direction of Cambiano, the outlet is on the right. Parking on the left of the factory, ring bell. The entrance in the courtyard on the right

Sheets and bedspreads in very good quality at adequate prices but inferior to shop prices. Coupons in leandra (a heavy cotton that looks like linen) for sheets and pillowcases or for tableclothes, napkins are discounted at 30-40%. A set of sheets for a queensize bed € 95,00 + € 50,00 made to measure, in a quality that will last a life time. Friendly service.

Le Particolarità

Via Don Lorenzo Giordano, 23/27 - 10073 Cirié (TO)   011 9214225
15.30-19.30. Fri. & Sat. also 9.30-12.30. Closed Mon.   C.C.: None

Clothing, military
VINTAGE

*Autostrada A4, exit Brandizzo towards Leini-Caselle and Cirié or the Torino
Tangenziale/ringroad to the Caselle airport and Cirié.*

A fascinating spot for collectors of military memorabilia. Military great coat €
15,00, bathrobes in basket-weave € 6,00, unused gasmask anno 1938 € 18,00,
plus boots, T-shirts. Also medals, buttons, pins, ribbons. A good address for trekking boots. They speak French.

Carrera Jeans

Via Torino, 168 - 10093 Collegno (TO)   011 4037727
9.00-12.30/15.30-19.30. Closed August   C.C.:All Major

Clothing, sportswear, casual, jeans
FACTORY OUTLET

*From Torino take the Corso Francia. At the traffic light before the railway bridge turn
right into Via Antonelli, before the overpass turn left under the bridge. the outlet is on
the right. Parking.*

The Carrera factory outlet is large and modern, selling jeans at regular prices or
visit the corner with discounted items. There are some bargains which don't
appear to have anything wrong with them, maybe they are only a bit shop soiled.

Diffusione Tessile

Corso Francia, 313 - 10093 Collegno (TO)   011 4157840
10.00-19.30   C.C.:All Major

Clothing
FACTORY OUTLET

Autostrada A4, exit Rivoli/Collegno. Corso Francia is right there, the shop is on the right.

This is the Max Mara outlet selling last years collection (minus the Max Mara
labels) and a special line of clothing for their outlets. Casual and elegant clothes
also in Marina Rinaldi styles (but no labels) all discounted 30% - 50%. There is a
corner with leatherwear, a lot of handbags (€ 40,00 and up) and shoes (€ 50,00
and up). Sizes from 38 to 50 plus XXL sizes up to 60.

Telerie di Poirino - Tessitura Gioda

Via Indipendenza, 14/ang. Via Arpino, 2 - 10046 Poirino (TO)   011 9450107
9.00-12.00/14.30-18.30. Closed Saturday and August   C.C.:None

Fabrics, home furnishings, household linen
FACTORY OUTLET

*Autostrada A21, exit at Santena and go towards Poirino. The factory is on the main
road and Via Arpino just before the IP gas station. Ring bell at Via Arpino 2.*

Two rooms selling cotton by Poirino, a special fabric that is very strong and
heavy, it resembles a good quality linen. A set of sheets, double, plus 2 pillow
covers € 65,00 - € 70,00, cotton per meter € 7,50, linen € 17,50, all in long
lasting, good quality.

Griffes Diffusion Revedi

Via Italia, 69 - 10036 Settimo Torinese (TO) 011 8002296
9.00-12.30/15.00-19.30. Mon. 15.30 - 19.30 C.C.:All Major

Clothing
FACTORY OUTLET

Bus 49 from Porta Susa. Near the central pedestrian zone.

Large outlet of 250 sqm which is part of the Mariella Burani Group. Great choice of suits, jackets, pants, shirts, ties, skirts, coats, handbags in classical or sporty styles for W/M. All sizes, also XXL. They give a 30% discount on their regular prices.

Antica Passamaneria

Via Bava, 21/b - 10100 Torino (TO) 011 8178754
10.00-18.00 C.C.:None

Fabrics, home furnishings, household linen
FACTORY OUTLET

Bus 30, 55, tram 15. Parking.

The right place to furnish a house in style since it is no longer that easy to find a passementerie factory that produces tassels, ribbons, braid in dozens of colours at reasonable prices. They can make tassels or trimmings to order, coordinated with curtains or cushions. Very knowledgeable personnel.

Arsenico & Breakfast

Via Gaudenzio Ferrari, 12/c - 10124 Torino (TO) 011 8172855
9.30-12.30/15.30-19.30. Sunday phone first C.C.:All Major

Clothing
VINTAGE

In the center, near Palazzo Nuovo and the Mole Antonelliana. Tram 16, 68, 13, 15, and 56.

Vintage fashions from the USA, UK, leather, jeans, surplus military or street style with brandnames like Converse, Levi's, Miss Sixty, Freesoul, Alpha Industry, Dr. Martens. Large collection of classical pieces, smoking, cashmere knitwear, crocodile handbags at reasonable prices. They have clients of every age group and speak English and French.

Eta Beta

Via Principi d'Acaja, 51 - 10138 Torino (TO) 011 4340008
Tuesday 13.00-19.30 C.C.:All Major

Clothing
BARGAIN BASEMENT

Bus 56, near the market on Piazza Benefica (Giardini Martini).

They import/export and buy directly from the factory. All items marked at half price plus another 50% off during the sales period. Fidelity card. Quantities of ErreUno dresses at € 225,00, shoes € 60,00, Pal Zileri fur trimmed jackets at € 175,00. Friendly saleshelp.

Ettore Confezioni
Via Cibrario, 84/A - 10144 Torino (TO)   011 7710808
9.00-12.30/15.00-19.00   C.C.: None

Clothing
BARGAIN BASEMENT

From Piazza Castello tram 13, from Porta Nuova tram 2, the basement is near the Maria Vittoria hospital. From the Tangenziale exit Corso Regina Margherita. Parking difficult.

Two floors of showroom samples: jackets by Dior, Cardin, Krizia, Zegna € 175,00, suits € 190,00 and up. Lightweight car coats in microfiber or cotton, plain or reversible start at € 60,00. Feraud jeans € 35,00. Go up one floor and prices are lower.

Factory
Via Vassalli Enaudi, 32/a - 10138 Torino (TO)   011 4335585
9.00-19.30.   C.C.:None

Clothing, casual, jeans
BARGAIN BASEMENT

Bus 55, 65, near the Piazza Benefica market. Parking is difficult.

Young and casual clothes by Anna Po, Bob & Paul, Rinascimento, jeans by Guess. The place is a bit of a jumble, baskets with special offers at € 10,00, suits for men at 50% discount but there is a good chance to find a true bargain especially for women since the selection for them is much larger.

Gant Flydocks.68
Via Valprato, 68 - 10155 Torino (TO)   011 231402
10.00-19.00. Monday closed   C.C.:All Major

Clothing, casual, jeans
FACTORY OUTLET

In the 'Docks Dora' area of Turin, an old warehouse that has been transformed in a shopping center. Parking in or outside the building.

Large and luminous, an outlet for 'Gant USA' fans, all merchandise is discounted 30% and up to 60% during the sales period. Jeans, sweatshirts, T-shirts, polo shirts and jackets, very well made and in authentic USA designs. All sizes are available, large choice, (less so for kids). Friendly personnel.

Griffes Diffusion Revedi
Corso Emilia, 8 - 10152 Torino (TO)   011 2485913
9.00-19.30. Monday 15.30-19.30   C.C.:All Major

Clothing, leatherwear
FACTORY OUTLET

Autostrada A4 exit Torino, at the end of Corso Vercelli. Bus 52. There is another outlet nearby in Corso Giulio Cesare 31.

Large warehouse type building of 850 sqm. Vast choice of suits, pea coats, trench coats, pants, shirts, ties, handbags in classical, middle of the road or sporty styles for W/M. All sizes, also XXL. They give a 30% discount on their regular prices and also sell seconds and showroom samples.

Il Grifoncino

Via G.N. Bodoni, 5 - 10123 Torino (TO)
9.30-12.30/15.30-19.00. Thursday 9.30-19.00

011 8179260
C.C.:All Major

Clothing
BARGAIN BASEMENT

Near the Parcheggio Bodoni, or the underground parking in Piazza Carlo Felice.

Lovely clothes for kids. Brummel cotton dungarees € 18,00, pretty appliqued shirts for girls € 22,00 by Amore, Henry Cotton's cute jodhpurs € 24,00, Best Company sweatshirts for teenagers. For W. showroom samples and brandname casuals by some major griffe. Sales from 10/7 and 10/1 at 50%. They speak English and French.

Il Grifone

Corso Turati, 15b - 10128 Torino (TO)
9.30-12.30/15.30-19.30. Friday 9.30-19.30
Saturday 9.00-12.30/15.00-19.00

011 596127
C.C.:All Major

Clothing
BARGAIN BASEMENT

Tram 4,16,12; bus 63,42,64. By car from Porta Nuova (Central Station) take Via Sacchi which becomes Corso Turati.

Lovely Armani Basic summer jackets for W. € 125,00, rather mad Moschino jackets € 70,00, clothes by New York, Luisa Via Roma, Henry Cotton's at 50% off. The men's store is a separate shop in the same complex: jackets in classical tweeds or wool and cashmere € 175,00, heavy cotton sweaters, shirts in the finest cotton by Yves St. Laurent € 30,00. As bargain basements go, worth the detour.

Il Vestigente

Piazza Solferino, 14a - 10121 Torino (TO)
10.30-12.30/15.30-19.30

011 538648
C.C.:All Major

Clothing
BARGAIN BASEMENT

In the center of town, 10 minutes walk from Stazione di Porta Nuova.

Strictly for the fearlessly fashions conscious looking for utterly up to the minute tailoring by Ralph Lauren, Via Maggio, F. Alpi, Iceberg and Bluemarine at prices that are slightly lower than the fashion boutiques in via Roma nearby.

Kid's Factory Store

Via XX Settembre, 56B - 10121 Torino (TO)
9.00-12.30/15.00-19.00

011 533284
C.C.:All Major

Clothing, casual, jeans
BARGAIN BASEMENT

Tram 4, Bus 57, 58, 72. Parking impossible.

Clothing for children from 0 to 10 years old and one can wander around and find plenty of bargains, remainders, special offers. Not all sizes are available but there is a lot of merchandise to choose from. Their corner with super discounts is worth a look.

La Murrina

Via Cigna, 2 - 10152 Torino (TO)   011 5217168
9.00-12.30/15.00-19.30   C.C.:All Major

Crystal, glassware
DISCOUNTS

The La Murrina shop is on the corner of Corso Regina Margherita/Via Cigna. Tram 3, 10, 16, bus 52. Parking.

On the ground floor lights, vases, objects in Murrano glass are for sale at normal prices. In the basement a sales area offers some handsome glass objects and lamps at 30-50% discount. They also sell plates, wine glasses in crystal, tea and coffee services, all end of line or discontinued. A good address to find colourful gifts. Other shops in Rome and in the Como and Venice area.

Lo Zio d'America

Via Palazzo di Città, 14 - 10122 Torino (TO)   011 4361423
11.00-13.00/15.30-19.30   C.C.:All Major

Clothing
VINTAGE

Close to Piazza Castello, trams 4,12,15, buses 57,58,63,68.

Mostly 50's/60's clothes, bell-bottomed Levis, velvet jackets in Beatles style, gilets, leather jackets € 80,00. Small devoted clientele, friendly atmosphere, for the under 25. Small selection of original platform shoes and winkle-pickers straight from the 60's!

Montebello Road

Via Montebello, 22/a - 10124 Torino (TO)   011 882356
10.00-19.30. Saturday 10.00-13.00/15.30-19.30   C.C.:All Major

Clothing, casual, jeans
DISCOUNTS

In the center of Turin between Corso S. Maurizio and the 'Mole Antonelliano'.

A shop that sells the jeans showroom collection of Miss Sixty and Killerbabe at sharply reduced prices. They also sell jeans by Roy Rodgers and Levi's at less and have a large assortment of casual sweatshirts and T's by Hangten, Ring Spoon, Cycle. Odd sizes are discounted all year round. They speak English.

Nuovodinuovo

Via Guastalla, 6 - 10124 Torino (TO)   011 883606
10.00-13.00/15.00-19.30. Saturday 15.00-19.30   C.C.:None

Clothing
VINTAGE

Near the University of Turin, between Corso San Maurizio and Corso Regina Margherita.

This is quite an interesting address for those who manage to dress with flair in vintage and secondhand clothing. One pays per kilo, shirts, blouses and dresses € 35,00, Levi's and other jeans € 12,00, jackets and coats € 8,00, trousers € 25,00 per kilo. One can try everything on and there is a change of stock every week.

Opificio Serico Fiorentino

Via Martiri della Libertà,42 - 10131 Torino (TO)　　　011 8196296
10.00-18.00. Saturday closed　　　C.C.:All Major

Fabrics, home furnishings, household linen
GOOD PRICES

Bus 56, 61, 66.

Silks, fabrics and velvets for high quality interior decorating at a 50% discount. The choice is not vast but prices are very competetive: linen or cotton velvet € 12,00 p.m., cotton € 10,00, also cushions and quilts in velvet. First and second choice items and a special sales corner that's worth a visit. They also sell fabrics from other manufacturers. Friendly and multilingual personnel.

Polar Outlet - Texitalia

Lungo Dora Colletta, 113 int. 8 - 10153 Torino (TO)　　　011 2487089
10.00-19.00. Closed Monday & August　　　C.C.:All Major

Clothing, blankets
GOOD PRICES

Go along the Lungo Dora following the current as far as Lungodora Colletta 113 and turn into the private road to N. 8. Parking in the court yard.

Their own production of casual wear in fleece (cardigans, twinsets, vests) or sporty wear like jackets and long sweaters for M/W/Ch. Also a lot of accessories, scarves, stoles, capes, gloves and hats and a special corner with homewear, blankets and cushion covers in various dimensions, all in fleece. They are distributors of Norwegian and Icelandic sweaters and speak English and French.

Robe di Kappa Gigastore

Via Foggia, 42 - 10152 Torino (TO)　　　011 2617850
10.00-19.30. Sat. 9.30-19.30. Monday 12.30-19.30 Open in August　　　C.C.:All Major

Clothing
FACTORY OUTLET

Autostrada A4, exit Torino, take Corso Giulio Cesare towards the center. After 4 km turn left to Corso Brescia. The Robe di Kappa Gigastore is now part of a commercial complex, entrance behind the bar or the supermarket. Parking nearby.

A gigantic complex selling woollen sweaters, track suits and skisuits in splashy colours by Linea Kappa, Robe di Kappa and Jeans Jeans at low prices. For those who like digging into baskets full of special offers, this is it! On the right their current collection, coordinates, blazers, skirts, all in sturdy no-nonsense styles and fabrics, ideal for sporty families.

Superga Outlet

Via San Marino, 31 - 10134 Torino (TO)　　　011 5690954
10.15-19.30　　　C.C.:All Major

Clothing, shoes
FACTORY OUTLET

Tram 4, 10, bus 14, 63, 74. Parking on the road.

A new address for the Superga outlet. Remainders, unsold, first and second choice quality shoes and sneakers by Superga. Tennis in bright colours, all sizes € 15,00 - € 25,00. Outerwear by K-way, quilted jackets € 48,00 - € 125,00, cotton polos with Superga logo € 20,00, jackets or skirts in suede € 75,00. Sales at 20-50% less, lots of special offers.

Ziccat

Via Bardonecchia, 185 - 10141 Torino (TO)   011 7723018
8.30-18.30   C.C.: None
Saturday 9.00-12.00

Food, chocolate
FACTORY OUTLET

Bus 33, 42 near the Corso Brunelleschi market.

An autentic outlet inside the factory. Great choice in chocolates and the local speciality gianduia soft chocolates sold per kilo, or handmade chocolates also sold per kilo. Special offers of pralines in presentation boxes, all in very good quality at low prices.

Holding Tessile

Via Torino, 50 fraz. Palazzo Grosso - 10070 Vauda Canavese (TO)   011 9251777
10.00-13.00/14.45-19.00   C.C.:All Major

Clothing, accessories
FACTORY OUTLET

Take the 'tangenziale' for the airport. Just after the airport turn right for S. Maurizio Canavese and S. Francesco al Campo. Palazzo Grosso is on the main road and the outlet is on the right.

A modern outlet offering all kinds of clothing for the 30/40 year age group with brand names like Gash Gash, Utility. Ladies' suits € 125,00, coats € 175,00. Evening gowns, scarves in silk, and knitwear by Vanity and Real. Don't miss the basement with woollen jackets for men by Holds and Sevres at € 75,00. Worth a visit.

Outlet Diadora - Invicta

Corso Toscana, 15 - 10078 Venaria Reale (TO)   011 730231
10.00-19.30. Saturday 10.00-19.30. Monday 15.00 - 19.30   C.C.:All Major

Handbags, leathergoods
FACTORY OUTLET

Bus 31. Near the new Stadio delle Alpi and Città Mercato di Venaria, behind the Auchan supermarket. Parking.

Famous brand names, Diadora, Invicta, for backpacks, bookpacks, sporty outer-wear, sneakers and mountain boots. A relatively small outlet with seconds, unsold, and showroom models. Discounts circa 30-40% and during the sales period 50-60%. Good prices on backpacks, travelbags and shoes. It's nice to browse.

F.lli Calderoni

Via G. Marconi, 3 - 28881 Casale Corte Cerro (VB)   0323 60335
8.00-12.00/14.00-17.30. Closed Saturday   C.C.: None

Household goods, various
FACTORY OUTLET

After Alessi, continue towards the center of Casale. The showroom is just before the church.

Ideal for brides, looking for traditional, beautifully finished flatware and stainless steel. Cutlery in elegant designs (serie Classica), in silverplate or stainless, pots and pans 'La Cuoca' or 'Cerro' in many different sizes and shapes, massive restaurant trolleys with hotplates & antipasta dishes. No 2nds but a saving of circa 30% on their whole collection is guaranteed.

Sergio Tacchini Factory Outlet

Via 42 Martiri, loc. Stazione - 28025 Fondotoce (VB)   0323 406928
9.30-12.30/15.00-19.00   C.C.:All Major

Clothing, sportswear, casual
FACTORY OUTLET

Autostrada A26, exit Verbania, to Verbania Pallanza for 2 km. Parking.

Corduroy trousers in nice autumnal colours for men at € 15,00 in summer weight
and € 37,00 in winterweight, polo shirts in pure cotton with the Tacchini logo €
20,00, longsleeved € 25,00. Tennis- and track shoes, tennis skirts and bermudas are
all discounted. They stock all sizes, but don't offer any seconds. They speak German.

Pretti - Toce Center

Via 42 Martiri, 195 - 28924 Fondotoce (VB)   0323 585011
9.30-19.00. Open on Sunday   C.C.:All Major

Household linen, various
FACTORY OUTLET

*Autostrada A26, exit Gravellona Toce in the direction of Verbania, on the right one can
see an ocre-yellow building, just before the railway.*

A shopping center of circa 2000 mq. selling household linen by Pretti, pots and
pans, sets of carving knives by Lagostina, various local food products, but also
parmesan cheese, lingerie and gift items in wood. Plenty of special offers in bathrobes and terrytowels, small hold-alls for travelling, large brand name beachtowels. They speak English, French and German.

Alessi

Via privata Alessi - 28882 Omegna - Crusinallo (VB)   0323 868611
9.30-18.00. Monday 14.00-18.00   C.C.:All Major

Household goods, gifts
FACTORY OUTLET

S.P. 229 Omegna-Gravellona Toce. After Omegna on the left, follow sign posts for Alessi.

Alessi is world-famous for it's strictly avantgarde designs in kettles, and tableware. Price depends on the colour of the label, which will tell you if it's a second
choice item or not (defects are minimal, and savings considerable). It's a large
outlet, busy in summer, with multi-lingual sales personnel, and plenty of parking.
Recommended.

Alfonso Bialetti

Via IV Novembre, 106 - 28887 Omegna - Crusinallo (VB)   0323 887228
9.30-12.30/14.30-19.00. Sunday 14.30 - 19.00   C.C.:All Major

Household goods, various
FACTORY OUTLET

S.S.229 Lago d'Orta from Omegna towards Gravellona Toce, on the left.

A great choice in electric espresso machines by Faema but also kitchen utensils
by 'La Cucina', or a 'designer' Chinese wok in stainless steel at € 25,00 + reci-
pe book. Discounts of up to 40% on regular merchandise, more on seconds.
Especially worthwhile for lovers of a true cup of Italian espresso. They also sell
clothing by Nazareno Gabrielli, Sergio Tacchini and shirts by Coveri.

Fratelli Piazza Effepi

Via IV Novembre, 242 - 28882 Omegna - Crusinallo (VB) 0323 643595
9.00-12.30/15.00-19.00 C.C.:All Major

Household goods, gifts
FACTORY OUTLET

From Omegna towards Gravellona Toce. The outlet is on the local road on the right.

The perfect place to stock up on kitchen implements: slotted spoons, measure-pints, large bowls in stainless steel for perfect pastry at € 7,00, 2nd choice, bowls for mixing omelets, fruit bowls, small jars and platters for a thousand different uses. Their regular stock is reduced at 30%, more when it is a second choice. An ideal outlet for the serious cook.

Lagostina

Via 4 Novembre, 39 - 28887 Omegna - Crusinallo (VB) 0323 652255
9.00-12.30/15.00-19.00 C.C.:All Major

Household goods
FACTORY OUTLET

A large outlet on the S.S. 229 Novara-Gravellona Toce, on the left. Ample Parking.

A large showroom, laid out like a supermarket with shopping carts, showing all the main lines in pots and pans in regular and 2nds. Important reductions and special offers like a pasta cooker 'Weekend' 22cm, or a 'Silverstone' frying pan. Gift items like fondue sets in stainless steel or sets of kitchen knives, trays, and trolleys for outdoor cooking.

Estyl di Erba

Via Belvedere 7 - Possaccio - 28923 Verbania (VB) 0323 571218
8.00-12.00/14.00-19.30 C.C.:All Major

Optician
FACTORY OUTLET

Autostrada A26, exit Gravellona Toce. Go through Verbania, Pallanza and Intra. At the traffic light at the Banca Popolare turn left and continue straight, past two squares, another traffic light to the right, go over the bridge, sign post Possaccio. The Estyl factory is on the right.

They produce their own line in prescription glasses and sunglasses. One can have a checkup and choose Rodenstock lenses at factory prices. They also sell objects in acetate, rather nice and unusual.

Lanerie Agnona

Via Casazza, 7 - 13011 Borgosesia (VC) 0163 291111
9.00-13.00/15.00-19.00. Sunday 10.00-19.00 C.C.:All Major

Fabrics, clothing
FACTORY OUTLET

Lanerie Agnona is on the other side of the river Sesia. Take the picturesque bridge to cross, it's a worthwhile experience. Parking outside of the gate.

They tend to sell a bit of everything, woollen fabrics in massive quantities, plus various bits of haberdashery. Wool costs around € 30,00 p.m. and cashmere starts at € 100,00 p.m and up. The choice in blankets and plaids in wool or wool/cashmere is fairly extensive, less so their collection of cashmere scarves € 70,00 - € 125,00 depending on size. Baskets with special offers.

Tessitura di Crevacuore

Corso Vercelli, 141 - 13011 Borgosesia (VC)   0163 23041
9.30-12.30/14.30-19.30. Closed Monday   C.C.:All Major

Fabrics, home furnishings, household linen
FACTORY OUTLET

From the center of Borgosesia, take the road towards Biella. On the left, shortly after their sign post.

Excellent address for Chanel type tweeds or anything in fancy woollen material. Prices are low! Count on € 7,00 per meter for the most unusual or elaborate woollen laces, tweeds. Cashmere/wool 50/50 € 25,000 per meter. They have enlarged their premises and now also sell handbags, ties and suit for W and some sweaters for M. They speak English. Sales in February and July.

Manifatture di Carisio

Via Torino, 2 fraz. Crocicchio - 13040 Carisio (VC)   0161 858211
9.30-19.30. Sat. & Sun. 10.30-19.30   C.C.:All Major

Knitwear, cashmere
FACTORY OUTLET

Autostrada A4, exit Carisio. Turn right, continue for 200 meters. It's the first building on the right, well indicated.

A new outlet for cashmere of their own production close to the autostrada exit. Casual and fashionable knitwear made for famous brandnames. A cashmere cape € 140,00, scarves € 45,00, also very luxurious coats in cashmere. Friendly personnel and a made to measure and alteration service. Sales in July and January/February. They speak English.

Ceramica Vogue

Strada Statale 143, no. 100 - 13882 Vergnasco di Cerrione (VC)   015 672327
8.30-12.30/14.00-18.00. Saturday 8.30-12.30   C.C.:All Major

Furniture, tiles
FACTORY OUTLET

Autostrada A4, exit Santhia towards Biella for approximately 20 minutes. A large factory that is immediately noticeable.

A visit to Ceramica Vogue is only worthwhile for those who want to buy large quantities of tiles. They specialize in single colour tiles and stock a lot of different shades to choose from. One can find 1st, 2nd and even 3rd choice plus end of line. They need 2 days to fulfill an order.

La Galleria Outlet Center

Via Tonale, 101 - 24061 Albano S. Alessandro (BG)
10.00-21.00. Sunday closed

035 584611
C.C.: All Major

Clothing, accessories
OUTLET CENTER

Autostrada A4, exit Seriate to S.S. 42, Sarnico/Lovere. Large parking.

A recently opened outlet center with about 30 indoor shops mostly selling clothing and lingerie. You'll find Playtex, Cacharel, Dim, Boggi, Vestebene, Coin, Golden Lady and many more. There is a bar on the first floor.

Cotonificio Albini

Via Manni, 7 - 24021 Albino (BG)
9.00-12.00. Saturday 15.00-18.00. Closed Thursday

035 777111
C.C.: None

Fabrics, shirts
FACTORY OUTLET

Autostrada A4, exit Bergamo towards Val Seriana. In Albino at the traffic light in Via Libertà turn left, follow Via Roma on the right. At the level of Via Bonelli to the right, a narrow road. Entrance on the left, the outlet is at the end on the left.

Fabric for shirts sold per meter or coupons sold by weight (€ 12,50 per kilo). 2nd choice shirts sell at € 50,00 for 4 shirts, all sizes. They work for various European markets: men's shirts by Thomas Mason, Arthur & Fox, Daniels & Korff, or Brooksfield, Crawford ecc. All fabrics are first quality, worth the detour.

Outlet Road - Gipsy

Via Sottoprovinciale, 24 - 24021 Albino (BG)   035 753419
9.30-12.30/15.00-19.00   C.C.:All Major

Clothing, sportswear, casual, jeans
FACTORY OUTLET

Autostrada A4, exit Bergamo continue towards Valle Seriana, past Albino to Comendono, the next village. At the traffic light turn right and immediately left into a narrow road to an industrial zone. Follow the road and the sign Outlet Road till the intersection and turn right.

This outlet offers great choice in sweatshirts and T-shirts by Sailor's, Point Loma USA, Ellesse sportswear, or Polartec parkas all at vastly reduced prices. Scorpion Bay sweats, seconds, in large bins at € 10,00, Ellesse mountain boots, very smart, € 35,00, corduroy pants € 22,50. Personnel is fairly scarse, there are lockers to leave bags and coats.

Trussardi Factory Outlet (Ditta Sisal)

Via Milano, 40 - 24011 Almé (BG)   035 634111
10.00 - 19.00   C.C.:All Major

Clothing, accessories
FACTORY OUTLET

Autostrada A4, exit Dalmine. Take the road to Val Brembana for circa 11 km. The Trussardi outlet is in a glass building on the left, parking.

The unsold items from all the Trussardi shops end up here, which means sizes can be a bit erratic, size 50 next to 36, a single sexy evening gown next to a series of spare tweed suits. For men there are a lot of delectable cable knit sweaters, also small leather goods, belts, shoes and jackets € 150,00 circa, pants € 65,00. Occasionally there is a fair selection of clothing for children.

Brand Store Factory Outlet

Via Verdi, 3 - 24100 Bergamo (BG)   035 231582
9.30-12.30/15.30-19.30   C.C.:All Major

Clothing
BARGAIN BASEMENT

In the center of Bergamo, near the Post Office in Via Verdi. Second traffic light to the right. Parking.

Quite an interesting choice of festive clothes and daywear: waistcoats € 35,00, skirts start at € 30,00, pants by Kookai, Armani, Valentino and Versace from € 25,00. Winter coats by MaxMara € 150,00, Henry Cotton's € 175,00, W's suits € 175,00. Everything is discounted 50%.

Scaglione Cashmere

Via Lochis, 12 - 24129 Bergamo (BG)   035 4373338
9.30-12.30/14.30-19.00   C.C.:All Major

Knitwear, cashmere
FACTORY OUTLET

Autostrada A4, exit Bergamo take the S.S. 342 towards Lecco-Como and the Longuelo area.

Ladies knitwear in merinos € 30,00, in 30%/70% cashmere/merinos € 75,00. Cardigans for M/W in 4-ply cashmere € 210,00. Chanel type suits € 110,00. Styling is classical as are the colours. All sizes available. Other address: Piazza S.Pietro in Gessate, 2 in Milan.

La Compagnia della Pelle

Via Lega Lombardo, 3 - 24048 Bonate Sopra (BG)
10.00-18.30. Saturday 8.30-12.30/14.30-18.30

035 4995011
C.C.:All Major

Handbags, leather goods, suitcases
FACTORY OUTLET

Autostrada A4, exit Capriate, towards Ponte S. Pietro, a very busy road.

They work for Benetton and Sisley, which means a great deal of casual and practical hand bags and book packs are for sale plus a smaller offer of small black
evening bags with strass clips. Large sporty hold-alls for travelling, for tennis or
golf in canvas with leather trimming, shopping bags and small leather goods with
the Benetton logo. Prices are comnpetitive.

I Pinco Pallino Factory Outlet

Vl. Mattei, 31 Z.I. - Entratico (BG)
14.00-19.00. Saturday 9.00-19.00

035 4255186
C.C.:All Major

Clothing, shoes
FACTORY OUTLET

*Autostrada A5, exit Seriate o Grumello. Take the S.S. 42 to Lovere. Just before the sign
for Entratico at the beginning of the village, turn right, at the roundabout right again.
The factory is in an industrial area.*

I Pinco Pallino is a very well known brandname for children's clothes, they have
a shop in Milan with elegant and casual clothes for children from 2 to 16 years
old. At their outlet they sell end of line, unsold and samples. Small velvet blazers
for Christmas, patent leather shoes, smock dresses at reduced prices. They have
another outlet at The Mall in Reggello (FI).

Ladyberg

Via per Azzano, 32 - 24050 Grassobbio (BG)
11.30-19.30. Saturday 10.00-18.00. Monday closed

035 525388
C.C.:All Major

Lingerie, underwear
FACTORY OUTLET

*Autostrada A4, exit Bergamo to Orio al Serio Airport. After the overpass at the crossing
turn left, at the traffic light left again, then left to Grassobbio. On the main road to Azzano.*

Lingerie, underwear, pareos, bikini's by 'Io Donna', 'Roberta', 'Olalà' and
'Papillon'. Beach hats by Blumarine, sandals in bright colours. Bermuda's for men
€ 9,50. Baskets with briefs € 1,00 - € 2.00, bras 3 for € 12,00. For small sizes
(2) their showroom collection is worth a look. A good source to stock up on
quality lingerie, friendly and competent personnel. Fidelity card.

Lovable Outlet - Sara Lee

Via Boschetti, 53/55 - 24050 Grassobbio (BG)
10.00-13.00/15.00-19.00. Tues/Thurs/Sat. 10.00-19.00

035 678334
C.C.:All Major

Lingerie, underwear
FACTORY OUTLET

*Autostrada A4, exit Bergamo to Orio al Serio Airport. After the overpass at the crossing
turn left, at the traffic light left again, then left to Grassobbio. At the traffic light right,
first street on the left. Parking outside. One needs a pass from the porter.*

Lingerie, underwear by Lovable. Large baskets with briefs in polyester, 2nds, € 4.00-€
5.00, bras € 13,00 up to size 8a. Corsets and nightdresses, p.g.'s for men € 15,00, special offers. They also sell DIM, Playtex, Wonderbra and Fila at discounts of circa 20%.

Spaccio Sagitta

Via Nazionale, 17 - 24069 Luzzana (BG) — 035 822842
9.30-12.00/15.00-19.30 — C.C.:All Major

Clothing, shirts
FACTORY OUTLET

From Bergamo S.S. 42. After Entratico towards Lovere on the right. Well indicated.

The best time to visit their summer collection is towards the end of April.
Clothes for romantics; long summer dresses in linen or linen/viscose by
'Veronica Damiani' or 'Closed' € 67,50, shirts € 22,50, long skirts that were fun,
worn with a crocheted stole, sizes up to 46, cashmere twinsets and scarves.
Racks with 2nds. Nice shirts for men, as were the parka's and cardigans with
leather elbow patches.

RJ Outlet

Via G. Galilei, 2 - 24050 Orio al Serio (BG) — 035 702141
10.00-19.30. Monday 14.00-19.30 — C.C.:All Major

Clothing
DISCOUNTS

*Autostrada A4, exit Bergamo, continue to the Airport Orio al Serio, pass the airport and
turn right under the autostrada after 50 meters. Is on the left, a shop of circa 1.000 sqm.*

Clothing and accessories for M/W by all the trendy brandnames: Armani, Roberto
Cavalli, Fendi, Gucci, MiuMiu, Moschino, Prada, Dolce & Gabbana, Valentino, Church,
Levis, Morgan, Versace and others. Prices are discounted 30% - 70%, with an average reduction of 40% on list price. They also sell their own line of up to date fashion, brandname RJ, in line with the latest styles. Worth a visit.

New Marbas

Via Groppina, 8 - 24020 Parre (BG) — 035 702141
16.30-18.30. Closed Saturday — C.C.: None

Knitwear
FACTORY OUTLET

*Autostrada A4, exit Bergamo. Take the direction of Valle Seriana. After Ponte Nossa at
the fork in the road for Clusone continue towards Parre. The factory is after the second
curve. Entrance to the outlet is at the last gate.*

Shirts and polos in mercerized cotton, made for some well known brand names
like Alfred Dunhill, Celine, Valentino. Polos for men, shortsleeved € 18,50, 2nds
€ 12, for women polos and T-shirts often with nautical or floral motifs at the
same price. The polos made for Callaway and Bobby Jones will please golfers.

Gruppo Bartoli-Cotton's Industries

Via Nazionale, 2 - 24060 Pianico (BG) — 035 981210
9.30-12.30/15.00-19.00. Closed Tues & Wed morning — C.C.:All Major

Clothing, sportswear, casual, jeans
FACTORY OUTLET

*Autostrada A4, from Milano exit Bergamo. From Venice exit Brescia Ovest. Take the
direction of Lovere. The outlet is on the S.S. 42 on the right and well indicated.*

An enormous factory hall offering plenty of good deals for sporty men. Jeans,
outerwear jackets, sailing parkas, hiking shorts, hunting and travel vests, ski overalls largely in size 48. Jeans Red Hawk € 15,00, bomber € 25,00, down ski jacket € 40,00, pants and bermudas by Brunik and Harbourmaster, only in size 52,
€ 10,00. Really worthwhile.

Spaccio Cassera Casa

Piazza Caduti 6 Luglio 1996 - 24040 Stezzano (BG)   035 4545011
10.00-12.30/15.00-18.30 (July 15.00-18.30). Sat. 10.00-12.30   C.C.: None

Household linen, various
FACTORY OUTLET

Autostrada A4, exit Dalmine turn right towards Stezzano, after 2 kilometers circa at the first roundabout look for the Cassera Casa sign. From Bergamo S.S. Francesca towards Treviglio. Ample parking on the square in front of the factory outlet.

Their home collection has lovely table and bed linens for discerning housewives. Garden cushions, cotton per meter in famous flower prints € 8,50 p.m., coupons € 8,00 per kilo. We recommend the linens in white or cream at € 20,00 per m., 180 cm w. for sheets. A small corner with lingerie and Victorian night dresses, linen tea towels make good presents. Also, numerous discounts and special offers..........

Perletti

Via Gaetano Scirea, 5/7 - 24060 Telgate (BG)   035 831001
8.00-12.00/13.30-17.30. Closed Saturday   C.C.: None

Umbrellas
FACTORY OUTLET

Autostrada A4, exit Grumello. Follow the signs for the 'Campo Sportivo' and Perletti. Parking outside. The modern factory stands in a new development, and their outlet is consequently spacious.

Large choice in umbrellas and parasols. They work for G. M. Venturi, Balestra, Laura Biagiotti and others. A small foldable in bright colours with the Biagiotti initials € 6. Large golf umbrellas € 8,50 in Blackwatch, Stuart or Buchanan clan prints, bamboo handled business umbrellas € 12. Some very jolly little parasols by Venturi at € 18,50. Also handbags beachbags, polyester scarves. Ideal for presents.

Virgy Chemises

Via F.lli Calvi, 4 - 24018 Villa d'Almè (BG)   035 639759
9.30-12.30/15.00-19.30   C.C.:All Major

Shirts
ARTISAN'S WORKSHOP

Autostrada A4, exit Dalmine, a road with heavy traffic. At Villa d'Almè continue towards San Pellegrino till the Esso gas station on the right. The shop is on the corner after the traffic light.

Virgy makes rather nice sporty shirts, good looking and modern, like the brownish shirts made with Armani type fabrics, wellmade, in classical taste. Normal shirt collection € 32,50 - € 62,50, great choice, various collars/fabrics. Seconds by McPherson with tiny imperfections € 20,00. For women some velvet or classical cotton shirts with long sleeves € 37,50.

Sheratonn Italiana

Via Lizzere, 2 - 25021 Bagnolo Mella (BS)   030 620281
9.00-12.00/13.00-17.00. Closed Saturday   C.C.: None

Silverware/Pewter
FACTORY OUTLET

Autostrada A4, exit Brescia Centro, take S.S. 45/bis towards Cremona, for 5 kms. At the beginning of the village, a narrow street opposite the API service station.

An excellent address for wedding presents or anyone in need of metal or silverplate table settings. Champagne flutes in silverplate € 11,00 each, with a gold rim € 12,00, sets of 6 tea glasses with silverplate handles, trays in various sizes, snail or oyster platters, brandy warmers, vodka glasses, frames in various styles and sizes, perfume bottles and hundreds of other objects.

Rebelot

Corso Cavour, 29 - 25100 Brescia (BS)
9.30-12.30/15.30-19.30

030 48587
C.C.:All Major

Clothing
DISCOUNTS

Autostrada A4, exit Brescia Est towards the center. We suggest to park around the Porta Cremona and walk to the center.

A small shop selling the unsold collection of Penelope, a boutique in the center of Brescia famous for their avantgarde clothing. Sizes are mostly small and prices are halved but still hefty. Worth a visit for the perky and unusual brandnames and highly innovative styles, either Italian or imported.

Rose & Thin

Via Orzinuovi, 93 - 25125 Brescia (BS)
9.30-13.00/14.30-19.00. Saturday 9.00-13.00

030 348005
C.C.:All Major

Clothing
FACTORY OUTLET

Autostrada A4, exit Brescia Ovest for the center. After Hotel Industria and in front of the Q8 service station, a corner shop.

Rose & Thin makes modern, slightly off-beat clothes in original fabrics and unusual colours. Slinky shirts in cotton voile and orange velvet, short mini dresses in white cotton hanging together with buckles and ribbons, all in small sizes, up to 44. Special offers € 10,00 - € 20,00. There is lots of choice, quality is ok but sizes are a bit erratic.

Efercal

Via Cavour, 147 - 25011 Calcinatello (BS)
8.00-12.30/14.00-18.00

030 9636600
C.C.:None

Hosiery
FACTORY OUTLET

Autostrada A4, exit Desenzano to Ponte S.Marco and S.S. 11. Take the road to Calcinatello, under the railway bridge, continue for 50 m, look for a large shop window.

Hosiery for M/W in excellent quality, Alta Moda, brandname Fergical, Breitex, Hamilton. They have everything, knee high net stockings € 1,25, pantyhose in cotton, in microfiber, support stockings, with lacey tops, in black lace ecc. Men's socks in cotton or wool, long or short with a diamond pattern, very up to date. They export to Germany.

Bulgari Camicie

Via Trento, 188 - 25020 Capriano del Colle (BS)
9.15-12.30/15.00-19.00. Saturday 9.15-19.00

030 9749222
C.C.:All Major

Shirts
FACTORY OUTLET

Autostrada A4, exit Brescia Ovest. Take the road to Quinzano d'Oglio. Bulgari camicie is on the left, well before the center of Capriano, in Fenili, and just before Italpresse.

More than 3.000 shirts to choose from in a great variety of colours, fabrics, styles. Either with a buttondown collar, diagonal, French collar, with 3 buttons, white collar on striped shirt ecc. Sizes go up to 52 which is a size 60 or XXXL. Prices from € 40,00 - € 49,00, special offers at € 19,00.

Brescia Factory Outlet

S.S. Brescia - Mantova - 25014 Castenedolo (BS)   030 2731225
9.00-19.30   C.C.:All Major

Clothing, accessories
FACTORY OUTLET

Autostrada A4, exit Brescia Est, take the provincial road to Mantova and then to the village of Castenedolo. At the beginning of the village on the right. Look for a large blue and yellow sign 'Henriette'.

An outlet of 3.000 sq. m. with various brandnames, Belfe, Fausta tricot, Donna Enrica, L'Equipe Plus, Freepride, Kenté, Basile, Tommy Hilfiger, Jantzen, offering general clothing, sportswear, leatherwear, household goods, linens at factory prices. Nice leather jackets by Pozzi € 200,00-€ 250,00. This is a rather recent outlet center with a bar on the premises and a play ground for children.

Bialetti Gruppo Rondine

Via Fogliano, 1 - 25030 Coccaglio (BS)   030 7703600
8.30-12.30/14.30-18.30. Closed Monday   C.C.:All Major

Household goods
FACTORY OUTLET

Autostrada A4, exit Rovato, S.S.11 then S.S.498 towards Bergamo. The factory is on the left coming from Brescia, the outlet is 50 m further on. Parking.

Teflon coated cooking pots start at € 3,50 in excellent quality. Grills in heavy cast iron € 7,00, for large fish € 8,00. Bialetti electric espresso machines in various models, discounted up to 35%. Racks full of kitchen utensils at €1,50 for a stainless steel pizza cutter. Nice presents are small pink-coloured espresso pots, good for two cups € 2,50. They now sell other Made in Italy brandnames.

Scab

Via Castrezzato, 44 - 25030 Coccaglio (BS)   030 7702558
Only on Wednesday. Saturday 9.00-12.00 from 1/4-1/8   C.C.: None

Furniture, various
FACTORY OUTLET

Autostrada A4, exit Rovato then take the direction for Chiari. After the sign 'Coccaglio' turn right at the traffic light.

Garden furniture in resina and steel resina. Comfortable chairs, long folding chairs, benches, trolleys for drinks, dining tables either in white, green, bordeaux or blue and can be ordered with a faux marble top. A sofa for three costs € 65,00. Prices are very competitive (citrca 35% less), and everything comes with a 3 to 5 year guarantee. In September phone first.

Outlet Cinzia Rocca - Rodel

Via Borgo Belvedere, 23 - 25033 Dello (BS)   030 9719121
9.00-12.30/15.00-19.30   C.C.:All Major

Clothing
FACTORY OUTLET

Autostrada A4, exit Brescia Ovest to Quinzano on the main road. A Dello continue for 200 m., the Rodel factory is on the right next to their outlet.

Large and well laid out, impressive choice of classical two and three piece suits in fashionable colours & styles. Smart suits € 100.00-€ 130.00, dresses, skirts, shirts that will last, sizes from 40 to 55 (XXL). Their sample size is 44 or for the XXL collection 43. It's all impeccable, very wearable and stylish.

Gallo Outlet

V.le Motta, 125 - 25015 Desenzano del Garda (BS)   030 9110465
9.00-12.00/13.00-19.00. Saturday 9.00-12.00/15.00-19.00   C.C.:All Major

Hosiery
FACTORY OUTLET

Autostrada A4, Desenzano exit, turn left, through Desenzano following the indications for Sirmione. Immediately after the town limit but before Rivoltella, on the right, well indicated.

Gallo produces high quality socks for the whole family in a great variety of styles. Dress socks in wool with a diamond pattern for M. start at € 3,00, also special hiking socks, winter socks, long socks. For W. beautiful printed or embroidered lacy panty-hose. Lots of cute, colourful fantasy socks for Ch. Check out their seconds!

RJ Outlet

Via Dei Colli Storici, 181 - 25015 Desenzano del Garda (BS)   030 9108084
10.00-13.00/15.00-19.30. Sat./Sun. 10.00-19.30   C.C.:All Major

Clothing
DISCOUNTS

Autostrada A4, exit Sirmione, after circa 800 m on the road towards Desenzano, on the right. A large shop of 1.000 sq.m.

Clothing and accessories for M/W by all the trendy brandnames: Armani, Roberto Cavalli, Fendi, Gucci, MiuMiu, Moschino, Prada, Dolce & Gabbana, Valentino, Church, Levis, Morgan, Versace and others. Prices are discounted 30% - 70%, with an average reduction of 40% on list price. They also sell their own line of up to date fashion, brandname RJ, in line with the latest styles. Worth a visit.

Luca's Gruppo Boglioli

Via Brescia, 47 - 25020 Gambara (BS)   030 9567241
9.00-12.00/15.00-19.30   C.C.:All Major

Clothing
FACTORY OUTLET

Autostrada A21, exit Pontevico for Gambara. Luca's is on the road towards Gottolengo/Brescia, on the left before an IP service station. A house with a large garden in front.

A rather elegant shop, understated, offering men's clothing in a distinctly English style. Jackets € 150,00, coats € 250,00 by 'David Burnett', rather dapper and tightly cut in mustard yellow velvet. Suits by Boglioli € 240,00, summer pants € 69,00. Shirts by Harrisons at € 68,00. All very striking, elegant and well made. Fidelity card.

Frabosk Casalinghi

Via Massimo d'Azeglio, 61 - 25067 Lumezzane (BS)   030 8250611
8.30-12.00/14.30-18.30   C.C.:All Major

Household goods
FACTORY OUTLET

From Brescia take the road to the Val Trompia and Lumezzane. Turn right at the 2nd traffic light, continue for 100 m. In front of the cemetry and immediately after an IP service station take the narrow road up to the left, follow the sign Frabosk.

A large showroom with a separate room for stock and seconds on the right. Frabosk is the producer of the original Capuccino Creamer for instant frothy milk and produce lovely tea kettles, rice cookers, steamers, termos flasks and plates and platters in stainless steel. Also ceramics and articles in wood made by others. Good deals are the pressure cookers and small espresso pots.

Mepra

Via Montini 176 - 25067 Lumezzane (BS)   030 8921441
9.00-12.00/14.00-17.30. Saturday closed   C.C.: None

Household goods
FACTORY OUTLET

From Brescia take the road for Val Trompia, Concesio, Sarezzo. Turn right for Lumezzane, continue straight. Go past two traffic lights, after 300 m the outlet is on the left, in front of an IP service station.

Lumezzane is a production center of kitchenware in stainless steel. Mepra produces kitchen ware, platters, serving dishes, fruit juicers, salt and pepper sets and whatever else the modern kitchen needs, all dishwasher safe. Fun designs, knives and forks with brightly coloured handles, sky blue or apple green, sold at very reasonable prices.

Cotonella

Via Nazionale, 137 - 25040 Malonno (BS)   0364 635596
8.30-12.30/15.00-19.00. Open in August   C.C.:All Major

Clothing, lingerie, underwear
FACTORY OUTLET

From Boario Terme and Brescia take the S.S. 42 towards Edolo. Cotonella is just after Malonno, on the left and is well indicated. Ample parking.

2 floors of family style underwear, pyamas, stockings and shirts. Two shirts for M € 20,50, brand name Gandolfi, men's T-shirts in elasticized cotton € 9,50, socks € 2,55. All the Playtex lingerie is discounted 30%: the original Wonderbras € 22,00, briefs and panties at € 4,00 or take 3 pay 2.

Gruppo Manerbiese

Via Cremona, 57 - 25025 Manerbio (BS)   030 99391
15.00-19.00. Saturday 9.00-12.00/15.00-19.00   C.C.:All Major

Clothing
FACTORY OUTLET

Autostrada A21, exit Manerbio. Take the local road to Pontevico and look for the sign Moda Donna, on the left. Parking.

A large outlet with samples and seconds on the left of the entrance and the current collection on the right, brandname Laura Lindor. A casual/classical style, a bit Nordic, easy to wear and well made. Their showroom collection size is 42, seconds can be found in any size, also XXL. A pair of trousers in cotton, 2nds, € 14,00 like the tops in viscose. The baskets with fabric remnants are also worth a look.

Mos Melior

Via Artigianale, 9 - 25025 Manerbio (BS)   030 9380028
9.00-12.00/14.00-19.00. Saturday 9.00-12.00/15.00-19.00   C.C.:All Major

Clothing
FACTORY OUTLET

Autostrada A21, exit Manerbio. Follow signs for the center and the station. After the bridge turn right and continue towards the industrial zone, turn right, Mos Melior is on the left. The entrance to the outlet is behind the factory.

Very presentable and elegant clothes by Elena Brunelli in size 40 to 48/50. Two piece sophisticated suits € 175,00. Rather etheral dresses in champagne silk voile, coats in wool, bombers in camel coloured tweed. The spring collection is for sale in March. Friendly atmosphere, a lot of choice.

Charly Boy

Via Lungo Oglio C. Battisti, 21 - 25036 Palazzolo sull'Oglio (BS)   030 732279
8.30-12.00/13.30-18.00. Closed Saturday & August   C.C.: None

Clothing
FACTORY OUTLET

Autostrada A4, exit Palazzolo sull'Oglio, turn right and continue for 3 km until a metal bridge. After the bridge turn right, continue 50 m to a small gate. The outlet is next to a beautifully restored villa.

The place to visit when in need of a very special, very festive dress for a little girl. Prices start at € 75,00 up to € 225,00 for a super de luxe creation.

Abert

Via Don P. Mazzolari, 17 (Z.I.) - 25050 Passirano (BS)   030 6577121
10.00-14.00/15.00-19.00. Saturday 9.00-12.00   C.C.:All Major

Household goods
FACTORY OUTLET

Autostrada A4, exit Ospitaletto. Turn immediately to the right and then to the left for Passirano.

An outlet for brides to be, stainless steel cutlery with or without brightly coloured handles in sets of 12 or 36, special offers and seconds. Modern and cheerful designs in bread baskets, trays and serving platters.

IPA Easy Cook

Via Industriale, 21 Z.I. S. Giovanni - 25060 Polaveno (BS)   030 8940035
9.00-18.00. Closed Saturday   C.C.:All Major

Household goods
FACTORY OUTLET

From Iseo take the road towards Polaveno. IPA Easy Cook is in the industrial zone after Polavena, turn right into the industrial zone S. Giovanni.

Easy Cook produces unusual kitchen wares in stainless steel, woks, special pasta cookers, steamers for slimmers, special models for cooking very large fish, a round electric oven with a silver finish € 125,00, quite striking. Also tins in original shapes to bake cakes, puddings or lasagna. Discounts 20% - 70%. Interesting outlet.

Caliban

Via E. Mattei, 1 - 25026 Pontevico (BS)   030 9307761
9.00-12.30/14.30-19.30   C.C.:All Major

Clothing, shirts
GOOD PRICES

Autostrada A21, exit Pontevico. From the exit Caliban is 100 m further on towards Gambara. Ample parking.

Large building stocked with clothing in the latest trends (Canali, Avirex, Penny Black). Their men's shirts are very good value at € 24,00, brand name Caliban or Nazareno Gabrielli, shirts by Luca Palazzi, Carlo Pignatelli or Ungaro € 29,00, by Balthazar Paris or Krizia € 32,00, A small room behind the shirts department holds deep discounts for second choice shirts, mostly for men and worth a look.

Spaccio Ciocca

Via L. Ciocca, 11 - 25027 Quinzano d'Oglio (BS)   030 9923522
9.00-12.00/15.00-19.00   C.C.:All Major

Knitwear, cashmere, hosiery
FACTORY OUTLET

Autostrada A4, exit Brescia Centro to Autostrada A21, exit Pontevico to Quinzano d'Oglio where we suggest to ask for directions.

The Calzificio Luigi Ciocca was founded in 1912 and produces more than 15 million pairs of men's long socks per year. In their outlet they offer long socks in wool at € 1,33 a pair, or packs of six at discounts. They also sell knitwear in wool or cashmere (a sweater € 65,00) in lovely colours and 2nds in polo shirts by Hardy Crobb's, Alan Scott and Rossopuro at € 6,50. Nice flowery pants and T-shirts by Ken Scott at low prices. Worth the detour.

Franciacorta Outlet Village

Piazza Cascina Moie, 1 - 25050 Rodengo Saiano (BS)   030 6810181
10.00-20.00. Fri. & Sat. 10.00-21.00. Open on Sundays   C.C.:All Major

Clothing, accessories
OUTLET CENTER

Autostrada A4, exit Ospitaletto. Follow the directions for Moie and Franciacorta Outlet Village. It takes about 5 minutes to reach the outlet village from the autostrada.

Another fairly recent addition to the Italian outlet centers/villages, done in a rustic Lombard style, very pleasant, with bars, a restaurant, an icecream parlour, a gym and lots of parking. Mostly clothing shops and household linen by Bassetti, Bottega Verde, Benetton, Conte of Florence, Frette, Levi's, Mila Schon, Nike, O'Neill, Para, Pompea, Pupa, Stefanel, Swinger, Versace and others. Average savings between 10% and 30%.

Fausta Cinquini

Via Lavoro e Industria, 431 - 25030 Rudiano (BS)   030 7060011
Only Saturday 10.00-12.00/14.00-18.00   C.C.: None

Clothing
FACTORY OUTLET

Autostrada A4, exit Palazzolo to Rudiano. From Milan it is more convenient to take the road to Linate and then the S.S. 11 to Urago d'Oglio. The outlet is before Rudiano in their Industrial Zone.

'Elegance in any size' is their slogan and they do indeed a very good job dressing XXXL ladies, by brand name Fausta Cinquini, Fausta Cinquini Sport and Cinquini Collection. Basic black dresses can be combined with untold combinations of jackets, shawls, vests in turqoise or pink, all very fluid and becoming. Their outlet only sells the showroom collection, end of series and unsold items.

Pintinox

Via Antonini, 87 - 25068 Sarezzo (BS)   030 8935111
9.30-12.30/15.00-18.30   C.C.: None

Household goods
FACTORY OUTLET

Autostrada A4, exit Brescia Ovest towards Sarezzo and Lumezzane. Pintinox is on the road for Lumezzane on the left. Parking is difficult.

A large showroom on the 1st floor with a good part of their collection on view, masses of stainless steel cutlery in practical styles or more elaborate implements for hotels and restaurants discounted 35%. Interesting are the 'Catering' articles on sale: very large professional kitchen pots and pans, seconds, at € 13,00 per kilo. You'll have to weigh these yourself. Also knives, forks, spoons, in silverplate, seconds.

Lam Argenti

Via Consolare, 52 - 25030 Zocco di Erbusco (BS)　　030 7760269
9.00-12.30/14.30-19.00. Sat. 9.00-12.30　　　　　C.C.:All Major

Silverware/Pewter
FACTORY OUTLET

Autostrada A4, exit Palazzolo sull'Oglio to S. Pancrazio. At the roundabout to the left, pass the church and continue. Argenterie Lam is on the left. Parking.

An elegant showroom with ample choice of small silver objects, picture frames, candle sticks, silver baby presents, ashtrays, presentation keys in silver, caraffes for wine with silver handles, hart or diamond shaped serving platters for bridge players, all discounted 20% and beautifully gift wrapped. Worthwhile.

Unionseta

Via Pirandello, 5 - 22070 Bulgarograsso (CO)　　031 9720211
9.00-19.00　　　　　　　　　　　　　　　　　C.C.:All Major

Clothing, beachwear
FACTORY OUTLET

Autostrada A9, exit at Fino Mornasco towards Cassina Rizzardi. After Bennet at the traffic lights to the right. Another 500 m, before the garage turn to the right for Unionseta.

Bathing costumes, beach shirts, lingerie by Moschino, Antonio Fusco and G. Mattioli. Overstock, seconds and showroom models. Bathing suits by Moschino € 24/€53 , beach dresses by Mattioli €93, Moschino T-shirts M/W € 18 Ties in silk by various wellknown 'griffe' €18 . Possible to find unusual and amusing pieces.

Seterie Ratti

Via Vivaldi, 6 - 22071 Cadorago (CO)　　　　031 8866280
9.30-19.00. Monday 15.00-19.00　　　　　　　C.C.:All Major

Silks
FACTORY OUTLET

Autostrada A9, exit Lomazzo, follow indications for Cadorago and Seterie Ratti. You can actually see the Ratti sign from the autostrada. We suggest to telephone ahead for groups. Ample parking.

Large showroom with high fashion items and Ratti Group products. Huge variety of silk fabrics for sale per m., fashion accessories like scarves, shawls, ties, also cushions and plaids, small silk/leather purses. The clothing for men and women is manufactured with Ratti fabrics, classical, unbeatable prices, all sizes. Seasonal sales and bargains every month. Worth a visit.

Emporio Pinto

Via Roma, 9 - 22070 Casnate con Bernate (CO)　　031 398634
9.00-12.30/15.00-18.30. Closed Saturday afternoon　C.C.: All Major/Taxfree

Silks
FACTORY OUTLET

Autostrada A9, exit Fino Mornasco, turn right, continue to the first traffic light. Turn left onto the S.S. 35 and keep going till the traffic light of Portichetto/Luisago, turn right. The Pinto outlet is at the beginning of the village on the right.

A modern outlet, completely renovated, offering all the silks that makes the Como region famous. Very large choice of ties € 15,00, scarves € 17,00, shawls € 14,00, cotton or silk fabrics for upholstery, shirts, objects for the home all at factory prices. Brandnames a.o. Bulgari. Discounts up to 50% and fidelity card, sales in July and August. They speak English.

GMG Seta Egon Furstenberg

Via della Chiesa, 5 - 22070 Cassina Rizzardi (CO)   031 921270
8.30-12.30/14.30-18.30. Saturday 8.00-12.00   C.C.: None

Silks
FACTORY OUTLET

Autostrada A9, exit Fino Mornasco to the left towards Villa Rizzardi. At the traffic light turn right.

Men's shirts with matching boxer shorts € 42, silk ties € 12 - € 18 by Egon von Furstenberg, who also designs the silk foulards at € 18,50. Silk fantasy waist-coats € 24, all in classical, tasteful designs.

Spaccio Aziendale

Via Risorgimento, 15/a - 22070 Cassina Rizzardi (CO)   031 881092
9.30-12.30/15.30-19.00   C.C.:All Major

Shirts
FACTORY OUTLET

Autostrada A9, exit Fino Mornasco, turn left to Cassina Rizzardi. The shop is in a gallery close to a bar, circa 300 m on the left after the roundabout with the fountain. Parking.

Men's shirts by Enrico Coveri and others at € 20,00 and up. A nice shirt, long sleeved, € 44,00, short sleeves € 40,00, In autumn they also sell knitwear in big, bulky knits by Coveri, Linea You Young. Discounts of up to 30% compared to shop prices. Fidelity card and sales in January and July.

Mister OK

Via per San Fermo, 57 - 22020 Cavallasca (CO)   031 536575
8.30-12.30/15.00-18.00. Closed Saturday   C.C.:All Major

Silks
DISCOUNTS

Autostrada A9, exit Como Sud towards San Fermo. The first village after San Fermo is Cavallasca at approximately 6 km. The outlet is on the main road.

Shawls, foulards, scarves, pareo, ties, ascots, stoles in polyester or silk, wool or acrilycs. Tremendous choice in polyester scarves in the latest designs and colours at € 3,50 standard size or € 25,00 for a silk scarf. Unbeatable prices, friendly multilingual staff.

Accademia Tessile Ivo Walter

Via Matteotto, 39 - 22070 Cernobbio (CO)   031 3347082
By appointment only   C.C.: None

Fabrics, home furnishings
DISCOUNTS

From Como towards Cernobbio-Maslianico to the industrial zone. After the Pizzeria Valverde continue 100 m on the left.

A wharehouse selling various types of decorating fabrics in natural fibers, plus window curtains and household linens like tablecloths and bed sheets. There are many special offers, discontinued items or end of series. Their shop in Como, Via Diaz 2, has a permanent sales corner.

Emporio Lario 1898
Via Vitt. Veneto, 52 - 22070 Cirimido (CO)   031 3523255
9.30-19.00   C.C.:All Major

Shoes
FACTORY OUTLET

Autostrada A9, Milano-Como, exit at Lomazzo. Turn right and at the traffic light again right. Lario is in the center of the village on the right. Ample parking.

An enormous hall, 450 sq.m. full of fashionable and sporty shoes by Susan Bennis, Jill Sander and their own brand name Lario. Some racks with their sho-wroom collection in size 37 for women and size 41 for men sell at € 62,00 circa. The Lario house collection is for sale at 30% below shop price, circa € 110,00 and available in all sizes. Also some Lario handbags. They speak English and their sales twice a year are major events.

Diffusione Seta Outlet
Via P. Paoli, 3 - 22100 Como (CO)   031 523800
10.00-18.00. Open on Monday morning   C.C.:All Major

Silks
FACTORY OUTLET

Autostrada A9, exit Como Sud. Follow the directions to the center. After the roundabout and befo-re the traffic light of Piazza Camerlata there is a sign Seta Outlet on the right. Large parking.

An enormous, modern outlet for silks: ties, scarves, stoles, clothing, nightwear, accessories. 2 rooms with special offers in ties and foulards by Ken Scott, Kenzo and Balestra near the entrance and a large space with ties by Dior € 65,00, Givenchy € 49,00, stoles by Genny, scarves, silk robes € 40,00, small handbags, evening bags € 39,00. Lots of special offers.

La Tessitura
Viale Roosevelt, 2/A - 22100 Como (CO)   031 321 666
9.30-12.30/14.00-18.00. Saturday closed   C.C.:All Major

Silks
CONCEPT STORE

Autostrada A9, exit Como Centro, follow directions for Cernobbio. At the level of the train station turn back at the traffic light. The Mantero complex is on the right after the super market and near the Sant'Abbondio church.

Mantero has created an avantgarde concept store in one of their old factory halls. Some gorgeous silks are for sale: masses of ties, € 7,50 - € 45,00, silk scar-ves € 32,50 circa and up depending on size, the choice is overwhelming (Trussardi, Donna Karan, Mantero). Superluxurious presents: slippers in silk, quilted bedspreads and pillow cases. Baskets with scarves on special offer € 10,00. All purchases will be nicely wrapped. Multilingual personnel.

Luan Saré
Via M. Cumano, 7 - 22100 Como (CO)   031 592124
9.00-12.00/14.00-18.00   C.C.: None

Clothing
FACTORY OUTLET

Autostrada A9, exit Como Sud. After the traffic light in Via Varesina/Piazza Camerlata, fifth road on the right in the direction of Como. Then third road to the right.

Very elaborate, feminine but pretty dresses with lots of glitter, for 30/40+ year olds. Masses of evening and cocktail wear, snazzy, lace edged or fur bordered dresses that will attract attention, but also more classical outfits, end of series at discounts, a wool-len suit € 156, silk polo with buttons in different colours € 63. Very friendly sales help.

Seterie Martinetti

Via Torriani, 41 - 22100 Como (CO)   031 269053
9.00-12.00/14.30-18.00 also Monday & Saturday   C.C.:All Major

Silks
FACTORY OUTLET

Via Torriani is a parallel street to Viale Varese where parking is available. Martinetti is at the beginning near Via Borsieri.

Silks, silks and more silks but also woollen crepes, linen cretonnes, cotton velvets and interesting combinations thereof can be bought at very good prices. A polyglot staff assists you. One room is totally dedicated to the sale of scarves/ties with all the major brand names. If you feel life is not worth living without a Versace scarf or tie, a silk kimono, ascots, paisley shawls or white fringed evening scarves for discerning men, this is the place to go.

Villa Sucota - Ratti

Via per Cernobbio, 17 - 22100 Como (CO)   031 576000
9.00-18.30. In summer Mond. 9.00-18.30 (closed winter)   C.C.:All Major

Silks
FACTORY OUTLET

Autostrada A9, exit Como Nord (last exit for Italy). Take the road to Cernobbio and at the 2nd roundabout to Como. On the right, parking in front of the gate. From Como bus n. 6 and 11.

Display with high fashion items and other Ratti Group products. Huge variety of silk fabrics, cashmere and wool. Furnishing fabric, cushions, fashion accessories like scarves, shawls, ties, perfumes and dressing gowns. Seasonal sales and bargains every month.

Larioseta

Via Asiago, 35 - 22100 Como Tavernola (CO)   031 512014
9.45-12.45/14.00-18.45   C.C.:All Major

Silks
FACTORY OUTLET

Autostrada A9, exit Como Nord towards Cernobbio. Approximately 200 m on the right after the overpass and Toyota. Parking.

A modern, well designed outlet inside the LarioSeta factory, offering a vast choice in ties and scarves. Ties start at € 10,00 up to € 42,50 (Les Copains, Leonard de Paris), scarves are circa € 32,50 for a standard size in pure silk. Large shawls in silk/wool mixtures € 45,00, plus accessories by some major 'Made in Italy' names like Moschino, Les Copains, Barbieri.

Fenegrò Cashmere

Via XXV Aprile, 3 - 22070 Fenegrò (CO)   031 3520070
10.00-13.30/14.30-19.00   C.C.:All Major/Taxfree
Closed Monday and 6/8 -28/8 . Sunday open in December

Knitwear, cashmere
FACTORY OUTLET

Autostrada A9, exit Lomazzo, follow the road to the right. At the traffic light to the right, go past the Lario shoe outlet. In Fenegrò in front of the cemetery to the left, then first gate on the left.

A factory store known for the high quality of its products. The knitwear collection is made in cashmere, merino wool, silk and other precious materials. Fenegrò produces modern designs in knitwear but also accessories like throws, blankets etc. They have a shop in Milano, Via Spartaco, 2 (in front of the Etro outlet).

Emporio della Seta Frey

Via Risorgimento, 49/51 - 22073 Fino Mornasco (CO)   031 927538
9.00-12.30/14.30-19.00. Sunday open in Dec. Open Monday   C.C.:All Major

Silks
FACTORY OUTLET

Autostrada A9, exit Fino Mornasco, to the right, continue for 500 m, the outlet is on the right and well indicated.

This emporium (1889) offers something for everybody. Accessories, ties (€ 10,00 - 17,50 styled by Krizia. Frey), shirts, jackets, weekend-wear, scarves 90 x 90 € 32,50, blouses, lingerie, silk material. Good taste, reasonable prices, nice silk and cashmere knitwear. They speak French, English and German. Sales in January. Alteration service.

Ines Crea Factory Outlet

S.S.35 dei Giovi, 40 - 22073 Fino Mornasco (CO)   031 928128
9.00-12.00/14.30-18.30. Saturday 10.00-12.00   C.C.: None

Clothing, beachwear
FACTORY OUTLET

Autostrada A98, exit Fino Mornasco towards Como. In front of the Shell service station.

Large choice of bathing costumes, bikinis, bermuda's and slips for M/W/Ch, also in XXL sizes and a fair choice of pareos and kaftans for the beach. One piece costumes € 17,90, two pieces € 16,90, XXL sizes € 18,90, kaftans € 15,90, bermudas € 15,80, bikinis for girls € 13,90. Special offers of shirts for men € 25,00.

Loris Abate Schontess

Via Garibaldi, 118 (S.S.35 dei Giovi) - 22073 Fino Mornasco (CO)   031 3542172
10.30-19.00. Monday closed   C.C.:All Major

Clothing, accessories
FACTORY OUTLET

Autostrada A9, exit Fino Mornasco to the center. At the traffic light turn right. Loris Abate is circa 100 m on the right. There is a sign to the outlet in the back of the factory complex.

Clothing made to very high standards for M/W in classical styles. Unsold items from their boutique in Milan but also a series of coats and jackets specially made for their outlets. Important discounts on evening dresses € 200,00, jackets and tailleurs in silk € 200,00, a silk sweater € 60,00. For men suits € 260,00, linen jackets € 200,00, cashmere sweaters € 160,00, ties € 15,00, also handbags and byoux. They have another outlet in Porto Cervo, Sardinia.

Artigiansalotti

Via Don Gnocchi, 14 - 22044 Inverigo (CO)   031 607101
9.30-12.00/15.00-19.00. Closed Monday & August   C.C.: None

Furniture, various
ARTISAN'S WORKSHOP

Approximately 26 km from Milano in the direction of Erba, on the main road to Valassina. From Switzerland take the state road Como-Bergamo, then at Lurago d'Erba towards Milano. Large show room of 600 sqm.

Since 1960 Artigiansalotti produces sofas, chairs, sofa-beds, from classical styles to the latest trends. All made to measure in top quality materials, with slip covers also in leather. Great choice of decorating fabrics by Rubelli, Marcato, Nobilis, Zimmer-Rhode or slipcovers in washable Alcantara at true factory prices. They speak English and French. Highly recommended.

Calzaturficio Brunate

Via del Seprio, 54 - 22074 Lomazzo (CO)
9.30-12.30/14.00-19.00. Saturday 9.30-19.30

02 96779393
C.C.:All Major

Shoes
FACTORY OUTLET

Autostrada A9, exit Lomazzo. Turn to the right, at the traffic light again right. After the bridge over the autostrada, turn immediately to the right. Parking.

500 mq of shoes by Krizia, Giesswein, Clarks, N.O.D., Nina Quei, well-known for their smart looks. Showroom models for W, size 37, are € 45,00, for M size 41 € 67,50. The rest of their vast (more than 1000 models) collection sells for € 75,00 circa for W and € 75,00 - € 150,00 for M. Short, pointed boots, stilettos, mocassins, handbags, some belts and small purses and wallets. They speak English and German.

Avon Beauty Club

Via XXV Aprile, 15 - 22077 Olgiate Comasco (CO)
9.00-19.00. Monday 13.00-18.45

031 998396
C.C.:All Major

Beautycare, perfumes
FACTORY OUTLET

S.S. 342 Como-Varese. Avon Beauty Club is well indicated. Drive inside the gate and pass the entrance, to the left.

Large and pleasant outlet with the complete cosmetics collection by Avon and lots of accessories like byoux, scarves, lingerie, also household linen and gift items. Best buys: goldplated earrings without nickel, moisturizing creams, anti-age creams for face and decolleté. Avon is the worlds largest producer of bijoux and cosmetics.

Tessitura Serica G. Canepa

Via Trinità, 1 - 22020 San Fermo della Battaglia (CO)
8.30-12.00/14.00-16.00. Saturday closed

031 219111
C.C.:None

Silks
FACTORY OUTLET

Autostrada A9, exit Como Sud to Como and San Fermo. Follow the road going down towards the river.

Rolls of silk fabric in a great variety of prints and colours, all very chic. Large tables covered with scarves, ties, shawls and stoles in excellent quality. Bed spreads in silk patchwork, handmade in Sicily. Lots of quilted table mats, covers and other gift items all in good taste.

La Murrina - Murano

Via Isonzo, 15 Z.I. - 22078 Turate (CO)
9.30-12.30/15.00-19.00

02 96975200
C.C.:All Major

Crystal, glassware
FACTORY OUTLET

Autostrada A 9, exit Turate. At the roundabout turn left to the industrial zone. One can see the factory from the autostrada.

Wall lights, chandeliers, candlesticks, vases in colourful Murano glass. Wine or whiskey glasses in crystal, tea and coffee cups, it's a good address for finding wedding presents or bits and pieces for the house. Lights, various decorative objects in crystal, vases, there is even a collection of German china, all discounted between 30% and 70%.

Albisetti

Via Nazionale, 3 - 22070 Vertemate (CO)   031 901190
9.30-12.30/14.30-19.00   C.C.:All Major

Silks
FACTORY OUTLET

S.S. 35 Milano-Como. Albisetti is in front of an IP service station on the left and next to a supermarket.

Modern, cheerful designs in clothes, scarves and ties by Iceberg, Byblos, Coveri, Fendi, D&G. Ties € 15,00, 2choice € 7,50. Enormous collection of silk scarves for sale at € 25,00 and up. Knitted jackets in linen/viscose or wool, colourful sweaters by Missoni. Skirts in matelassé washed silk, silk blouses € 45,00 and up. Special offers all the time: traditional men's shirts in fine cotton, lingerie by Roverto Cavalli, Missoni sweaters.

Armani Factory Store

Prov. per Bregnano, 13 - 22070 Vertemate (CO)   031 887373
9.30-19.00. Closed Monday   C.C.:All Major

Clothing, lingerie, underwear
FACTORY OUTLET

Autostrada A9, exit Fino Mornasco and then S.S.35. From Milano take the S.S. 35 towards Como. The outlet is housed in a specially built, East Coast USA style building of 3 floors.

All the Armani brandnames are for sale, Armani, Emporio, Armani Jeans. W. suits € 112,50 (Emporio) - € 375,00 (Armani), dresses € 99,00 - € 375,00, evening dresses € 400,00 - € 1,500,00, pants € 60,00 circa. All sizes but mostly size 42. For men a separate floor with shirts € 25,00, pants, coats € 250,00, all sizes. The last floor is dedicated to children. There are seconds and special offers. Other outlets in Trissino (VI) and Matelica (MC).

Dolce Mercato Sorini

S.S. 415 Castelleonese - 26012 Castelleone (CR)   0374 350150
9.00-12.30/15.00-19.00   C.C.:None

Food, biscuits, sweets
FACTORY OUTLET

From Crema take the S.S. 415, at the beginning of Castelleone turn right at the traffic light. A large outlet with ample parking.

Sorini produces chocolates, marrons glacés and a host of other sweets and biscuits for the seriously sugar dependent. Row upon row of biscuits, cakes, pasta, liquorice, desserts, often in 1 kilo packs and discounted. Unbeatable prices for very tasty marrons glacés in presentation boxes: € 8,50 for 900 grams.

Stockhouse

Via Macello, 30 - 26013 Crema (CR)   0373 86524
9.15-12.30/15.30-19.30   C.C.:All Major

Clothing
BARGAIN BASEMENT

From Milan take the S.S. 415 to Crema Ovest and follow the directions for Brescia. The Stockhouse is near the SMA supermarket and after the hospital (Ospedale).

This is a very popular shop, not only with the locals, but also with the Japanese tourists. All the most trendy and fashionable Italian designers are well represented especially in size 42 for W and size 48 for M but even in size XXL there is a lot of merchandise for sale.

Cabodà

Via Mantova, 141 - 26100 Cremona (CR)
9.00-12.15/15.15-19.30

0372 434018
C.C.:All Major

Clothing
BARGAIN BASEMENT

Autostrada A21, exit Cremona, continue for 1 km towards the center. Caboda is on the left next to a service station.

Raincoats, woollen coats, bomber jackets, dresses, suits, many with a Henry Cotton's, Norton & Wilson or Caractère label. All sizes available, even XXL for M/W. The new winter collection arrives at the end of September. Discounts of 30 - 50% for modern, practical clothes with or without famous labels and a super discount corner, everything at 70% off.

Griffes Diffusion

Via Dante, 108 - 26100 Cremona (CR)
9.00-13.00/14.30-19.30

0372 33221
C.C.:All Major

Clothing, shoes
FACTORY OUTLET

Autostrada A21 Cremona - Brescia, exit Cremona, follow the indications for the center and the train station.

This is one of the outlets of the Mariella Burani Fashion Group, selling last seasons collections at very competitive prices. All their 15 brands (Mila Schon, Mariella Burani, Revedi) are well represented, not only in clothing but also shoes and accessories, in all the most popular sizes for M/W. A good choice in leatherwear makes this outlet worthwhile to visit.

Creazioni Saint Michael

Via dei Partigiani, 7 - 26010 S.Michele di Ripalta Cremasca (CR)   0373 68474
8.30-12.00/13.30-18.30

C.C.: None

Household linen, various
FACTORY OUTLET

From Milano S.S. 415 'Paullese'. At the Crema ring road exit for Credera and Moscazzano and then left for S. Michele. After the church 150 m on the left.

A good address for decorating fabrics in a rustic, practical style, stripes or Scottish tartans, very heavy quality, ideal for slipcovers or curtains and printed on both sides € 21per meter, 270 cm wide. Tablecloths, napkins in jacquard or satin cotton, terrytowel robes and coupons.

Stefania Confezioni

Via L. da Vinci, 54 - 22062 Barzanò (LC)
8.30-18.30. Saturday 8.30-12.00; open Xmas week

039 955344
C.C.: None

Household linen, various
ARTISAN'S WORKSHOP

From Milano take the provincial road (Superstrada) to Lecco, exit Nibionno toBergamo. At the end of the village in an industrial zone.

The right address to buy very luxurious sheets, competitively priced. Two double sheets € 83 - € 155, sheets in jacquard, various colours, rather smashing and unusual. They also sell sheets in silk € 315 circa and table clothes and quilted bedspreads made to measure.

Punto Scarpe

Corso Dante, 20 - 24032 Calolziocorte (LC)
9.00-12.30/15.00-19.00

0341 630733
C.C.:All Major

Shoes
DISCOUNTS

From Lecco on the provincial road to Bergamo, in the middle of the village on the left. Parking.

Ideal place for large families on a budget. A self service selling shoes, slippers, gaiters, working/hiking/dress boots by Stonehaven, Lumberjack, Levi's, Barbie, Kevin Klain etc. for 0 - 100 years, for babies, trendy teens, grannies, all at less than € 50,00. Other address in Lecco, C.C. Le Piazze, C.so Carlo Alberto 120, tel 0341 285850 and in Cernusco Lombardone, C.C., tel. 039 9908612.

Famar Interior Design

Via N. Sauro, 36 - 23893 Cassago Brianza (LC)
9.00-12.00/14.00-19.00. Closed in August

039 955365
C.C.: None

Furniture, various
DISCOUNTS

From Lecco take the direction of Valsassina. The factory is immediately after the bridge.From Milan take the superstrada for Lecco, exit at Nibionno, direction of Bergamo and to Cassago for 1 km.

Special sales of Flou, Poliform, Poggenpohl, Flexform, Saporiti, and others at 40% less. Get on their customer list for their special sales of beds, wardrobes, deckbeds, curtains etc. all used during expositons. We suggest to phone first, they speak English.

Diana Store

Z.I. Olgiate Molgora - 23807 Merate (LC)
Closed Monday

039 9908551
C.C.: None

Clothing, sportswear, casual, jeans
FACTORY OUTLET

From Milano take the Tangenziale Est in the direction of Lecco. Diana is on the left, after Merate. Follow the sign 'Diana Store' before the Shell service station.

Everything for the beach, gymnastics, trekking, ballet, from XS to XXL. Sweatshirts, shorts, bathcaps, beachtowels, beachbags, bodysuits. Good quality products that last. Savings of 40%. It is possible to find prototypes of beachwear, designed for major brandnames. The best time for a visit is from May to September.

Lorenzini

Via Como, 39 - 23807 Merate (LC)
14.00-18.00. Saturday 9.00-12.30. Closed Monday

039 9906315
C.C.:All Major

Shirts
ARTISAN'S WORKSHOP

From Milan take the Tangenziale Est to Lecco, exit Agrate, continue to Cernusco Lombardone. At the first traffic light to the right, continue for 200 m, Lorenzini is on the right. Parking inside the gate.

Luxury shirt makers, well known for the high quality and elegance of the fabrics. One can order a shirt made to measure from a vast choice of sample models, in different fabrics, button down, three button collars ecc. They also produce sporty shirts, for W there is less choice. Sales in January and July, they speak English, German and French.

Tessitura Donghi

Via Don L. Sturzo, 1 - 23895 Nibionno (LC) 031 690895
15.30-19.30. Saturday 9.30-12.30 C.C.:All Major

Household linen, various
FACTORY OUTLET

Superstrada Milano-Lecco, exit Cibrone to Masnago. The outlet is at the beginning of the village on the right. Large parking.

A small space but full of very promising bargains. They produce sheets and eider-downs for the Fenice Home Collection, Royal Cover and Abitare in very good quality and taste. The eiderdowns, either single or double, seconds, are sold at 50% discount and start at € 30,00 - € 50,00. Very very nice! Some baskets with coupons, some cushion covers in jacquard, very original small carpets, tea towels and other bits and pieces make this a worthwhile address. They speak English.

Cererie Amos Sgarbi

Via per Lecco, 24/26 - 22048 Oggiono (LC) 0341 266611
9.00-12.00/14.00-18.00. Sat. 9.00-12.00. Only Tue. morning & Wed. C.C.:All Major

Candles
ARTISAN'S WORKSHOP

On the Milano-Lecco Superstrada take the Oggiono exit and then the direction of Lecco.

Any kind of candle can be bought, by weight or in packs of 12. Good choice of colors, fantasy candles, anti smoke or church candles, perfumed candles or large torches for the garden, with Citronella oil that will keep insects away. All at competitive prices.

Fontana Pret a Porter

Via Edison, 39 - 23899 Paderno d'Adda (LC) 039 512098
10.00-12.30/14.30-19.00. Closed Monday C.C.:All Major

Clothing
FACTORY OUTLET

On the edge of the village towards the bridge on the Adda on the left. The outlet is open to everybody, ring bell to enter.

Fontana stands for classical clothes with fancy touches like fur trimmed sleeves or embroidered blouses, all very luxurious and elegant, Alta Moda made to measure or adapted on the spot. Prices reflect all this super chic perfection €1.552 for a 3-piece suit, silk blouses €265. Sales in July and January at 30% - 50% less.

Imec

P.zza Nino Colnaghi, 1 - 23899 Paderno D'Adda (LC) 039 9515121
9.00-12.30/15.30-19.00. Saturday 9.30-18.30 C.C.: None

Lingerie, underwear
FACTORY OUTLET

From Milano S.S. 36 until Cernusco. At Paderno d'Adda continue towards the Adda river. Ample parking on the square in front of the factory.

Massive quantities of nightgowns, kimonos, pyamas, baby-dolls, housecoats and beach gowns are for sale, 80% with the Imec brandname, but also dresses by Franca von Wunster. Downstairs a special lingerie department with You Young underwear by Coveri in animal prints/metallic colours. For large ladies sturdy black and white sets. T-shirts/briefs & striped pyamas for men. Discounts up to 40% on regular merchandise.

Coltelleria Rusconi Art

Via Roma, 6 - 23834 Premana (LC)   0341 890432
9.00-12.00/15.00-19.00. Closed Monday   C.C.:All Major

Household goods, various
GOOD PRICES

From Lecco take the direction of Val Sassina (from Bellano the road is rather narrow). Premana seems to be glued to the mountain and Rusconi is in the center of the village near the church.

The whole village of Premana is involved in the production of scissors and knives, not any old knife but special models to slice raw ham, to up-root funghi, to cut frozen foods, to fillet salmon. The scissors are also made for every possible purpose. Prices are definitely lower but the real advantage is the great variety of utensils on offer.

Pompea Calze

Via Mantova, 48 - 46041 Asola (MN)   0376 719655
9.00-12.30/15.30-19.30   C.C.:All Major

Hosiery
FACTORY OUTLET

Autostrada A4, exit Desenzano del Garda then take S.S. 567 towards Mantova. Follow directions to Carpenédolo, Asolo. Pompea is just after Carpenédolo.

Socks and stockings by Calze Pompea for M/W/Ch and their collection of underwear and lingerie at especially low prices for their outlet. Pantyhose are sold under the brand name AC Art Collant.

Fashion District

Via M. Biagi, Loc. Basse di Mezzo - 46031 Bagnolo S. Vito (MN)   0376 25041
10.00-20.00   C.C.:All Major

Clothing, household linen
OUTLET CENTER

Autostrada A22, exit Mantova Sud, the outlet center is right there.

Large, 35,000 sq.m., designed like a medieval village, with circa 60 shops representing more than 180 brand names: Mariella Burani, Just Cavalli, Gianfranco Ferré, Corneliani, Extè, Bassetti, Rosenthal, Villeroy & Boch. Also gourmet food, musical events, bars, restaurants and kindergarten. English spoken. There is another Fashion District outlet center at Valmontone near Rome.

Calze Filodoro

Via Brescia, 6 - 46040 Casalmoro (MN)   0376 7281
9.00-12.30/14.00-19.00. Closed Monday   C.C.:All Major

Hosiery
FACTORY OUTLET

Autostrada A4, exit Desenzano del Garda then take S.S. 572 in the direction of Castiglione. Continue on 343 for Asola approximately 8 km. At the beginning of Casalmoro on the left. Entrance at the Filodoro parking.

The outlet is attached to the facory. They sell the Filodoro collection of collant, stockings, kneehighs plus brand names like Philippe Matignon, Figura, Filoverde at an average saving of 35%. Lingerie by Playtex, Wonderbra, Cacharel and Omero at discounts.

CSP International- Oroblu

Piazza Castello - 46040 Ceresara (MN)
9.00-12.30/15.00-19.30. Closed Monday

0376 8101
C.C.:All Major

Hosiery
FACTORY OUTLET

S.S. 236 from Brescia to Mantova. Ceresara is near Castel Goffredo, another area known for the production of hosiery.

Oroblu is a well known brand name and their shop in the center of Ceresara sells the regular collection of hosiery at reduced prices. Large choice of fantasy stockings and tights in lace, geometric designs, tartan designs, net stockings, in wool, cotton or lycra for extra support.

Manifattura del Mincio

S.S. Goitese, 448 - 46044 Cerlongo di Goito (MN)
9.00-12.00/15.00-19.00 from Tue. to Fri.
Saturday 9.00-12.00. Closed in August

0376 607061
C.C.: None

Household linen, various
FACTORY OUTLET

From Mantova S.S. 236 'Goitese' towards Brescia. The outlet is on the main road on the right in the village of Cerlongo. Parking. From Autostrada A4 take exit Desenzano, or Autostrada A22 exit Mantova Nord.

They have enlarged their sales point next to the factory. Sheets, towels, beach towels with fancy designs and some sporty sweatshirts and T-shirts in polypropilene. Possible to buy terrytowel material by weight at €6 per kilo or € 14 for finished towels. Special offers on bathrobes by Cacharel, Les Copains, Benetton.

BBF di Gambetti

Via H. Dunant, 26 - 46040 Guidizzolo (MN)
8.00-12.00/14.00-18.30. Mon open, Sat 8.00-12.00

0376 819359
C.C.: None

Hosiery
FACTORY OUTLET

S.S. 236 from Brescia towards Mantova. On the left at the beginning of Guidizzolo.

A large outlet offering every kind of stocking, tight, pantyhose, knee-highs, socks imaginable. Support or net stockings, neon-coloured pantyhose, long stockings for men in cotton or wool, sports socks and childrens socks with tiny ducks. Knee-highs in lycra net, black or cream coloured € 1,30. Very patient and efficient personnel.

Laboratori Piazza

Via H. Dunant, 25 - 46040 Guidizzolo (MN)
8.30-12.00/15.00-19.00

0376 819002
C.C.: None

Hosiery
FACTORY OUTLET

S.S.236 from Mantova to Bresciia, pass the village, at the traffic light after 1.5 km on the left is the Fiat dealer, continue for 500 m. on the S.S. 236, you'll find Piazza on the left.

Terapeutic stockings and tights knit with a gradual compression of 40 den, 70 den. or 140 den. in Lycra. Also special knee-highs, tights and stockings premaman, knee-highs for men in cotton/lycra. Large choice of specialized stockings anti trombosis, anti varicose veins, bad circulation ecc.

Lottario Secci
P.za D'Arco, 5 e 5/b - 46100 Mantova (MN)　　　0376 327264
9.15-12.30/15.30-19.15　　　　　　　　　　　　　C.C.: None

Shoes
DISCOUNTS

In the center of Mantova, we suggest to go on foot.

Well known and popular with Italians coming from afar to buy the latest styles in shoes at heavily discounted prices. Sample shoes by Moschino, size 37, € 80, lace-ups or queenies by The Saddler, men's shoes, English style, by Dawson, Made in Northampshire € 93. They also sell handbags by Celine and Moschino. Great choice and great confusion.

Lubiam
Viale Fiume, 55 - 46100 Mantova (MN)　　　　　0376 309321
9.00-12.30/15.00-19.30　　　　　　　　　　　　C.C.:All Major

Clothing
FACTORY OUTLET

From Modena and the Autostrada A22, exit Modena Sud and then S.S. 413. After the hospital complex turn right and take the third on the left. Viale Fiume is on the left. Look for the Lubiam shopping sign. Parking in front. From Verona exit Mantova Nord.

A large outlet that should be of interest to the career conscious. Lubiam works for Cerruti, Benci and Osvaldo Testa, and produces the kind of very well-made and with-it suits that look right anywhere. They only sell their recent collection here, but at circa 35% less than elsewhere and it is possible to have suits made to measure. They speak English.

Spaccio Corneliani
Via Panizza, 5 - 46100 Mantova (MN)　　　　　0376 304410
9.00-13.00/15.30-19.30　　　　　　　　　　　　C.C.:All Major

Clothing
FACTORY OUTLET

From Mantova take the road to Ferrara-Rovigo, continue until the Corneliani complex on the right. The outlet entrance is after the factory, a shop front with parking.

For the man in search of a new wardrobe, go and see the Corneliano collection of suits and jackets, coats and trousers in a great variety of designs, colour, sizes and styles. A saving of 35% is guaranteed! On the first floor there is a small collection of women's clothes, some made by other manufacturers.

Emporio Carla Carini
Via IV Novembre, 32 - 46024 Moglia (MN)　　　0376 556100
15.00-19.30. Sat 9.00-12.00/15.00-19.30　　　　C.C.:All Major

Clothing
FACTORY OUTLET

Autostrada A22, exit Reggiolo/Rolo. The Emporio is near the artisan's zone in Moglia on the main road. The entrance is on the left of the factory, parking in front.

Large premises, enormous choice in all sizes but mostly in showroom size 42. Elegant dresses and festive suits, seconds € 175,00 in silk. Last year's remainders are discounted 50% to € 115,00. Embroidered T-shirts € 55,00, deceptively simple embroidered linen blouses, 2nds, € 62,50 and up. This is a good address to find something special for a wedding or a very festive evening.

Cantina Soc. Quistello

Via Roma, 46 - 46026 Quistello (MN)
8.00-11.45/14.00-18.00. Saturday 8.00-11.45

0376 618118
C.C.:None

Wine
GOOD PRICES

Autostrada A22, exit Mantova Sud, to Quistello. The cantina is near the train station.

A very good address to stock up on the local wines: Lambrusco Mantovano Doc, a fizzy white wine, a nice Chardonnay, either in bottles or per liter. All in all they sell about 12 different types of wine. Special offers in December and an excellent price/quality ratio.

Dismero Factory Outlet

Via Custoza, 128 - 46048 Roverbella (MN)
9.30-12.30/15.30-19.30

0376 693556
C.C.:All Major

Clothing
FACTORY OUTLET

Roverbella is near Villafranca di Verona. From Verona/Mantova take the S.S. 62 or from the Autostrada A22 take the Mantova Nord exit.

Jeans in tiger prints, tartans, uni-coloured, fantasy, always with an embroidered D on the back pocket. In summer linen Capri's with velcro flaps, T's in stretchy cotton, tops and skirts in sky bly, it's all cheerful and well-made. Desmero is a well known brandname in Germany. Other outlets in Bussolengo (VR) and Tezze (VI).

Diamant

Viale Kennedy, 18 - 46019 Viadana (MN)
9.00-12.00/15.00-19.00

0375 782194
C.C.: None

Household linen, various
FACTORY OUTLET

From Casalmaggiore follow the road on the left towards the industrial zone. Diamant is part of the Dondi complex with a separate entrance just after the factory on the right.

Their strong point is the bed linen collection by Blumarine. Two double beds, totally covered in Blumarine pillows, sheets, shams and quilts are the dream of every young bride. Prices lower than average but don't count on finding seconds, remainders or samples, it's all the latest of the latest.

Emporio Caleffi

Via Belfiore, 24 - 46019 Viadana (MN)
9.00-12.30/15.00-19.00

0375 788350
C.C.:All Major

Household linen, various
FACTORY OUTLET

From Casalmaggiore on the S.S. 358, the Emporio is at the beginning of Viadana, on the left and well indicated, parking.

A spacious showroom with their regular collection at regular prices, but there are plenty of special offers: quilted bedspreads, eiderdowns, sheets, terrytowel robes, all 1st choice but last years collection and therefore reduced 20%. With a bit of luck one can find good looking summer quilts at € 45,00 for a double or a winter weight for 1 person at € 32,50.

C.I.T.

Via Matteucci, 19 - 20043 Arcore (MI)
9.00-12.00/16.00-19.00

039 60681
C.C.: None

Clothing, shirts
FACTORY OUTLET

From Milano take the Tangenziale Est to Vimercate. Take the Arcore exit. C.I.T. is on the left, half way on the road towards Arcore, a new factory with a large outlet.

Quantities of sophisticated men's shirts by Cerruti and Bagutta € 30,00, Trussardi € 35,00 plus Armani seconds, all sizes. Lovely tweed winter coats for W € 75,00 - € 225,00 (made for Bloomingdale). Very classy city suits in Armani type colours and styles, sizes 42-46, € 175,00. Pants and skirts in wool € 35,00 all had labels by Bagutta.

Griffes Diffusion

Via Guido Rossa, 1 - 20010 Arluno (MI)
10.30-19.30. Closed Monday. Saturday 9.30-19.30

02 90119004
C.C.:All Major

Clothing
FACTORY OUTLET

Autostrada A4, exit Arluno continue in the direction of Corbetta. At the round-about turn left into Via Castiglioni, a parallel road to the autostrada. This very large outlet is at the end after the Mercedes Benz dealer.

This is one of the outlets for the Mariella Burani Fashion group. Nice classy clothing for men, also casuals and accessories. Dresses and suits, nice spring jackets in bright rainbow colors for W. an ample choice of leatherwear, all sizes available. There is something for everybody from the 15 brandnames that make up this fashion group.

Angelo Rusconi

Via Repubblica, 35 - 20020 Barbaiana di Lainate (MI)
9.00-18.00. Open Saturday, in the Xmas season call first

02 93255385
C.C.: None

Handbags, suitcases
ARTISAN'S WORKSHOP

Autostrada A8/9, exit Lainate, take the direction to Nerviano. At the round-about go left to Lainate, then right to Barbaiana. Via della Pace is a narrow road with villas on the right.

An artisan's workshop that produces handbags and travel bags in farmbred crocodile. A Bugatti type bag, quite large € 875.00, a classic Gucci style with bamboo handle € 550,00, a large travel size Kelly € 900,00. An attache case, big enough to carry a computer € 1000,00, a suitcase in crocodile € 2,000,00. Also agendas, wallets, belts.

Intimo Fashion Group

Via del Lavoro, 23 - 20010 Bernate Ticino (MI)
9.00-12.30/14.00-19.00. Closed in August

02 97255931
C.C.:All Major

Lingerie, underwear
FACTORY OUTLET

Autostrada A4, exit Boffalora S.T. proceed on the Padana Superiore S.S.11 to Magenta. After the bridge over the autostrada turn immediately left to a dirt track.

More than 10.000 products are for sale: underwear, sweatshirts, socks, and their strong point pyamas, night shirts and robes. Special offer of 3 pyamas for M/W at € 40,00, 2nd choice 3 for € 25,00 (the defects are well indicated), robes 2nds € 12,00, sweatshirts for kids € 5,00. Beach T-shirts € 8,00. Brand names Gianca, Frette e GattaMatta. Sizes up to 54 for W and 60 for M. Very competitive prices, definitely worth the trip.

Pozzi Group
Via per Desio, 24c - 20030 Bovisio Masciago (MI)　　　036 2591713/4
8.00-12.00/14.00-19.00　　　　　　　　　　　　　　　C.C.:All Major

Clothing, leatherwear
GOOD PRICES

Take the superstrada Milano - Como, exit 8, turn right to Bovisio, Pozzi is on the left. Parking.

An ample showroom with a large collection of leatherwear: skirts, pants, blazers, jackets, furs. They also work to order. Prices are convenient, a leather or suede skirt € 40,00 - € 110,00. Coats in cashmere and fur, in mohair, lined with lapin chinchilla. Styles tend to be classical with the occasional very fashionable prototype.

Tessuti Raponi
Viale Gramsci/ang.Via Strada - 20091 Bresso (MI)　　　02 6104794
9.00-12.30/15.30-19.30　　　　　　　　　　　　　　C.C.:All Major

Fabrics, home furnishings
BARGAIN BASEMENT

From Milano take Viale F. Testi and turn left at the major Sesto S. Giovanni intersection to Bresso. At the traffic lights in Bresso Raponi is in front.

Silks circa € 12.00 per meter, some jolly nice designs. Wool from € 6,00 per meter up to € 12,00 for an authentic Scottish clan design in merino wool. Velvet € 6,00 per meter. Great cartons with bits of cotton, wool, velvets, stretchy material from €0,50 to € 1,00 per etto. Naj Oleari plastified fabric pieces € 6,00 per kilo. Definitely worth the trip for able seamstresses.

Wenk
Via Galileo Galilei, 7 - 20091 Bresso (MI)　　　　　02 66501934
9.00-12.30/14.00-19.00　　　　　　　　　　　　　C.C.: None

Silverware/Pewter
FACTORY OUTLET

From Milan take Viale Zara, Viale F. Testi and at the major intersection for Sesto S. Giovanni turn left to Bresso. At the next traffic light turn right, go straight and at the third traffic light turn left, then the first right and the first left.

Two small rooms, one with a collection of pillboxes, frames, glass and silver statues, bottles with fancy taps, baby gifts. Prices are to be discounted by 40%. Sterling silver salmon knives at € 58,00 or nutcrackers, bottle openers, butter knives in silver all at 20% below shop price make good wedding gifts. 76-piece silver table setting € 2,200. Hagerty large size silver cleaning bath € 9,00 minus 20%.

Erreuno Outlet
Via Veneto, 11 - 20090 Buccinasco (MI)　　　　　　02 48882238
10.00-18.00. Closed Monday　　　　　　　　　　　C.C.:All Major

Clothing
FACTORY OUTLET

Tangenziale Ovest, exit Assago to Buccinasco. After Milano Più turn to the left towards a small church, Via Veneto is behind a gas station (Manfredo) in an industrial zone.

In their new factory building Erreuno has recently opened an outlet. Last season's tailleurs, dresses, coats, very elegant and well finished at discounts of 30% - 50%. Sizes from 40/42 up to 46/48. They have another, smaller outlet in Milan, Via Morgantini, 28, tel. 02 48701310 where there is less choice. Prices, though often slashed in half, are not low!

Benetton Factory Outlet

Viale Europa, 9/15 - 20010 Buscate (MI)
9.00-12.30/15.00-19.00. Sat. 10.00-19.30. Mon. 15.00 - 19.00

0331 803048
C.C.:All Major

Knitwear, cashmere
FACTORY OUTLET

Autostrada A4, exit Arluno to Castano Primo. In Buscate the Benneton Outlet is near the traffic light on the left, next to a tile shop, with parking in front.

An outlet of circa 150 mq offering woollen knitwear for the whole family at reduced prices. Merchandise is all by Benneton, mostly knitted goods for adults but this is a good place to stock up on childrens clothes and sweaters too. Sales at 50% in January and July.

MA.TE.BA.

Via Alfredo di Dio, 77/79 - 20020 Busto Garolfo (MI)
9.00-12.30/14.30-19.30

0331 568419
C.C.:All Major

Clothing, household linen
DISCOUNTS

Autostrada A4, exit Arluno towards Busto Garolfo. From Parabiago take Viale Lombardia, at the roundabout 50 m on the right. Ample parking.

An authentic outlet for the true-blue bargain hunter. Large tables covered with knitwear in merino wool or cashmere, racks with the latest showroom collections of Reporter, Pancaldi B and Esologue all in size 42. Soft furnishing fabrics at € 7,00 per meter, 280 cm. wide + scotchguard. Also lots of material, sheets, bits and pieces sold by weight.

Maglieria Gemma

Via Tiziano, 6 - 20022 Castano Primo (MI)
9.00-12.00/14.00-18.00. Saturday 9.00-12.00

0331 881314
C.C.: None

Knitwear, cashmere
ARTISAN'S WORKSHOP

From Busto Arsizio to Castano Primo. After the first traffic light turn immediately right, then after 100 m, following the canal, look for a narrow track on the right.

Small outlet full of beautiful knitwear with very well known brand names like Gemma or TSE. They make deceptively simple twinsets in cashmere € 160,00, but also heavier cable sweaters for men in wool € 85,00. Cashmere/silk vests € 100,00, cashmere & filo jumpers € 120,00, their remnants & second choice tops at € 30,00 were a steal.

Outlet Sposa

Via Cremona, 4 - 20063 Cernusco sul Naviglio (MI)
10.00-18.00. Open on Sunday

02 92181630
C.C.:All Major

Clothing, bridal wear and formal
FACTORY OUTLET

From Milan take the S.S. 11 - Padana Superiore or S.P. 103 - Nuova Cassanese to Cassano d'Adda and via Torino.

An outlet dedicated to new brides. Wedding dresses start at € 250,00, either very sober and elegant in white or ivory or in unusual designs and pastel colours. There is a large choice of natural fabrics like silk georgette, taffetà, organza, muslin. From the end of september they sell a special collection of dresses for bridesmaids.

Diffusione Tessile
Via Benedetto Croce, I/A - 20090 Cesano Boscone (MI)   02 45862300
10.00-19.30   C.C.:All Major

Clothing
FACTORY OUTLET

In the Lorenteggio area.

One of the Max Mara outlets selling off last years collection (minus the Max Mara labels) plus a special line of clothing for these outlets. Casual and elegant clothes also in Marina Rinaldi styles (but no labels) all discounted 30% - 50%. There is a corner with leatherwear, a lot of handbags (€ 40,00 and up) and shoes (€ 50,00 and up). Sizes from 38 to 50 plus XXL sizes up to 60.

Luciano Marcato
Via Bizet, 36/d - 20092 Cinisello Balsamo (MI)   02 660714
14.00-18.00. Saturday closed. Friday 14.00-16.30   C.C.:All Major

Fabrics, home furnishings, household linen
FACTORY OUTLET

From Milan take Via F. Testi. At the traffic light continue to the center of Sesto S. Giovanni, turn left for Cinisello. Continue to Via Lincoln and after the Centro Commerciale (Il Ventaglio) at the traffic light turn left and then immediately right. Continue until Via Ciaikovsky then turn right. Last gate on the right.

Their outlet is on the first floor and offers a limited series of Luciano Marcato fabric, either end of series and remainders, for curtains and furniture, all in refined good taste. Glass curtains € 5,00 p.m. and up, heavier curtain material in cotton or jacquard € 6,50 -€ 29.00. Very heavy silk in colorful squares € 30,00 either 140cm or 280cm wide. They speak English, French and German.

Donisia
Via R. Sanzio, 7 (Buonarotti) - 20093 Cologno Monzese (MI)   02 26708342
10.00-14.00/15.00-19.00. Closed Monday   C.C.:All Major

Clothing
FACTORY OUTLET

Tangenziale Est, exit Cologno Sud. At the rotonda the first right then again right and at the traffic lights right again for the entrance to Donisia (in front of the supermarket). Parking inside.

Spacious first floor sales point, lots of choice for 30/40 year old career women in search of wearable dresses and suits. Sizes from 40 up to XXL. Brand names Andie Di, Elisabetta Burni, Cyd & Samm, Harrod's of London. Linen dresses € 90,00, suits € 175,00 circa. A couple of racks with seconds are worth a look.

Hitman
Via G. di Vittorio, 8 - 20094 Corsico (MI)   02 48856214
10.00-13.30/14.30-19.00. Sat. 9.30-13.30/15.00-19.00   C.C.:All Major

Clothing
FACTORY OUTLET

From Milan by car, after reaching Corsico and after the traffic light turn left to cross back towards Milan at the level of the Omnitel shop. It's a freestanding, walled-in building. From the Tangenziale Ovest, exit Trezzano, Corsico to Milan, on the right.

A paradise for the well-dressed 'Cerruti' man in search of classical or formal suits in wool and cashmere. Men's 4-ply cashmere sweater € 185,00, polos in wool € 45,00, 2 piece suits € 265,00, cashmere jackets € 380,00, raincoats € 125,00, all sizes available, tremendous assortment. For women less choice, mostly sporty things. Special offer of Andrea Pfister shoes at € 75,00. Jeans Cerruti € 60,00.

Spaccio Antonio Fusco

Via Ex Cascina Lavagna, 5 - 20094 Corsico (MI)
10.00 - 19.00

02 4471966
C.C.:All Major

Clothing
FACTORY OUTLET

From Milan take the Viale Lorenteggio (which will become the Vigevanese) to Corsico. The Fusco Outlet is on the left, between an Esso gas station and a Chiccolandia signpost. Take the sliproad and turn back at the next stop light. Parking in the back of the building.

Best time to visit is during the sales period when prices are halved. Antonio Fusco is famous for his faultless jackets for men and women, the kind that becomes a basic part of one's wardrobe. For W sizes from 40-46, for men up to 54. Suits for W during sales € 234 jackets € 185, for men classical jackets €207, suits € 258. Shirts €39, cashmere cardigans with zip € 289, all very well made. There are no 2nds or special offers.

CZ Cizeta Paramedicali

Via IV Novembre, 46 - 20012 Cuggiono (MI)
10.30-12.00/15.30-17.00. Saturday closed

02 9721811
C.C.:All Major

Hosiery
FACTORY OUTLET

Autostrada A4, exit Boffalora towards Castano Primo. In Cuggiono follow indications for Zona Industriale. At the intersection for Castano Primo turn right, continue for 50 m.

Support stockings, tummy warmers, knee supports, step-ins, corrective shoulder straps, gloves and breast feeding bras in all sizes. Very good offer of stockings, tights and kneehighs, in relaxing and supportive lycra mixtures, second choice, 40 and 70 denier € 2,00 per pair. Thights with lace briefs, regular € 4,00. Definitely worthwhile.

MHWay

Via Campania, 46 - 20090 Fizzonasco (MI)
10.00-13.00/14.00-17.00. Fridays till 16.30

02 90781960
C.C.:None

Handbags, leather goods
FACTORY OUTLET

From Milan take the tangenziale Ovest, exit Rozzano per Fizzonasco. After via Brodolini and the crossing, turn right, after 10 m. turn left.

MHWay is a well known brandname producing handbags, travel bags in leather or imitation leather with synthetic fabrics like nylon to great effect. Black city-chic cases for P.C.'s, shopping bags or backpacks fit to carry baby. They export all over the world.

Mascheroni 2 Discount Sport

Via Prealpi, 28 - 20034 Giussano (MI)
9.30-12.30/15.00-19.30

0362 850179
C.C.: None

Clothing, sportswear
DISCOUNTS

From Milano, Viale F. Testi, superstrada for Lecco, exit Giussano. The shop is well indicated, at the rotonda on the left.

Every kind of sports wear and outdoor gear can be found here at discounts. Fishing, hunting, travel vests, tennis and riding gear, hiking boots and mountain gear. A husky jacket by Best Company € 25,00 (instead of € 45,00), a jacket in boiled wool by Giesswein € 85,00 (instead of € 175,00).

Alberto Aspesi

Via Salvatore Quasimodo, 32/34 - 20025 Legnano(MI)   0331 579565
9.30-12.00/14.00-18.00. Saturday 9.30-17.00. Closed Monday   C.C.:All Major

Clothing
FACTORY OUTLET

*Autostrada A8, exit Castellanza, towards Rescaldina. Take the road between two 'Gran Casa',
turn right towards an anonymous looking gate at the end of the road . Parking in front.*

A large factory hall with last years Aspesi collection, mixed in with row upon
row of 2nds discounted 30-50%. Two piece suits, 2nds, in linen/viscose € 140,
sizes run from 36 up to 46 for W. This is not a place for the rounder figure. For
men some ties, bermudas and a fair choice in shirts. For children there is less
choice. It needs an eagle eye to find a bargain.

Dolce & Gabbana Industria

Via Rossini, 70 - 20025 Legnano (MI)   0331 545888
10.00-13.30/14.30-19.00   C.C.:All Major

Clothing, shoes
FACTORY OUTLET

*Autostrada A8, exit Legnano. Continue on the main road and pass 9 traffic lights. At
the roundabout turn right, then seventh road on the left.*

A large factory hall, all open space, selling last year's Dolce & Gabbana collection, samples and some seconds (but not much). For men sizes 44 to 56, sample size 48 is well represented, for women size 38 to 48 with far more choice
in 40/42, less so in 46/48. A two piece suit, tight party style € 185,00-€ 300,00,
for men € 225,00 circa. (During sales everything sells at 20-40% less).

Maglificio Lia Sforte

Via A. Moro, 4/6 - 20020 Magnago (MI)   0331 658444
8.00-12.00/14.00-18.30   C.C.:All Major

Clothing
FACTORY OUTLET

From Busto Arsizio S.S.527 to the Lonate Pozzolo 'Zona Industriale'.

A small outlet that sells very cute baby clothes in cotton. Tiny T-shirts € 3.00,
salopette € 10,00, nice quality. Some bins with end of series € 5.00. Very busy
with local mums and crying babies.

Borsettificio di Marcallo

Via Clerici, 19 (interno) - 20010 Marcallo (MI)   02 9761141
9.00-12.00/14.00-19.00. Saturday 9.30-12.00/14.30-18.30   C.C.:All Major

Handbags, leathergoods
GOOD PRICES

*Autostrada A4, exit Boffalora. After the main square in Marcallo turn left. From
Magenta before the main square, turn right.*

Very well-made and amusing handbags (they sell samples and second choice La
Cage aux Folles and Anna Brown) € 40,00, in ostrich print, or nifty fabric/lea-
ther, also some good looking attache cases. Fantastic men's shoes in English leather, size 40/41 and for W size 37. They speak Portugese and French.

Nuncas Italia

Via Curiel, 40 - 20017 Mazzo di Rho (MI)　　　　　　02 9317961
9.00-13.30/14.30-18.00. Sat. 9.30-12.30. Closed in August　　C.C.:None

Detergents, cleaning material
FACTORY OUTLET

From Milano S.S.233 (Varesina). Before Baranzate turn left in front of the Sacco hospital. A narrow road, after the autostrada bridge 1st. right, straight then 1st. left, 1st. right and 2nd left. From Tangenziale Ovest, exit Pero. Take S.S. Sempione, at traffic light left Via Buonarotti, right into Via Gasperi. Then 3rd right and 1st left.

Their first best selling cleaning product was White Nuncas and Neutro Nuncas for shoes, made in 1935. Since then they have diversified into highly specialized cleaning products for the house in excellent quality, for windows, chandeliers, glassware, silver, perfumed moth strips, lemon scented waxes, spot removers for marble etc. They also sell Goddard's Silver Polish, Enka bleaches, Marsiglia soap, Crackfree starch.

Alpo

Via M. Bandello, 4/1 (interno) - 20123 Milano (MI)　　　02 4814130
9.00-13.00/14.00-18.00. Sat. open in Nov./Dec. Closed in Aug.　C.C.:None

Gloves
FACTORY OUTLET

MM1 exit Conciliazione. Bus 54,18. Tram 21. Enter the courtyard.

A large space with a good choice of gloves in leather and suede, lined & furlined, in various colors, sizes, weights, qualities but all at discounted prices, since this is their showroom collection. Don't count on finding too many sports/ski gloves. They speak English, hold twice-yearly sales and can do alterations.

Alviero Martini

Via L.A. Muratori, 13 - 20135 Milano (MI)　　　　02 59990206
10.00-19.00. Monday 15.00-19.00　　　　　　　　C.C.:All Major

Clothing, accessories
FACTORY OUTLET

MM3, exit Porta Romana. Via Muratori is behind the newsstand.

The outlet is attached to the Alviero Martini factory and sells end of line, remainders and showrooom models of this famous brand name. Global travellers will find bags and matching travel cases, shawls and scarves, umbrellas and hats in 'parchment coloured, geographic' fantasies. Prices are between 30 and 50% less but still at a certain level. Sales and they speak English.

Basement Outlet

Via Senato, 15 - 20021 Milano (MI)　　　　　　02 76317913
10.00-12.30/15.30-19.00　　　　　　　　　　　C.C.:All Major

Clothing
BARGAIN BASEMENT

In the fashion triangle of Milan, from Via Sant'Andrea to the left, left again, a flight of stairs in red.

Remainders by Polo R.L., Donna Karan, Calvin Klein and all the famous Made in Italy brandnames like Armani, Blumarine, Ermanno Scervino either Alta Moda or PretaPorter at very comepetitive prices. The sales people are helpful but let you browse, sizes tend to be smallish with some sizes in 46/48 but not much.

Bianco e No

Via Lorenzetti, 4 - 20146 Milano (MI)   02 48705057
9.30-12.30/14.30-19.00. Closed Monday   C.C.:None

Household linen, various
FACTORY OUTLET

MM1 exit Gambara. Corner of Via Palma, Piazza Gambara.

Mainly Zucchi products. Remnants in half linen/half cotton € 12,00 per kilo, guest towels Valentino 2nds, sold per weight, colored cushions in linen/cotton € 5,00, stretchy slipcovers called 'Zapping'. New offers every week, always at competitive prices.

Calzature Fabiano

Piazza Fidia, 3 - 20159 Milano (MI)   02 6887418
9.00-12.30/15.00-19.30. Friday 9.00-19.30   C.C.:All Major

Shoes
BARGAIN BASEMENT

Tram 4,11. Bus 82 or walk from Stazione Garibaldi.

Endless racks of shoes & boots in all sizes, starting at 34 for women up to 40 and at 39 for men up to 46. Average price € 55,00 circa for women and € 75,00 for men. Amid the masses of practical shoes it's possible to find Pollini Sport, Mario Cerruti, Aknethon, Forest Land, Casadei, Roberto Cavalli, Sergio Rossi. Towards December they also stock a respectable line in high heeled evening shoes. Sales at 50%.

Centro Stock Scarpe

Via Torino, 64 - 20123 Milano (MI)   02 72094075
Monday 14.00 - 19.30   C.C.:All Major

Shoes
BARGAIN BASEMENT

MM1 exit at Duomo or Cordusio. Tram 2,3,8. From Piazza Duomo on the right.

For tourists in a hurry this central shop might be useful. Shoes for men start at € 45,00, either in classical or more trendy designs, not always all sizes available. For women 2 floors of Texas boots, cute evening sandals or embroidered slippers at € 30,00 and up. Ankle booties with high heels at € 35,00 were good buys. Mocassins in supple leather € 20,00. Worth a visit for the budget conscious.

Corso Como Outlet

Via Tazzoli, 3 - 20154 Milano (MI)   02 29002674
9.00-19.30. Tues. & Wed. open till 20.30   C.C.:All Major

Clothing, accessories
DISCOUNTS

Metro 2 Garibaldi, towards the Cimitiero Monumentale, on the left.

This is the famous 'Corso Como' boutique's outlet for last year's unsold clothing and accessories. Discounts vary from 30% to 60%. Brand names Helmut Lang, Prada, Givenchy, Gucci, J.P. Gaultier, Marni, Watanabe and many more. Sizes tend to be smallish and every discounted item for sale has a modern and streamlined appeal. Worthwhile to visit before a serious bout of shopping in the center of Milan.

Crazy Art

Via Lambrate, 14 (interno) - 20131 Milano (MI)
9.00-12.30/14.30-19.00

02 2847003
C.C.:All Major

Furniture, various
VINTAGE

Bus 55,62.

Butcherblock tables, duck decoys, marble garden ornaments, ancient leather golf bags with wooden clubs plus a delightful kitsch department on the first floor. Fun to browse, their whole inventory is either for sale or for rent. Their shop in Via Pietro Custodi 4 is a touch more upmarket as is the one in Via Madonnina 11.

Cristiano Fissore

Via Alessandria, 5 - 20144 Milano (MI)
10.00-19.00. Monday closed

02 83241799
C.C.:All Major

Knitwear, cashmere
FACTORY OUTLET

MM2 Porto Genova.

The Cristiano Fissore collection in cashmere, cashmere silk or wool is well known in Italy. In their outlet prices are circa 50% below list price. Baggy sweaters in wool € 75,00 to € 400,00 in cashmere, a cardigan in silk and cashmere € 75,00. Designs are casual/chic: twinsets, two-ply tops or a six-ply cashmere jackets with zip in a rib-knit, all very wearable.

Diffusione Tessile

Galleria San Carlo - 20122 Milano (MI)
10.00-19.30. Monday 15.30-19.30

02 76000829
C.C.:All Major

Clothing
DISCOUNTS

MM1 San Babila exit.

A bargain basement on Corso Vittorio Emanuele selling last year's Max Mara collection, practically opposite their beautiful flagship store. You'll find Max Mara, SportMax, Blues Club, Pianoforte, Rinaldi, Weekend, I Blues, all at 30-50% less in all sizes. It's impossible not to find a bargain!

D Magazine Outlet

Via Montenapoleone, 26 - 20121 Milano (MI)
9.45-19.45. Open on Sun. and in Aug.

02 76006027
C.C.:All Major/taxfree

Clothing
BARGAIN BASEMENT

MM1 San Babila exit, MM3 Montenapoleone exit (which is closer).

Some of the unsold merchandise of Armani, Moschino, Nikos, Romeo Gigli, Fendi and others can be found in this cave like shop right on Milan's most expensive shopping street. One has to be slim to fit into their offerings, faultless legs help, the skirts were minimal chic! Men's shirts in the finest of cotton start at € 25,00. Also silks and lingerie. Friendly multilingual personnel (English, French, German, Spanish and also Italian).

Double B

Viale Lancetti, 28 - 20158 Milano (MI)
10.00-19.00. Monday 15.00-19.00

02 45475324
C.C.:All Major

Clothing
DISCOUNTS

Viale Stelvio turns into Viale Lancetti, parallel to Viale Jenner. On the north side of Milan towards Como. A gate with a flight of stairs.

There are really 4 shops in this complex, 2 to the left with sporty clothing by Brian & Berry and two to the right with the remainders of the Boggi shop in the center of Milan. On the ground floor super discounts of 50 to 70%, downstairs more recent collections discounted 30 to 50%. Sizes for men start at 38 up to 58, for women there is less choice and sizes are more erratic, lots of 40, 42, very few 46,48. The Boggi winter collection is available as of september 1.

Emporio 31 Design Outlet

Via Tortona, 31, (int. 10) - 20144 Milano (MI)
10.00-13.00/14.00-19.30. Closed Monday

02 4222577
C.C.:All Major

Furniture, various
DISCOUNTS

From Via Stendhal by car, on the left. After the ING complex to the right. Parking in the courtyard.

A large hall of 600 square meters selling furniture, objects, lights used for publicity shots. Possible to find flawless designs by Poltronova, Tronconi, Acerbis Int., Matteo Grassi, Zeus, Zoltan and others at a saving of 15% - 50%. Interesting and modern objects, a must for those who are furnishing a house. They speak English and French.

Emporio Isola

Via Prina, 11 - 20154 Milano (MI)
10.00-19.30. Monmday 15.00-19.30

02 3491040
C.C.:None

Clothing
BARGAIN BASEMENT

From the autostrada take Viale Certosa and then Corso Sempione. In front of the Milan headquarters of RAI (Italian Sate Television). Tram 1,29,30,33 Bus 57,94.

L'Emporio is aiming at an upmarket type of client in search of the latest fashions at a lower price. Small sizes will do well here: Moschino, Aspesi, Gaultier, Kenzo. Upstairs cashmeres only. For men, casual/sporty wear by Gentry Portofino, Gaultier, Armani. Aspesi, D&G. Last year's collections at 30-40% less. Other address: Foro Bonaparte 70 near the Sforza castle. They speak English and French.

Etro

Via Spartaco, 3 - 20135 Milano (MI)
10.00-13.45/14.45-19.00

02 55020218
C.C.:All Major

Clothing, fabrics
FACTORY OUTLET

Tram 9,23,30. Bus 84. Outlet is next to the factory.

Last year's Etro collection is sold in a small shop next to the factory in Via Spartaco. All merchandise discounted up to 50%. There is a fair choice in soft-furnishing material: € 12 and up p. meter and of course piles of cashmere sweaters, Indian shawls € 37, and embroidered bags. Downstairs tweed jackets, hunting boots, parkas, polos at -50%, all very luxurious!

Fashion Factory

Via Zumbini, 37 - 20143 Milano (MI)   02 89159068
9.30-19.30   C.C.:All Major

Clothing
BARGAIN BASEMENT

MM2 Romolo Famagosta exit. Bus 71,76,95. In the Barona area.

Large factory hall, well ordered, great choice of clothes, modern city styles, by
Patrizia Pepe, Liu-Jo, Moschino, Kookai, Manifatture Italiane: skirts € 45,00 - €
80,00, dresses € 90,00 circa and fun. Men's sizes from 46 - 58/60, for women
a lot of size 42, but even a few sizes in 46 can be found. Men's jackets by Henry
Cotton's, Loro Piana, Versus at 50% less. Corner with promotions, books, Indian
articles.

Floretta Coen Misul

Viale Beatrice d'Este, 15 - 20122 Milano (MI)   02 58307365
9.00-17.00. Closed in July and August   C.C.: None

Clothing
BARGAIN BASEMENT

Tram 9, 29, 30 Viale Bligny.

A Milanese institution and very popular with housewives trying on dresses, suits
and coats by Ferré, Yves St. Laurent, Missoni and Blumarine at very competitive
prices. A Blumarine sweater € 83, a Ferré coat € 210. Less choice for men: knitwear by Codice and Blumarine, even some cashmere. Sales in January and June:
everything at 30%-50%.

Fontana di Trebbia

Via Trebbia, 26 - 20135 Milano (MI)   02 55194353
8.00-12.30/13.30-17.00. Sat closed. Closed 15/7 - 1/9   C.C.: None

Handbags, leathergoods
FACTORY OUTLET

MM3 exit Lodi. Bus 90,91,92. Near Piazza Trento. On the 3rd floor, take the ancient lift.

Fontana produces beautifully made handbags under their own brand name and
for D&G. The two large rooms on the third floor show prototypes, samples and
remainders. Nice large travelling bags in leather or glove soft attaché cases
brand name Fontana. Furry bags by D&G in cheerful colors start at € 32.50, a
'shopping' in lambskin with metal handles € 65,00. Overwelming choice, reasonable prices.

Franco Jacassi

Via Sacchi, 3 - 20121 Milano (MI)   02 86462076
By appointment only   C.C.:All Major

Clothing, accessories, fabrics
VINTAGE

MM1 - Cairoli, MM2 Lanza.

After collecting all the famous Italian 'sarte' or couturiers of the fifties and sixties like Biki, Sorelle Fontana, Gattinoni and the jackets and coats by Armani
from the late seventies, Franco Jacassi now sells to museums and by auction.
Not only the clothing but also handbags by Roberto di Camerino, Gucci ecc.
are all in splendid condition as are the prices.

Galli Pelletterie

Via Cesare Balbo, 13 - 20136 Milano (MI)   02 58302665
9.00-12.30/14.00-19.30   C.C.: None

Handbags, leathergoods, suitcases
ARTISAN'S WORKSHOP

Tram 24, corner of Via Bellezza.

In this small showroom you can admire day and evening bags made for Celine, Valentino and admire Hermes-style Kelly bags € 140,00, Gucci style bamboo-handle bag € 160,00, a Bugatti design or a bucket shoulder bag made for the Japanese and French market. Bags in the prettiest of colors and in superior scratch-resistent calf's leather. They work to order and stock attaché cases for men.

Grandi Firme

Via Manzoni, 26 - 20121 Milano (MI)   02 799240
10.00-13.00/15.00-19.00   C.C.:All Major

Clothing
DISCOUNTS

Tram 1. MM3 Montenapoleone exit.

A charming second floor outlet for the showroom collections of Caroline Roehmer and Weil, Paris. All at half price, very tasteful and becoming, in sizes that will climb to 46 and in a variety of styles, all suited to ladies that lunch.

Gru.p Italia Factory Outlet

Via Riva di Trento, 5 - 20139 Milano (MI)   02 57455228
10.00-19.00. Monday 13.00-19.00   C.C.:All Major

Handbags, leathergoods
FACTORY OUTLET

exit Brenta or Bus 95. Better to go by car.

Their outlet stocks remainders, seconds, end of line handbags and travel bags by 'Made in Italy' names like Valentino, Laura Biagiotti, Oxus, GMVenturi, Soprani. A handbag by Valentino € 125,00 circa, Biagiotti € 55,00 and up. Leather jackets in antiqued brown nappa € 380,00, also men's raincoats and masses of belts & small leather goods.

I Mercanti

Via M. Macchi, 32 (interno) - 20124 Milano (MI)   02 6696638
9.30-12.30/14.30-19.00   C.C.:All Major

Household goods, gifts
DISCOUNTS

MM1 and 2 exit Stazione Centrale. Bus 90,92.

For household goods in general and a nice selection of gift articles and glassware. Reputable products made by Tefal, Prestige, Microonde, Lagostina, Pirex, Barazzoni, Leifheit, Aeternum and many more at a nice 30% discount. This place is ideal to fit out a kitchen.

Il Mercatino di Tatiana

Via Cavallotti, 13 - 20122 Milano (MI)
9.30-13.00/15.00-19.30

02 798786
C.C.: Le maggiori

Clothing
DISCOUNTS

Tram 23, autobus 60, 73, 84, 37. MM1 San Babila.

Tatiana specializes in Anglo-American sporty looks at decidedly upmarket prices. But there is hope! In the courtyard, last season's merchandise: Scapa of Scotland, George Hogg, Harry & Moore, Chashmere and Coton, Harton % Benson, Saks, Les Copains, Versace, Chevignon, Iceberg, Boss, Alpi are sold at 30-50% off. A prevalence of small sizes.

I Santi

Via Corio, 2 - 20135 Milano (MI)
8.30-12.00/14.00-17.00. Saturday closed

02 5416981
C.C.: All Major

Handbags, leathergoods, suitcases
FACTORY OUTLET

MM3 exit Porta Romana. Tram 9,29,30,13.

The showroom of the I Santi collection is on the second floor of this building close to Porta Romana. Every kind of travel bag or duffel bag is on show, attachè cases, overnight bags in leather and canvas, daypacks and backpacks, tennis bags. Good deals on their collection for women too. They speak English.

Il Salvagente

Via Fratelli Bronzetti, 16 - 20129 Milano (MI)
10.00-12.30/15.00-19.00. Wed & Sat 10.00-19.00

02 76110328
C.C. AE only

Clothing
BARGAIN BASEMENT

Tangenziale Est, exit Forlanini. In Milan Bus 54,60,61,62.

The largest bargain basement in Milan, well organized, spacious and full of sassy fashions! They sell all the big Italian designers at a discount and some French and American labels too. (Donna Karan mini skirt €10). For W. sizes from 38 to 46, for M. from 46 to 54. Prices are reputedly 50%-70% lower but still stratospheric at times. Twice-yearly sales are major events: 30% off 1st. week of sale, 60% off 2nd week. This place is always busy.

Il Salvagente Bambini

Via Balzaretti, 28 - 20133 Milano (MI)
10.00-13.00/15.00-19.00. Closed July & August

02 26680764
C.C.: None

Clothing
BARGAIN BASEMENT

In Città Studi, MM2 Piola exit then 5 minutes on foot or Bus 62.

Ample choice, all merchandise is sorted on age/sex, from toddlers up to 14 yrs. old. Reporter, Coveri, Kenzo, Ralph Lauren, Kickers, CP Company, Aspesi, Kauten, Brooksfield, Cheapie, Magil at 50% discount. Busy with young mums and screaming kids. Unbeatable for fashion and price conscious upwardly mobile families.

Kian

Corso Vercelli, 51 - 20144 Milano (MI)   02 460785
9.30-19.30   C.C.:All Major

Shoes
DISCOUNTS

MM1, exit Conciliazione, tram 24, bus 18.

Very trendy stiles for the young. They produce their own brand name but also sell remainders and showroom models from various shoe factories in the Florence area. Good prices for sandals and summer clogs, mules and stilettos in all sizes.

Kookai

Via Quintiliano, 33 - 20138 Milano (MI)   02 58016368
10.00-20.00. Closed Tuesday   C.C.: None

Clothing
FACTORY OUTLET

From Milano take the road to Linate, turn right immediately after the railway bridge, at the square take the second right and then the second left.

A cheerful and large selling point, brightly painted. Kookai fashions in size 40 up to size 46 (but a smallish 46). Jeans start at € 60. up to € 62, dresses from € 26 up to € 68. There are also handbags at € 12 and up and other modern accessories. It's all definitely for the very young.

La Scialuppa

Via M.Melloni, 75 - 20129 Milano (MI)   02 717239
9.30-12.30/15.30-19.30. Wed 9.30-19.30   C.C.:All Major

Clothing
DISCOUNTS

Near Piazzale Susa. Bus 54 or 61.

La Scialuppa caters to the more mature and classical dresser in search of good quality coats and jackets in a wearable Italian style. Cashmere woollen coats for men €362 circa. Tweed jackets by Pasquale Felpi €154, 4-ply English cashmere sweaters at €223. Their basic strength remains their men's department: trousers in Loro Piana fabrics at €58. For W cashmere/woollen coats by Edwards €135, skirts, classical dresses.

Larusmiani Outlet

Via U. Ollearo, 8 - 20155 Milano (MI)   02 33002600
15.00-19.00. Saturday 10.00-13.00/15.00-19.00   C.C.:All Major

Clothing
FACTORY OUTLET

West of the center towards the A4 to Torino. Via MacMahon, Ponte della Ghisolfa.

Larusmiani produces very elegant cotton fabrics since 1922 used for suits and jackets. In their outlet they sell not only fabrics at a 50% discount but also elegant suits for men € 375,00, casual/trendy jackets, pyjamas, cashmere sweaters, leatherwear, lots of choice and worth a visit!

Le Vintage

Via Garigliano, 4 - 20159 Milano (MI)   02 69311885
11.00-14.30/15.30-20.00. Saturday 10.30-18.30. Sunday 13.00-19.00
Mon. & Tues. only afternoons   C.C.:All Major

Shoes
BARGAIN BASEMENT

Viale Zara, Piazzale Lagosta. North of the center near the Porta Garibaldi station.

Le Vintage sells the unsold merchandise of the 'Le Solferine' shop in the Brera area. Rather striking and avangarde shoes by John Richmond, Anna Sui, Vivienne Lee, Stephan Janson at half price but not all sizes are available. Those who wear shoe size 37 will have better luck! They also sell clothing from the 70's.

Leuce

Via Panizzi, 6 (interno) - 20146 Milano (MI)   02 48950907
9.30-12.30/15.30-19.00   C.C.:All Major

Clothing
BARGAIN BASEMENT

In the Lorenteggio area on the outskirts of Milan. Bus 54 to the last stop. The entrance to the basement is inside the gate.

An amazing quantity of flamboyant merchandise is on display, but be aware that the two rooms are cramped. Christian Lacroix PAP suits € 350,00, dresses, sweaters or Cinderella style ball-gowns by Krizia, Sonia Rykiel, Dolce Gabbana, Les Copains. For M suits by Valentino in woollen checks or pale yellow silk and linen. Evening capes in black lined with white silk. Show this book to Tonino, the owner, and he'll give you a healthy discount. They speak English and French.

Lo Spaccio 1

Via Newton, 12 - 20148 Milano (MI)   02 4046445
9.30-12.30/15.00-19.00. Saturday 9.30-12.30   C.C.:All Major

Clothing, lingerie, underwear
FACTORY OUTLET

Between Via Civitali and Via Zamagna. Car advisable.

Kentelle produces lingerie for various designers plus a collection under it's own brandname. A good selection of kimonos, robes, housecoats, pyamas, some in heavy Chinese silk. Nighties by Chiarugi € 97, terrytowel Armani robes € 94, Armani boxer shorts € 18. It's possible to find Valentino lingerie either in silk or nylon, mainly small sizes or sets by La Perla.

Marni

Via Fratelli Tajani, 1 - 20133 Milano (MI)   02 71040332
11.00-16.00. Saturday 11.00-18.00. Closed 15/7-15/9   C.C.:All Major

Clothing, accessories
FACTORY OUTLET

MM2 Piola, near the exit in a court yard.

Dresses, coats, knitwear in the latest fashions (even though it's last year's) because of the innovative and original designs. Well organized, large choice, discounts of 50% but still steep - coats € 200,00- € 750,00. Sizes from 36/38 to 46 with lots of 42. Also shoes, handbags. Sales in January and July, busy busy.

Mulino Docks Dora

Via Toffetti, 9 - 20139 Milano (MI)   02 56810393
10.30-13.00/14.00-19.30. Closed Monday   C.C.:All Major

Clothing
VINTAGE

From Corso Lodi take Via Marochetti to Piazza Mistral. Via Toffetti is the first on the left. Docks Dora is on the left corner of Via Boncompagni. Parking. MM3 Rogoredo exit, Bus 95,84.

Housed in an old mill, most of their merchandise comes from the Netherlands or the U.S. Jeans € 10,00, leather jackets € 25,00, hats, some furry € 2,50, crimplene dresses straight from the sixties, T-shirts by OshKosh. In all 500mq of clothing to invent a new look. Corner with household linens sold per kilo at € 10,00. It's all fun.

Raponi

Via Ronchi, 2 (P.za M. Titano) - 20134 Milano (MI)   02 2153900
9.00-12.30/15.30-19.30   C.C.:All Major

Fabrics
BARGAIN BASEMENT

MM2 exit Lambrate. Take the passage way under the station to exit in Piazza Titano. Tangenziale Est exit Lambrate.

Stock up on precious silks and natty woollens, linens and ribbons. Designer silks € 11-14, 140 cm w. or woollen gabardine at € 8,50 per meter. They always stock bridal silks. Good deals in designer fabrics sold by weight. Other adresses: Via Panzeri 10, Milano, Via A. Strada 73, Bresso (MI).

Renna Sport Off

Via Paolo da Cannobio, 8 - 20123 Milano (MI)   02 72094638
10.00-19.30   C.C.:None

Clothing
BARGAIN BASEMENT

MM1 exit Duomo. Near Piazza Diaz.

An outlet for unsold merchandise from the Renna e Sport stores. Prices are reportedly 50% below shop price, for merchandise that is at least one season (sometimes more) old. In winter a fair offer in leather and sheepskin coats. Close to Piazza Duomo.

RJ Outlet

Via Zumbini, 37 - 20143 Milano (MI)   02 89159068
Monday 14.00-19.30   C.C.:All Major

Clothing, accessories
GOOD PRICES

Metro MM2 Famagosta where there is also a large parking.

Great choice in accessories and clothing by all the most trendy designers: from Armani to Roberto Cavalli, from Fendi to Gucci, Prada, Moschino, MiuMiu, Dolce & Gabbana, Valentino, Church's, Levis, Morgan, Versace and many others; Prices are 30% - 70% below list price, with an average of 40% compared with the official list price.

Scarparium
Via Pietro Custodi, 4 - 20136 Milano (MI)   02 89422823
10.00-13.00/15.30-19.30   C.C.:All Major

Shoes
BARGAIN BASEMENT

From Viale Col di Lana towards Piazza Tito Caro.

A large shop stacked with shoes, boots, sandals and slippers with various brand names, either famous or totally unknown. Not all sizes are always available but there is a good chance to find a bargain at € 19,00 next to a pair of ankle boots in lizard at € 200.00. One has to browse, prices are competitive. They also sell handbags, accessories and clothing.

Serapian
Via Jommelli, 35 - 20131 Milano (MI)   02 280121
8.00-12.30/14.00-19.00. Saturday 8.00-12.30/14.00-18.00   C.C.: None

Handbags, leathergoods, suitcases
FACTORY OUTLET

Bus 75, tram 33. By car from Piazza Loreto take Via Porpora, seventh cross road on the left. Parking difficult.

One of the snazzier factory outlets and popular with Milanese ladies for the excellent quality of their handbags, (a Bugatti shape in ostrich € 1,000). Their own line of sturdy travelbags and suitcases in PVC and leather are best sellers. Small leather envelopes, soft enough to wear on the skin, a must for safe, anti pickpocket travelling € 30,00.

Shabby Chic
Via B.Cellini, 21 - 20129 Milano (MI)   02 76018149
10.30-19.30. Monday 14.30-19.30   C.C.:All Major

Clothing
VINTAGE

Tram 9,23,30. Near to Viale Premuda and in front of Via Lincoln.

A small shop, very neat and chic, offering a savvy mixture of 60's and 70s American/Austrian/English styles, Harris tweed, Burberry's, kilts. Summer dresses, spotlessly ironed € 40,00 and up, sweaters € 15,00, polo Lacoste € 17,50, Tyrolean jackets with matching linen skirts € 60,00, leather bombers € 60,00. Mostly small sizes. They speak English and French and keep their clients informed via email.

Spaccio Bassetti
Via Procaccini, 32 - 20154 Milano (MI)   02 33450125
9.30-18.30   C.C.: None

Household linen, various
FACTORY OUTLET

Near Corso Sempione.

Household linens with small defects called 'Primetta' that are only sold in their 12 outlets all over Italy at low prices. Ample choice of last year's remainders like terrytowel robes, sheets, slipcovers, quilted bedspreads, duvets & duvet covers, Gran Foulard and end of line blankets, all discounted 30/40%. There is another outlet in Via C. Botta 7a.

Spaccio Luciano Soprani

Via Morosini, 30 - 20135 Milano (MI)   02 55183913
10.30-14.00/15.00-19.00. Closed Monday   C.C.:All Major

Clothing
FACTORY OUTLET

Towards Linate, between Via Spartaco and Via Fogazzaro. Not far from the Etro outlet.

Large and well laid out. A worthwhile place for those in search of original party dresses or elegant bridal suits. Highly innovative designs, made in unusual fabrics. Striking taffeta blouses, linen/silk tunics with pants. Strictly for fashion forward men beautiful winter coats or leather car coats. Prices become especially interesting during the sales period when they take 70% off label price: an Alta Moda suit in silk € 225,00, fur coat € 600,00. Recommended.

Tissuteam

Via Lambro, 12/A - 20129 Milano (MI)   02 29517883
9.00-12.30/15.00-19.00. Closed Monday & August   C.C.:All Major

Fabrics
FACTORY OUTLET

MM1 exit Porta Venezia. Tram 1,9,23.

Highly recommended for curtain/soft furnishing fabrics. Tissuteam sells end of series, seconds and remainders of the Lorenzo Rubelli collection. Silks and cotton chintz per meter € 14-19, silk velvets € 29, English linen/cotton damask € 37, (70% less than the Rubelli pricelist). Some Indian cottons. Multilingual personnel.

Tommaseo 2 di Pupi Solari

Piazza Tommaseo, 2 - 20123 Milano (MI)   02 433648
10.00-13.00/15.00-19.00   C.C.:All Major

Clothing
DISCOUNTS

MM1 exit Conciliazione. Entrance at the first door.

Remainders, unsold, stock and showroom samples of the main Pupi Solari shop next door. Clothing for toddlers and kids in excellent taste and very good quality at prices that are not exactly low but still better than elsewhere for the same quality.

Valextra Outlet

Via Cerva, 11 - 20122 Milano (MI)   02 76003459
10.00-13.00/14.00-19.00   C.C.:All Major
Sat. 10.00-13.00/14.00-19.00. Closed Mon., Wed & Fri 10.00-19.00

Handbags, leather goods, suitcases
FACTORY OUTLET

In the center of Milan, MM1 San Babila, 5 minutes on foot and near their main shop.

Handbags, attache cases, small leather goods, wallets, travel bags all by Valextra and all end of line or seconds. Handbags in fabric, ecrù, € 122,00, small envelopes € 50,00. The seconds are discounted a further 25%, their end of line 40 - 50 %. The shop is small but offers a lot of choice especially in shoulder bags in that very wearable brandy color.

Vibec

Via Marco d'Agrate, 33 - 20139 Milano (MI)   02 57407443
9.15-19.15. Sat. 9.00-13.00/15.00-19.00   C.C.:All Major

Jewelry
FACTORY OUTLET

In the Ripamonti area. Tram 24, bus 95. Parking inside.

Large, well-protected outlet of silver objects, ideal for wedding presents or gifts: picture frames, animals in silver, cups and platters, mirrors with heavy silver frames, cutlery, some china, baby toys, all discounted between 20 and 30%. Special corner with Ferrari silver fountain pens or Mikawa pearls, plus gold chains, earrings, bracelets. They present a small gift at the cashier, but no further discounts.

Vintagespirit Multistore

Piazza Generale Cantore, 3 - 20123 Milano (MI)   02 8373814
10.00-13.00/15.30-19.30. Sabato 10.00-19.00   C.C.:All Major

Clothing, accessories
VINTAGE

MM2, Porta Genova.

This is the first multi-store of vintage clothing in Milan with 6 different shops: Elizabeth the First, etnic clothing. Miss Ghintig, Sartoria Italiana. A.N.G.E.L.O. with brandnames like Pucci, Y.st.L, Missoni, Ungaro, Pierre Cardin. Elite Vintage with pieces from the Pescetti store Genova, Letty & John, american byoux. Voss & Kompani, byoux from Scandinavia.

Adidas Outlet

Via Monte San Primo, 3 - 20052 Monza (MI)   039 27151
10.00-19.00. Sat. 10.00-20.00   C.C.:All Major

Clothing, sportswear, shoes
FACTORY OUTLET

Take the Superstrada to Lecco, exit Monza to Muggiò. At the beginning of the village.

This is a new outlet selling the clothing, sportswear, underwear and lots and lots of shoes, tennis, sneakers, boots, mocassins all by the famous Adidas brandname. There are special offers galore, enormous choice and savings on average of circa 30%.

Philips Outlet

Via Vasari, 23 - 20052 Monza (MI)   039 2036645
15.00-19.00. Afternoons only   C.C.:All Major

Electric appliances, household goods
FACTORY OUTLET

Towards Concorrenza, Viale Libertà and inside the Philips factory complex.

A very useful outlet for buying coffee makers, TV's, hair driers, microwaves, cameras, electric toothbrushes, and small appliances for pedicure or massage. All seconds (because of small surface blemishes) or end of series. Special offers abound. This is the only Philips outlet in Lombardy.

Calzaturificio Wilsonsport

Viale I° Maggio, 15 - 20014 Nerviano (MI)
9.30-12.00/15.00-19.00

0331 585735
C.C.: None

Shoes
FACTORY OUTLET

Autostrada A8/9 exit Lainate towards Nerviano. At the traffic light (Città Mercato) continue towards the Nerviano 'Zona Industriale'. Wilsonsport is on the right after the curve in the road. From Milano S.S.33 (Sempione). At Città Mercato turn left towards the Nerviano Zona Industriale.

An authentic factory outlet where one has to fight one's way in over piles of shoe boxes. Men's shoes, sample size 43, well made €52 and up, made to measure € 21 extra. They work for Donna Karan, Valentino, Trussardi, Polo and others. American preppy/college styles also for women but less choice. Sample size 37 € 37 - € 62.

Factory Outlet Levi's e Dockers

Via Giovanni XXIII, 2 - 20014 Nerviano (MI)
9.30-19.30

0331 415316
C.C.:All Major

Clothing, casual, jeans
FACTORY OUTLET

Along the main road S.S. del Sempione from Milan to Nerviano, at the traffic light in front of the commercial center Auchan.

600 mq. selling space, parking inside the building. All the Levi's and Dockers jeans, sweats, T's on the market, discounted 40% to 70% on list price. This is the ideal outlet for families and active youngsters. Pleasant and helpful service, multilingual personnel. An American style outlet, worth a visit.

Luciano Padovan

Via Bergamina, 10 - 20014 Nerviano (MI)
10.00-12.30/15.00-19.30

0331 584223
C.C.:All Major

Shoes
FACTORY OUTLET

Autostrada A8, exit Legnano, follow the main road, at the traffic light turn left, take the Sempione S.S. 33 towards Milan, pass Parabiago to Nerviano. Follow the signs for Padovan. Parking.

Very fashionable women's shoes 'Designed by Luciano Padovan', elegant sandals, slippers, ballerinas or stilettos. Not the kind of shoes to take a long walk in. Sample size 37 € 50, with paillettes or in snake skin € 62. Other sizes € 83 circa. Fancy beach bags € 42.

Kartell

Via delle Industrie, 1 loc. Noviglio
20082 Noviglio/Binasco (MI)
9.00-13.00/14.00-19.00. Closed Monday

02 900121
C.C.:All Major

Furniture, various
FACTORY OUTLET

Autostrada A7, Milano-Genova, exit Binasco. The factory is visible from the autostrada. Call first to make sure that the outlet is open.

Special sales three times a year with discounts between 20-40% for furniture used for photo sessions. All pieces are in plastic material and in very bright colors, designed by famous names like Magistretti, Citterio and Starck. Casa Kit and Standard, distributed by Kartell can also be found.

Calzaturificio Riccardo Banfi

Via Mons. Pogliani, 2 - 20015 Parabiago (MI)   0331 551335
9.00-12.00/14.30-19.00. Sat. 9.00-19.00. Sun. open in Dec.   C.C.:All Major

Shoes
FACTORY OUTLET

Autostrada A8/9, exit Lainate towards Nerviano-Parabiago. From Milano S.S.33 (Sempione) towards Legnano. At the level of S. Lorenzo turn towards the center. Follow the yellow sign posts to an an ochre colored building on a corner.

Banfi works for some well known Italian designers and exports to major European countries. Their men's collection is especially well represented, some classical models, some avantgarde models. For women the latest fashions are in stock, sample size for W is 36, prices are definitely convenient also for purses, small leather goods, sales at 40%.

Claudio Morlacchi

Via Castelnovo, 24 - 20015 Parabiago (MI)   0331 555411
9.00-12.00/14.00-19.00   C.C.: None
Saturday 9.00-13.00/14.00-16.00

Shoes
FACTORY OUTLET

In the center of Parabiago, in a charming old building. Follow the indications for the railway station and the cemetery.

Cross the court-yard to their outlet. Their shoe collection is classical and very well made, the type of shoe that looks right with everything, a bit Milanese/understated but stylish € 75.00 - € 150.00. Nice handbags and shoulderbags, backpacks in high-tec fabric trimmed with lizard € 160,00. It's a small place, but friendly.

Colette Pretty Shoes (Fashion Point)

Via E. de Amicis, 24 - 20015 Parabiago (MI)   0331 551526
9.30-12.30/15.30-18.30   C.C.:All Major

Shoes
FACTORY OUTLET

From Milano S.S.33 (Sempione), turn left at Nerviano/Città Mercato. In Parabiago continue towards the center and follow the Colette signs. The outlet is in a green and white building, on the right from the entrance.

They produce fashionable shoes of great quality and those very nice evening bags by Judith Leiber! Women's shoes start at €84, men's shoes €115, boots are well over €135. Their collection is really smashing and very refined since they work for some major national and international designers. Showroom models for women size 37, for men 41 at circa € 83. Sales at 40%.

Fratelli Rossetti

Via Cantù, 24 - 20015 Parabiago (MI)   0331 495217
9.30-12.30/14.00-19.00. Saturday 9.30-19.00   C.C.: None

Shoes
FACTORY OUTLET

From Milano Autostrada A8/9, exit Lainate, to Nerviano Z.I. continue to Parabiago and Via S. Maria. Coming from Turin and the A4, exit Arluno to Parabiago and the train station, the outlet is well indicated. Parking.

Very large premises, good choice. Men's shoes € 90,00 and up, their famous Flexa Line sells at € 120,00. Showroom models size 42 at € 65,00. For women tremendous choice, classical, refined, latest trends, all colors, prices between € 70,00 - € 125,00. Showroom models, size 36 start at € 55,00. Good choice in irregular sizes like 34/35 and 40/41 for W and 39/40 and 46/48 for M. There is another outlet in Serravalle (AL) and they have a mailing list.

Parabiago Collezioni

Via Caldara, 4 - 20015 Parabiago (MI)   0331 495007
15.00-19.00. Sat. 10.00-19.00. Thurs. & Fri. 10.00-20.00   C.C.:All Major

Shoes
FACTORY OUTLET

From Milan take the S.S. Sempione to S. Lorenzo di Parabiago, at the traffic light turn left, after two roundabouts at the first traffic light to the right. There is a parking area next to the factory.

Great choice in shoes, all sizes, sample sizes are 37.5 for W and 42.5 for M. There are some shoes used at fashion shows, available in larger sizes. Brandnames are Thierry Rabotin (rather trendy) and Karin Rose, (a well known brand name for mature feet in the U.S.). The handbags and small leather goods were modern and low priced.

Rede di Parabiago

Via S. Maria, 60/Via Veneto - 20015 Parabiago (MI)   0331 550257
9.30-12.30/14.00-19.00 Closed Monday   C.C.:All Major
Saturday 9.00-12.30/15.00-19.00

Hosiery
FACTORY OUTLET

In front of the municipality and 400 mtrs. from the train station. Plenty of parking. The outlet is in a basement on the left of the piazza.

Men's long socks in wool or mercerized cotton € 4,00, with the Trussardi brand name € 4.50. Pantyhose 13 denier, silk-finish, sheer, € 2,90, panty fish-net in lycra € 6,00. Baby socks € 1,20, very cute. Excellent quality, lots of offers and ample choice!

Ugo Rossetti Spaccio

Viale Marconi, 57 - 20015 Parabiago (MI)   0331 494522
9.30-12.00/15.00-19.00. Sat. 9.30-19.00   C.C.:All Major

Shoes
FACTORY OUTLET

From Milano S.S. 33 (Sempione) to Parabiago. In S. Lorenzo turn left at the traffic light, continue for 500 meters. The Ugo Rossetti outlet is on this street just before the center.

They offer enormous choice. Some corners with special offers, trendy or classical & well-made. Men's shoes Etnos/UgoUomo € 105,00, golf shoes, leather € 95,00. For W. all sizes tremendous choice, last years collection is discounted 50%: € 60,00, recent collection (Vivalei) -30%: € 65,00. They speak French and English. Sales in January and July.

Timberland Factory Outlet

Via Piave, 26 - 20016 Pero (MI)   02 3536687
10.00-19.30. Monday 16.00-19.30   C.C.:All Major

Clothing, shoes
FACTORY OUTLET

From Milano take S.S.33 (Sempione). After reaching Pero and immediately after an IP service station, turn to the right.

Large and filled to the brim with Timberland clothes, shoes, boots and bags. End of series, samples, and seconds. Timberland shoes are well represented, from kids tennis shoes at € 25,00 to € 70,00 for a men's trekking boot. A shirt in lamb skin € 220,00, special offers in duffel bags in canvas and leather € 100,00, bermudas, samples, € 45,00 and jeans in every possible shape and size.

Spacci Bassetti
Via Legnano, 24 - 20027 Rescaldina (MI)   0331 448512
9.30-18.30. Saturday 9.00-12.30/14.30-18.30   C.C.:None

Household linen, various
FACTORY OUTLET

Autostrada A8, exit Castellanza, continue towards Rescaldina, turn left at the first traffic light.

Bassetti products like Gran Foulard are well represented, either as seconds or samples, or remnants sold per kilo. Large wire baskets with unfinished towels are good value as are the colorful cushions in cotton. There is also a respectable range of their normal collection and an enormous choice in every type of household linen be it duvets, blankets, robes, or sheets discounted between 30-40%.

Babycresci Bellavita Magnolia
Corso Europa, 323 - 20017 Rho (MI)   02 9399011
9.30-12.30/14.30-18.30   C.C.:All Major

Clothing, underwear
FACTORY OUTLET

From Milano S.S. 33, at the intersection in Rho to the right. Babycresci is immediately on the right. Parking in front of the gate.

Children's clothing in brushed cotton, sweatshirts by the shipload, all made on the premises. Practical but cute clothes that are not scared of the washing machine. Busy with young mothers who might find a jogging outfit for themselves. Corner with second choice articles, brand name American Place, 2 salopettes in cotton for toddlers € 10,00, 3 colored T-shirts € 7,50.

Duccio del Duca - Oregon
Via Manzoni, 9 - 20028 San Vittore Olona (MI)   0331 518208
9.00-12.00/14.00-18.30. Sat. 9.00-12.30   C.C.: None

Shoes
FACTORY OUTLET

From Milano S.S.33. In the center of San Vittore turn right. The entrance of the outlet is the door on the right of number 9.

Well made shoes with a high fashion content, booties in the latest styles, snakeskin loafers, sandals with stiletto heels.   Shoes € 65-93, showroom sizes 36.5/37 sell for € 53 and bags by Coccinelle are discounted 30%. Some French brand names, some platform shoes, very well made boots. Best time to buy: March and end of September.

Siport
Centro Dir. Il Quadrato, Via Giotto, 1 - 20090 Segrate (MI)   02 26920899
10.00-14.00/15.00-19.00
Sat. 9.30-13.30/15.00-19.00. Closed Monday   C.C.:All Major

Shoes
FACTORY OUTLET

From Milan to Linate, San Felice and then to the left for Segrate. At the first traffic light to the left. The Centro Direzionale is the last complex on the left. The entrance for Siport is on the right side of the building. Parking.

Shoes by Avirex, Missoni Sport for men €38-€70. Mocassins, sandals of the Birkenstock type, hiking boots. Showroom size is 41 and sell at €26 but few available. They make kid's shoes for Barbie (Mattel), Kid Land and Fisher Price €6-€18,50. Little dresses with the Barbie brand name for real girls €18, all ages.

Superga Outlet

Via Olgia, 18 - 20090 Segrate (MI)
10.00-19.00. Monday 14.30-19.00

02 2133378
C.C.:All Major

Clothing, shoes
FACTORY OUTLET

Tangenziale Est, exit Lambrate take Via Cassanese. In Segrate, fraz. Lavanderie on the left. Parking.

A very large hall selling remnants and last year's collection of Superga sneakers, boots, and casual clothing. Cashmere tennis shoes € 72.50, in canvas € 22.50, all sizes and colors. Kids' sports shoes €15,00, special offers in hiking/work/rubber boots, prices start at € 30,00. Superga ski overalls, 3 for the price of 2, special offers all year round, they speak English, German and Spanish.

Settimocielo

Via Cesare da Sesto, 1 - 20099 Sesto San Giovanni (MI)
9.30-13.00/15.00-19.00. Open on Sunday

02 26229931
C.C.:All Major

Ceramics, terracotta, porcelain
FACTORY OUTLET

From Milan take Viale Monza and at the turn off for Sesto San Giovanni keep going straight. Follow the road parallel to the train track till a small square with a pyramid statue, Via C. da Sesto is the third on the right. The shop is on the corner. Parking difficult.

The Rosenthal outlet for unsold or returned goods, end of series, from the 130 shops that sell Rosenthal in Italy. Discounts from 35-80% (Tax free possible). Large and airy shop, lots of tea & dinner sets for sale, all classical. Prices half shop price: teaservice for 6, €109 circa, complete dinner services €260-518. Versace ashtrays, lots of knick knacks, a blue dot means an aditional discount but no seconds available.

Puntopeggy

Via Cassino, 9 - 20067 Tribiano (MI)
8.30-12.30/13.30-18.30. Closed Saturday

02 90632429
C.C.:None

Beauty care, perfumes
FACTORY OUTLET

From Milano S.S. 415 (Paullese). At the roundabout for Caleppio di Settala turn right to Melegnano, and immediately left for Paullo and right for Tribiano, then left at the next roundabout, go past the bridge, second street on the right. Ring bell on the gate.

Small outlet selling some wonderful products at extremely competitive prices. Big tubes of anti cellulite cream, creams for stretchmarks, drainage, firming and whatever other part of the body needs toning up. Also mud packs, oils, bleaching creams, bath oils, shampoos, sun screens. They work for some well known Italian stylists.

Canali

Via S. Pellico, 2 - 20050 Triuggio (MI)
Only Saturday 8.30-12.00/14.00-17.30

039 2014226
C.C.:None

Clothing
FACTORY OUTLET

From Milan take the Tangenziale Est, exit Arcore, follow the indications for Arcore - Canonica - Triuggio. In the center of the village, close to the the post office.

Canali epitomizes Italian good taste, prime materials and the kind of design that turns every male into a Greek god (or nearly). Count on spending approximately € 100,00 for trousers, € 225,00 for jackets, and € 325,00 for suits. There is plenty of expert saleshelp and a large selection to choose from.

Civas

Via Dante, 8 - 20050 Triuggio (MI)
9.30-12.30/15.00-19.00

0362 943052
C.C.: None

Clothing
FACTORY OUTLET

From Milano, Tangenziale Est, exit Arcore proceed towards Arcore - Canonica - Triuggio. In Triggiu take the road for Seregno. Civas is 50 m further on after the pharmacy.

Production of rain coats and jackets by Guido di Riccio for Pluvex. Sharp city styles in trendy colors. 3/4 length jackets in satin with pearl buttons € 35,00, trouser suits € 110,00. Second choice casual jackets € 25,00. Sizes from 36 to 50. Sales 1/5 - 1/6 and 1/11- 1/12. There are many French brand names which makes this outlet worth a visit.

Irge Pigiami

Via Patriotti, 29/31 - 20029 Turbigo (MI)
9.30-12.30/15.00-19.00

0331 871160
C.C.:All Major

Lingerie, underwear
FACTORY OUTLET

Autostrada A4, exit Boffalora towards Castano Primo then take S.S.341 to Galliate/ Novara. A little before the cross road on the right.

Well ordered, plenty of choice and the possibility to find a genuine bargain. Housecoats in chenille € 26, pyjamas, nighties, babydolls € 18,50 and up in excellent quality that will last for years and doesn't fear the washing machine. Styles are sober, not frivolous. Lingerie for women (also XXL) upstairs, together with expert help.   Moneysaver!

Infiore by Emmeci

Viale C. Battisti, 127/ang.Via Carducci
20057 Vedano al Lambro (MI)
9.30-19.00

039 2324255
C.C.:All Major

Lingerie, underwear
FACTORY OUTLET

On the local road along the Monza-Biasonno park, look for a sign 'spaccio' at the beginning of Vedano. The entrance is on the left down a flight of stairs.

Sets of bra and panty in silk in spring colors like yellow and bright blue, sizes up to 4, in black and white up to 5. Bodysuits with built-in bra € 14,00, 'Super dream up' bras (a sort of Wonderbra) € 9,00. Good deals can be found in their baskets with seconds, briefs, bras in lace for as little as € 5,00, support hose € 2,00. Sales and they speak English.

Spacci Bassetti

Via Bolzano, 3 - 20059 Vimercate (MI)
9.30-18.30. Monday 14.30-18.30

039 668634
C.C.:None

Household linen, various
FACTORY OUTLET

Autostrada A4, exit Agrate, in front of Star go right or coming from the Tangenziale Est, exit and direction of Burago. Next to the Marzotto clothing outlet.

Bassetti products like Gran Foulard are well represented, either as seconds/ samples, or remnants sold per kilo. Large wire baskets with unfinished towels are good value as are the colorful cushions in cotton. There is a respectable range of their regular collection for sale and an enormous choice of duvets, blankets, robes, or sheets discounted between 30-40%.

Crealis Tutto Bimbi

Via Capo di Vico, 47 - 27022 Casorate Primo (PV)
9.30-12.30/14.30-19.30

02 90097885
C.C.:All Major

Clothing
FACTORY OUTLET

Autostrada A7, exit Binasco. At Casorate take the ring road for Visconti Motta, then third exit left for Casorate.

All baby and toddler clothes with the Chicco label and all articles for new borns are 20% discounted and there are many special offers of baby carriages, beds, baby chairs. The maternity wear is sold at 50% less than shop price and available in all sizes. There is a large playing area for kids with very competent personnel.

Cantina di Casteggio

Via Torino, 96 - 27045 Casteggio (PV)
8.30-13.00/15.00-18.30. Sunday 8.30-12.30

0383 806311
C.C.:All Major

Wine, liqueurs
GOOD PRICES

Autostrada A21 exit Casteggio in the center, circa 300 m. from Piazza Cavour.

Pinot Grigio Oltre Pavese, Chardonnay del Casteggiano, Rieslling Italico D.O.C, Olterepò Pavese, spumanti. Special offers, a catalogue, they ship and speak English, Spanish and French.

Distilleria Bellomi

Via Torino, 101-103 - 27045 Casteggio (PV)
8.00-12.00/14.00-19.00

0383 82353
C.C.:All Major

Wine, liqueurs
GOOD PRICES

Autostrada A21, exit Casteggio, then S.S.10 to Voghera. At the beginning of Casteggio, coming from Voghera.

Judging by their machinery they must handpress the grapes, very interesting. Their best grappa sells at € 8,50; they also produce sambuca (minus the coffee bean) and digestive liqueurs based on artichokes or various other very wholesome herbs.

Tanino Crisci

Via Garibaldi, 9 - 27045 Casteggio (PV)
15.30-19.30. Sat. 10.00-12.00/15.30-19.30
Closed Monday. Sun. 9.00-12.30.

0383 82254
C.C.:All Major

Shoes
FACTORY OUTLET

Autostrada A7 to Pavia then the S.S.35. On the main square, Piazza Cavour, the Tanino Crisci shop is at the beginning of the narrow street opposite Hotel Cavour.

Luxury boots and shoes, all handmade, either classical or in the latest fashion. This outlet offers unsold stock from the various Tanino Crisci boutiques situated in prime locations all over the world and samples from their showroom collections in size 42 for men and 36-36,5 for women. Prices are circa 50% less.

Il Bottegone

Via Petrarca, 2 - 27010 Giussago (PV)
9.00-12.00/14.00-19.00. Sun. 14.00-19.00. Monday closed

0382 927244
C.C.: None

Furniture, various
VINTAGE

From Milan take the S.S. 35 dei Giovi, from Binasco turn left to Giussago, then turn right past the village in the direction of Certosa.

A farmyard holding veritable treasures: old doors, beams, ladders, balconies in cast iron, ornamental gates and entrance doors, window shutters, stone balustrades. Inside rustic furniture, cupboards, side-boards, kitchensinks. All to be restaurated. It's impossible not to find something interesting especially since their prices are reasonable.

Riso Scotti

Via Torretta, 23 - 27100 Rivanazzano (PV)
8.30-12.30/15.00-19.00. Saturday 8.30-12.30

0382 5081
C.C.:None

Food, pasta, rice
FACTORY OUTLET

Autostrada A7, exit Bereguardo/Pavia Nord to Pavia. At the roundabout turn left towards Milan and the tangenziale. After 1,5 km take the Pavia Stadio exit, at the Stop sign continue straight, at first traffic light left, second traffic light right, at the crossing left, at the third traffic light left for a further 300 m.

Riso Scotti is a well known producer of rice and pasta made of rice. A their 'spaccio' they sell various types: Arborio, Roma, Carnaroli or unpolished rice from 1 to 5 kilo in cheerful cotton bags. Their 1/2 kilo packs of rice with mushrooms, vegetables or asparagus are ideal to prepare a quick risotto. Wafers made of rice, rice milk, biscuits, crackers and spaghetti made of rice are all low in calories.

Calzaturificio A. Garzia

Via Valllere, 291 - 27029 Vigevano (PV)
8.00-12.00/14.00-18.30

0381 326566
C.C.:None

Shoes
FACTORY OUTLET

In Vigevano take the road to Mortara. At the level of Alfa Romeo go towards Novara.

There are two things to do in Vigevano: see the stupendous Piazza Ducale, and visit the Garzia shoe factory. On show are shoes from the current collection, mostly sample size 37 but other sizes are available at € 65,00 circa. Also handbags. The shoes are known for their workmanship and original designs. Sales middle of January and July. They speak English.

Ravizza Country Store

Via Bereguardo, 38 Cascina il Boscaccio
27020 Zerbolò (PV)
10.00-19.00. Closed Mon, Tues morn & August

0382 818341
C.C.:All Major

Clothing, sportswear, casual, jeans
BARGAIN BASEMENT

Autostrada A7, exit Bereguardo, towards the Ticino river, continue across the famous 'boatbridge'. Take first on the left.

Pretty setting, dripping with country charm. The unsold items of the Ravizza Milano store are sold at half price here. Barbour, Burberry, Alpi, Donaldson, Irish Aran sweaters, flannel blouses, waders, hunting bags, various objects all discounted. English and German spoken, sales in January and July, alteration service.

Gabel Industrie Tessile

Località Villapinta, Via ai Piani - 23010 Buglio in Monte (SO)
9.00-12.30/14.30-19.00. Sat. 9.00-19.00

0342 620173
C.C.:All Major

Household linen, various
FACTORY OUTLET

S.S.38. Halfway between Morbegno and Sondrio, 200 m after the Brace restaurant on the left. Look for the sign for Buglio and turn left. Continue another 100 m, turn right, a narrow dirt track in the middle of fields.

A large outlet that's part of the factory. It sells all the Gabel household linens at discounts of 30% - 50%. Lots of offers: slipcovers 'Poncho', remnants by weight, bathroom carpets € 6,50, sheets and pillow cases in many colors and at low prices, duvets, blankets and bed spreads by Gabel and Somma or in very pretty, Made in Asia, patchwork.

Samas Italy Outrage

Via Nazionale dello Stelvio - 23030 Chiuro (SO)
9.00-12.30/15.00-19.00. Closed Tuesday

0342 48501
C.C.:All Major

Clothing, sportswear, casual, jeans
FACTORY OUTLET

From Sondrio to Tirano on the busy S.S.38, on the left. If it is difficult to turn, continue and take the next turn off. Parking inside the gates near the outlet.

A rather packed space with rows of performance fleece jackets for W, corduroy ski pants in heavy stretch € 40,00, for M Poachers jackets € 65,00. Ski parkas with fur hood € 90,00 by Icelander, Goretex rain jackets € 85,00. A small room on the left with the Outrage ski/sailing/golf collection or clothing by Jantzen, Ploumanagh and Icelander is recommended. Prices used to be more competitive. Sales in August.

Bernina Manifattura

Via Mazzini, 1 - 23104 Delebio (SO)
8.00-12.00/13.30-17.30. Saturday closed

0342 685206
C.C.: None

Lingerie, underwear
FACTORY OUTLET

S.S. 38 from Colico towards Sondrio, in the center of Delebio, follow signs for Bernina on the right.

Bernina produces underwear in stretchy wool, angora or cashmere, support stockings, elbow straps, shoulder straps, tummy warmers etc. Chemises and slips in mixtures of wool and cotton, vests with short sleeves in angora/wool € 20,00, in anti-allergy knits or all cashmere € 30,00. Also tiny newborn baby wraps in the finest of washable wool. Non-run stockings/collants € 5,50. Friendly atmosphere, very good prices.

Coam Industrie Alimentari

Via Nazionale dello Stelvio, 286 - 23017 Morbegno (SO)
8.00-12.30/14.00-19.00

0342 482103
C.C.: None

Food, local products
FACTORY OUTLET

From Milan S.S. 36 to Lecco/Colico and another 15 km to Morbegno. After Morbegno Coam is on the right, take the secondary road in the industrial zone. The factory has a garden in front with the sign of a mushroom. Ample parking.

The right address for gourmets in search of local food specialities. Dried porcini mushrooms 'Boletus Edulis' in sachets of 200 grams or more, tinned champignon de Paris, jars with dried tomatoes in olive oil, salt-packed capers, olive paté, smoked salmon, sword fish, sturgeon, tuna and trout either in presentation boxes or sold by weight.

Pezzotti Ruffoni

Via Rivolta, 45 - 23017 Morbegno (SO)   0342 610806
9.00-12.00/14.30-18.30 or ring bell   C.C.: None

Furnishings, moquette, carpets
ARTISAN'S WORKSHOP

S.S. 38 dello Stelvio. At the beginning of Morbegno, turn right after the bridge.

A pezzotto is a rag-type carpet, typical of the Valtellina area. Strips of cotton, chenille or velvet are woven on wooden hand looms into colorful carpets or wall-hangings. They work to order. Starting price for the smallest size, a bathroom rug, € 9,00. They speak English.

Emporio Marzotto - Tessuti di Sondrio

Via Tonale, 4 - 23100 Sondrio (SO)   0342 533111/230
9.00-12.30/15.00-19.00   C.C.:All Major

Clothing, fabrics
FACTORY OUTLET

S.S. 38 from Morbegno towards Sondrio. Take the circular road to Bormeo, exit Via Vanoni, turn left to the center and at the roundabout turn right. The outlet is next to the entrance of the factory, immediately on the right.

A mixed offer of fabrics, household linens, men's shirts, sporty jackets and sweaters. Best offers are their men's pants, seconds or showroom collection made by Incotex for some very famous names and sold here at € 25,00 - € 45,00 a pair. Men's shirts € 25,00 - € 40,00 and quite elegant. In the back room rermnants in fabrics, linen or viscose for curtains 150cm wide, all in beautiful quality.

Maglificio Corona

Via Mario Greppi, 109 - 21021 Angera (VA)   0331 960200
8.30-12.00/14.00-18.00. Sat. 9.30-12.00/15.00-18.30   C.C.:All Major

Clothing, lingerie, underwear
FACTORY OUTLET

From Sesto Calende to the center of Angera, after the Piazza Parocchiale continue straight into a narrow street. Or park on the lake front near the church and walk to Via Merzagora on foot. Recommended: a visit to the Museo della Bambola (a museum of dolls) in Rocca Borromeo.

Production of men's underwear, brand name Lisanza. T-shirt in cotton € 7,50, mercerized cotton € 17,50. Polo shirts € 17,50, mercerized cotton € 45,00 all in very good quality. Also knitwear, pyamas, handkerchiefs and some special offers but not much. A corner with wind jackets and sailing parkas by SLAM at a 35% discount is worth investigating. They speak English.

Saporiti Italia

Via Marconi, 23 - 21010 Besnate (VA)   0331 273333
15.00-18.00   C.C.:None

Furniture, various
FACTORY OUTLET

Autostrada A8, exit Besnate, turn right. At the first raffic light turn right and just before the second traffic light turn left.

Special sales of tables, cupboards, chairs and sofas made by Saporiti and used at fairs, films, photo sessions, or end of series and stock. Prices are circa 40% lower than normal, a quick saving. The best time to visit is after an important furniture fair, for example at the beginning of April.

MarcoRossi

Verdi, 5 - 21020 Bodio Lomnago (VA)

14.30-18.00. Sat. 9.30-12.30/14.30-18.30

0332 949788
C.C.:All Major

Handbags, leathergoods, suitcases
FACTORY OUTLET

Autostrada A8, exit Lago di Varese/Buguggiate to Bodio Lommago. In Bodio take the first road for Inarzo after a sign "Ippica". L'Emporio di Rossi is on the left at the back of the complex. Parking.

Very large outlet of handbags, travel bags, briefcases and wallets with labels by Valextra, Magli, Fendi, Jean Paul Gaultier, Escada and Giuia. Prices range from € 25,00 up to € 275,00 for a really snazzy number. Also ostrich handbags with matching stilettos in bright red with their own brand name. Umbrellas € 15,00, silk ties by Escada € 20,00. Small leathergoods, seconds, on offer at € 10,00. Worth the trip.

La Perla - Zanotex

Via per Cadrezzate, 12 Z.I. - 21020 Brebbia (SO)

10.00-12.30/15.00-18.30. Only open on Mon., Fri. and Sat.

0332 982805
C.C.:All Major

Lingerie, underwear
FACTORY OUTLET

Autostrada A8, exit Sesto Calende and the Superstrada to Laveno. At Travedona Monate take the road to Cadrezzate. Continue on the local road, after the Motocross and halfway past the industrial zone, Zanotex is on the left.

Production of underwear and lingerie for La Perla, GrigioPerla (for men), Joelle, Occhiverdi, Malizia. They also produce luxurious summer-evening tops and body suits, bathing costumes, beach wraps and pareos, bikinis and long T-shirts, mostly in smallish sizes, maximum 46/48. For men bathrobes and kimonos in silk or linen, bermudas and slips.

Barbara Shop-Mirtillo

Via Lega Lombarda, 7 - 21052 Busto Arsizio (SO)

9.30-12.30/15.30-19.30. Closed in August

0331 327111
C.C.:All Major

Clothing
FACTORY OUTLET

Autostrada A8, exit Castellanza take the direction for the center of Busto Arsizio. Turn left after the Palazzo delle Esposizioni.

Mirtillo produces amusing sweatshirts for kids from 0 up to 16 years, in all the latest colors, with slogans and little touches, by Mirtillo, Mirtillino, MirtilloNotte. Dresses by I.K.K.S. € 49,00, cute shirts € 29,00. Loyal customer card 10%, discounts, special offers all year round. Sales at 15% off.

Fjordoblu

Via per Cassano Magnago, 120 - 21052 Busto Arsizio (VA)

9.00-12.30/15.00-19.00, Fri & Sat only. Open Sunday in Dec.

0331 681155
C.C.:All Major

Food, fish
FACTORY OUTLET

Autostrada A8, exit Busto Arsizio, after 300 m follow the road to Cassano Magnago on the right. The factory can be seen from the autostrada. Ample parking..

The right place to buy smoked salmon, either whole or in special cuts, from various parts of the world. Whole frozen salmons, cooked or smoked, offers of small chunks for pasta dishes or paté. Sliced, smoked sturgeon, caviar, crab, fish soup in tins, tuna and salmon paté. Savings on average 35%.

Kenté
Corso Sempione, 194 - 21052 Busto Arsizio (VA)
9.30-12.30/15.00-19.30

0331 681766
C.C.:All Major

Knitwear, clothing
FACTORY OUTLET

Autostrada A8, exit Busto Arsizio. Take the local street to Gallarate, Kenté is on the right, ample parking.

A large showroom with their current and last year's collection discounted at circa 50%. This is a place for the young and skinny, looking for the latest colours and trends. At the time of visiting there were a lot of 70's style jeans and striped blouses for sale, also handbags and accessories. In the back are the deep discounts: tops and shirts € 14,50 - € 19,50, mini skirts € 14,50 in sizes up to 46.

Steber P&C
Via Vizzolone di Sotto, 5 - 21052 Busto Arsizio (VA)
9.00-12.30/14.30-19.00. Saturday 9.00-12.30

0331 381981
C.C.:All Major

Lingerie, underwear
FACTORY OUTLET

Autostrada A8, exit Busto Arsizio then Superstrada for Malpensa, second exit to Gallarate. Follow indications for Busto Arsizio Nord, continue straight after the overpass, at the second traffic light after CC Coop look for the sign Steber P&C, turn right. Parking.

Homewear and underwear for the well dressed child, from 0-16 years by Pappa&Ciccia, La Perla, Grigioperla, Malizia. Last year's collection and end-of-series are discounted 30%. T-shirts, bibs, small tops and vests are all very well made and very pretty. All sizes available but no seconds, prices start at € 15,00. Sales in January and July, new collection March and September.

Gruppo Europeo Jersey
Via Volta, 48 - 21010 Cardano al Campo (VA)
9.00-12.30/14.30-18.30. Sat. 9.00-12.30/15.00-19.00
Tues & Thurs only mornings, Mon & Fri only in afternoon

0331 262271
C.C.:All Major

Clothing
FACTORY OUTLET

From the Autostrada A8 take the Superstrada for Malpensa, exit Cardano al Campo, follow the road to the right, under the bridge. After the Fiat car dealer and the stop sign the outlet is straight ahead.

For young and snappy dressers, sizes from 42 to 46, brand name Pietrogrande and Nantucket Island. Clothing in modern fabrics, mixtures of linen, rayon, wool, acrylics, a bit influenced by the 70's. It's all very wearable, large choice. Tight fitting shirts € 58,50, short jackets € 135,00, skirts/trousers € 60,00. Their current collection is discounted 20%. Corner with seconds and end of line at 50%.

Maglificio "AR-VA",
Via Belvedere, 15 - 21020 Casciago (VA)
9.00-12.00/14.30-18.00. Only Mon/Tues/Thursday

0332 826460
C.C.:All Major

Knitwear, cashmere
ARTISAN'S WORKSHOP

From Varese towards Laveno, at the Esselunga rotonda in Masnago turn left and follow indications for Casciago. Continue for approximately 700 m after the church, then follow indications at right hand corner. The factory is in a cul de sac to the left. Private parking.

For cashmere and woollen cardigans and polos in excellent quality and classical styles, all sizes available. A cardigan in 'cool wool' € 80,00, short sleeve tops in cashmere € 75,00, jacket in cashmere, tweed design € 130,00. Prices are very reasonable and the colors are stupendous. Sales and showroom samples.

Lindt & Sprungli

Via Tintoretto, 15 - 21012 Cassano Magnago (VA)
9.30-13.00/14.30-19.00. Sat. 9.30-19.00.
Open on Sundays. Closed from 1/7 - 1/9

0331 285442
C.C.:All Major

Food, chocolate, coffee
FACTORY OUTLET

Autostrada A8, exit Gallarate. The factory is well signposted, you can actually see their building from the autostrada. Parking, cafeteria, services for the disabled.

For serious chocaholics. A very spacious and clean sales point with special offers all the time, written on a blackboard at the entrance. The complete range of Lindt chocolates is for sale at 30% less, either by weight or in presentation boxes.

Spacci Bassetti

Via Provinciale, 5 - 21030 Cuveglio (VA)
9.30-13.00/14.00-18.30. Monday 14.30-18.30

0332 624154
C.C.:None

Household linen, various
FACTORY OUTLET

Autostrada A8, exit Buguggiate, follow indications for Laveno. After Gemonio take the provincial road to Valcuvia on the right for 4 km. The outlet is on the left, a large factory complex with parking.

Spacious outlet selling the Bassetti collection of household linens: the famous Gran Foulard either quilted or as cotton throws, cheerful bed sheets with giant oranges or lemons, bathrobes and towels. Terrytowel material is sold per kilo, 2nd's in Gran Foulard, quilted, € 25,00. Blankets and duvets are discounted 30-40%.

Spaccio Valcuvia

Via Battaglia S. Martino, 110 - 21030 Cuveglio (VA)
9.30-12.30/15.00-19.00

0332 624540
C.C.:All Major

Lingerie, underwear
FACTORY OUTLET

Next to the Cuveglio Centro Commerciale shopping center. From Varese just before the town on the right.

A very useful outlet to stock up on briefs, bras and camisoles. All sizes available from XS to XXL at € 0,80 to € 10,75. Bras in cotton € 9,50, also large sizes, only in white. Their boxes with fluffy thongs, lamé tangas, glittery briefs and strings, seconds, are great fun and good value, brand name Debenham, Bloomingdale (those famous Bloomies), H&M, For children great choice. They also sell 'Pierre Cardin Pour Homme' and bathing suits and fabric remnants. Worthwhile.

Polinelli

Via Roma, 57 - 21020 Daverio (VA)
10.00-13.00/16.00-19.00. Sabato 10.00-13.00

0332 942011
C.C.:All Major

Optician
FACTORY OUTLET

Autostrada A8, exit Lago di Varese, continue towards Azzate, Daverio. Follow the signs for Polinelli. The outlet is next to the church, parking inside the gate.

Sun glasses, prescription glasses, goggles, brand name Riccardo Polinelli. Reading glasses start at € 35,00, metal frames. Great choice in sunglasses for kids. They produce eyeglasses for Guy Laroche, Blast, Park Avenue, Kaleido and Catherine Spaak.

Bellora Giuseppe

Via C. Cantù, - 21054 Fagnano Olona (VA)
8.30-12.30/15.00-19.00. Closed Monday

0331 619641
C.C.:All Major

Household linen, various
FACTORY OUTLET

Autostrada A8, exit Busto Arsizio towards Solbiate and Fagnano Olona. Follow the signs.

An elegant outlet for household linens. Good taste, good quality and good prices: embroidered linens € 32,50 per kilo, cotton € 20,00 per kilo. The width of most material is 2.70 meters. They produce a 'Classic' line, linen towels with handmade fringes, tableclothes in damask, or a 'country' line, printed with floral designs, or in honeycomb cotton. They also produce the Ferré line 'I Corredi', the pinnacle of quality. Savings from 25% up to 70% for seconds and end of line.

Il Guardaroba (Parah)

Via P. da Gallarate, 7 - 21013 Gallarate (VA)
9.00-12.30/15.00-19.30

0331 785219
C.C.:All Major

Lingerie, underwear
FACTORY OUTLET

Autostrada A8, exit Gallarate/Samarate. At the roundabout turn right, continue 100m, at the intersection turn to the left. Continue straight until Via da Gallarate which is on the left. The outlet is next to the SuperDi supermarket. Parking.

A fairly small collection of bra/panty sets by Parah, sizes up to 4, bras € 25,00-€ 37,50, panties € 7,50, all very pretty, nicely hanging on wall racks. Bathing costumes W   (lots of XXL), they also sell some general homewear and fabric/ribbon remnants.   Special offers of lingerie by Off-Limits in 100% cotton, sweats and T's, customer cards.

Tonali Marina Bravin

Via C. Battisti, 3 - 21045 Gazzada (VA)
10.00-12.30/14.00-18.30

0332 464233
C.C.:None

Clothing
FACTORY OUTLET

Autostrada A8, exit Castronno towards Gazzada. On the main road on the right, well indicated.

Spacious, well-ordered 2nd floor outlet selling the showroom collection (mostly size 42) and last year's unsold (also size 46/48). Vey good looking two piece suits in silk or linen € 200,00. Special offers of jackets and dresses € 50,00, pants and mini skirts € 25,00, fantasy T-shirts € 25,00. Their collection is well made, fit for any kind of social event, but definitely designed for slim ladies.

Felli

Via Clivio, 2 - 21036 Gemonio (VA)
8.00-12.00/14.00-17.30

0332 601062
C.C.:All Major

Accessories, various
FACTORY OUTLET

From Varese take the S.S. 394 towards Laveno. In Gemonio at the traffic light to the left for Besozzo. Felli is on the right.

Felli specializes in clothing for priests, various articles for catholic churches, memorial plaques or plates. In November they sell a respectable range of Christmas articles, in particular nativity scenes (presepio) made in various parts of the world.

T&J Vestor
Via Roma, 71/b - 21010 Golasecca (VA)
9.00-12.30/14.30-19.00

0331 950331
C.C.:All Major

Household linen, various
FACTORY OUTLET

Autostrada A8, exit Sesto Calende/Vergiate, towards the center of Golasecca.

A large choice in towels, tableclothes and bed linen, but they are especially known for the Missoni carpets, for sale in various dimensions and patterns and the Missoni terrytowel robes (€ 45,00 circa). Great choice in men's pyamas at € 19,00 - € 25,00, also baskets with seconds, special offers. Their address in Milan: V.le Elvezia 22.

Botteguccia Richard Ginori
Via Diaz, 10 - 21014 Laveno Mombello (VA)
9.30-12.30/15.00-18.30. Closed Monday

0332 666309
C.C.:All Major

Ceramics, terracotta, porcelain
FACTORY OUTLET

From Laveno take the road for Mombello and the Zona Ceramica.

Smaller than the Richard-Ginori outlet in Sesto Fiorentino (Florence) but still worth a visit: a table centerpiece with 8 serving dishes, € 60,00, statuettes of violin and cello players in white china € 40,00, special offers of discontinued dinner sets for 12, in various, mostly classical, designs. Coffee and tea sets, ashtrays, mugs and cheese plates, ideal for gifts.

Simonetta Confezioni
Viale Kennedy, 986 - 21050 Marnate (VA)
9.00-12.00/14.30-19.00. Saturday 9.00-12.00

0331 389081
C.C.: None

Clothing, sportswear, casual, jeans
FACTORY OUTLET

Autostrada A8, exit Castellanza towards Marnate and the Zona Industriale, Campo Sportivo. Follow the signs, the outlet is at the end of Viale Kennedy next to Giesse.

An ideal place to stock up on everyday practical but fun sweatshirts, pants, jackets in fleece, mostly made for the German market with brand names like Olsen, High Society, Basic Nouveau, at very low prices. Spending more than € 30,00 for any item, be it a heavy outdoor sweatshirt or an anorak in pile, will be difficult. All their knitwear is 50% wool, 50% acrylic, jeans by Ferrucci € 15,00 to € 25,00.

Maglificio Enfi
Via Stazione, fraz. Crugnola - 21020 Mornago (VA)
15.00-19.00. Sat 9.00-12.00/15.00-19.00

0331 904400
C.C.:All Major

Knitwear
FACTORY OUTLET

Autostrada A8, exit Sesto Calende, take the provincial road Vergiate-Varese. Enfi is before the railway overpass and in front of the Somma factory.

A well ordered outlet, airconditioned in summer. Knitwear in good quality, often destined for northern european markets (Holland, Germany). Remainders in 50/50 wool acrylic € 12,50, polo in wool € 9,50, cute sweatshirts by Karin Kling. For men knitwear by Hey, Homewear V&D. All sizes available. There is another outlet is Sesto Calende, Via Sempione, 96.

Gabel Somma

Via Stazione, 125 - 21020Mornago - fraz. Crugnola (VA)　　0331 900384
9.00-12.30/15.00-19.00. Sat. 9.00-19.00　　　　　　　　　C.C.:All Major

Household linen, various
FACTORY OUTLET

Autostrada A8, exit Sesto Calende, take the provincial road Vergiate-Varese. Near the railway overpass and Maglificio Enfi.

A large factory hall selling quilted bedspreads, covers, duvets by Borbonese, Trussardi or Gabel in lush designs and beautiful quality. Beach towels € 13,00. Remnants in cotton fabric, lovely quality 2.80 m wide € 9,00, woollen blankets € 9,00 per kilo and terry towel p.m.€ 5,00, 2.00 meters wide. Satin ribbons € 0,50 per m.

Garda Intimo

Via della Prava, 61 - 21017 Samarate (VA)　　　　　　　0331 721173
10.00-12.30/15.00-19.00. Sat. 10.00-17.00　　　　　　　C.C.:All Major

Lingerie, underwear
FACTORY OUTLET

From Busto Arsizio take the superstrada towards Malpensa, exit Samarate and continue towards Novara. After Samarate at the traffic light before the Esso gas station turn right and follow the signs for Garda.

Small outlet with very good quality, family style underwear in sizes from XS to XXL. Camisoles in linen/viscose at € 6,50 that will come out of the washing machine looking as new. They produce Charro underwear, Garda Intimo, Unicà, Green Generation, Ginni and Ginni Uomo. T-shirts € 4,00, remainders start at € 4,00.

Inside

Via Aspesi, 37 - 21010 Samarate S. Macario (VA)　　　　0331 234377
14.30-18.30. Sat. 9.00-12.30　　　　　　　　　　　　　C.C.:All Major

Household linen, various
FACTORY OUTLET

Autostrada A8, superstrada to Malpensa airport, exit Samarate/Gallarate, after the roundabout straight, at the traffic light take the second of the three streets towards the center of S. Macario. Straight and after the roundabout first to the right.

Production of sheets and quilts for Trussardi and Farnese, lots of special offers! The current collection is discounted 35%, seconds are 50% off. There is a table covered with remnants, bits of blanket, quilts at € 7,50 per kilo. Decorating pillows in velvet € 10,00, robes € 24,50 - € 64,50. It is all in good taste and very well made.

Sylvie Italy

Via Gandhi, 9 - 21010 Samarate San Macario (VA)　　　0331 235670
16.00-19.00. Saturday 9.00-12.00　　　　　　　　　　　C.C.:All Major

Clothing, sportswear, casual
FACTORY OUTLET

Autostrada A8, exit Busto Arsizio, superstrada towards Malpensa, exit Samarate. Take the provincial road to Oleggio. After Samarate and before the Esso service station turn left at the traffic light, then follow signs for Sylvie Italy.

Sylvie Italy produces sportswear for Eddy Bauer USA, Arrow, Pro-Man, de Wall, Alain Manoukian, Cerruti mostly for men. Sweatshirts, polos for hiking, golf, sailing, Casual sweats in soft colours € 27,00 sizes up to 58 in an interesting mix of cotton/viscosa/polyamide/angora/cashmere, long sleeved polo, striped collar € 18,00. For women there is little of interest.

La Rotonda Factory Store

Viale L. Lazzaroni, 25 - 21047 Saronno (VA)
10.00-19.30. Open on Sun. Mond. 13.30 -19.30

02 96280082
C.C.:All Major

Clothing, household linen
FACTORY OUTLET

Autostrada A9, exit Saronno, turn right and then again immediately right for the Rotonda di Saronno. Parking.

A first floor outlet with lots of cute things for children. Also clothing, underwear and handbags by Bonfanti Borse, Marina Yachting, Henry Cotton's, Levi's, Ralph Lauren Polo, Diesel. Competitive prices, circa 30% less then shop price. Levi's jeans € 40,00, Polo R. Lauren € 42,00. There is a corner with household linen by Coin Casa, a wellknown department store, at great discounts.

Lazzaroni

Via Novara, 55 - 21047 Saronno (VA)
9.00-19.00

02 967661
C.C.:All Major

Food, biscuits, desserts
FACTORY OUTLET

Autostrada A9, exit Saronno. Turn right into the parking area for the Rotonda di Saronno. The outlet is near the parking exit on the right.

A nicely air conditioned outlet for the famous 'amaretti di Saronno'. Packs of I kilo € 5,50. Smaller quantities can be bought in presentation boxes and cost relatively more. Special offers of plumcakes, 3 bags of chocolate pastry € 7,50, various types of pasta, and of course amaretto liqueur.

Lisanza

Via Angera, 60 - 21018 Sesto Calende - Lisanza (VA)
9.00-12.00/15.00-18.30

0331 989355/989111
C.C.:All Major

Lingerie, underwear
FACTORY OUTLET

Autostrada A8/A26, exit Sesto Calende, take the S.S.629 towards Angera. After Lisanza the factory is on the right.

A favorite of all the foreign (German) tourists in the area. Elegant nightdresses € 37,50, in woollen jersey or cotton, bodysuits in silk or in linen jersey € 12,50, sets of bra and panties in silk € 25,00, men's dressing gown in terry velours/cotton € 37,50. Occasionally there are special offers like the two piece suits in summer wool for M/W at € 138,00.

El Charro Griffe Center

Via XXV Aprile, 15b - 21048 Solbiate Arno (VA)
9.00-12.30/15.00-19.30. Sat. 9.30-12.30/14.30-19.30

0331 991922
C.C.:All Major

Clothing, sportswear, casual, jeans
FACTORY OUTLET

Autostrada A8, exit Solbiate. In the center of town behind the church where parking is available.

The El Charro outlet is in a vast warehouse. Cowboy looks for everybody, jeans € 35 circa, cotton polos € 24, T-shirts by Ferrucci € 6, bombers in leather € 260. Nice series of T-shirts by Schott. Accessories, bandanas, bibs, denim work jackets, coveralls and tanks. All sizes.

Forest Tower

Via Milano, 140 (S.S. Sempione) - 21019 Somma Lombardo (VA)
9.00-12.15/15.00-19.30

0331 256521
C.C.:All Major

Household linen, various
FACTORY OUTLET

Autostrada A8/A9, exit Gallarate. Take the S.S. Sempione towards Somma Lombardo. Just before Somma, on the left of the Gigante supermarket, look for the Old Vic building.

Many small gift items like quilted knitting bags, potholders. Lovely patchwork bedcovers 270x270, € 100,00, garden cushions € 6,00 and Borbonese and Trussardi bed linens at a discount. A corner with remnants sold per kilo is worth a look. Busy and popular with the local housewives.

Anna Lisa

Via Pacinotti, 25 - 21100 Varese (VA)
9.30-12.30/15.30-19.30

0332 240064
C.C.:All Major

Clothing
FACTORY OUTLET

Autostrada A8, exit Varese. Go past the two stations in the direction of Viale Valganna towards Induno Olona. The second road on the right after Viale Ippodromo. Parking.

Vast choice of suits, coats and elegant skirts full of little details that make them stand out by brandname Anna Lisa and Altre Cose. Suits start at € 105,00, skirts € 45,00. The jeans are gold embroidered, to be worn with colourful, splashy tank tops. Offers of remnants and showroom samples, a lot of size 42, but some 46/48 can be found. Their sales are not to be missed.

Calzaturificio Carabelli

Via Pisacane, 9 - 21100 Varese (VA)
8.30-12.00/13.30-17.30. Sat 8.30-12.00

0332 286758
C.C.:All Major

Shoes
FACTORY OUTLET

Autostrada A8, exit Varese, in front of the hospital take Via Gasparotto which is a paralel street to Viale Borri. Via Pisacane is a cross street and the Carabelli factory is well indicated.

Shoes in very good quality in the softest of leather in a classical style and especially designed for older feet at discounts from 30% to 50% compared to shop price. Men's sandals € 25,00, lace ups in soft deer skin € 50,00, sandals and clogs for W € 55,00, shoes with inlays € 45,00 - € 65,00. The latest Oxfords € 99,80. Men's sizes go up to 46, for women up to 42.

Calze Malerba

Via Gasparotto, 77 - 21100 Varese (VA)
10.00-13.00/14.00-19.00

0332 259233
C.C.:All Major

Hosiery
FACTORY OUTLET

Autostrada A8, exit Varese in the direction of Laveno/Gavirate. After the stop sign turn right, after 200m and two traffic lights the factory is in front near a busy intersection, a new complex with ample parking.

A very large outlet with lots of choice. Men's socks in cotton or wool, very cute baby socks, net stockings, support stockings, kneesocks in packs of 2. Friendly sales help and a corner with special offers at rock bottom prices. They also sell Ragno underwear and some jeans but mostly their own production of socks for any kind of sport in any kind of weight.

Valigeria Principe

Via Duca degli Abruzzi, 166
21100 Varese - fraz. Calcinate d.Pesce
8.30-12.15/14.15-18.15. Open on Sundays. Open in August

0332 327611
C.C.: None

Handbags, leathergoods, suitcases
FACTORY OUTLET

Autostrada A8, last exit for Lago di Varese, then towards Gavirate along the lake. The showroom faces the lake but to park, turn right (towards Calcinate) and then left into the parking area.

Large outlet with very well-made classical and fashionable handbags by Principe, Cerruti 1881 at 30 to 40 % discount - (medium price €78 circa). Samples at 40%, very trendy XXL clutch bags. Also belts, small leather goods, umbrellas. The Astrolabius series of travel bags and attache cases are interesting and discounted 30%.

Maglificio Isabel

Via Peschiera, 5 - 21029 Vergiate (VA)
9.30-12.30/14.30-19.00. Sat. closed

0331 947243
C.C.: None

Knitwear, cashmere
FACTORY OUTLET

Autostrada A8, exit Vergiate, follow the directions for 'Scuola Elementare'. From Varese go to the center of Vergiate, in front of the church on the right, across the village. Isabel is opposite the Scuola Elementare.

High quality knitwear in merinos, cashmere, lambswool in winter and in 100% cotton, linen or silk in summer. Casual or classical/understated styles, very wearable, in a wide range of colors and sizes, up to 48/50 for W. Special sales and samples all year round. Sales in January and July. They speak French, Enlish and German.

Samsonite Italia

Via Clivio - 21050 Viggiù (VA)
9.00-12.30/15.30-19.30. Closed Monday

0332 275811
C.C.:All Major

Handbags, leathergoods, suitcases
FACTORY OUTLET

Coming from Varese, follow the road towards Viggiù and then towards Baraggio. At the rotonda take the second right.

On sale are mostly travelbags and suitcases made out of sturdy material, but also hard shell Oyster suitcases, Samsonite shoes, all seconds at 35% less than shop price. Defects are of the 'hardly noticeable' kind. Definitely worthwhile for the frequent traveler and fans of the Samsonite brandname.

Spaccio Zucchi

V.le Varese, 113 - 21059 Viggiù (VA)
9.00-12.30/14.00-18.30. Monday 14.30-18.30

0331 948688
C.C.:None

Household linen, various
FACTORY OUTLET

Autostrada A8, exit Gazzada and continue for Gaggiolo. At the traffic light before the frontier, turn left towards Viggiù, continue for approximately 300m. The outlet is just before Viggiù.

The Zucchi collection of household linens, cotton blankets, bedspreads, baskets with guest towels, pan holders, giftboxes with aprons, some racks with sweatshirts by Jantzen, plenty of choice and low prices, discounts of 30-40% for remainders, end-of-series Grand Foulard and blankets.

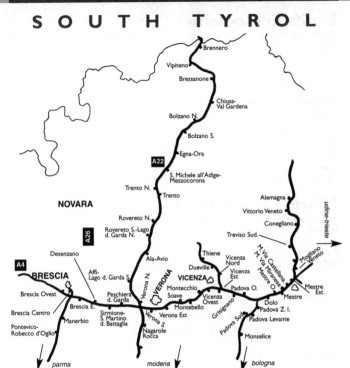

Merlet Loden Outlet

Via Museo, 54 - 39100 Bolzano (BZ)
9.00-12.30/15.00-19.00. Saturday 10.00-12.00

0471 323512
C.C.:All Major

Clothing
FACTORY OUTLET

In the center of Bolzano, in front of the 'Otzi' Museum.

This is a worthwhile address for those in search of loden coats and jackets at a discount. Their showroom collection is sold at a 50% discount, they sell second choice items in loden and boiled wool, and their collection of loden coats goes from the classic Tirolean style to fancy creations with fur collars, ribbons and leather trimmings.

Thun Store Thuniversum

Via Galvani 29, Z.I. Sud - 39100 Bolzano (BZ)
9.00-18.00. Sunday open in December

0471 245255
C.C.:All Major/Tax Free

Ceramics, terracotta, porcelain
FACTORY OUTLET

Autostrada A22, exit Bolzano Sud, follow the indications for the Fiera di Bolzano, towards the southern industrial zone. Thun is opposite the Fair.

The new Thun store offers spacious surroundings and an elegant bistrot where one can observe all the first choice Thun products. Their outlet of 500m2 is dedicated to ceramics or china objects, either 2nd choice or end of line, minimum discounts of 35% on clocks, angel candlesticks, coffee or tea cups, or vases and decorative wall plates. Special offers at 50%. In February there is a 'ceramics party' with discounts of 45%-60%. To make group arrangements phone 0471-245272. Worth a visit.

Lanificio Moessmer

Via Walther von der Vogelweide, 6 - 39031 Brunico (BZ)   0474 411267
7.00-12.30   C.C.:All Major

Clothing, fabrics
FACTORY OUTLET

Autostrada A22 towards the Brennero, exit Bressanone, S.S. 49. In the center of Brunico, after the bridge on the right. Well indicated.

Spacious shop with loden coats, loden fabric, blazers, hats, scarves all in a distinct Tyrolean style. Classic loden coat circa € 300,00, fancy coats with pleats, ribbons and leather trimmings can go as high as € 900,00. Racks with special offers in coats € 175,00, Tiroler hats € 70,00, loden fabric, boiled wool € 37,50 p. m. Corner with remnants. Very busy with mostly German and Austrian tourists.

Ulbrich Tessitura

Passeggiata Tielt, 17a - 39031 Brunico (BZ)   0474 555900
8.30-12.00/14.30-19.00   C.C.:All Major

Household linen, various
FACTORY OUTLET

Autostrada A22, exit Bressanone then S.S. 49 towards Brunico. Following the indications for Moessmer, Ulbrich is just before the bridge. Parking.

A well known producer of table and bed linen. Old local designs and motifs are woven into table clothes, towels, cushion covers, bed spreads and curtains, all in very high quality linen, cotton or wool. Their end of series and seconds are only for sale here in their outlet, all year round, at a discount of 40 to 50%.

Ankershoffen

Via Brunico, 19 - 39030 Brunico - S.Lorenzo di Sebato (BZ) 0474 474599
9.00-12.00/14.30-18.30. Sat 9.00-12.00   C.C.:All Major

Furs
FACTORY OUTLET

Autostrada A22 towards the Brennero, exit Bressanone towards Brunico Ovest. Ankershoffen is in the Industrial Zone just befor Brunico on the left.

There are Ankershoffen shops in Munich and Paris but here at their factory, prices are lower. Their speciality: mink coats, reversibile coats in persian lamb and shearling coats with sable collars. One whole floor is dedicated to minks in a bewildering choice of styles.

Spadafora

Via Lahn, 3 Ora - 39040 (BZ)   0471 815301
8.45-12.00/12.30-18.00. Sat 9.00-12.00   C.C.:None

Knitwear, cashmere
FACTORY OUTLET

Autostrada A22, exit Ora turn left towards Bolzano on the S.S. 12. Turn right for the Industrial Zone of Ora, then left. The outlet is in front of the factory, large, well laid out.

A very avantgarde knitwear collection by Marina Spadafora in all sizes. Micro/maxi skirts or suits/dresses/shawls in mixtures of wool and silk or cashmere, polyester and wool, all very striking and in unusual colours, browns wih grey, black with ghreyish flecks, some dark blue and winterbeiges or orange with bordeaux. Jackets € 220,00 microskirts € 75,00. Interesting designs that are easy to wear.

Timberland Factory Outlet
C.C. City Center, Statale del Brennero
39049 Vipiteno (BZ)   0472 767670
9.00-12.00/14.30-18.45. Sat. 9.00-13.00/14.30-18.30   C.C.:All Major

Clothing, shoes
FACTORY OUTLET

Autostrada A22, exit Vipiteno/Sterzing, turn right to the main road. After the traffic light to the left for the Centro Commerciale.

An American style outlet with a profusion of jeans, sweatshirts, shoes and all kinds of jungle gear. Samples and seconds galore, special offers in canvas travel bags € 94.50, bermudas and jeans start at € 29,50. Lots of Timberland boat shoes € 72,50 and boots.

Calzedonia
Via del Lavoro, 30 - 38063 Avio (TN)   0464 688323
9.00-19.00   C.C.:All Major

Hosiery, lingerie
FACTORY OUTLET

Autostrada A22, exit Ala/Avio. After the center of Avio in the industrial zone on the right. The outlet is in Via Carri and well indicated.

All the unsold and end of series socks, stockings, lingerie of the Calzedonia /Intimissimi franchises all over Italy end up here. For children there are cute rubber soled socks and bathing shorts, for M/W underwear, lingerie and fun socks and hosiery. This is not a large store but well stocked with a lot of special offers.

Pelletterie Anna Valli
Via del Lavoro, 26 - 38063 Avio (TN)   0464 684367
9.00-12.00/15.00-19.00. Sat. 9.00-13.00/15.00-19.00. Open on Sunday   C.C.:All Major

Handbags, leather goods
FACTORY OUTLET

Autostrada A22, exit Ala/Avio. After the center of Avio on the right in the industrial zone and near Calzedonia.

Production of handbags, professional bags, diaries, travel bags for famous national and international brand names. It's worth the trip to buy holdalls, small leather goods, attache cases, back packs and purses by Cacharel, Samsonite, Hugo Boss and other well known designers. They give additional discounts for quantity buying and speak English, French and German.

DalSasso
Piazza Dante - 38050 Bordo (TN)   0461 782041
8.30-12.00/15.30-19.00   C.C.:All Major

Clothing, fabrics
FACTORY OUTLET

From Trento on the S.S. 47 towards Feltre. A shop front between Bar Roma and Bar Cusso.

Production of loden coats and jackets in boiled wool and loden fabric by the meter. DalSasso W. coats with great fur collar € 300,00, boiled wool jackets € 115,00, men's loden coats € 135,00, loden coats by Merlet € 285,00, all very classical and lasting. There is a special corner with coupons in wool and silk, knitting wool, and 2nds in coats.

Calze Malerba

Loc. Broletti - 38050 Castelnuovo (TN)
9.00-12.30/15.00-19.00. Closed Mon.

0461 752635
C.C.:All Major

Hosiery
FACTORY OUTLET

On the S.S. 47 from Trento to Feltre, on the left. Large factory. Parking and their outlet are on the right of the entrance.

Large shop with more or less the same collection as in their Varese outlet, socks galore, special offers, collant, jeans and some Ragno underwear. Net stockings and thights € 3,70. Offers of men's woolen dress socks.

Blu Center

Via G. Catoni, 147 - 38060 Mattarello (TN)
9.00-12.00/15.00-19.00. Sat. 9.00-12.00/14.00-19.00

0461 943224
C.C.:All Major

Clothing
FACTORY OUTLET

From Trento to Verona on the S.S. 12, on the left after Mattarello. Parking.

A very stylish men's department on the ground floor with clothes by a famous 'Made in Italy' brand name. Coats cashmere/wool € 300,00 and up. Jackets in cashmere, € 270,00 circa, sturdy cardigans, shirts and ties. On the 1st floor fairly classical, very good quality W. jackets € 275,00, pants, skirts, blouses, dresses € 175,00 and up, brand name Lory Valente. Small offer of seconds in suits & jackets with flaws indicated and sometimes hardly noticeable.

Trapuntificio C.A.T.

Località le Basse - 38060 Mattarello (TN)
8.30-12.30/15.00-19.00

0461 945386
C.C.:All Major

Household linen, various
ARTISAN'S WORKSHOP

Autostrada A22, exit Trento Centro or Rovereto, then take S.S. 12. The Le Basse area is after Mattarello on the left just after the Blu Center outlet.

This area is well known for the production of eiderdowns. One can order special sizes, patterns or eiderdown mixtures. A 155x220 size in 100% eiderdown super € 210,00, in 'Magic' 80/20 € 175,00, in a square stitch € 150,00. Also merinos wool blankets, quilts and curtains made to measure.

Trapuntificio Patiflex

Via della Stazione, 7 - 38060 Mattarello (TN)
9.00-12.00/15.00-19.00

0461 945333 /809
C.C.:All Major

Household linen, various
ARTISAN'S WORKSHOP

From Trento on the S.S. 12 to Verona. To the right at the flashing traffic light in the center of Mattarello

They sell anything to do with beds and bedding: eiderdowns, quilts, woollen blankets, latex matresses, pillows. An eiderdown stitched in a square pattern, 155x200, superior quality € 225,00, acceptable quality € 72,50. A double quilt will start at € 125,00 to € 340,00 and up.

Bailo

Loc. Coldané - 38050 Pieve Tesino (TN)
9.00-12.00/15.00-19.00. Closed Mon.

0461 591241
C.C.:All Major

Clothing, sportswear, casual, jeans
FACTORY OUTLET

From Trento S.S. 47. After Borgo Valsugana at the intersection go left towards Pieve Tesino and continue for approximately 12 km. At the beginning of Pieve to the right for Cinte Tessino. The outlet is behind the main factory.

Sportswear of high quality, ski and casual clothing, specialised high-tech mountain jackets, performance wear. Large choice of seconds, end of series and prototypes. All in cheerful, bright colours and extremely practical, washable materials. Weekly special offers tied in to the tourist season in the area. They speak English, French, German. Sales in December/January and August/September.

Metex

Lagarine, 5 - 38050 Scurelle (TN)
8.30-11.30/14.00-18.30. Sat 8.300-11.00

0461 762331
C.C.:None

Fabrics
DISCOUNTS

From Trento S.S. 47 towards Castelnuovo. Afetr Castelnuovo turn left for Strigno. The factory is in an industrial zone on the left.

Metex cuts fabric in patterns for some major Italian designers. Their remnants are sold per meter or per skirt or jacket length. Tremendous choice of wool and wool/ cotton in city colours like taupe, grey, neutral beige, bordeaux at € 13,00 per meter. A skirt length € 7,50. Brightly patterned silks € 18,00 per meter. These are very high quality fabrics in innovative designs.

Dolomiten Sportswear

Via Piera, 2/A - 38038 Tesero (TN)
8.00-12.00/15.00-19.00

0462 813106
C.C.:All Major

Clothing
FACTORY OUTLET

Autostrada A22, exit Ora/Egna and then S.S. 48 for Cavalese. After Cavalese and half way to Tesero, the Dolomiten factory is on the right.

Dolomiten has a chain of shops all over the Alto Adige region, but this is their center of production. The complete Dolomiten collection is for sale here: loden coats lined with fur, jackets in boiled wool, quilted woollen vests, flannel shirts and knitted sweaters. There is a corner with irregular sizes and end of series. They work with 'Tiroler Loden' fabric from Innsbruck in Austria.

Cavit

Via del Ponte di Ravina, 31 - 38040 Trento (TN)
9.00-12.30/14.00-18.30. Closed Sat.

0461 381711
C.C.:All Major

Wine, liqueurs
FACTORY OUTLET

Autostrada A22, exit Trento Centro, take the tangenziale towards Verona (S.S.12). Exit Ravina I. Z., under the autostrada bridge, turn left, and continue past the Ferrari factory. After the servicestation the Cavit enoteca is reached by a narrow road past their offices, on the left.

It's possible to taste wine with a group of people, but we suggest to phone beforehand. They produce a great deal of different wines, Grigio di Cavit, Prime Rose, Cabernet Sauvignon, Fiori d'Inverno, Casteller, Val d'Adige, plus grappas and olive oils all at 20% discount. Their Cavit Brut, methode champenois costs € 6,45, a sparkling wine € 4,00. They ship and speak English and German.

Ferrari, F.lli Lunelli

Via Suffragio, 77 - Trento 38100 (TN)
9.00-12.00/15.30-19.30. Open in Aug.

0461 981566
C.C.:All Major

Wine, liqueurs
GOOD PRICES

From Autostrada del Brennero exit Trento centro, take the tangenziale to Verona. At Ravina Z.I turn right under the autostrada bridge, then left. You can see the factory from the autostrada. Near the Cavit winery.

The main office building is a glass pyramid with a beautiful entrance hall showing the classical Ferrari Brut bottle, first produced in 1902. Prices are circa 10% less on a minimum purchase of 36 bottles Ferrari Brut methode champenois. The Lunelli group also produces the Villa Margon white wine, grappa Segnana and the Surgiva mineral water.

V E N E T O

G 5 di Lozza G. & C.
Via Stadio, 4 -32041 Auronzo di Cadore (BL)
9.00-12.00/15.30-19.00. Sat. 8.00-12.00

0435 40037
C.C.:None

Optician
FACTORY OUTLET

From Cortina, in summer, take the S. P. 48 over the Tre Croci pass with it's splendid panorama. Lozza is at the beginning of the village, after the stadium, a narrow road on the right. From Belluno take S.S. 51b and at the level of the Esso service station, before the stadium, turn left.

Their own production of eye and sun glasses. Their frames for reading glasses cost € 26, whatever model you choose, in metal or in plastic. They also sell glasses by Sting, Gucci, Burberry, Ferré and others. Last year's collection is discounted 50%, recent collection 30%.

Morotto
Loc. Fiames, 5 - 32043 Cortina d'Ampezzo (BL)
8.30-12.00/15.00-19.00

0436 884419
C.C.:All Major

Clothing, sports accessories
DISCOUNTS

From Cortina take the direction for Fiames, approximately 2 km, on the right.

Morotto produces cross country skis, for sale in the shop next to the factory with a discount of circa 10%. They also sell sportswear by Patagonia, Invicta and Dolmar, discounted between 20 - 50%, which makes it possible to find bermudas by Patagonia at € 21 and Invicta T-shirts at € 11.

Manifattura Valcismon - Sportstore

Via G. Marconi, 81/83 - 32030 Fonzaso (BL)
8.30-12.30/15.30-19.30

0439 571217
C.C.:All Major

Clothing, sportswear, casual
FACTORY OUTLET

From Feltre to Trento on the S.S. 50, take the direction to Artèn on the right. Large factory with parking inside the gate.

Great choice in brandname 'Sportful' gear for mountainbike, cycle, rollerblade and ski enthusiasts at a 30% discount. Also tenniswear by Sergio Tacchini, sport bras in Drytex fabric, hiking boots, (2 pairs of bad weather shoes by Versan at € 55,00 were a good deal). Large baskets with remnants. Friendly & very busy.

Outlet Diadora Tempo di Sport

Zona Industriale Fonzaso - 32030 Fonzaso (BL)
9.00-12.30/15.30-19.30

0439 56553
C.C.:All Major

Clothing, sportswear, casual, jeans
FACTORY OUTLET

On the S.S. 50 from Trento, just before Feltre on the left.

Large outlet, busy, great choice in sport shoes for tennis, jogging, mountain climbing and football. Diadora fleece jackets € 35,00, Diadora socks, colored tennis shoes € 12,50, also jeans, shirts and T-shirts. Special corner with 2nds and remainders at half price plus 25% off on last season's merchandise. All very sporty and practical stuff but worth a look especially for their shoes.

Maglificio A.M.D.

Località Cesa - 32020 Limana (BL)
Phone first.

0437 967582
C.C.:All Major

Knitwear, cashmere
FACTORY OUTLET

Take the state road from Belluno towards Trichiana. First floor outlet, ample parking.

They work for some well known 'Made in Italy' names. Tops by 'Le Bambole' in viscosa or silk/linen mixtures € 55,00. Brightly colored, rustic sweaters in pure Merinos wool, Missoni style, circa € 95,00, shortsleeved tanks in 60/40 cashmere/silk € 40,00 a good deal but few sizes and colors left. Corner with special offers € 15,00, mostly sweaters in mixtures of acrylic/wool.

Borca Occhiali

Via Roma, 76 - 32040 Lozzo di Cadore (BL)
8.00-12.00/13.30-18.15. Sat. 8.00-12.30/14.00-18.30

0435 76323
C.C.:None

Optician
GOOD PRICES

Autostrada A27, exit Cadore/Cortina to Auronza/Sappada. After Domegge di Cadore go to the center of Lozzo di Cadore. Borca is on the main square between Caffe Milano and the Banca Veneta, on the first floor.

For more than 40 years Borca produces eye glasses. Frames start at € 12,50 for reading or sun glasses. They sell a fair selection of designer frames by Byblos, Armani, Persol, Vogue, Genny, Valentino, Web, Bulgari and YSLaurent at discounts. Eye checks and glasses ready in one day.

Cesco 2000

Via Rin Inf. 9/11 Mare - 32040 S. Pietro di Cadore (BL)
8.30-12.30/15.00-19.00. Closed Tuesday

0435 460012
C.C.:All Major

Optician
FACTORY OUTLET

Autostrada A22, exit Belluno, continue towards Pieve di Cadore. Pass through all the villages until Stefano. The outlet is approximately 10 km further on in the hamlet of S. Pietro Mare.

Prescription glasses and sun glasses for M/W/Ch, either with their own brand name or by Dolce & Gabbana, Police, Dior, Sting. Frames start at € 35,00 for their own brand to € 50,00 and up for brand names (with a small discount). Also contact lenses and progressive lenses. They speak French, English and Spanish.

New Koko's

Via Cavassico Inf. 183, fr. Cavassico - 32028 Trichiana (BL)
9.00-18.00

0437 555616
C.C.:None

Socks/stockings
FACTORY OUTLET

From Belluno take the S.P. 348. In a ,small industrial zone, fraz. Cavassico, near the Incon shopping center.

A small outlet selling sports socks made for various well known brandnames like the 'High-Tech' tennis, golf or hiking socks made for Fila and Lotto or the red racing socks made for the Ferrari racing team. Offers of 6-pack children socks, very cute, and second choice items at low prices.

Kalaki Occhiali

Via dell'Occhiale, 54 - 32040 Vallesella di Cadore (BL)
9.00-12.30/15.00-19.00

0435 520190
C.C.:All Major

Optician
FACTORY OUTLET

On the main road towards Auronza di Cadore, on the left in front of the Fina service station. First floor outlet. Parking.

Large choice of sunglasses in the latest models, with coloured lenses, pink, green, bright blue, € 37,00. The eye glasses with nose pads in precious stones are a speciality of the house, they are called 'Precious Mineral Pads' and made for those who believe in their curative power: quartz for the astral sign Leo, moon stoon for Cancer etc. at € 75,00.

Metal Dream Occhiali

S.S. per Auronzo, Loc. Campopiano, 11
32040 Vigo di Cadore (BL)
9.30-12.00/15.00-18.00. In summer 9.30 -19.30

0435 77129
C.C.:All Major

Optician
FACTORY OUTLET

From Lozzo di Cadore take the main road to Auronzo di Cadore, On the right, a free standing house with parking. In the front shop they sell only sun glasses, in the back of the building the prescription glasses.

Great choice in sun glasses, coloured, reflecting lenses € 32,00, but also Jacky O large tortoise frames. Progressive lenses for sun glasses € 155,00 a pair, coloured lenses € 36,00 a pair. Reading glasses without frames, their own production, brand name Babylon. Special offers in sun glasses 2 pairs € 25,00. In nearby Calalzo di Cadore a visit to the museum, dedicated to the optical industry in this area, is worthwhile.

Camicerie Shirt

Via Trieste, 3 - 35010 Cadoneghe (PD)
9.00-12.00/16.00-18.00. Sat. 8.30-12.30. Phone first

049 8871954
C.C.:None

Shirts
ARTISAN'S WORKSHOP

Autostrada A4, exit Padova Est towards Ponte di Brenta, Cadoneghe. Follow Via Garibaldi and Via Matteotti towards Meianiga di Cadoneghe. Via Trieste is a cross road to Via Gramsci.

A small workshop that produces some very nifty mens' shirts. A shirt in light blue with collar and cuffs in white, deadly chic, made to measure € 35,00. Shirts with French collar or button down, various designs and fabrics, all ready made € 30,00. Worth the detour.

Coop.Pellicciai Riuniti

P.zza della Memoria - 35030 Cervarese S.Croce - Fossona (PD)
8.00-12.00/14.30-17.30

049 9915398
C.C.:All Major

Furs
FACTORY OUTLET

Autostrada A4, exit Grisignano. After Cerverese continue to Fossona. The Coop Riuniti is in a large 'palazzo' on the right. Parking outside the gate.

Their outlet is large and pleasant, with some beautiful Alta Moda furs on show (they work for some big fashion names). Mink coats start at € 2,500,00 up to about € 6,000,00 full length, it all depends on the skins used. Beaver coats € 1,500,00 - € 2,500,00, sheepskins in blu with highly original finishing € 500,00. Also many mink lined sheepskins or raincoats. They work to order. Worth the trip, savings can be as high as 40%.

Antica Ceramica d'Este

Via Rovigo, 13 (Zona Commerciale II) - 35042 Este (PD)
8.00-12.00/14.00-18.00. Sat. 8.00-12.00

0429 3493
C.C.:All Major

Ceramics, terracotta, porcelain
ARTISAN'S WORKSHOP

From Este take the provincial road to Deserto-Villa Estense. 500 m after the only traffic light, to the left. The warehouse is at the end on the right.

Plates in a 'Vecchia Este' design, with intials, coat of arms, all made to order. Book ends in the shape of a faun, small boxes in 'biscuit' € 12,50. Little mandarins and pumpkins € 7,50, bases for lamps, handpainted, € 37,50. It is possible to browse and find a nice present. They work to order and produce those colourful Twinings promotional teapots.

Ceramiche Estensi

Via A.Volta, 26 - 35042 Este (PD)
9.00-12.00/14.30-18.30. Sat. 9.00-12.30

0429 4848
C.C.:All Major

Ceramics, terracotta, porcelain
FACTORY OUTLET

At the beginning of Este on the S.S.10 on the right to the Zona Industriale. The outlet is at the back of the factory, on the first floor where one can park.

Large showroom full of discontinued objects, seconds, prototypes and over- production. Cheerful wall plates with big paprikas € 7,50, vases € 12,50, table center set (12 pcs) € 37,50, handpainted ashtrays € 10,00. Seconds in large white or cream platters and spaghetti bowls are good buys for garden entertaining. Xmas ceramics at € 5,00. They speak, English, French, Spanish and German.

Este Ceramiche

Via Sabina, 31 - 35042 Este (PD)
8.00-12.00/14.00-18.00. Saturday phone first

0429 2270/3064
C.C.:None

Ceramics, terracotta, porcelain
FACTORY OUTLET

Autostrada A13, exit Monselice then S.S.10 towards Este. In the center of Este and near the Duomo, first road to the right, the outlet is at the end on the left just before the small bridge. Anonymous entrance on the first floor.

Everything here is beautiful, they work for well known brand names (and European royal families). Large handpainted cachepots with shell-design, Mammy cooky-jars € 60,00, underplates done in a sponge technique € 5,50, 2nds, in gold or silver € 10,00. Strawberry platters with cream jug, pyramids, big ashtrays, ideal for presents.

Gallia Confezioni

Via Villetta, 79 - 35015 Galliera Veneta (PD)
15.00-19.30. Wed & Fri only
Sat 9.00-12.30/15.00-19.30

049 5969241
C.C.:None

Clothing, shirts
FACTORY OUTLET

From Vicenza take the S.S.53 towards Treviso. After Cittadella follow signs for Galliera Veneta. In the center of Galliera take the direction of Tombola.

Shirts for men in a large assortment, well made with brand names like Gallia & Roberto Guiducci. Price per shirt circa € 37,50, all sizes, during their sales € 17,50 - € 25,00, also flannel shirts for winter. For W. less choice, some blouses by Charlotte Davis or Mulberry, England straightforward and classical. Sizes up to 50.

Bata Factory Outlet

Via del Santo, 183 - 35010 Limena (PD)
9.30-12.30/15.00-20.00. Fri. & Sat. 9.00-20.00

0498 843799
C.C.:All Major

Shoes
FACTORY OUTLET

Autostrada A4, exit Padova Ovest. Just before the center, near the Porsche car dealer.

Larger than their outlet in Albignasego (PD) and well stocked with shoes in every kind of colour or style. There are always special sales, promotions, irregular sizes at low prices, average savings circa 30% - 50%. The new Bata collection sells at regular shop prices.

Storehouse

Via Vittorio Veneto, 32 - 35043 Monselice (PD)
9.00-12.30/15.30-19.30
Open Mon. morning; closed Tue. morning

0429 781109
C.C.:All Major

Clothing
BARGAIN BASEMENT

Autostrada A13, exit Monselice, take the S.S.16 towards Rovigo. Storehouse is on the main road after a service station on the right.

A spacious shop selling end-of-line, remainders by WP store, Henry Lloyd, Invicta and others. The recent Ralph Lauren collection is for sale at a discount of 30%, polo R.L. for men € 47,00, shirts by Haller € 23,00, polo Superga € 26,00. For W. suits by Melrose € 150,00 circa, small sizes only.

Donatello
Via Martiri della Libertà, 15 - 35100 Padova (PD)
9.30-12.30/15.30-19.30

049 8753836
C.C.:All Major

Clothing
BARGAIN BASEMENT

In the center of Padova, in front of the Max Mara store.

Like its sister store in Mestre, though smaller, Donatello offers great choice in contemporary clothes for men and women. Shoes by Prada, Alma, Gabrielli and dresses and evening suits by Donna Karan, Genny, Fendi, Versace, Prada, D&G, Moschino. Good deals in shearling coats in mad colors, all at 50% less. Sales another 20%.

Magicoral
Via Cappelli, 20 - 35122 Padova (PD)
9.00-13.00/14.30-18.00

049 655922
C.C.:None

Handbags, accessories, various
FACTORY OUTLET

In the center of Padova near the basilica of S. Antonio.

Bags, clogs, slippers, hats, scarves by Mali Parma, a very well known name for amusing and fun accessories. A must for those who frequent fashionable seaside resorts to wear beach bags decorated with fishing nets, and small embroidered fish, straw hats with bits of fruit and flowers, mules with paillettes.

RJ Outlet
Via Po, 58 - 35135 Padova (PD)
10.00-19.30. Monday 15.00 - 19.30

049 619481
C.C.:All Major

Clothing
DISCOUNTS

Autostrada A4, exit Padova Ovest, turn left - Padova Centro-Fiera; after the by pass turn right onto the fly - sign for RJ Outlet. From Padova take Via Altichiero, and Via Due Palazzi on the left: after 50 m take Via Po.

A shop of circa 800 sq.m. with a large assortment of clothing by major designers: Armani, Roberto Cavalli, Fendi, Gucci, MiuMiu, Moschino Prada, Dolce & Gabbana, Valentino, Church's, Levis, Morgan, Versace and many others; prices are 30% to 70% lower than list price. There is a Special Sales room and lingerie by Roberta at a discount.

Belvest
Via Corsica, 55 - 35016 Piazzola sul Brenta (PD)
Sat. only 8.30-12.30. Open last Sun of month 8.30-12.30

049 9699111
C.C.:All Major

Clothing
FACTORY OUTLET

From Padova S.S.47 to the left for Campo S. Martino, after the bridge continue straight. In Piazzola at the second traffic light turn right in the direction of Carmignano. Belvest is approximately 300 m further on the right.

The right address for smart dressers in search of cashmere coats, jackets and double- or single-breasted suits. Luxurious classical styles, important materials and prices, but discounts can go as high as 50%. Best time for a visit: October/November. For W. their very chic suits, showroom size 42, are a steal.

I Pierpaoli

Via L.Einaudi, 55 - 35016 Piazzola sul Brenta (PD)
9.00-12.00/15.00-19.30

0499 600800
C.C.:All Major

Knitwear, cashmere
FACTORY OUTLET

Autostrada A4, exit Padova Ovest. Take the direction of Piazzola sul Brenta, Zona Industriale. It's the last building, behind the Opel car dealer.

Well-made, high quality, fashionable designs and colors for every age group. Two distinct collections, one classical, the other very avantgarde with brand names like 'Le Twinset' and 'Francesca Pierpaoli'. Twinsets in silk and viscosa € 110,00, cardigan with a border in very fine steel thread € 115,00, baskets with showroom samples at € 15,00.

Calzaturificio Laudino Caccin

Via Roma, 2 - 35010 San Giorgio delle Pertiche (PD)
8.00-11.30/14.00-18.00

049 5747930
C.C.:None

Shoes
FACTORY OUTLET

Autostrada A4, exit Padova Est then S.S. 307 towards Castelfranco Veneto and Borgoricco, then turn left and continue till the intersection, turn right for San Giorgio d. P. Calzaturificio Laudino Caccin is just after the bridge on the right.

A large factory hall, good choice in luxurious shoes for M/W, either classical or absolutely latest style. Mocassin in brownish colors sit next to purple stilettos, in fact they work for two globally known 'names' in the shoe business. Shoes for W circa €78 and up. Very good choice for men, classical styles €94 and up, all sizes, but no sample sizes.

Bolgheri

Via Sant'Antonio, 2 - 35030 Sarméola di Rubano (PD)
10.00-19.00. Closed Monday

049 8731023
C.C.:All Major

Clothing
GOOD PRICES

From Padova take the S.S.11 towards Vicenza. Bolgheri is at the first traffic light of Rubano on the left after a discount food store in the old factory of Levorato.

Snazzy men's fashions in a large space. Jackets by Ermenegildo Zegna, Les Copains and Givenchy in summer wool or wool/cashmere € 175,00. Also raincoats, windbreakers, anoraks. Ties by Aquascutum, Church's, Memphis € 25,00, 2nds € 10,00. Ties by Leonard de Paris € 40,00 regular, € 20,00, 2nds. Lots of cashmere. Sales in January & July at 50%.

G.T.A. Moda

Via Padova, 115 - 35030 Tencarola di Selvazzano (PD)
9.00-12.00/15.00-19.00

049 8685623

Clothing
FACTORY OUTLET

On the local road S.S. 250 Pavia - Abano Terme.

A good address to stock up on basics for one's winter or summer wardrobe. Men's jackets in summer wool € 115,00, trousers € 45,00, women's jackets € 110,00, trousers in fabric by Loro Piana € 70,00, short skirts by Belford € 30,00. It's all very wearable, classical, practical.

Pepper

Via Marco Polo, 1 - 35010 Trebaseleghe (PD)
9.30-12.30/15.00-19.30. Closed Monday

049 9387226
C.C.:All Major

Clothing, casual, jeans
FACTORY OUTLET

From Mestre or Castelfranco Veneto take the S.P. 245. From Padova Est take the S.S.515. In the center of the village, it's difficult to miss, large parking.

Casual wear, sweatshirts, parkas, jeans, ski wear, seconds at discounts by CerrutiJeans, Merit Cup, Best Company, Marina Yachting, Henry Cotton's. Ski sweaters in pure wool from S to XL € 35,00, jeans € 20,00. Long linen tank dresses and skirts in vague colours and a sporty look, it's all cheerful and fun. Sample size 42 for W and 48 for M.

Ombrellificio Sardella

Via S.Zeno, 27 - 35030 Veggiano (PD)
8.00-12.00/14.00-18.30. Saturday closed

049 5082256
C.C.:None

Accessories, various
ARTISAN'S WORKSHOP

Autostrada A4, exit Grisignano towards Padova on the S.S.11.

Various types of umbrellas are for sale: a classical Burberry, Stewart or Blackwatch or other Scottish clans at € 12,50 to € 17.50 for the more elegant handles. Interesting umbrellas for special purposes, a white parasol type for brides-to-be, a large golfing umbrella with incorporated saddle handle in leather € 25,00 or an XL model for fisherman.

Centro Calzature F.lli Rossi

Via Venezia, 10 - 35010 Vigonza (PD)
9.30-12.30/15.15-19.15

049 625039
C.C.:All Major

Shoes
FACTORY OUTLET

On the right on the S.S.515 towards Treviso. The entrance is on the side of the factory. Parking.

Beautiful shoes by Yves St. Laurent, Genny, Fendi and Fendissimi, Banfi, Anne Klein and their own brand name Rossi at € 59,50 - € 129,50. Showroom collection Y.St.Laurent in size 36/36.5 or 37/37.5 at € 59,00, other brand names only size 37 and size 41.5 for men at € 65,00. Tennis shoes by Superga or Keds € 12,50. Also clothes by Henry Lloyd, Husky, Think Pink. Large place and always busy.

Spaccio Calzature Zanin

Via Venezia, 88 - 35010 Vigonza - Capriccio (PD)
9.30-12.30/15.00-19.00

049 9801430
C.C.:All Major

Shoes
FACTORY OUTLET

Autostrada A4, exit Padova Est, towards Stra. The shop is on the right with parking in the front.

A large selling space of 120 sq.m. with an ample assortment of shoes for M/W by various prestigious brand names. City shoes, sporty shoes, lace ups either in neutral or fashion colors, the kind of shoes one wears all the time because they are comfortable and combine with everything. Special offers and showroom models in excellent quality at very competitive prices. It's easy to browse, knowledgeable and helpful personnel.

Calzaturificio F.lli Caccin

Via Cornara, 64 - 35010 Zeminiana di Massanzago (PD)
9.00-12.30/15.00-19.00. Open on Monday morning

049 5720011
C.C.:All Major

Shoes
ARTISAN'S WORKSHOP

Circa 20 km from Padova, take the new road S.S. del Santo to Borgoricco - S. Maria di Sala (VE) and Z.I. Massanzago. The outlet is well indicated.

Practically handmade shoes in excellent quality and with double leather or rubber soles only for men. English styles like a classical Church's type shoe (€ 85,00 and up) or original mocassins, very comfortable, starting at € 95,00, modern or sporty styles and matching belts. Shoes in ostrich, croccodile, lizard or snakeskin can be ordered. Ready-made sizes from 39 to 48 (with half sizes available), made to measure, inlays, repairs.

Calzaturificio Luval

Via Padovane, 19 - 35010 Zeminiana di Massanzago (PD)
14.30-18.30. Sat. 9.00-12.00/14.30-18.30

049 5720055
C.C.:None

Shoes
ARTISAN'S WORKSHOP

Circa 20 km from Padova, take the new road S.S. del Santo to Borgoricco - S. Maria di Sala (VE) and Z.I. Massanzago. Close to F.lli Caccin.

High class ladies shoes, brand name Paola Cipriani at € 50,00 and up in very good quality and classical but certainly not boring designs. Ankle boots in lambskin or pony € 75,00, cute red hobo bags with zippers for Xmas, € 75,00. Best time to buy: end of October, and before Easter.

Maglificio Grecotex

Via U. Saba, 18 - 45035 Castelmassa (RO)
9.00-12.00/15.00-19.00. Sunday open in December

0425 840086
C.C.:All Major

Knitwear, cashmere
FACTORY OUTLET

From Bologna or Padova Autostrada A13, exit Occhiobello. Just before Castelmassa there is a small industrial zone. The outlet is on the corner. Parking.

The best time to snap up knitwear by Umberto Tricot is at the end of October or the beginning of March. Men's ribbed sweater in cashmere 3-ply € 170,00 in camel, grey or beige. For young women cropped sweaters with matching A-line skirts, in mixtures of wool, viscose, or cashmere/wool in pinks € 97,50 and up. All sweaters, cardigans around € 45,00 in wool/silk/viscose or in linen/viscose in summer.

Stefanel

S.S. Romea, 309 km 67 - 45014 Contarina (RO)
8.30-12.30/14.30-19.00

0426 322855
C.C.:All Major

Clothing, casual, jeans
FACTORY OUTLET

From Chioggia after porto Viro towards Ravenna, after the Motto Morecola building and before the shopping center, on the right.

Stefanel produces mountains of medium quality clothes for the young in the latest trends and fashion colours. Sizes tend to be smallish, tight fitting hipster pants, midriff baring T's. We suggest a visit during the sales period to obtain a better discount. Other outlets in Ponte di Piave (TV) their headquarters and Marostica (VI).

Einstein Outlet

Via Eridania, 113 - 45030 Occhiobello (RO)
10.00-12.00/15.30-19.30

0425 760232
C.C.:All Major

Clothing, sportswear, casual
FACTORY OUTLET

Autostrada A13, exit Occhiobello, to the left, at the Stop sign to the left for circa 1 km. The outlet is well indicated.

Terribly trendy clothes by brandname Bray Steve Alan in violent colours with black slogans, strategically placed. Mountains of T-shirts and hipster pants, striped jeans with zippers and chains, all for the very young.

Outlet Logitex

Via Toniolo, 7 - 31030 Altivole fraz. Caselle (TV)
9.30-12.30/15.30-19.30. Sat. 10.00-12.30/16.00-19.30
Open on Sunday. Closed on Monday

0423 915940
C.C.:All Major

Clothing, casual, jeans
FACTORY OUTLET

Along the S.S. 667 from Altivole to Caselle, on the left. The entrance is in the back. Parking.

Excess inventory and end of line sporty/casual clothing by Bailo, Silvy and Woolrich. High-tec, practical, well-made wind jackets and rain coats for men € 50,00, flanel shirts € 29,00. For women Woolrich jeans, seconds, € 15,00, jeans shirts € 15,00, also underwear Extyelle by Keon for men. Large space, lots of choice, fidelity card.

Angelo Miotto

Via Sartori, 6/8 Z.A. - 31020 Bosco di Vidor (TV)
9.00-12.00/15.00-19.00

0423 987956
C.C.:All Major

Clothing, lingerie, underwear
FACTORY OUTLET

From Treviso take the S.S.348 and continue past Vidor to the Zona Industriale of Bosco di Vidor. Miotto is well indicated on the left at the roundabout.

Bikinis and bathing costumes in 'Cool-Max' fabrics at € 29,50 circa. Sets of lingerie in 'Dentelle de Calais' lace at € 37,50, Bodysuits and bras also for larger sizes up to cup size D, slips and camisoles by brandname Madonna Visconti and Feeling.

Conf. SanRemo

Via San Marco, 4 - 31031 Caerano S. Marco (TV)
9.00-13.00/14.30-18.30

0423 659296
C.C.:None

Clothing
FACTORY OUTLET

From Castelfranco Veneto on the S.S.307, turn right just before the rotonda of Caerano. The San Remo factory is on the right at the end of Via San Marco.

A very large factory hall filled with men's suits by Steve Linford, Hugo Boss, Biagiotti Uomo, San Remo and Young Club. A woolen suit by Peter & Sons € 165,00, winter coats € 195,00 - € 400,00. Dress pants € 52,50, special offer in jackets € 50,00, shirts € 32,50, all well made and wearable. For W less choice, some two piece suits in linen, some skirts, all classical.

Candel

Via G. Verdi, 23 - 31030 Candelu' (TV)
9.00-12.00/14.00-18.00. Sat. 9.00-12.00

0422 686144
C.C.:None

Knitwear, cashmere
FACTORY OUTLET

Autostrada A27, exit Treviso Nord towards i Ronchi. The outlet is on the main road that crosses Candelù, on the right.

Small showroom with the recent collection of clothes by 'Marisa Monti by Candel'. Dresses, skirts and classical knitwear in sizes 42 - 54 in the kind of shapes and colors that look good on the taller XL woman. A linen dress with gold embroidery and decorative zippers € 95,00, a polo with golf logo in gold € 20,00, all in lovely quality.

Trevigiana Confezioni

Via Gentillin, 4 Biban Z.A. - 31030 Carbonera Biban (TV)
9.00-12.30/15.00-19.30

0422 445027
C.C.:All Major

Clothing
FACTORY OUTLET

Carbonera is on the east side of Treviso and Trevigiana is in the 'B' district of Biban.

Large shop, large choice especially for men. Their strong point are the classical men's suits in tasmania wool, the kind of suit that lasts for years, € 275,00 - € 325,00 and up, also in XXL or made to measure. Racks of pants, well made, all sizes. For W there is little, some very classical trouser suits.

Rugby Colours

Via Belvedere, 19 - 31032 Casale sul Sile (TV)
16.00-19.00. Sat. 8.30-12.00

0422 821354
C.C.:None

Clothing, sportswear, casual
FACTORY OUTLET

Autostrada A7, exit Mogliano Veneto direction Casale. There are no indications of the outlet on the provincial road from Casale to Roncade but it is in the immediate vicinity of the rugby field. It is a warehouse and the name is written on a tiny bell.

Production of Rugby and Lotto sweats and T-shirts for hyper-active adults and kids. Extremely colorful knitwear, with wide stripes, exactly the kind used by rugby players, € 30,00 - € 40,00 in very sturdy quality. Same models for kids € 25,00, brand name Lotto. Overalls start at € 40,00 - € 60,00. They also sell Lotto sport shoes at low prices.

Tognana Sebring Porcellane

Via Capitello, 22 - 31030 Casier (TV)
9.30-12.30/15.30-19.30

0422 6721
C.C.:All Major

Ceramics, terracotta, porcelain
FACTORY OUTLET

Autostrada A7, exit Treviso Sud. Tognana is on the Casier-Treviso local road, on the left. Mountains of ceramics can be seen from afar.

White china, flowers and fruit-decorated china, bowls and vases in various shapes and price levels. Their 'seconds' corner offers white plates & colored underplates all in 'dishwasher/kids/continual use' quality. They have special offers from time to time: white fish-shaped platters, fit to carry a whole salmon, € 7,50.

Commerciale Veneta Abbigliamento

Via Borgo Treviso, 131 - 31033 Castelfranco Veneto (TV)   0423 722204
15.30-19.00. Sat. 9.00-12.30/15.00-19.00. Mond. closed   C.C.:All Major

Clothing
FACTORY OUTLET

On the circular road around Castelfranco Veneto look out for the sign for the Centro Commerciale, at the traffic light to the left, go straight past the C.C. at the roundabout turn back and enter into the first courtyard on the right.

Very elegant and well made clothes, either traditional or more daring and frivolous by Abitificio Black, Lewel fashion, Basile, Y.St.Laurent. All sizes are available, a really useful address for those in search of a (bridal) party outfit. Men's suits by Y.St.Laurent € 245,00. A small room on the right holds some surprisingly well made skirts and jackets at low prices.

Liberti

Via Circonvallazione Est, 48-50 - 31033 Castelfranco Veneto (TV)   0423 4243
9.30-20.00   C.C.:All Major

Lingerie, underwear
FACTORY OUTLET

After Castelfranco Veneto on the road towards Treviso. On the right. A large factory. Parking.

Very large shop front next to the office building. Prototypes in the latest colors at 20% discount, also cotton bras & panties (pretty, with lace and in spring colors) sizes up to 6/7, striped cotton pyjamas € 20,00 - € 35,00, cotton petticoats & bodysuits € 19,00. Baskets with seconds up to size 5 heavily discounted. Brandname Liberblu by Liberty.

Maglificio Petersant

Viale XXIV Maggio, 56 - 31015 Conegliano (TV)   0438 410484
9.00-12.00/15.00-19.30   C.C.:All Major

Knitwear, cashmere
FACTORY OUTLET

Autostrada A27, exit Conegliano and take S.S.635. Maglificio Petersant is on the right on the local road to Formeniga, Vittorio Veneto.

A shopfront next to the factory. One can't browse, everything is folded, but the salesladies will show you polos and high necked sweaters, heavy woollen jackets or short cardigans with zipper in spring colors, diamond patterns or heathery type hues. For men ample choice in Burlington sweaters, English autumn colors and boxy shapes, diamond design, € 32,50 and up. Seconds by Studio GFF for M/W start at € 10,00.

La Reginetta

Via del Commercio, 9/11 - 31041 Cornuda (TV)   0423 639521
8.00-12.00/13.30-18.15. Saturday 8.00-12.00   C.C.:None

Shoes
FACTORY OUTLET

Towards Feltre on the S.S.348 exit Cornuda and the Zona Industriale. The outlet is visible from the road, a little before Flavis. Ring bell.

A good choice in hiking boots and shoes, mountain boots, work boots, casual shoes. Mountain boots € 20,50 - € 47,50, in leather € 55,00, brand names Wildebeest and Garmish. Wool lined hunting boots € 19,50. Very pretty little booties for children decorated with edelweiss Heidi style.

Lotto Factory Outlet

Via Padova, 23 - 31041 Cornuda (TV)
10.00-13.00/14.30-19.30

0423 821400
C.C.:All Major

Clothing, casual, jeans
FACTORY OUTLET

On the S.S. Dolomiti, from Montebelluno turn left to Cornuda, Lotto is before the 'La Crocetta' commercial center and 'Bernardi' and close to the North Face outlet

A very large shop selling the Lotto sporty articles and casual clothes at reduced prices. Mountain boots, special offer, € 20,00, sneakers T-lite, large sporty bags, tops Fast Web/Juventus, sweatshirts and T-shirts with the 'Italian Sport Design' logo. There is a lot of choice, savings circa 30%.

Sporttrenta Outlet

Via Ru' Bianco, 5 - 31041 Cornuda (TV)
9.00-12.30/15.30-19.30. Sunday only in Nov./Dec.

0423 639801
C.C.:All Major

Clothing, sportswear, casual
DISCOUNTS

On the S.S. Dolomiti, from Montebelluno turn left to Cornuda, the shop is opposite 'Bernardi', their outlet is on the left. If the outlet is closed enter their main shop.

Clothing and sports shoes from all the most prestigious brandnames (Napapijri, Bolton, Fred Perry, Patagonia, Postcard, Columbia Sportswear Company, Dainese, Dolomite, Rossignol, Eisbar, Fischer, Jilbo, Ockey, Atala, Cor Sport ecc.) discounted circa 30%. These are unsold or out of season items from their main shop, all in perfect condition.

The North Face Outlet

Via Padova - 31041 Cornuda (TV)
10.00-13.00/14.30-19.30. Sat. 9.00-13.00/14.30-19.30

0423 839133
C.C.:All Major

Clothing, sportswear, casual
FACTORY OUTLET

On the S.S. Dolomiti, from Montebelluno turn left to Cornuda before the commercial center 'La Crocetta' and 'Bernardi'. It is practically next to the Lee Factory Outlet.

Sportswear 'Never stop exploring' for hiking and mountaineering. Large, lots of special offers and end of series like the trousers for men € 10,00 - € 25,00. Backpacks, boots, Goretex finished jackets, summer parkas € 35,00, sleeveles shirts for W € 20,00, shirts in tactel material € 40,00.

Think Pink

Via Guizza, 53 - 31030 Covolo di Pederobba (TV)
9.00-12.30/15.30-19.30. Closed Mon.

0423 86264
C.C.:All Major

Clothing, sportswear, casual, jeans
FACTORY OUTLET

Covolo di Pederobba is on the S.S.348 between Treviso e Feltre. The factory is on the right with parking in front.

Think Pink sweatshirts and parkas are renowned for their cheerful colours and original prints. Great choice in current and last seasons collection plus baskets with seconds and odds and ends. Wind breakers € 37,50 - € 110,00, M/W pants € 29,50, sweats with Think Pink logo, seconds € 20,00, polos in cotton M/W € 15,00, gloves and hats € 4,00. It's all very vibrant and attractive.

Paoletti di Follina
Via Cartiera, 5 - 31051 Follina (TV)
9.00-12.30/15.30-19.00

0438 970345
C.C.:All Major

Clothing, accessories
FACTORY OUTLET

Autostrada A27, exit Vittorio Veneto to Follina. From Treviso S.S.13. After the Priula bridge turn right. Paoletti is at the beginning of Follina, on the left.

Perfectly clipped hedges will lead you to this very elegant store, where time seems to have stopped. Mountain style knitwear, Scottish plaids in twilled wool, kilts, Austrian boiled wool jackets, walking sticks and scarves, pretty cotton blouses, all in refined good taste. Good offers in fabrics, also remnants.

Axo Factory Store
Via Fabio Filzi, 66 - 31036 Istrana (TV)
9.30-12.30/15.30-19.00. Sund. 9.30-12.30. Closed Mond.

0422 832300
C.C.:All Major

Clothing, sportswear, casual
FACTORY OUTLET

From Treviso, turn left at the traffic light in the center of Istrana. The Axel factory is on the right after circa 300 m.

Specialized clothing for motor bikes, mountain bikes, trekking in pure macho style One and two-piece outfits in leather and/or high-tech fabrics with the Axel brand name. Their current collection is discounted circa 20% but there is an ample choice in seconds, samples and remainders at very good prices. All sizes available from S to XXXL for men and XS to XL for women.

Meeting
Via Volta, 5 - 31020 Lancenigo di Villorba (TV)
9.30-12.30/15.00-19.00. Closed Monday

0422 919845
C.C.:None

Clothing, sportswear, casual, jeans
FACTORY OUTLET

From Treviso S.S.13 towards Conegliano. To the left between Pneumatici Pirelli and Datasys. On the left near 'Civis'.

An outlet for bodybuilders, ballet, arobics and gym enthusiasts, looking for T-shirts, sweats, performance wear in natural fabrics and with a used look but rigourously new. Bodysuits and bibs in neon colours, brand name Dimensione Danza. Prices are half shop price and there is a lot of choice in all sizes, also in seconds.

Carella
Via Roma, 90 - 31050 Miane (TV)
9.15-12.15/15.30-19.30

0438 971110
C.C.:All Major

Clothing
FACTORY OUTLET

Autostrada A27, exit Alemagna and then towards Follina. From Treviso S.S.348 to Valdobbiadene.

Woollen jerseys and fabrics with a high fashion content for the fuller figure. Their showroom collection is produced in size 44 and sells at 50% discount, but sizes start at 40 and can go up to 54 and beyond. Good looking, modern designs, an average saving of 35% for woollen suits that will hold their shape, prices are not exactly low but very reasonable for this kind of quality.

Il Punto Tricot

Via Raffaello, 19 Zona SPZ - 31021 Mogliano Veneto (TV)   041 5937008
14.30-18.30. Sat. 9.00-12.30   C.C.:All Major

Knitwear, cashmere
FACTORY OUTLET

Autostrada A27, exit Mogliano Veneto towards Casale. At the roundabout follow indications for the Zona Industriale, turn right and then left.

A large outlet on the first floor. Knitwear in excellent quality and designed to look good on larger sizes - up to 52. Flat front skirts with matching twinset in nordic colours, blues, greens, bright yellow. Short sleeve tops in viscose € 35,00 and up. Baskets with 2nds and remnants start at € 15,00.

In-Out Industries (Nigi)

Via Marconi, 157 - 31021 Mogliano Veneto (TV)   041 5937522
9.00-12.00/14.00-18.00. Closed Mon.   C.C.:None

Lingerie, underwear
FACTORY OUTLET

From Mogliano Veneto take the S.S. 13 to Treviso. Just outside the city limits, on the left, a large factory complex before the road bends to the left. Parking inside the gate.

A useful address for those in need of woollen underwear for cold climates. Camisoles in good quality wool and wool and cotton € 5,00, panties, baskets full of underwear for the whole family, terry towel robes for men by Valentino € 45,00, bodysuits. Always busy, they also work for Krizia Underwear.

Sartorial Homme

Via Vallio, 15 - 31050 Monastier di Treviso (TV)   0422 898068
9.00-12.15/14.30-18.30. Sat. telephone first. Closed in August   C.C.:None

Clothing
ARTISAN'S WORKSHOP

From Roncade a little before the Zona Industriale 2, take a narrow road to the left, 100 m further on the right, a small building. Parking.

A small showroom with mens' coats and suits, brand name Homme. They call themselves industrial tailors which means they can adjust, make to measure and do alterations. Well made suits in Tasmania wool €225,00-€325,00. Good choice of different fabrics and styles, like the coat with a pellegrin capelet (called a 'tabarro' in Italian) in English grisaglia wool, very unusual, or the lovely coat in toffee coloured cashmere.

Fila Store

Via Feltrina Sud, 192 - 31044 Montebelluna (TV)   0423 605868
9.00-12.00/15.30-19.30. Saturday 9.30-19.30   C.C.:All Major

Clothing
FACTORY OUTLET

On the S.S. 348 Feltrina, from Treviso on the left, a building with a turret near the industrial zone of Montebelluno.

Three floors of Fila clothing and accessories, recent collection, samples and showroom collection and last years remainders. Trousers in brushed cotton for W € 30.00, suede boots for M, ski jackets with fur border by Ciesse Piumini or Fila, polos and sweatshhirts. Average savings circa 30%, more discounts on the 3rd floor. Other outlet in Verrone, prov. of Biella.

Maglificio Leonello Spagnol

Viale Boccavalla, 1 - 31044 Montebelluna (TV)   0423 285745
10.00-12.30/14.30-19.00. Sunday open in Dec.   C.C.:All Major

Knitwear, cashmere
FACTORY OUTLET

From Treviso on the S.S.348 towards Feltre. On the last overpass look out for three warehouses, one with a sign "Spaccio Spagnol".Take the narrow road on the left, (this is not easy because of the traffic).

Knitwear for M/W (but more choice for W), very stylish, up market prices but in beautiful quality. Samples are sold at cost, some prototypes are smashing, some are understated, very chic novelties, seconds, remnants, accessories and gifts, knitted throws ecc. They work for international designers known for their minimalist designs. There is another outlet in Bigolino where prices are slightly lower. Sales 1/1-1/3 and 1/7-1/8.

Sport Outlet

Via Feltrina Sud, 160 - 31044 Montebelluna (TV)   0423 303667
9.00-12.30/15.30-19.30   C.C.:All Major

Clothing, sports articles
FACTORY OUTLET

From Treviso on the S.S.348 just before Montebelluna on the left and past the Fila outlet. A shop front with ample parking.

Clothing and sporting goods by Benetton Sportsystem, Nordica, Asolo, Prince, Kastle, Rollerblade, Killer Loop. The right place for hiking, cycling, tennis and roller blade enthusiasts. Snowboards start at € 172,50, large choice of sweats and sports shirts with logos € 30,00 - € 40,00. Prices on the whole are 35% less than shop price but no seconds or end of line items are being offered for sale.

B.C. International

Via S.Ambrogio, 2/B - 31050 Morgano fraz. Badoere (TV)   0422 739999
9.00-12.00/15.00-19.00. Monday open all day   C.C.:All Major

Clothing
FACTORY OUTLET

S.S. 53 Treviso - Castelfranco Veneto, turn left at the traffic light in the center of Istrena. In Badoere, past the center for 50 m in a small shopping area on the right.

Children from 2 years to 16 years old (max. size is 44) will do well here. Large baskets with seconds, sweaters, dresses, pants or shirts, all at € 5,00, modern and cheerful. For small girls, 6 years, cute dresses in pink linen € 10,00, sporty linen shirts for boys € 8.00.

Maglificio Morgano

Via Bosco, 22 - 31050 Morgano fraz. Badoere (TV)   0422 739392
9.00-12.30/15.30-19.30   C.C.:All Major

Knitwear, cashmere
FACTORY OUTLET

From Treviso towards Castelfranco Veneto on the S.S.53, turn left at Istrena at the traffic light. In Badoere di Morgano, past the center, at the traffic light turn right. After the roundabout of the Zona Artigianale turn right. Morgano is on the right.

Large first floor outlet with metal containers full of knitwear, either seconds, samples or end of line at low prices. V-necks, polos in merino wool, cotton or rayon € 9.00- € 12,50. Their current collection is sold at shop prices, all sizes available. Interesting discounts on men's trousers in brushed cotton, flannel blouses with the Morgano label and miriad other very wearable/classical knitted items.

Montello

Via Priula, 97 S.S. Schiavonesca - 31040 Nervesa della Battaglia (TV) 0422 726702
9.30-12.30/15.00-19.00. Closed on Monday C.C.:All Major

Knitwear, cashmere
FACTORY OUTLET

Autostrada A27, exit Treviso Nord and S.S. Pontebbana to Conegliano/Udine. At the Nervesa/Vicenza intersection and just before the bridge over the Piave river, turn left to Nervesa, after 150 m. the outlet is on the left.

Enormous quantities of knitwear in merino wool and an equally large choice of colours, sizes and shapes, classical, fashionable, trendy or sporty for every age group. In summer also cotton and rayon/viscose or silk knits. A polo in cotton melange, € 22,00, a cardigan in cotton with zip, very well finished and washing machine resistent € 37,00. Also lingerie and knitting wool. Sales 1/1-1/3.

Maglificio Colombo

Via delle Industrie - 31010 Paderno di Ponzano (TV) 0422 440382
9.30-12.30/15.00-19.00. Saturday 9.30-12.30 C.C.:None

Knitwear, cashmere
FACTORY OUTLET

From Treviso towards Ponzano, at the roundabout turn right in the direction of Castrette, then left for the Via delle Industrie and then left again.

High level knitwear at good prices. They work for the German market, brand name Gaby Laudon, so their collection is geared towards the larger sizes. Long sleeve tops in viscose € 32,50, jersey dresses € 65,00, longish twinsets € 65,00, a corner with remnants is worth investigating at € 25,00 a sweater.

Setaveneta

Via Pedeguarda, 18 - 31050 Pedeguarda (TV) 0438 842409
9.00-12.00/15.00-19.00. Open all day on Monday C.C.:All Major

Silks
FACTORY OUTLET

From Pieve di Soligo towards Follina, Seteveneta is on the left. A well indicated villa complex with a garden.

A large showroom selling scarves by Furstenberg at € 32,50, also stoles, ties, and remnants in silk. It is possible to buy silk per meter, fantasy or neutral, shantung or moiré € 15,00 - € 25,00, natural silk (bourette), 140 wide € 22,00 per meter. Also cushion covers, small presents.

Stefanel

Via delle Industrie, 19 - 31047 Ponte di Piave Levada (TV) 0422 819576
10.00-19.00. Monday 15.00-19.00 C.C.:All Major

Clothing
FACTORY OUTLET

Autostrada A4, exit Noventa di Piave to Ponte di Piave e Levada/Oderzo. At the Levada traffic light turn left for 50 m. The parking area for the outlet is well before the factory.

Two large factory halls selling Stefanel seconds, samples, unsold and even their most recent collection (at a 20% discount). There is a corner with Marithé Gibaud jeansy wear at 50% discount, a corner with remnants at € 5 - € 10, racks with rayon knitwear in strange colours. Sizes tend to be small, maximum 46 for W, 50 for M. Ideal for the budget conscious.

Selina

V.le dell'Industria, 22 - 31055 Quinto di Treviso (TV)
9.00-12.30/15.30-18.30. Sat. 9.00-12.30

0422 476299
C.C.:All Major

Lingerie, underwear
FACTORY OUTLET

From Treviso S.S.515 "Noalese" to Padova past Quinto di Treviso. Selina is in the I. Z. on a road parallel to the main road. The outlet is on the first floor of the factory. Parking in front.

Large choice of underwear for the whole family in medium/high quality. Sets of slip/bra € 8,50, colored T-shirts for men € 1,80. Woollen camisoles, 2nds, € 3,75, lace panties € 4,90. Brand names Vajolet, Axiom, Toujours, Notte. This place is always busy and offers multiple choice in light and mid-weight high performance underwear, especially for men. They speak English.

Alpinestars

Via Arsure, 2 - 31039 Riese Pio X (TV)
12.00-20.00/9.00-20.00. Sund. 13.00-20.00. Closed Tues.

0423 750472
C.C.:All Major

Clothing
FACTORY OUTLET

On the road from Castelfranco Veneto to Asolo, on the left and near Nefer Intimo.

Boots for bikers, leather motor jackets, one piece coveralls, jackets and moto-cross pants from recent or last year's collections. Special offers at super discounts, seconds, their prices are competitive and they offer everything for the true biker.

Nefer Intimo

Via Castellana, 42 - 31039 Riese Pio X (TV)
17.00-19.00. Closed Sat.

0423 454343
C.C.:None

Lingerie, underwear
FACTORY OUTLET

Near Castelfranco Veneto, on the left on the local road to Asolo, just after Alpine Stars.

Lovely lingerie in elegant colors and shapes: matching bra & panty sets in 'Dentelle de Calais' € 30,00, or camisoles in silk, sizes up to 6, white cotton fantasy briefs € 3,00. Boxes with special offers galore. They stock bikinis and bathing costumes from May onwards. Very professional saleshelp.

Replay Factory Outlet

Via Castellana, 71 Loc. Vali - 31039 Riese Pio X (TV)
10.00-12.30/15.00-19.30
Sat. 9.30-12.30/14.30-19.30. Sunday 15.00-19.00

0423 7491
C.C.:All Major

Clothing, sportswear, casual
FACTORY OUTLET

From Castelfranco Veneto to Asolo, on the right, a large factory complex.

For fans of the Replay brandname. Jeans style clothing for the whole family, jeans shirts € 31,00, dresses € 49,00, jeans in indigo € 31,00, all seconds, for men T-shirts, jeans and shirts, seconds € 18,50 - € 31,00. This is a cheerful place with a playing area for kids amidst clothing for 6 months to 16 years, done in an East Coast USA style.

Spaccio M 3 Knitwear

Via Mare, 65 - 31020 S.Vendemiano (TV) 0438 400307
9.00-12.00/15.00-19.00. From 1/3-1/5 and 1/11-1/1 phone first C.C.:All Major

Knitwear, cashmere
FACTORY OUTLET

Autostrada A27, exit Conegliano, take the first road to the right, continue for 200 m. the outlet is on the right.

Very up-to-date, young, stylish fashions in cotton/linen/viscose or microfiber, designed by Georges Rech Synonime, Sarah Pacini and Anvers. Also some seconds, end of line in smallish sizes at € 30,00 and up. There is a separate collection for larger sizes. Sales in July/August and February/March, they speak English and French.

Giesse Scampoli

Via Bradolini, 14 Z.I. - 31020 San Fior (TV) 0438 409040
9.00-12.30/15.00-19.30. Open in August C.C.:None

Fabrics, home furnishings, household linen
BARGAIN BASEMENT

Autostrada A27, exit Conegliano to S.S.13 Conegliano-Pordenone, on the right.

Large wire baskets hold remnants in cotton or wool, big industrial spools with woollen or cotton yarn, (€ 0,25 per 100 grams), printed silk € 8,00 per meter, furnishing fabrics Made in Spain € 6,50 p.m. for double width, impossible not to find something interesting. There are Giesse shops all over Italy, for information phone 045 6702804.

Maglificio Innocenti

Via Resistenza, 9 - 31020 San Vendemiano (TV) 0438 410007
14.00-17.30. Saturday closed C.C.:All Major

Clothing
FACTORY OUTLET

From Treviso to Vittorio Veneto on the S.S. 51. Before the center of San Vendemiano to the right. The outlet is next to the main building on the left with parking in front.

First-rate address for the over 40 lady looking for elegant jersey dresses that last at € 200,00 and up. Suede jackets € 350,00. Sizes from 40 up to 52/54, twin-sets in wool, long tunics, American flag sweaters € 90,00 all in superior quality, very wearable, a classical collection with a very modern twist.

Spaccio Ape

Viale Italia, 30 - 31040 Segusino (TV) 0423 979911
9.00-12.30/15.00-19.30. Open in August C.C.:All Major

Clothing
BARGAIN BASEMENT

From Treviso or Feltre take the S.S. 348 to Segusino and the center. After the service station on the right, keep going for another 100 mt., the outlet is on the right in front of a factory.

This is the Think Pink outlet for children. Basically they offer the same type of merchandise, colourful sweatshirts, skirts and pants in a fantasy print, dresses in corduroy, bandanas, hats, gloves, but obviously in smaller sizes for toddlers (6 months) up to 16 years, which will dress a size 44/46. The very large Think Pink outlet for adults is in Covolo di Pederobba (TV).

Non Solo Cashmere

Via Galvani, 11 Z.I. Sud - 31027 Spresiano (TV) 0422 889747
15.00-19.00. Sat. 9.30-12.30/15.00-19.00 C.C.:All Major
Only on Wed., Thurs. and Friday afternoon

Knitwear, cashmere
FACTORY OUTLET

From Treviso take the S.S. 13 Pontebbana. After Visnadello, in an I.Z., at 'Zippy' turn right. The outlet is well indicated.

Large showroom, full of lovely cashmere sweaters, cardigans, dresses, mantellas. Very delicate colours, chic designs, frivolous feminine tops, macho rustic sweaters. They work for Walter Steiger, Ermanno Scervino and Marchesin, their own brandname and prices are very competitive for this kind of quality. A sleeveless high-necked cashmere top € 30,00, a gilet for M in wool/cashmere € 20,00.

Glooke Sport Outlets

Via Conegliano, 80a - 31058 Susegana (TV) 0438 435546
9.30-12.30/15.30-19.30 C.C.:All Major

Sports articles
DISCOUNTS

Autostrada A27, exit Conegliano, second intersection to the right to the center. At the first traffic light to the left for the 'Pontebbana' S.S. 13 to Treviso. Continue for 10 minutes on this road, on the left before the Mercedes car dealer.

500 mq stacked with pingpong tables, punch balls, stationary bikes, tennis and basket nets, rowing machines and weight lifting equipment, all discounted between 30% and 70%. Also sun glasses, shoes and clothing by Lotto, Filo and Benetton. Special offers 'Formula Tris' or 'Best Price' makes every purchase a very good deal indeed.

Vendramini Sporting Shoes

S.S. 348, Via Piavesena, 2 - 31040 Trevignano Signoressa (TV) 0423 670468
9.00-12.00/14.00-18.00. Sat. closed. Closed in August C.C.:None

Shoes/boots
FACTORY OUTLET

From Treviso S.S.348, 12 km to the north, Via Piavesena is immediately after 'recupero auto'. Parking.

A small outlet on the ground floor. Vendramini produces boots and shoes for skiing, trekking, hiking and biking since 1919. Their prototypes are called Courmayeur, Cortina, Tyrol etc. They also make biker boots in leather and winter boots that will resist frost (from € 40,00 upwards), all in sturdy designs and beautiful quality. Special offers and second choice at 25% - 66% less. They speak English.

Norton & Wilson

Via S. Antonino, 261/a - 31100 Treviso (TV) 0422 348028
9.00-12.30/15.00-19.00. Closed in August C.C.:All Major

Clothing
FACTORY OUTLET

Autostrada A27, exit Treviso Sud towards the Ca'Foncello hospital. At the roundabout take the first road to the left, after 1 km to the left, after the bypass and circa 600 m.

Very classy atmosphere, large tables showing shirts and jeans at € 60,00. Men's suits by Norton & Wilson are € 225,00. A two piece tailleur for W, very elegant, in pink silk € 350,00, with the 'Ritz the Saddler' label. Also racks with 2nds and remnants of high quality material, samples and prototypes in size 42. They speak English, German and French. Sales start the middle of January and July.

Spaccio Iana Unitessile

Via S. Antonino, 198 - 31100 Treviso (TV)   0422 402866
9.00-12.30/15.00-19.00   C.C.:None

Clothing, maternity clothes
FACTORY OUTLET

From Treviso take the road for Casier. On the Tangenziale take the Lido di Jesolo exit. The outlet is on the Jesolo-Casale road on the right.

Samples and seconds for 0-12 year olds, plus some maternity dresses. Little bomber jackets, seconds, € 12,50, blazers in Vichy prints € 17,50, large quantities of discounted overalls and bermudas. Baskets with special offers all arranged according to age, offer practical but cute clothes that will not fear the washing machine. Very busy.

Intreco - Papermoon

Via Feltrina, 71 - 31100 Treviso Munigo (TV)   0422 431490
9.30-12.30/15.00-19.00   C.C.:All Major

Clothing, lingerie, underwear
FACTORY OUTLET

From Treviso take the main road la Feltrina to Feltre, after 2 km on the left.

The cutest clothes by Cacoa and Papermoon for children from 0 - 15 years old. Large choice, a corner with samples (for 2 years old) and prototypes and last years' collection at half price. Seconds from € 20,00 - € 14,00. The dresses for 3 years old, last seasons collection by Papermoon, were a steal at € 28,00. It's all very well made and in good taste.

Cantina Produttori di Valdobbiadene

Fraz. San Giovanni - 31030 Valdobbiadene (TV)   0423 982070
9.30-12.00/14.00-19.00   C.C.:All Major

Wine, liqueurs
GOOD PRICES

From the S.S. 438 to the right direction of Vidor, then left to Bigolino di Valdobbiadene. The cantina with a large sign Valdoca is on the right in the hamlet of San Giovanni.

The Cantina di Valdobbiadene represents over 600 local wineries that produce more than 80.000 q.li of grapes of which 80% is used to make the famous Prosecco di Valdobbiadene which can be compared with the best French champagne. They sell various kinds of Prosecco either in bottles (€ 4,20 - € 4,70) or per liter (€1,70 per liter, minimum 10 liters). Red, white wine per liter € 1,15.

Pellizzari Vantaggi

Via Roma, 190 - 31050 Vedelago (TV)   0423 400145
Open in August   C.C.:All Major

Clothing, household linen
DISCOUNTS

S.S.53 Castelfranco-Treviso, at the traffic light. Two shops, the one on the right sells the new collection at 20% discount, the shop on the left sells samples, overruns and seconds.

Pelizzari Vantaggi sells the showroom collection, remainders and seconds by Trussardi, Guess, Papermoon, Cacao, Vestebene, Corneliani Uomo, Allegri, Missoni. Jeans by Trussardi € 47,50, 2nds for M/W, shirts for M € 20,00-€ 47,00. Also towels per kilo, furnishing materials, sportswear and nightwear. By the end of January and August they sell of next season's samples at a 40-50% discount.

Italmode

Via Galvani, 106 - 31029 Vittorio Veneto (TV)
8.00-12.30/15.00-19.00. Tues. 15.00-19.00 in summer

0438 521243
C.C.:All Major

Knitwear, cashmere
FACTORY OUTLET

Autostrada A27, exit Vittorio Veneto Sud, follow indications for the center. At the 1st traffic light continue, at the 2nd light turn right, Via Galvani is 500m further on the left. From Conegliano/Sacile go beyond the suburb of San Giacomo di Veglia. Via Galvani is on the right after approximately 1 km.

Past a beautiful, abandoned villa, a large, very decorative outlet with stacks of woollen sweaters and a great choice in colors and sizes. In summer cardigans and tops in viscosa and silk. A polo in cotton stretch € 32,00, and jackets in cotton with zip and pockets € 37,00. For men all the classical knitwear in great colours. Sales from 1/1-1/3.

Lanificio Bottoli

Via Caserma, 1 - 31029 Vittorio Veneto (TV)
9.00-12.00/15.00-18.30. Sat. 9.00-12.00

0438 554343
C.C.:None

Fabrics, home furnishings
FACTORY OUTLET

Autostrada A27, exit Vittorio Veneto Nord. Lanificio Bottoli is situated on the road to Vittorio Veneto, on the left, along a small stream. It is well indicated

They sell mostly woollen material, p.m. or a jacket length € 25,00, a skirt length € 8,00 in excellent quality and at low prices. Their bestsellers are the Scottish tartans in pure wool, with a choice of at least 75 different clans, quite mind boggling, in beautiful muted or striking colors. Mohair plaids and blankets € 18,00 and up. Silk scarves € 25,00 - € 35,00.

Viezzer Pizzin Tessile

Via della Sega, 4 - 31029 Vittorio Veneto (TV)
9.00-12.30/15.00-19.30

0438 552234
C.C.:All Major

Clothing
FACTORY OUTLET

Autostrada A27, exit Vittorio Veneto Nord and the S.S. 51 to Vittorio Veneto center. On the left, well before the center and near Lanificio Bottoli.

Very sophisticated fabrics in wool and wool/silk or cashmere and soft shades, all sizes for elegant men looking for well taylored grown-up suits. Price per jacket € 175,00 - € 225,00, also suits, trousers € 50,00-€ 70,00, coats and a series of shirts, ties and scarves.

Calzaturificio Ballin

Vicolo B.Cellini, 4 - 30032 Fiesso d'Artico (VE)
8.00-12.00/14.00-19.00. Closed Saturday

041 5137211
C.C.:All Major

Shoes
FACTORY OUTLET

Follow the indications for the Riviera della Brenta, at the beginning of Fiesso, immediately after the Agip service station to the left (from Mestre). Parking.

This place is a must for the fashion conscious. Small but overflowing with the latest styles. The best time to buy sample shoes, size 37, is the middle of October and middle of April at € 75,00 per pair. Other sizes are available at € 100,00. They work for major national and international avantgarde designers and these shoes sell for at least € 350,00 in cities like New York or London. Some handbags are also for sale and worth a look.

Spaccio Calzature La Serenissima

Via Prima Strada, 27/b, Quart. Ind. - 30032 Fiesso d'Artico (VE)   049 502 731
9.00-12.00/15.00-18.00. Saturday 9.00-12.30   C.C.:All Major

Shoes
FACTORY OUTLET

Autostrada A4, exit Dolo. In Dolo to the right in the direction of Padova for circa 2 km.
An industrial zone, 1 km from the Villa Reale in Strà.

Nearly all the shoes and sandals for sale are of the deadly stiletto type, two-
toned, in suede or nappa, with contrasting lizard trimmings and in bright
colours. Shoes for W circa € 55,00, a pair, for men € 70,00 (but less choice and
only in classical designs). They also sell handbags and evening bags, some matching the shoes, and casual leather wear.

Renato Angi

Via Provinciale Nord, 89 - 30030 Fossò (VE)   041 5170469
9.30-12.30/15.30-19.30. Closed Monday   C.C.:All Major

Clothing, accessories
BARGAIN BASEMENT

On the provincial road from Dolo to Piove di Sacco, almost in the center of Fossò. A
shop front next to the Eurospin supermarket.

A large, trendy showroom, city style. The right place for the young to buy handbags in avantgarde or very fashionable styles € 47,00-€ 70.00, in good quality
at   decidedly friendly prices. Shoes for W in sample size 37 € 50,00. Worth a
visit if only to get an idea of the latest in tiger, strass and rhinestone looks à la
Roberto Cavalli. Sales in July and February.

La Murrina - Murano

Via Alta, 28 - 30020 Marcon (VE)   041 5951140
9.00-12.30/15.00-19.30. Monday closed   C.C.:All Major

Crystal, glassware
FACTORY OUTLET

Autostrada A4, exit Mestre, take the tangenziale to Trieste and the first exit for
Marcon. Follow the signs or phone.

Lamps, wall lights, chandeliers, candlesticks, vases in colourful Murano glass.
Wine or whiskey glasses in crystal, tea and coffee cups, it's a good address for
finding wedding presents, clowns in coloured glass or objects for the house.
Lights, various decorative objects in crystal, vases, there is even a collection of
German china, all discounted between 30% and 70%.

Donatello Gloria

Via Antonio da Mestre, 15 - 30174 Mestre (VE)   041 975535
9.30-12.30/15.30-19.30   C.C.:All Major

Clothing
BARGAIN BASEMENT

On the tangenziale take exit Via Castellana to the hospital, a sign with a large H. In
the center of Mestre in a gallery. From Venice take Bus 2 or 8.

Donatello offers great choice in all the big Italian fashion names. Racks and racks of
sheepskin coats, dresses, suits by every big designer name one can imagine.   Tailleurs
Moschino € 253,00, also Plein Sud, Armani, Cividini, D&G, Les Copains, Fay. shoes by
Moschino, lingerie La Perla. Men's suits by Pal Zileri discounted 50% circa, ties by Brioni
€ 67,00, by Burberry € 46,00, jackets by Fay for men € 245,00. They speak English.

Outlet Store

Corso del Popolo, 255 - 30172 Mestre (VE)
9.30-12.30/15.30-19.30

041 5315301
C.C.:All Major

Clothing
BARGAIN BASEMENT

From the tangenziale to Corso del Popolo/Mestre Centro. Parking near Hotel Ambasciatori. On the railway overpass (in the old worker's union building).

This is the outlet for a chain of luxury boutiques (Al Duca d'Aosta) in the Veneto area. All the famous Italian brand names, either Alta Moda or Pret a Porter, plus some Americans like Donna Karan, Polo Ralph Lauren, Calvin Klein are sold at very competitive prices. Possible to browse, friendly sales personnel, large choice, especially good deals in PoloRL and Lauren Uomo.

Mazzorato

Via Orsato, 40 - 30100 Mestre Marghera (VE)
9.30-19.30. Sat. 9.30-20.00

041 5381766
C.C.:All Major

Clothing
FACTORY OUTLET

There is a boat/bus service every hour from Piazzale Roma in Venice. Phone for information.

Medium quality and low prices for the showroom collection of Marchese Coccapani and Pedrini, dresses for the young € 30,00, pants € 20,00, the boutique collection is sold at 50% discount, dresses in L and XL € 35,00 either in cotton or wool/acrylic mixtures.

Incotex

Via della Fornace, 15/17 - 30034 Mira (VE)
14.00-18.30. Sat. 9.00-12.30. Closed Monday

041 5629611
C.C.:All Major

Clothing, raincoats
FACTORY OUTLET

Via Fornace is 200 m from the Municipality building of Mira. Follow the walls of a large complex (Bankiser). The indications are poor, but follow the wall fencing to the outlet.

Incotex is a well known producer of pants for M/W, (but mostly for M) and they work for some major and minor luxury international brand names. Well made classically cut pants in brushed cotton € 35,00, in summer wool, corduroy or linen € 45,00. On the first floor rain jackets by Dupont, Paris € 130,00. Friendly and helpful personnel, but at times there is very little choice, we suggest to phone first.

Artexa

Via Salgari, 2/p - 30036 S.Maria di Sala (VE)
9.00-12.00/15.00-19.00. In summer closed on Sat.

041 487722
C.C.:All Major

Home furnishings, carpets
FACTORY OUTLET

Autostrada A4, exit Padova Est, take the main road, S.S. 515 to Treviso. Artexa is before the center of S. Maria di Sala, a narrow street to the right after the Pizzeria Gregorio.

An outlet for kitchen and bathroom carpets, non slip, fitted, kilim, oriental carpets, in coconut fiber, either samples, seconds or made to measure. This is an extremely useful address for those furnishing or redoing a house.

Ca' da Mosto Seventy
Via Venezia, 146 - 30077 Scorzé (VE)
9.00-12.30/15.00-19.00. Open in Oct/Nov & Mar/Apr.

041 5899555/539
C.C.:All Major

Clothing
FACTORY OUTLET

On the 'Castellana' a busy road between Mestre and Castelfranco. The outlet is just before Scorzè and well indicated.

The 'Seventy' showroom collection is only for sale during certain months of the year and their enormous outlet is well known in the area, full of locals snapping up pants, classical or trendy € 30,00 - € 50,00, a dress plus jacket in raw silk or a cool trouser suit € 80,00, men's shirts € 20,00 all at a good price/quality level. Also handbags, belts and fabric remants sold per meter. Busy with only a few changing rooms.

Pierobon
Via delle Industrie, 36a - 30038 Spinea (VE)
9.00-12.00/15.00-19.00

041 999512
C.C.:None

Clothing, lingerie, underwear
FACTORY OUTLET

From Mestre take the 'Miranese' just before the roundabout of Mirano. The factory is behind the PAM offices.

Great choice in kid's pants for 6-12 years old, € 7,50 - € 12,50, lovely beach sets for toddlers € 10,00, underwear and sweatshirts pre-maman € 12,50. Velvet blazers in 'little lord Fauntleroy' style, tartan kilts for girls € 22,00, brand names Le Filande, Calins, Coquins. All in very good quality, muted colors, accurately finished.

Vetreria Artistica Rosa
Via G. Ferraris, 26 - 30038 Spinea (VE)
8.00-12.00/13.00-17.00. Sat. 8.00-12.00

041 5410868
C.C.:None

Lamps
ARTISAN'S WORKSHOP

Autostrada A4, exit Mestre and take Via Miranese. In the Zona Industriale of Spinea.

An authentic laboratory where one can see the famous Venetian chandeliers made by hand by artisans blowing into long metal rods with roaring fires all around them. One can order an authentic Venetian crystal chandelier, with little pendants, speckled gold leaves, etc. and choose from a book full of designs. They ship anywhere in the world.

Balocoloc
Calle Lunga, S.Croce 2134-30125 - 30100 Venezia (VE)
9.00-15.00. Also by appointment

041 5240551
C.C.:All Major

Accessories, various
ARTISAN'S WORKSHOP

From Piazzale Roma it's 2 minutes on foot. After the church, in the Santa Croce area.

For carnaval hats, scarves, masks and mantelets all made on the premises, historically true copies, in lovely materials. Original and fun! They work to order and for special requests it's probably better to phone their laboratory in Mestre, tel 041 640273 rather than go to their shop.

Emporio Pettenello

Campo S. Margherita 2978 Dorsoduro - 30125 Venezia (VE)
9.30-13.30/15.0-20.00

041 5231167
C.C.:All Major

Toys
GOOD PRICES

At the level of Ca' Foscari and Ca'Rezzonico on the left.

This shop dates back to 1899 and stocks a respectable quantity of toys at competitive prices. They also sell books and typical Italian items like a Pinocchio in various sizes and nativity scenes during the Christmas period.

Mazzon "Le Borse"

Campiello S. Tomà 2807 - 30125 Venezia (VE)
9.00-12.30/15.00-19.00

041 5203421
C.C.:All Major

Handbags, leather goods
ARTISAN'S WORKSHOP

In Venice take the no 82 boat direction of S. Marco, and get off at S. Toma. On foot it is circa 10 minutes from the Central Station, cross the bridge in front and follow directions for the Accademia.

A small workshop and a good address for ladies in search of classical bags like a 'Birkin' or 'Garden Party' at €130,00, all very well made. A hobo bag with perforated H, € 80,00 a large Birkin for travelling in green canvas with leather€ 240,00 a small red leather envelope bag € 80,00. One can order different colors/leather and they ship. Also belts and attaché cases for M in black anti-scratch leather and metal coloured locks, very very chic.

Gilfor Pelle

Via Dante, 2 - 30030 Vigonovo (VE)
8.30-12.30/13.30-19.00. Open from 15/9 to 1/4

049 9830148
C.C.:All Major

Clothing, leatherwear
ARTISAN'S WORKSHOP

Autostrada A4, exit Padova Est or Padova Zona Industriale. In the center of the town. Look for a pink house.

Lush and lightweight fur-trimmed shearlings, sporty sheepskins, black leather jackets, pants, great choice. They make-to-order and prices are excellent considering the high quality. For appointments out of season, telephone 041-466305.

Dismero Factory Outlet

Piazza Nuova, 79 - 37012 Bussolengo (VR)
9.30-12.00/14.00-19.00

045 7156960
C.C.:All Major

Clothing
FACTORY OUTLET

Autostrada A4, exit Peschiera (from Milan) to Bussolengo and the center. The outlet is in front of the church.

Jeans in every possible colour, shape, size, elasticized, in canvas, corduroy, tiger prints or gold threaded, fringed etc. but always with a golden D embroidered on the back pocket. In summer linen capris with velcro closing, tops and T's with the D logo, all in very good quality and only for W. Dismero is a wellknown brandname in Germany. Discounts of circa 30%. Sizes up to 46/48.

Swinger International

Via Festara Vecchia, 44 - 37012 Bussolengo (VR)   045 6767759
9.00-12.30/15.00-19.30. Closed Monday   C.C.:All Major

Clothing, fabrics
FACTORY OUTLET

Autostrada A4, exit Sommacampagna. In Bussolengo look for the commercial center Grande Mela. Swinger is behind this center 100 m. further up the road.

Colored, embroidered, shredded, gold-trimmed jeans by Rocco Barocco, Fendi, 2nd choice € 24,50, equally embellished jackets, all fit for the disco € 44,50 and up, jeans by Swinger, Rocco Barocco, Video Music, Fendi € 35,00, dresses, mini-skirts, remnants in cotton, alcantara € 6,50 p.meter.

Aesse Technical Equipment

Via Ca'Magre, 33 - 37063 Isola della Scala (VR)   045 6630551
9.30-12.30/15.30-19.30   C.C.:All Major

Clothing, sportswear, casual, jeans
FACTORY OUTLET

Autostrada A4, exit Verona Sud and S.S.12 to Modena. Aesse is in a Zona Industriale on the left of the main road, about 3 km after Isola della Scala.

Their whole 'The great outdoor Aesse' collection is for sale; Aesse Mariner, Aesse Tick, light weight or heavy weight performance clothes for trekking, biking, canoeing, mountaineering. A shirt or jacket in trevira fleece € 40,00, ano-raks, T-shirts in polypropilene, a cycling suit € 35,00, bermudas € 8,00, 5 T-shirts Aesse € 17,50, good deals everywhere.

Diffusione Tessile

Via Padana Inferiore Ovest, 15 - 37045 Legnago (VR)   0442 602811
9.30-13.00/15.00-19.30. Saturday 9.30-19.30   C.C.:All Major

Clothing
FACTORY OUTLET

From Verona take the superstrada to Rovigo and exit at the second indication for Legnago. At the roundabout follow the sign for S.Pietro di Legnago, continue, after the disco 'Principe' on the right.

This is a Max Mara outlet selling last years remainders (minus the Max Mara labels) and a special collection made for their outlets. Casual and elegant clo-thes also in Marina Rinaldi styles (but again no labels) all discounted 30% - 50%. There is a corner with leatherwear, a lot of handbags (€ 40,00 and up) and shoes (€ 50,00 and up). Sizes from 38 to 50 plus XXL sizes up to 60.

Abital Confezioni

Via Preare, 6 - 37025 Parona (VR)   045 8085333
9.00-13.00/15.30-19.30   C.C.:All Major

Clothing
FACTORY OUTLET

From Verona, (exit Verona Nord) take the S.S.12 towards Trento. Just before Parona follow the S.S.12 and after the traffic light the factory is on the left. Ample parking inside the gates.

A large, elegant outlet with a vast choice of men's and women's suits, either super chic, formal or casual, all made by Corneliani. Also shirts, sweaters, accessories, all sizes and colours available. Prices are fair for the quality offered and discounted circa 35%. For women less choice but the same high level of quality/wearability. In the back of the store there is a small area with remnants and end of line clothing.

Thun Store Rivoli

Loc. Ca'Campagna - 37010 Rivoli Veronese (VR) 045 6205631
9.00-13.00/15.00-19.00 C.C.:All Major

Ceramics, terracotta, porcelain
FACTORY OUTLET

Autostrada A22 (Brennero), exit Affi to Rivoli Veronese for 3 km. Before Rivoli the shop is on the left. Ample parking.

A very welcoming store offering the complete collection of Thun ceramics, all first choice, but there is also a corner with seconds and end of series with discounts of 35 to 50%. Great choice of clocks, angel candle sticks, ceramic puppies and kittens, apart from their famous platters and plates and coloured oven dishes. Every week there are special offers in ceramics and china with a minimum discount of 45%. For group visits phone 045 7205631.

Maglierie Renato Guerra

Via Mazzini, 8 - 37055 Ronco all'Adige (VR) 045 6615390
9.00-12.00/14.30-18.00 C.C.:None
Sat. 9.00-12.00/15.00-19.00. Closed 1/7 - 1/10

Knitwear, cashmere
FACTORY OUTLET

Autostrada A4, exit Verona Est/Soave, 15 km to Ronco all'Adige. Near the Stizzoli outlet.

Some cartons with remnants all in merino wool. Spools of wool sold per kilo, some quilted cardigans in loden green with a faint nod to Tyrolean styles: € 90,00, a special series of water resistant knitwear for hunters in alpaca and alcantara plus samples, sweaters (2nds) € 25,00, knitting wool per kilo. The best time for a visit is October.

Stizzoli

Via XX Settembre, 2 - 37055 Ronco all'Adige (VR) 045 6608411
9.00-12.00/15.00-18.30. Sat. 9.00-12.00 C.C.:All Major

Clothing
FACTORY OUTLET

Autostrada A4, exit Verona Est from Milano, exit Soave from Venezia. In the center of Ronco on the main road.

Very well made clothes that will last for ever for the over-50 lady. Flowery blouses in viscosa with knitted borders € 60,00 - € 165,00, tunic style dresses in heavy woollen jersey € 60,00 - € 115,00, linen pants € 85,00. Some seconds, some remnants, plenty of choice, sizes up to 54. On the first floor last year's collection, discounted 35%.

Settimocielo

Via C. Battisti, 272 - 37057 S. Giovanni Lupatoto (VR) 045 8265060
9.00-12.30/15.00-19.30 C.C.:All Major

Ceramics, terracotta, porcelain
FACTORY OUTLET

Autostrada A4, exit Verona Sud to Rovigo/San Giovanni Lupatoto. Before the shoppingcenter Verona 1, near the Toys shop and behind the Chateaux d'Aix furniture store.

This is the Rosenthal outlet for unsold items, remainders, end of series of the 130 Rosenthal shops in Italy. There are no seconds but discounts of 50% to 70% on tea sets for 6 (€100,00), dinner sets for 12 (€ 250,00 - € 500,00), glasses and gift objects like ashtrays by Versace discounted 60%.

Cantina di Soave

Via Roma, 45 - 37038 Soave (VR)
9.00-12.30/14.30-18.30

045 6139811
C.C.:All Major

Wine, liqueurs
GOOD PRICES

Autostrada A4, exit Soave to the center. After the city wall, on the right is Via Roma. One can park in the courtyard.

No Italian holiday is complete without a glass of white Soave or Custoza or a caraffe of red Valpolicella or Bardone wine. In the cantina di Soave one can buy wine per liter but must bring a plastic container or large 5lt bottle. They also sell wine per bottle or in 6 bottle-packs and stock some presentation boxes of various local wines.

3A Antonini - Lumberjack

Via Pacinotti - 37135 Verona (VR)
11.00-17.00. Closed Monday

045 8291111
C.C.:All Major

Shoes
FACTORY OUTLET

Autostrada A4, exit Verona Sud to the center. At the first traffic light turn left, Via Righi, again left, at the end turn right. (Circle the factory to arrive at the outlet).

Manufacturers of Lumberjack & LJK casual and sporty shoes, great choice, all sizes available. Hiking boots, dress shoes, mocassins, boat shoes, sneakers and sandals, this is a good place to visit for families. In summer special offers of sports shoes, whereas September is a better time to find dress and city shoes. Prices are very competitive.

Brugi Astrolabio

Via Spallanzani, 29 - 37135 Verona (VR)
8.30-20.00. Open on Monday morning

045 8299148
C.C.:All Major

Clothing, sportswear, casual
FACTORY OUTLET

Autostrada A4, exit Verona Sud, take the underpass, continue towards the end, then to the right into a wide street. At the crossing go straight then first to the left. The outlet is in front of Glaxco and not far from Luck/Mavecon.

Large, well organized factory hall selling sportswear, casual wear, ideal for large families. A corner of special offers and super bargains is worth a look. New arrivals towards the end of September. In spring their skiwear is really discounted, jackets, ski overalls, light weight quilted jackets € 25,00. Very good prices too for children's casuals, a flannel lined jeans jacket € 26,00.

Emporio Mash, Acon

Via Col. Fincato, 262 - 37100 Verona (VR)
9.00-12.15/15.30-19.30. Sat. 9.00-19.30. Closed Mond.

045 525448
C.C.:All Major

Clothing, casual, jeans
FACTORY OUTLET

From the Brennero and autostrada A22 take exit Affi and S.S. 12 to Verona. Follow the directions for Bosco Chiesa Nuova. From autostrada A4, exit Verona Est towards the center, than at P.le Porto Vescovo to the right for Chiesa Nuova. Parking in the back of the building.

A large hall with row upon row of jeans in every possible colour, shape, weight and size. Their regular collection in the latest styles, brand name Mash, is available in all sizes at € 39,50. In the back of the shop a large section is dedicated to seconds at € 19,50 for M/W and € 8,00 for Ch, again with a lot of choice. Worthwhile also to find jeansy jackets, mini and maxi jeans skirts and non iron chinos. Prices are very competitive.

Giesse Scampoli

Via Ca' di Cozzi, 22 - 37100 Verona (VR)   045 8301099
9.00-12.30/15.00-19.30. Sat. 9.00-19.00   C.C.:None

Fabrics, home furnishings, household linen
BARGAIN BASEMENT

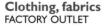

From Verona take the road to Parona. On the right, a large shop with ample parking.

Fabrics per meter or per kilo, impossible not to find some nice bit of material for a cushion or unfinished towels Made in U.S.A. sold per kilo, silk prints by famous designers, woollens from Scotland, furnishing fabrics for curtains or table clothes. Good deals also in fake fur, velvets, flannels, eiderdowns and notions.

Mavecon

Via dell'Esperanto, 20/b - 37135 Verona (VR)   045 9211611
8.30-12.30/14.30-19.00   C.C.:None

Clothing, fabrics
FACTORY OUTLET

Autostrada A4, exit Verona Sud. Follow 'altre direzione' and take the first road to the right 3 times. Mavecon is situated in a freestanding brown building just before the autostrada bypass and near Brugi. Parking.

Extensive collection of men's clothing in good quality and up to date designs. Suits € 135,00 in sizes up to 60 (XXL), jackets € 97,50, pants € 37,50, vests, knitwear 'Sèvres' in merino wool, bombers in kid skin € 238,00. A corner with remnants in summer wool sold per kilo € 8,00, jeans by Rica Lewis € 5,00, flannel shirts by 'The Golf Club' € 17,50.

Calzaturificio Itersan

Via Meucci, 62   Z.I. S.Agostino - 36057 Arcugnano (VI)   0444 288673
9.00-12.30/15.00-18.30. Sat. 9.30-19.00   C.C.:None

Shoes
FACTORY OUTLET

Autostrada A4, exit Vicenza Ovest and the Zona Industriale to the right, at the roundabout turn right, at the end of the road turn right, continue for two km. At Arcugnano continue till the supermarket and turn left, follow the signs for Itersan.

Itersan produces two different collections, one for hospitals, the other strictly for tired feet. The wooden sandals, leather clogs and rubber soled walking shoes are all made for those who are on their feet all day long, well made and low prices. For the more mature there is a small room stocked with comfort shoes, classical models, with inlays and laces, in soft deerskin leather, with double soles, extra width etc. at € 70,00, sample size 37 for W, 40 for M, € 35.00. Very helpful personnel.

A.B.C. Ceramiche

Vicolo Ca'Erizzo, 15 - 36061 Bassano del Grappa (VI)   0424 524364
8.30-11.30/14.30-17.00. Saturday closed   C.C.:None

Ceramics, terracotta, porcelain
ARTISAN'S WORKSHOP

From the center of Bassano take the direction of Trento for circa 2 km. In Via S. Vito look for a narrow road on the left with a sign A.B.C. Ceramiche.

All the typical ceramics of this region: large plates made of bundles of asparagus, a turkey shaped tureen complete with spoon, artichoke plates with matching sauce boats, pumpkin serving dishes and strawberry baskets. This is their showroom for wholesalers, sometimes they can not sell certain items, but choice is overwhelming and discounts can be as high as 50%.

Perdomello Ceramiche

Viale Vicenza, 93C - 36061 Bassano del Grappa (VI)   0424 502118
8.00-12.00/13.30-18.00. Saturday closed   C.C.:None

Ceramics, terracotta, porcelain
ARTISAN'S WORKSHOP

From the center of Bassano pass the river and take Viale Diaz and S.S. 248 to Nove/Marostica. On the left, after F.lli Cavalli and just after the Agip/Q8 service station.

The showroom is above the workshop, holding a large collection of highly unusual and decorative ceramic objects like greek columns, large vases with guirlands, life size statues, coffee tables, horses heads, gigantic baskets with fruit, busts and portrets in biscuit. They let you browse and ship everywhere.

Calzaturificio Kaina

Z.I. Capese - Via Div. Tridentina, 3   0424 80360
36061 Bassano del Grappa - Campese (VI)   C.C.:All Major
8.00-12.00/14.00-19.30

Shoes
FACTORY OUTLET

From Bassano take the superstrada to Trento. In Solagna there is a sign for Kaina on the left, a narrow road that will take you to the Campese-Campolongo road.

Everyday and bad weather shoes for M & W, super comfort slippers, 'Scholl's' type sandals, flexible clogs with leather uppers at good prices. Offers in Itersan slippers, cork soles, all sizes. Men's shoes in nabuk leather, brandname 'Roads' € 54,00, sandals for W by Anna Moretti € 49,50. There is a corner with special offers and lots of choice.

Space Outlet

Via Nazionale, 68 - 36056 Belvedere di Tezze (VI)   0424 564777
10.00-13.00/15.00-19.30   C.C.:All Major

Clothing
BARGAIN BASEMENT

On the S.S. Bassano-Cittadella, in the center of Belvedere, on the corner of the square on the left.

Dolce e Gabbana, Cavalli, Richmond, Voyage London, Tommy Hilfiger, Ballantyne e Patty Shelabarger all in Lolita sizes, terribly with-it and originating from showroom collections. A dress by Patty Shelabarger € 139,00, a knitted bolero € 79,00, tiger printed lingerie by Roberto Cavalli, tops covered in paillettes € 50,00.

Marzotto Factory Store

Via Einaudi, 5 - 36040 Brendola (VI)   0444 492422
9.30-12.30/15.00-19.00   C.C.:All Major

Clothing
FACTORY OUTLET

Autostrada A4 exit Montecchio. Turn left (difficult) and left again, into a narrow road before the autostrada bridge. Parking outside the gates.

Trendy and fashionable quality clothes to live & work in for young professionals, brand names Ferré, Ferré Studio, Ferré Forma, GFF, Borgofiori Marlboro, Lebole, Principe Seawind and Brenda Ashe. Tremendous selection, spacious suroudings, discounts of 50% for seconds, regular merchandise at 35%. Corner with remnants and ribbons, sold per meter, special offers on sample sizes 42/44 for women, 46/48 for men at 40% less. Friendly service.

Biemme Sport

Via Oltre Agno, 32 - 36070 Brogliano (VI) 0445 947366
9.00-12.00/15.00-19.00 C.C.:All Major

Clothing, sports accessories
FACTORY OUTLET

Autostrada A4, exit Montecchio. Follow the directions for Valdagno, S.S. 246. The factory is on the left, a free standing building, a bit before Cornedo V. Parking outside the gates.

A large outlet for mountain bikers & Tour de France racers who can find all the equipment and accessories they need. Underwear that will prevent saddleburn, neon colored tops with back pockets € 20,00, cycling suits with logos, cycling shorts by Fila, 2nds, € 10,00, Biemme Hi-Tech underwear, gloves, helmets at discounts of 30%-50%.

G.T.Erre

Via E. Fermi, 5/Via degli Alpini - 36043 Camisano V.no (VI) 0444 611224
9.00-12.00/15.30-19.30. Closed Mon. & 5/8 - 22/8 C.C.:All Major

Jewelry
DISCOUNTS

Autostrada A4, exit Vicenza Est, from Torri di Quartesolo follow the directions for Camisano V. G.T.Erre is on the right coming from Vicenza, in a cluster of new shops, on the main road at the beginning of Camisano.

Worth the trip for those looking for jewelry, watches and silver frames at nice discounts. Gold is sold per gram at fair market price, but one saves circa 25% on the finished product; rings, necklaces, bracelets and brooches in gold with or without precious stones. Silver frames and icons are 50% off, watches circa 15%. Busy, with a number system at the entrance.

Gold Knit

Via Roma, 13 - 36042 Breganze (VI) 0445 873156
9.00-12.00/15.30-19.30 C.C.:None

Knitwear, cashmere
FACTORY OUTLET

From the traffic light in the center of the village, take Via Roma to the left.

Knitwear in medium/high quality for M/W, classical, super trendy, flashy, sorted by color, large choice, for which you'll rarely spend more than € 79. Short cropped cardigans, miniskirts and in winter classical cashmere twinsets at equally competitive prices. In summer embroidered T-shirts, tops in viscose € 31-58, twinset in cotton € 53. For men V-necks in merino wool € 37.

Spaccio Nogara

Viale Italia, 77 - 36051 Creazzo (VI) 0444 520611
8.30-12.00/15.00-18.00. Closed Mon. C.C.:All Major

Clothing
FACTORY OUTLET

Autostrada A4, exit Vicenza Ovest to the Fiera and Verona and the S.S. 11 from Vicenza to Olmo di Creazzo. At the traffic light whith on the corner the Cantina San Matteo follow the sign for Creazzo. In the center, on the left, a tall factory building.

A very large outlet offering classical, very well made suits, jackets and pants for the more mature at extremely competitive prices. This is a good place to renew a wardrobe without going broke. The price for a woollen jacket starts at € 79,00. They also make to measure and do alterations.

Maglificio Brian Rita

Via Farneda, 17 - 36030 Fara Vicentino (VI)　　　　　0445 897103
8.00-12.00/13.30-17.30. Saturday closed　　　　　　　C.C.:None

Knitwear, cashmere
ARTISAN'S WORKSHOP

Autostrada 31, exit Dueville to Breganza. At the traffic light of Breganze turn right to Mason Vicentino, at the T to Salcedo turn left, pass S. Giorgio di Perlena, continue to Salcedo/Fara till the sign for Maglificio Brian Rita.

This address is a bit far out but worth it for those in search of lovely knitwear in cashmere, mohair and merino wool or shimmering gold, bronze or silver colored tops in viscose or cotton at low prices. Twinsets in cashmere in pale grey and taupe €110.00, special offers, 2nds, at € 10,00, nice ribbed sweaters for M, they work for some snazzy international brandnames. All sizes, also XXL.

Furetto

Via Giovanni XXIII, 47 - 36020 Fellette di Romano (VI)　　　0424 383345
9.00-12.00/16.00-19.00　　　　　　　　　　　　　　　C.C.:All Major

Shoes
FACTORY OUTLET

From Bassano to Fellette di Romano on the local road. At the church at the crossing turn left, continue for 50 m, immediately on the left.

Casual and sporty shoes like leather sneakers or wholesome Birkenstock type sandals by Trussardi. Kids' shoes by Furetto € 20,00, tennis shoes for men by Trussardi € 30,00, leather dress shoes for M € 55,00, special offers in Clarks loafers € 35,00. Showroom size for M 41, for W 37 at € 32,50 circa.

Christia Confezioni

Via Praelle,1 - 36063 Marostica (VI)　　　　　　　　0424 470065
8.30-12.30/14.30-18.00. Saturday closed　　　　　　　C.C.:None

Furs, leatherware
FACTORY OUTLET

From Marostica to Breganze, on the main road, about 800 m from the center after a service station, a large square on the left.

The shearling and sheepskin coats by Cristia are very well known in Northern Europe and Russia because of their unusual designs and beautiful workmanship. A long coat with a high collar in fur, a scarf made of pleated fur attached to a fur-lined hood, a cossack type coat with tresses, all made for Siberian temperatures. Special prices for showroom models and they make to order.

Spaccio Belfe

Corso della Ceramica, 76 - 36063 Marostica (VI)　　　　0424 75058
9.00-12.30/15.00-19.00　　　　　　　　　　　　　　　C.C.:All Major

Clothing, sportswear, casual
FACTORY OUTLET

The Belfe outlet has moved away from pretty Marostica. Take the superstrada from Bassano, exit Nove, it's 50 m. up the road. A free standing building with parking. On the right of the entrance is a Stefanel outlet.

Ski outfits, lightweight performance vests and jackets, bermudas, polos, down vests and sweaters, sporty clothing that is contemporary, never sloppy. Special offers, seconds and remainders at 50%. Prices are sort of okay for the quality they offer. There is another outlet selling their current collection at -20%, inside the actual Belfe factory in Via Festa. Follow the indications for the Carabinieri.

Prandina & Co.
Via Marconi, 59 - 36064 Mason Vincentino (VI)
8.00-12.00/14.30-18.00

0424 411792
C.C.:All Major

Clothing, leatherwear
FACTORY OUTLET

Autostrada A4 per Valdastico A31, exit Dueville, to Breganze. At the traffic light to the right, circa 4 km, at the beginning of Mason Vic. on the right.

A very up-to-date collection of leatherwear, very cool. A blazer in black nappa € 360,00, a men's jacket in deerskin € 250,00 - € 400,00, a three-piece nappa suit for W in red or taupe € 550,00, also made to measure. A coat with the Joseph label, grey and very smoothly styled € 375,00, a sheepskin in apple green, with long fur at the wrists, 70's style, cow girl pants, today's etno mix, interesting.

Dainese Top Ten
Via Roma, 63 - 36060 Molvena (VI)
9.00-12.30/16.00-19.30

0424 411624
C.C.:All Major

Clothing, leatherwear
FACTORY OUTLET

Autostrada A31 (Valdastico), exit Dueville to Marostica on the S.S. 248. Take the local road to Mason Vicentino.

Dainese Top Ten is a very famous brand name for leather motorcycle and mountain bike 'top to toe' outfits. Styles are super macho, primary colors or total black, with red, yellow or orange accents. This is not a place for shrinking violets. Gloves, boots, helmets, overalls in leather with bomber jackets (€ 870,00) all by Dainese. Large choice, all the latest models are on show.

German's
Via Villa, 45 - 36060 Molvena (VI)
8.00-12.00/13.30-18.15. Sat. 8.00-12.00

0424 708160
C.C.:None

Clothing, leatherwear
ARTISAN'S WORKSHOP

Autostrada A31, exit Dueville, turn left to S.S. Marosticana, past the bridge, left to Breganze, follow sign for Mason Vicentino. Once there, look for Banca S. Giorgio, take the small road in front to the outlet at the end.

Leatherwear of their own production: jackets, long coats, trousers and skirts. Sizes from 42 to 56, but they produce a lot of 'made to measure'. These are very fashionable and well made clothes that will look good anywhere, jackets start at € 350,00 and up, pants from € 200,00 and up.

Surplus Diesel
Via Ponticello, 34 - 36060 Molvena (VI)
9.00-19.00

0424 411811
C.C.:All Major

Clothing
FACTORY OUTLET

From Marostica take the local road to Mason Vicentino, Surplus is on the right, look for a sign saying 'Welcome', Surplus. Parking in front. The first floor sells the seconds and remainders.

On the 1st floor mountains of T-shirts, tops and jeans from € 10,50 - € 24,50, confusion and no hope to find larger sizes. Diesel is definitely for the young and slim, it's all a bit mad, with a used look, although brand new. Platform shoes, rhinestone boots, studded cowboy belts, all very amusing. On the ground floor other brand-names like Diesel, Betsey Johnson N.Y., Kookai, LiuJo, Fairley at normal shop prices.

Global Store Montècchio

Viale Europa, 98 - 36063 Montècchio (VI)   0444 496660
9.00-12.30/15.30-19.30   C.C.:All Major

Knitwear, cashmere
FACTORY OUTLET

Autostrada A4, exit Montecchio M. Turn right to Montecchio and the S.S. 246 and Viale Europa, Global store is on the left.

Knitwear in fashionable designs, in wool or cashmere, by Avon Celli or Fenzi, two brandnames known for their quality and workmanship. All sizes available from XS to XXL, classical V-necks, polos, twinsets, and every possible variation thereof. Very chic colours. They have another outlet in Longastrino, in the province of Ferrara.

Sorelle Ramonda Stockhouse

Viale Trieste - 36075 Montecchio Maggiore (VI)   0444 491575
9.00-12.45/15.30-19.45   C.C.:All Major

Clothing
BARGAIN BASEMENT

Autostrada A4, exit Montecchio Maggiore, to the right, at the traffic light to the right direction of Vicenza. The Sorelle Ramonda Stockhouse is on the left after circa 100 meters. Parking.

All unsold items from the large Sorelle Ramonda store further up the road at no. 45 end up here. A rather eclectic collection of dressing gowns next to evening dresses at low prices. Marlborough jeans, 2 for € 20,00, Jeans Energy 2 for € 45,00. Also special offers, seconds etc. They accept credit cards but only for purchases of € 75,00 or more.

Argenterie Rossi & Arcandi

Via Astico, 2e/2f - 36010 Monticello Conte Otto (VI)   0444 946676
8.00-12.00/14.00-18.00. Sat. 8.30-12.00   C.C.:All Major

Silverware/Pewter
FACTORY OUTLET

Autostrada A31 (Valdastico), exit Vicenza Nord to Monticello. In the center of the village.

Elegant collection of silverware from pill-boxes to cutlery to silver frames and major candelabras. Also gift objects in silver and Murano glass. Prices depend on the workmanship involved, they produce for some major designers. The Vicenza area is known for their production of gold and silver jewelry and silver objects.

Tessitura Eger & Figli

Via Tenente Eger, 17 - 36065 Mussolente (VI)   0424 878441
9.00-12.00/14.30-17.30. Sat. 9.00-12.00   C.C.:All Major

Fabrics, home furnishings, household linen
FACTORY OUTLET

From Bassano d. Grappa to Asolo S.S. 248, then left to Mussolente. Take the road to Borso del Grappa, the outlet is 30 m. after their main store, on the left. An old villa next to the factory.

An oasis of good taste, attracting clients from everywhere, in search of original, attractive curtain and upholstery material at very acceptable prices and service with a smile. Damasco € 10,95 p.m., taftà € 8,95, madras € 7,96, matelassé € 12,95, large choice of curtain material at € 6,00 p.m. Remnants per kilo € 3,00. Nice sets of hand towels, napkins, ideal for presents.

Ceramica V.B.C.

Via Molini, 45 - 36055 Nove (VI)
8.00-18.00. Saturday 8.00-18.00

0424 590026
C.C.:All Major

Ceramics, terracotta, porcelain
ARTISAN'S WORKSHOP

In the center of Nove take the road to Bassano, circa 800 meters, on the left.

Nove is an important production center for ceramics. Plates, platters, table settings in country style, with fruit or flower decorations. Very popular with tourists are the serving dishes or soup tureens in the shape of a cabbage or pumpkin. Ideal for small presents, salad spoons € 10,00, salt and pepper sets in various animal shapes. It's all cheerful and colorful. They ship complete dinner sets to the U.S.A.

Ceramiche Alessi

Via Brenta, 2A - 36055 Nove (VI)
8.00-12.00/13.30-17.30. Saturday closed

0424 590031
C.C.:None

Ceramics, terracotta, porcelain
ARTISAN'S WORKSHOP

From the center of Nove take the road past the Museum of Ceramics.

Alessi produces original modern, classical and 'antique' bases for lamps in an unending variety and shape. Their regular collection is not for sale to the private public but they will sell you their seconds and end of series at important discounts. A ceramic base, country style, € 27,50, in aged wood with gold finishes € 35,00. Phone for an appointment mentioning this book.

Ceramiche Ancora

Via Martini, 26/28 - 36055 Nove (VI)
8.00-12.00/13.30-18.00. Saturday 8.00-12.00

0424 590023
C.C.:All Major

Ceramics, terracotta, porcelain
FACTORY OUTLET

From the center of Nove take the street leading to the Ceramic Museum, on the right of the church.

The outlet is in their warehouse. Large offer (over 13.000 objects) of ceramics for table settings or purely decorative, either regular or seconds. One can browse amidst the shelves full of plates in the shape of a cabbage or jugs in the form of a rooster. Design is classical, platters with lemons, baskets for strawberries, flowery garlands on vases. This outlet is popular with Americans but prices are not exactly low.

Ceramiche Barettoni

Via Molini, 3 - 36055 Nove (VI)
8.00-12.00/14.00-18.00. Sat. phone first

0424 590013
C.C.:All Major

Ceramics, terracotta, porcelain
ARTISAN'S WORKSHOP

In the center of Nove, at the cross roads, next to a Bar.

The oldest ceramics factory in the Nove region. They still produce center pieces for tables, decorative statues of a pastoral nature, platters and vases inspired by the age-old molds (1700-1800) of their factory collection. You can order a traditional platter with a design to your choice, with your coat of arms or initials, all hand made. They have a room full of seconds and remnants.

Ceramiche Rita Dal Prà

Via Munari, 102 - 36055 Nove (VI)   0424 590001
8.30-12.00/14.00-18.00. Sat. phone first. Closed in Aug.   C.C.:None

Ceramics, terracotta, porcelain
ARTISAN'S WORKSHOP

A rather interesting and very old buidling in the center of Nove, a little past the museum of ceramics, on the right.

Elaborate, baroque and rococo figurines in a biscuit type of white, '18th century style' angels, or plump young cupids, pastoral scenes painted with a delicate hand, Victorian dogs, small dalmatians with gold collars, sets for crocuses and vases for tulips. Also more modern center pieces. For a visit with a large group phone first, since these are rather 'breakable' surroundings. They speak English and French.

Stylnove Ceramiche

Via Munari, 102 - 36055 Nove (VI)   0424 829313
8.00-12.00/14.00-18.00. Saturday closed   C.C.:None

Ceramics, terracotta, porcelain
ARTISAN'S WORKSHOP

Stylnove Ceramiche is next door to Rita del Prà.

They produce grandiose horse's heads in gold or the head of David, Greek torsos or Greek columns with an antique finish, ceramic tables with a base of wheat sheafs, or in the form of tassled cushions, life size lions or stallions. They export all over the world.

Staff International

Via del Progresso, 10 - 36025 Noventa Vicentina (VI)   0444 760753
Telephone first   C.C.:None

Clothing
FACTORY OUTLET

From Padova to Este, from Milan and the A4, exit Soave to Lonigo and Noventa Vicentina.

Twice a year they organize a special sale for a couple of weeks of their summer or winter showroom collection made up of famous avantgarde fashion names. Snap up rococo corsets by Vivienne Westwood Red Label or Gym jeans, tailleurs by New York, interesting pieces by Alberto Biani, Costume National, Martin Margiela and Bella Freud. Phone to find out the right dates.

Maglificio M.D.

Via dell'Industria, 2 - 36040 Orgiano (VI)   0444 874799
8.30-12.30/15.00-19.00. Sat. 8.30-12.30   C.C.:None

Knitwear, cashmere
FACTORY OUTLET

Autostrada A4, exit Montecchio, to the left (very busy) for Brendola, Lonigo, and the direction of Noventa Vicentino. Maglificio M.D. is in a small I. Z. on the right, next to the Susimoda shoes outlet.

Knitwear by Kathleen Madden, understated, cool and well made. Jackets € 97,50 and matching skirts € 42,50 in sizes up to 46, twinsets by Authentic Women in gold/white stripes, some baskets with remnants. Polos, sleeveless tops in excellent quality € 24,50. The showroom collection is half price. For men less choice, a V-neck sweater in merinos € 24,50, but still worth a look. Friendly personnel.

Calzaturificio Zamberlan

Via Marconi, 1 - 36030 Pievebelvicino (VI)   0445 660999
9.00-12.00/16.00-19.00. Closed Monday   C.C.:All Major

Shoes
FACTORY OUTLET

From Schio take the S.S.46 in the direction of Pasubio. Turn left for Pievebelvicino, Zamberlan is in the center of the village, on the left.

Hiking boots and shoes in various models and weights, with names like Travel lite, Alpin Lite and Lady Lite. The sturdiest model, the Norwegian is € 120,00 and beautifully made, prices for the other models start at € 30,00. These are superior boots in sizes from 36-49, continental half sizes from 38.5 to 45.5. Also nice backpacks in soft leather, perfectly wearable in cities, € 90,00 in natural colors.

Euromanteau

Via Schio, 92 - 36036 Pievebelvicino (VI)   0445 660038
8.30-12.30/15.00-19.00   C.C.:All Major

Clothing
FACTORY OUTLET

Take the S.S. 46 from Schio to Rovereto. The factory is visible from the main road, turn left and immediately left again. Close to the Zanebet and Zamberlan outlets.

Racks of wintercoats for W. with fur collars, large sizes € 195,00 - € 275,00. Loden coats, montgomery's for men by Steinbock € 165,00. Winter skirts € 25,00. Plenty of beautifully made Austrian and Bavarian (dirndl) garments in sizes up to 54, or half sizes. Jackets in boiled wool, jeans jackets, blazers in nappa lined with boiled wool, edelweiss embroidery everywhere. Sale of summer suits in linen in November, good deals! This is a very large outlet with very well made, classical clothes in all sizes.

Siri Preziosi

Via Ponte, 15 - 36020 Ponte di Castegnero (VI)   0444 730028
9.00-12.00/15.00-19.00. Closed Monday   C.C.:All Major

Jewelry
DISCOUNTS

From Autostrada A4, exit Vicenza Est take the S.S. 247 Riviera Beriga till Ponte di Castagnero. At the traffic light the shop is next to the bridge.

Original reproductions of Sheffield silverplate from Victorian times, watches, gold jewelry (also made to measure), brandname jewels, silverware. Special promotional offers of silver frames and icons, silver gifts in 925/..o silver. Baby gifts. Discounts of 10% to 50% all year round. They speak English.

Francesco Biasia

Via dell'Artigianato, 2 - 36030 Povolaro (VI)   0444 360167
14.00-19.00. Sat. 9.30-12.30/15.30-19.00   C.C.:All Major

Handbags, leather goods
FACTORY OUTLET

Autostrada A4, exit Vicenza Ovest to the S.S. 248 and Bassano. Just before Povolaro, on the right, before the Agip service station, well indicated.

A new outlet for handbags, evening bags and small leather goods with the Evolution or Francesco Biasi brandname. Lots of handbags on special offer, € 5,00 - € 85.00, nicely modern, in leather, straw, for the beach or smart city bags, all very feminine. Watches and small leather purses € 15,00 and up. Busy.

Giesse Scampoli
Via Cap. Alessio, 162 - 36027 Rosà (VI)   0424 75058
9.00-12.30/15.00-19.30   C.C.:None
Sat. 9.00-12.30/14.00-19.30. Open in August

Fabrics, household linen
BARGAIN BASEMENT

S.S. 47 Padova-Bassano or from the Trento/Vicenza superstrada to Padova exit Rosa.

Fabrics per meter or per kilo, it is impossible not to find some nice bit of material for a cushion or heaps of unfinished towels Made in U.S.A. at € 5,00 per kilo. Silk prints by famous designers, woollens from Scotland, furnishing fabrics for curtains or table clothes per meter at low prices. Good deals also in fake fur, velvets, flannels, eiderdowns and notions.

Marilena Confezioni
Via Cusinati, 12 - 36028 Rossano Veneto (VI)   0424 545530
9.00-12.30/15.00-19.30   C.C.:All Major

Clothing, casual, jeans
FACTORY OUTLET

Rossano Veneto is a small village on the S.S. 245, between Bassano and Castelfranco Veneto. After the Esso service station turn right after 50 meters. The outlet is well indicated.

The 'Goose & Gander' collection for children and adults, practical, casual and sporty clothes for young families. 2nds in polo shirts di Goose & Gander € 15,00, waxed jackets for M at € 45,00, long floaty 70's dresses for W in viscosa € 55,00. Special offers galore especially for children, 2nds start at € 8,00.

Spaccio Franco Ziché
Via Perlena - 36030 S. Giorgio Perlena (Fara V.) (VI)   0445851231
15.00-19.00. Wed. & Sat.00-12.00/15.00-19.00   C.C.:None

Knitwear, cashmere
FACTORY OUTLET

Autostrada A31, exit Dueville, to Breganze. At the traffic light to the right to Lusiana-Asiago, at the intersection turn left, the first village is S. Giorgio Perlena, the outlet is on the right in the center.

1/3 of their production is destined for export, mostly to Germany but also the U.S., Canada and the Far East with new collections every season. Brandnames Franco Ziché, Kafka, Miss Harlow, they also work for Nazareno Gabrielli and Windsor. Knitwear by Ziché in viscosa, very stylish, € 60,00, 2nds € 17,00. remnants Kafka, (avantgarde) € 50,00, dresses by Miss Harlow (larger sizes) € 90,00, striped polos for M, 2nds € 9,00. Worth the trip.

Vircos Pelle
Via Meucci, 10 Z.I. - 36066 Sandrigo (VI)   0444 750130
8.15-12.15/14.00-18.00. Closed in August   C.C.:None

Clothing, leatherwear
ARTISAN'S WORKSHOP

Autostrada A31 Valdastico, exit Dueville direction Breganze. Vircos is on the left in the Industrial Zone of Sandrigo and well signposted.

A good address for classical sheepskin coats for men and women. Their Spanish shearlings (in April and May) are priced just over € 500,00, the Australian sheepskins will be around € 375,00 (heavier to wear than the Spanish variety but longlasting and equally warm). Shirts in goat skin € 225,00. They speak English and French.

Dottus Spaccio

S.S. Nuova Gasparona - 36030 Sarcedo (VI) 0445 344190
9.00-12.30/14.30-19.00 C.C.:All Major

Gifts, local products
FACTORY OUTLET

From Bassano take the Nuova Gasperona towards Thiene. Sarcedo is just after Breganze and the outlet is on the right in a small commercial plot. Parking.

Dottus specializes in useful objects with a twist: hot water bottles in the shape of breasts € 25,00, foldable pocket ashtrays € 8,00, bottle openers in brightly colored resina. Small furniture in metal/zinc and floor lamps called 'Fright', some seconds, but most of their collection is brand new and sold at regular shop prices.

Outlet-Shop Finanziaria

Via San Giuseppe, 122 - 36030 Sarcedo (VI) 0445 344519
9.00-12.30/15.30-20.00. Mon. & Thurs. closed C.C.:All Major

Clothing
DISCOUNTS

In the center of Sarcedo, on the 'Gasparona Vecchia' road, at the traffic light on the right.

Very well made and up to date clothing for men in beautiful fabrics by Loro Piana, Cerruti. A suit in Tasmania by Loro Piana € 120,00, a linen jacket in clotted cream beige by Scuderi € 170,00. Also suits by Scuderi, knitwear by Morgana, a ribbed sweater in cotton € 45,00, jackets start at € 79,00, shirts from € 35,00. All sizes available, worth a visit.

Maglificio Sartori

Via Paraiso, 60 - 36015 Schio (VI) 0445 678156
9.00-12.30/15.30-19.30. Open in August C.C.:All Major

Clothing, sportswear, casual
FACTORY OUTLET

Autostrada A31, Valdastico, exit Thiene-Schio, follow the indications for Schio. Jockey is just before Schio on the left.

The current collection of Marc O'Polo, Peter Mass, Cacherel (3 printed T-shirts € 25,00), Daniel Hechter, Valeria Sartori, Bleifrei, Jockey underwear all at a 20% discount. The 1st floor is entirely dedicated to special offers and samples or prototypes. Also large bins full of seconds € 9,00. Sales from July to September and from January to March. Multilingual personel. Alteration service. Busy and popular.

Marzotto Factory Store

V.le dell'Industria, 126 - 36015 Schio (VI) 0445 693478
9.30-12.30/15.00-19.00 C.C.:All Major

Clothing, household linen
FACTORY OUTLET

Autostrada A31, exit Thiene to Schio. In Schio take VI.e Industria to the right, keep going to their enormous factory complex and large parking.

Blankets and quilted bedspreads by Lanerossi. Thermoblankets 2 pers. € 65,00, 'Samarkand' blankets 30% off, pale colors, velvet borders. Remnants in blankets, velvet ribbons and seconds at a 40% discount. Also sportswear, classical clothing and household linen by Ferrè, knitwear by Marlborough.

Cat Studio Spaccio

Via Colleoni, 18 - 36010 Thiene (VI)　　　　　0445370449
9.30-12.00/15.30-19.00. Closed Wednesday　　　C.C.:All Major

Clothing, sportswear, casual
FACTORY OUTLET

In the center of Thiene, on the level of Piazza S.Pio X. Parking.

Highly specialized outlet for fitness, dancing and ballet outfits, brandname Freddy. Sweatshirts, parka's, T's, bodysuits and warm-up pants, in cotton, very pale colours, old rose, white, pearly grey. Large containers with seconds and samples. Modern shop. All sizes.

Cristiano di Thiene

Via del Lavoro, 25 - 36016 Thiene (VI)　　　　0445 380330
8.00-12.30/14.00-18.00. Sat. closed　　　　　C.C.:All Major

Clothing, leatherwear
FACTORY OUTLET

Autostrada A31, exit Thiene. The main road to the center crosses Via del Lavoro in the industrial area. Cristiano di Thiene is on the right, on a corner after a rooundabout.

Superlight, supersoft sheepskins, short, 3/4 length or long, all Spanish skins, beautifully made, classical or fashionable. Count on circa € 600,00 for a long, nearly floorlength coat. Large choice in black leather blazers and bombers, skirts and trousers in spring colours. They also stock unusual pieces like the capri pants in embroidered suede. They sell the showroom collection in September.

Confezioni Campagnolo

Via Pasubio, 16/b - 36027 Rosa Cusinati (VI)　　0424 861185
9.00-12.00/15.00-19.00　　　　　　　　　　　C.C.:All Major

Clothing, leatherwear
ARTISAN'S WORKSHOP

From Cittadella to Bassano on the S.S. 247. In the center of Cusinati follow their sign to the left.

Their own production of leather wear and shearling coats. Shirts in kid skin, latest styles € 260, in peccary € 105. Sheepskin coats start at € 389, all in good looking flattering shapes, all sizes available. Very good prices.

Nuova Taela Guy Rover

Viale Europa, 47 - 36016 Thiene (VI)　　　　　0445 380965
9.00-12.30/15.30-19.30　　　　　　　　　　　C.C.:All Major

Clothing, shirts
FACTORY OUTLET

Autostrada A321, exit Thiene to the center. At the level of Hotel Torresin continue to Lugo, Sarcedo, Marostica, (Via Valsugana, Viale Val Cismon). At the roundabout turn left into Viale Europa. The shop is on the left in a small shopping center.

A lovely shop with lots of pretty clothes to choose from. They sell to some major luxury stores in Milan, Rome, New York and their style is sassy but chic. A dress with matching jacket in silk € 99,00, stupendous colours, sizes from 38 to 48. For men very nice shirts in xfine cotton € 25,00, polos € 20,00, all end of line or unsold. Worth a visit to update one's wardrobe at a fraction of the normal shop price.

Spaccio Borse

Via Roma, 108 - 36040 Torri di Quartesolo (VI)   0444 582367
8.30-12.00/15.00-19.00. Saturday 8.30-12.00   C.C.:All Major

Handbags
ARTISAN'S WORKSHOP

Autistrada A4, exit Vicenza Est, to the right and at the crossing with traffic light turn right, a very busy street. The shop is a bit further ahead, on the right and in front of a bank.

Handbags by Tosca Blu, Blumarine, Blugirl, Roberto Cavalli and their own brand-name Marisa. A shopping bag in fake crocodile € 50,00, a Kelly in fake croco with zip € 60,00, boxy bags, hobo bags in lizard printed leather or metallic red patent leather. The quality is ok, there are lots of up to date bags to choose from.

Antinea - Armani Factory Store

Via Stazione, 93 - 36070 Trissino (VI)   0445 492105
10.00-19.00. Monday 15,00-19,00   C.C.:All Major

Clothing
FACTORY OUTLET

Autostrada A4, exit Montecchio to Valdagno/Recoaro for circa 5/6 km. Antinea is on the right, a free standing building.

Large floor space devided in M/W areas offering the Armani collection of suits, dresses and jackets/trousers, mostly elegant, (The Emporio Armani collection is for sale in the province of Modena) but the inventory changes all the time. All the Armani colours, cream, pale beige, taupe, Milan grey and black, are well represented, more choice in size 42. Women's suits € 255,00, M pants € 75,00, M suits € 275,00. Armani underwear for M, a few Armani jeans at € 22,50, 2nds.

Marzotto Factory Store

Via dei Lanifici - 36078 Valdagno - Maglio di Sopra (VI)   0445 427512
10.00-12.30/15.00-19.00. Sat. 10.00-19.00   C.C.:All Major

Clothing
FACTORY OUTLET

Autostrada A4, exit Montecchio M and S.S. 246 to Valdagno for circa 18 km. The actual factory outlet is about one kilometer north of the main Marzotto complex, on the right with parking inside the gate.

Marlborough sportswear, two-piece suits by Borgofiori in wool or cotton up to size 52 and discounted circa 35%, bridal party dresses, tweedy jackets for office wear, chic grey pin stripe suits by Ferré for elegant men but also special offers in men's suits. Racks with samples, dresses in size 42 for W, discounted 40%. Large offer of blankets by Lanerossi. Impossible not to find something.

Al 94

Corso Fogazzaro, 94 - 36100 Vicenza (VI)   0444 546213
9.30-12.30/15.30-19.30   C.C.:None

Clothing
BARGAIN BASEMENT

Near Piazza S. Lorenzo in the center of Vicenza.

Al 94 sells the showroom collections of Max Mara, Prisma, Pianoforte, Basile and Marzotto at nice discounts and not only in 42 but also in the more popular sizes. This is really the kind of place to visit often since merchandise changes all the time. Fair offer of silk scarves and ties, shirts for discerning men and cashmere cable knitwear. Worthwhile for eagle eyed bargain hunters.

Bottega Veneta

Viale della Scienza, 15 - 36100 Vicenza (VI)
9.00-13.00/14.00-19.00. Closed Saturday

0444 396504
C.C.:All Major

Handbags, leathergoods, shoes
FACTORY OUTLET

Autostrada A4, exit Vicenza Ovest, to the left for the Zona Fiera, at the roundabout turn left, continue for circa 100 m., on the left, with a garden in front.

End of line and showroom models of the famous Bottega Veneta handbags in pleated leather. Prices are discounted 50% for black or brandy colored clutch bags or moss green and bordeaux satchel bags. During their sales W slingbacks, sample size 37, at € 75,00, boots in faux croco at circa € 125,00. For men less choice, one type of lace-up Oxford only, size 43 and up. Sales in July. Worthwhile outlet despite the prices because it's all so stylish.

Cash & Gold

Viale della Scienza, 14 - 36100 Vicenza (VI)
9.00-13.00/15.30-19.30

0444 965947
C.C.:All Major

Jewelry
GOOD PRICES

Autostrada A4, exit Vicenza Ovest, to the right for the industrial zone and at the roundabout to the left, circa 100 mt on the right, there is a large sign.

A 1200 sqm first floor outlet of silver and gold jewelry, picture frames, cups, small presents, a very large choice of precious objects from € 2,50 - € 15,000,00. One can wander around and choose something without pressure, prices are wholesale. They speak English, French and German.

Gold Lion

Via Lanza, 23 - 36100 Vicenza (VI)
9.00-12.00/15.00-19.00

0444 964417
C.C.:All Major

Silverware
ARTISAN'S WORKSHOP

Autostrada A4, exit Vicenza Ovest, Via Scaligeri, Viale Sole. Turn right, Strada Cattane and first to the right.

Small shop with beautiful silver objects, the address to get a really smashing picture frame, hand made and hammered with nails, which gives an uneven but very authentic surface. Very notable and attractive! They work to order. Also antique tea services in silver, plates, objects in crystal and silver.

Green Tree Shop

Viale della Scienza, 46/48 - 36100 Vicenza (VI)
9.00-12.30/15.30-19.30. Monday closed

0444 960456
C.C.:All Major

Clothing
FACTORY OUTLET

Autostrada A4, exit Vicenza Ovest. At the roundabout turn left. Castelli Green Tree is on the right, just before super market 'Il Gransole'.

A place to visit often. Polo shirts by Jaeger, Bogner or Etienne Aigner, (all seconds) € 18, knitwear in avantgarde styles and innovative mixtures of wool by Kathleen Madden at very competitive prices. Suits for W in linen € 69, tops in viscose or viscose/linen start at € 11. For men, apart from the polo shirts, less choice.

Zenith Maria Elena Lovison

Via del Fabbro, 13 - 36100 Vicenza (VI)
9.30-12.30/15.30-19.00. Saturday 9.30-12.30

0444 303063
C.C.:All Major

Handbags, leather goods
FACTORY OUTLET

Autostrada A4, exit Vicenza Est, to Caserme Ederle. At the traffic light go straight, pass 2nd traffic light. After two service stations turn left, another 500 m and Via Gasparella is on the left. Zenith is at the level of the stop sign.

Production of handbags and small leather goods by Zenith and Maria Elena Lovinson in modern, streamlined and high-tech styles at medium quality. This is the right place to stock up on gifts for the young and trendy: shopping bags, trunk or hobo bag styles in unusual colours, faux reptile with metal lockets, book bags and city backpacks. Good prices.

Spaccio Milton

Via Manzoni, 119 - 36010 Zané (VI)
9.00-12.30/15.30-19.30. Closed Monday

0445 362350
C.C.:None

Shirts
FACTORY OUTLET

Milton is just after Thiene, towards Schio, on the right and in front of the shopping center Emisfero.

Very cool and goodlooking men's shirts in pure cotton by David Freeman € 30,00, very stylish, jackets in pure wool, classical, nice. Soft corduroy women's shirts, cotton and washed silk blouses start at € 22,50. Seconds in shirts and blouses start at € 15,00.

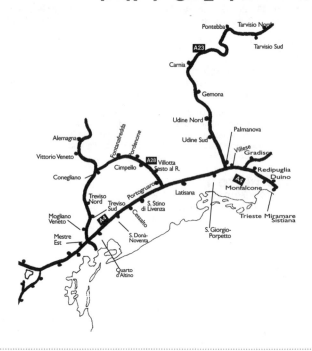

Sedialand

Via Udine, 26 - 33044 Manzano (GO)   0432 745547
9.30-12.30/14.30-19.30. Saturday 9.00-19.30.   C.C.:All Major
Monday closed

Furniture
FACTORY OUTLET

Autostrada A23, exit Udine Sud to Manzano. Sedialand is the first shop on the left in Manzano and close to the Agip service station.

The area around Manzano is known for the production of chairs. The furniture in this large factory hall is produced by the Italsvenska company and apart from chairs they sell tables and some office furniture but no cupboards or garden furniture. Transport and assemblage is up to the client.

Allo Spaccio

Via Terza Armata, 30 - 34074 Monfalcone (GO)   0481 410600
9.00-12.30/15.00-19.30   C.C.:All Major

Clothing, sportswear, casual
FACTORY OUTLET

Autostrada A4, exit Monfalcone est, at 200 m.

A large complex full of woollen sweaters, track suits and skisuits in splashy colours by Linea Kappa, Robe di Kappa and Jesus Jeans at low prices. For those who like digging into baskets with special offers, this is it! On the right their current collection, coordinates, blazers, skirts, all in sturdy no-nonsense shapes and fabrics, ideal for sporty families.

La Delizia

Via Udine, 24 - 33072 Casarsa della Delizia (PN)   0434 869564
8.30-12.00/15.30-19.30   C.C.:All Major

Wine, liqueurs
FACTORY OUTLET

On the local road S.S. 13 Pordenone - Udine on the right in the middle of the village.

A major producer of white & red wines and spumante. Pinot Grigio La Delizia € 3,50, Pinot Bianco € 2,50, Cabernet € 2,30, Refosco € 2,60. A 'Gran Spumante', € 5,00. There is a tasting bar next to the factory full of locals sipping their 'bianchino' or glass of white wine.

Consorzio Coltellinai

P. Italia, 11 - 33085 Maniago (PN)   0427 71744
8.30-12.30/15.30-19.30   C.C.:All Major

Household goods, various
FACTORY OUTLET

Maniago is north of Pordenone, follow the Strada Provinciale 251. The Consorzio Coltellinai is in the center on the main town square.

Maniago is known for the production of fine hunting knives, pocket knives, knives for kitchen use, table knives etc. Gift sets of hunting or barbecue knives with horn handles or inlaid with walnut or other fine woods, highly specialized, beautiful workmanship.

De Antoni Carnia

Via Roma, 41 - 33023 Corneglians (UD)   0433 60451
9.00-12.30/15.00-19.30   C.C.:All Major

Clothing
ARTISAN'S WORKSHOP

Autostrada A23, exit Carnia, at the beginning of the village in a free standing house.

Jackets, vests, capes and wall hangings in wool. Production of the Walkjanker, famous jackets in boiled wool, very soft and warm, all hand made and in beautiful colors, € 210,00 circa, the kind of jacket that never wears out. Long scarves € 50,00.

Nuova Tiglio

S.S. Udine-Spilimbergo, 175 - 33030 Fagagna (UD)   0432 8108801
15.30-19.30. Saturday 9.00-12.00/15.30-19.30   C.C.:All Major

Clothing
FACTORY OUTLET

From Udine to Fagagna, on the main road on the left in the same building as the 'Rivendita Auto'.

A very good address to find men's suits made with fabrics by Loro Piana, Zegna and Policarpo. All suits are in refined good taste, sober but elegant. All sizes available. They also work for Pal Zileri. Worth the detour.

Spaccio Caffi
S.S. 352, V.le Grado, 5 - 33050 Lauzacco Pavia di Udine (UD)   0432 675276
9.00-12.30/15.30-19.30   C.C.:All Major

Household linen, various
FACTORY OUTLET

Autostrada A4, exit Palmanova (a famous renaissance city founded in the late 16th century and worth a visit), to the S.S. 352 and Udine. At the level of Risana, on the left.

They sell anything to do with the furnishing of a bedroom: bedspreads, either quilted, in jacquard or in chenille, sheets, mattress covers and plaids. Also fabrics for curtains and bedspreads, in linen/cotton or stretchy mixtures to cover sofas and chairs. Always busy so prices must be good!

Cab Salotti & Dintorni
S.S. 352, Loc. Lauzacco - 33050 Pavia di Udine (UD)   0432 675136
9.00-12.30/15.30-19.30. Open on Sunday from 1/10 - 1/5   C.C.:None

Furniture, various
FACTORY OUTLET

Autostrada A23, exit Udine Sud to the S.P. 352 and Lauzacco di Pavia di Undine. From Udine on the right, near Linea Caffi.

Production of upholstered furniture, sofas, chairs, beds, from the sleek and streamlined to classical Victorian. All the covers are removable, even in alcantara. Large choice of exclusive fabrics, (more than 3000) in prime materials at very competitive prices.

Nonino
Via Aquillea 104, Percoto - 33050 Pavia di Udine (UD)   0432 676331
8.30-12.00/14.00-17.30. Saturday closed   C.C.:None

Wine, liqueurs
FACTORY OUTLET

Autostrada A4, exit Palmanova, take the S.S. 352 to Udine, turn right at Percoto.

Their outlet is inside the factory, a pleasant tasting room offers the possibility to sample the various grappas and amaro liqueurs. A bottle of Superior grappa € 13,00 their famous amaro € 8,00. Very nice gift packs and 'Italian design' bottles make this an ideal place to buy presents.

F.G.M.
Vicolo Taglio, 8 Z.I. - 33050 Rivignano (UD)   0432 774554
8.30-11.30/13.45-17.00. Saturday 9.00-11.30   C.C.:None

Clothing
FACTORY OUTLET

Autostrada A4, exit Latisana. At the intersection turn left to Rivignano and the center. At the traffic light turn right, continue for 800 m. then to the left for the Industrial Zone.

Production of very well made trousers in various styles (€ 60,00 - € 80,00) with fabrics by Loro Piana, Luigi Botto and others in wool, flannel, corduroy, cover, summer wool, shetland and stretch fabrics. All sizes are available, but no seconds. It's possible to find remnants to match for a jacket. They export all over the world and work for major brandnames. Worthwhile.

Zilco Due

Via Madonna di Strada, 22 - 33048 S.Giovanni al Natisone (UD)   0432758025
8.30-12.00/13.30-18.00   C.C.:None

Furniture, various
FACTORY OUTLET

Autostrada A4, exit Palmanova to San Giovanni/Manzano, continue for 10 km, look out for the Zilco Due sign on the left.

An important producer of furniture, chairs and tables in wood, brandname Zilco Due. Circa 45% of their production is destined to furnish hotels, offices, congress rooms outside of Italy. Design is modern (but not too modern).

La Casa del Prosciutto

Via T.Ciconi, 24 - 33038 San Daniele del Friuli (UD)   0432 957422
8.30-12.30/14.30-18.30. Tuesday closed   C.C.:None

Food, local products
GOOD PRICES

In the center of San Daniele, pass the Hospital, go up to Piazza 4 Novembre, turn to the left.

San Daniele is famous for the production of raw ham. In this shop one can find raw ham, cooked or smoked ham, ham cooked in a bread crust, in a paper bag, grilled etc. Also excellent salami from the Friuli area.

L I G U R I A

Arianna Cashmere

Via Repubblica, 29 - 16013 Campo Ligure (GE)
9.00-12.00/15.00-18.00. Sat. phone first

010 921054
C.C.: None

Knitwear, cashmere
ARTISAN'S WORKSHOP

From Genova to Alessandria on the A26, exit Masone. Turn left to Campo Ligure, it's immediately on the right, after the Carabinieri.

Long scarves in cashmere and silk € 35,00, cardigans in cashmere € 165,00, twin sets in cashmere € 195,00. It is possible to find some very good bargains during the sales period at low prices for excellent quality.

Maglificio Elsa Massucco

Via de Gasperi, 60 - 16030 Casarza Ligure (GE)
8.00-12.00/14.00-19.30

0185 46032
C.C.:All Major

Knitwear, cashmere
ARTISAN'S WORKSHOP

Autostrada A12, exit Sestri Levante to Casarza. After the church and the bridge turn right. Elsa Massucco is immediately after Champion.

Cashmere, cashmere/wool, merinos, well made knitwear for M/W in classical shapes and soft colours. Cardigans in 6-ply rib knit with zip, twinsets in pastel colours, also made to measure. Even in summer there is always a good choice and their new winter collection arrives in September.

F.lli Levaggi
Via Parma 469 - 16043 Chiavari (GE)   0185 383092
8.00-12.00/14.00-19.00. Saturday 16.00-19.00   C.C.: None

Furniture, various
ARTISAN'S WORKSHOP

Autostrada A12, exit Lavagna, turn right and follow the directions for Chiavari after the bridge.

Chiavari has been famous as the center of production for Chiavari chairs, elegant chairs on spindly legs, often gilded. At this artisan's workshop it is still possible to find the original version and many variations thereof at reasonable prices.

Ferrari Roberto
Vc. Casano, 18r - 16123 Genova (GE)   010 2474511
8.30-12.30/15.00-19.00   C.C.:None

Fabrics, home furnishings, household linen
BARGAIN BASEMENT

In Genova's old town, near Piazza De Ferrari. On the side of the Carlo Felice theater, on the corner of the Farmacia and the Banca di Lodi, follow the road into the old city for 80 m.

Give-away prices for curtain material, glass curtains, and various remnants sold per meter or per kilo. Old world atmosphere, topsy-turvy merchandise, friendly and very polite personnel. True bargains.

Liapull
Via Frà Vincenzo da Fiorenzuola, 72 - 16127 Genova (GE)   010 2423177
9.30-18.00. Saturday 9.30-12.30   C.C.:All Major

Knitwear, cashmere
ARTISAN'S WORKSHOP

Autostrada A7, exit Genova Ovest to the center, Piazza Principale, Salita Granarolo.

Knitwear in cashmere, silk and other precious fibers at prices from € 50,00 to € 250,00. Samples (size 44 for W.) and showroom collection at half price. Sizes for W up to 48, for M. up to 64. They produce a special collection in cashmere for children from 2 years and up. Nice discounts on end of season, samples or display articles.

Magazzini del Cotone
Via Morin, 32r - 16129/1 Genova (GE)   010 5704399
9.00-19.30 . Sat. closed   C.C.:All Major
Friday 9.30-13.00/15.30-19.30

Clothing
BARGAIN BASEMENT

Near the Fiera area.

Their inventory changes daily, the kind of place to check out from time to time to find elegant dresses or sporty pant suits and swimwear. Especially during their sales period prices are rockbottom! Young and helpful personnel. It is a large place, a visit is always worthwhile. Other address: Via S. Vincenzo, 101/r.

Maglificio Ferro

Lungobisagno Dalmazia, 71, int. 13 - 16141 Genova (GE) 010 8360380
9.00-13.00/14.00-18.00 C.C.:All Major

Knitwear, cashmere
FACTORY OUTLET

Autostrada A12, exit Genova Est to Molassana for 1 km, near the Coop.

Brand name Linea Yachting Nautica for knitwear in cashmere and merino wool, cotton and cashmirette at half price for last season's collection. Very good offers during their sales. Short sleeved tops in cashmere € 75,00, cardigans in cashmirette with zip € 60,00. Good prices for classical models, certainly not trendy.

Diffusione Tessile

Corso Perrone, 19 - 16100 Genova Campi (GE) 010 6591235
10.00-19.30 C.C.:All Major

Clothing
FACTORY OUTLET

Autostrada A7, exit Sampierdareno, follow the signs to IKEA.

This is one of a series of Max Mara outlets selling off last years collection (minus the Max Mara labels) and the special series designed for their outlets. Casual and elegant clothes also in Marina Rinaldi styles (but no labels) all discounted 30% - 50%. There is a corner with leatherwear, a lot of handbags (€ 40,00 and up) and shoes (€ 50,00 and up). Sizes from 38 to 50 plus XXL sizes up to 60.

Viva Brasil

Via del Commercio, 27 - 16167 Nervi (GE) 010 321250
9.00-19.30 C.C.: None

Clothing, beachwear
FACTORY OUTLET

Autostrada A12, exit Nervi. At the beginning of Nervi there is a sign Viva Brasil. Turn left into Via del Commercio.

An outlet that sells swimwear, bermudas, slips, bathing costumes, bikinis plus athletic wear for children and adults at factory prices, brand name Viva Brasil. Sizes for W from 36 to 60, plus pre-maman and they also make to measure. For men there is a good choice in swimming briefs and bermudas and the possibility to have XXXL sizes made especially.

Maglificio Iroide S.N.C.

Via Bressanone, 17/2 - 16153 Sestri Ponente (GE) 010 6140474
8.30-12.30/14.30-18.30. Saturday 9.00-12.30. Closed in August C.C.:All Major

Knitwear, cashmere
FACTORY OUTLET

Autostrada A10, exit Genova-Pegli or autobus 1, 2 or 3 Genova Voltri, at the stop for the COOP in front of Via Merano.

On the 2nd floor, large collection of cotton, wool and cashmere knitwear. Short sleeved cotton sweaters € 30,00, various woollies € 80,00, cashmere, their speciality, circa € 125,00 all made for the fashion conscious. They work to order and give an extra discount of 10%-20% during the Genova boat fair. They speak English.

Tessitura Gaggioli

Via Liggia, 1 (Via Aurelia 208) - 16030 Zoagli (GE)   0185 259057
9.00-12.30/14.30-18.30   C.C.:All Major

Fabrics, home furnishings
ARTISAN'S WORKSHOP

Autostrada A12, exit Rapallo to Via Aurelia and the direction of Sestri Levante. At Zoagli after the tunnel Gaggioli is at the level of Via Aurelia 208.

Velvets, damasks, shantungs and taffetà in cotton, linen, silk or mixtures thereof, woven by hand which takes absolute ages to produce. This is a genuine product, very striking, especially their silk damasks, super quality that lasts a life time if not more.

Velluti e Seterie Cordani

Via San Pietro, 21 - 16030 Zoagli (GE)   0185 259141
9.00-18.00   C.C.:All Major

Fabrics, home furnishings, household linen
ARTISAN'S WORKSHOP

Autostrada A12, exit Rapallo and the Strada Aurelia to Chiavari. After the long tunnel of 1.5 km, the service station Fina and another 500 m, take the first to the left, continue for 200 m. Follow the signs.

Silks, velvets, damask in silk organza of their own production, also wool and linen. Shantung and taffetà in silk or mixtures, woven by hand. Lots of choice, lovely fabrics for luxurious home furnishings here at their outlet at a fraction of the normal price.

Olio Crespi

Corso Italia, 81 - 18034 Ceriana (IM)   0184 551013
8.00-12.00/14.00-17.30. Saturday closed   C.C.:All Major

Food, olive oil
FACTORY OUTLET

Autostrada A10, exit Arma di Taggia to Sanremo. Continue for 2 km, turn right at the intersection to Ceriana Baiardo.

Their sales point is next to the factory and offers the possibility to buy extra virgin olive oil pressed from Taggiasca olives, local products like pesto, olive paste, olives in oil, dried tomatoes, chili oil, bottled artichokes, tuna, special aromatized truffle oils. They speak English, German and French.

Griffes Diffusion

Largo Nuvoloni, 5 - 18038 Sanremo (IM)   0184 500209
9.00-12.30/15.30-19.30   C.C.:All Major

Clothing, shoes
FACTORY OUTLET

Along the sea front, zona Casinò, and in front of the Russian church.

Griffes Diffusion is part of the Mariella Burani Fashion group. Spring jackets in bright rainbow colors, raincoats, men's sweaters in wool plus suits and pants. Also casual clothing, shoes and accessories, an ample choice of leatherwear, all sizes available. There is something for everybody but don't count too much on finding famous brand names.

Slam
Corso O. Raimondo, 123 - 18038 Sanremo (IM) 0184 591890
9.30-12.30/15.30-19.30 C.C.:All Major

Clothing, sportswear, casual
GOOD PRICES

In the center of Sanremo, Piazza Colombo towards the fountain, the shop is on the left.

They are specialized in clothing for sailing: wind breakers, water resistent parka's and anoraks, vests with pockets everywhere, coveralls, polos and bermudas, all made to keep one warm and dry and all discounted circa 30%. They speak English.

Outlet Diadora - Invicta
Corso Limone Piemonte, 15 - 18039 Ventimiglia (IM) 0184 238020
9.00-19.00. Sat. 9.00-19.00. Monday 14.30-19.30 C.C.:All Major

Clothing, sports accessories
FACTORY OUTLET

In the center of Ventimiglia, near the shopping center.

Mountains of sporty shoes, sneakers, climbing boots, trekking, jogging, tennis shoes (also coloured € 12,50), football and basket. Good offers of jackets in pile Diadora € 34,50. Backpacks and sporty clothing by Invicta. There is a special section with samples and end of line. The average discount is 30%-40% and up to 50% - 60% during the sales period.

Brands Store Factory Outlet
Via Benessea, 25 - 17035 Cisano sul Neva (SV) 0182 595067
9.30-13.00/15.30-19.00 C.C.:All Major

Clothing, accessories
BARGAIN BASEMENT

Autostrada A10, exit Albenga, to the left for Garessio, continue for 2 km till a grey factory building on the left. Brands Store is below Eurobimbo.

Large hall with an even larger choice of clothing, accessories, shoes, knitwear all discounted between 20% and 50%, some of it stock or samples. Sizes from XS to XXL with a special section dedicated to oversizes. Dresses by Ferré, tops by Whistles London, shoes by MiuMiu, Geox. For children cute things by Fiorucci, NafNaf. In January and July everything is discounted another 50%.

Piombo
Via Savona, 38 - 17019 Varazze (SV) 019 930273
9.00-13.00/15.00-19.00. Saturday 10.00-12.30/16.00-19.00 C.C.:All Major

Clothing
FACTORY OUTLET

Autostrada A10, exit Varazze, turn right, go through the village, on the right before the harbor (Cantieri).

Important and unusual dress suits, very fashionable, with some interesting color combinations. Especially for men there is a large choice of luxury suits, jackets, shirts and coats in the latest trends. Sizes from 46 up to 54, some pants go up to 56/58. Less choice for women, tailleurs, dresses, blouses and jackets from 40 - 48, but mostly smaller sizes.

E M I L I A R O M A G N A

Nella
Via Giovannini, 12 - 40052 Baricella (BO)   051 879651
9.00-12.30/15.00-19.00. Closed 24/7-21/8 and Thursd. aft.   C.C.:All Major

Fabrics, home furnishings
GOOD PRICES

Autostrada A 13 Bologna - Padova, exit Altedo. At the church of Altedo continue towards Baricella

Beautiful fabrics in luxurious Alta Moda quality: linen, cotton, silk, wool and cashmere, either per meter or remnants. Prices from € 4,95 - € 32,50 per m. Also
material for soft furnishing, accessories, scarves in silk and wool, handbags. There
are samples all year round. They have a large clientele and lots of foreign clients
from all over the world.

All' Area Aperta
Via Irnerio, 17 - 40126 Bologna (BO)   051 247586
8.30-19.00   C.C.:All Major

Clothing
BARGAIN BASEMENT

In the center of Bologna, near the weekly market La Piazzola.

They only sell brand name clothing at major discounts and have a very good
selection of suits and leather jackets for W and even more choice for M, also in
XXXL sizes, men's suits € 270,00 circa. T-shirt by Onyx, Calvin Klein, D&G,
Ferré, Cacharel, Cavalli, Trussardi, Versace from € 20,00. Jeans Cavalli € 100,00.

Bruno Magli Outlet Store

Via Larga, 33 Z.I. Roveri - 40138 Bologna (BO)   051 6015879
9.30-14.00/15.00-18.30. Monday morn. open   C.C.:All Major

Shoes, handbags
FACTORY OUTLET

Tangenziale Nord, exit 12, S. Vitale. The Magli outlet is in Via Cerodolo, second on the right after the train overpass. Large parking.

A large well appointed sales outlet, pleasantly air conditioned in summer. Magli shoes are world famous and very dashing. Sizes for women start at 34 up to 42 and for men from 39 to 45. Special offers in sample pairs size 37 and size 42. Matching handbags, small leather goods or suede and nappa jackets in spring colours were equally tempting.

Griffes Diffusion

Via Ducati, 5 - 40100 Bologna (BO)   051 6415873
9.00-13.00/15.30-19.30   C.C.:All Major

Clothing, shoes
FACTORY OUTLET

Autostrada A1, exit Bologna Borgopanigale, 2 km in the direction of the center.

This is an outlet for the Mariella Burani Fashion Group, selling last seasons collections at very competitive prices. All their 15 brands (Mila Schon, Mariella Burani, Revedi) are well represented, not only in clothing but also shoes and accessories, in all the most popular sizes for M/W. A good choice in leatherwear makes this outlet worthwhile to visit.

Gruppo Arcte - Il Negozio

Via Trilussa, 4/a - 40132 Bologna (BO)   051 6173711
9.30-12.30/16.00-19.30   C.C.:All Major

Lingerie, underwear
FACTORY OUTLET

Tangenziale exit n. 2 Borgo Panigale, then towards the center. At the first traffic light to the left, Via della Pietra, the second street on the left is Via Trilussa. Arcte is tucked away in a corner on the left of the square.

The Arcte factory produces quantities of snazzy underwear brandname Arcte, Argentovivo, Julipet, Bacirubati, Azzuleja, Allen Cox, Amarena, Wander, Sogni e Bugie. Pyjamas for men € 25,00 brand name Argentovivo plus underpants, shirts, singlets, all from last year's collection. Some bermudas, some T-shirts. For women there are sets in linen lace, bra sizes up to 4. Sizes for M up to 56, up to 52 for W. In summer pareos, bikinis, tops, all very well made.

Hettabretz

Via Emilia Ponente, 130 - 40133 Bologna (BO)   051 3145311
10.00-13.00/14.00-19.00. Monday closed   C.C.:All Major

Clothing, leatherwear
FACTORY OUTLET

Take the Tangenziale or circular road around Bologna, exit 3, zona Ospedale Maggiore. The outlet is next to the main entrance of Hettabretz.

Leather and suede clothing, fur lined, unusual Alta Moda designs. Smart city coats with fur collars, midnight blue Victorian evening dresses or charleston dresses of the 20's with feathers and jais. For M softly tailored jackets in smoky colours, all very beautiful.

Pancaldi & B.

Via Marziale, I/I Via di Corticella 184/2 - 40128 Bologna (BO)   051 322052
10.00-13.00/14.00-17.00. Sat. closed   C.C.:All Major

Clothing, shirts
FACTORY OUTLET

Tangenziale Nord, exit Castel Maggiore, third street on the left, towards Zona Corticella.

Pancaldi is famous for classical men's shirts and silk blouses for W. but also suits
for elegant managers in a discreet grey wool € 245,00. Tailleurs for W. in linen,
linen/cotton, shirts, trousers. Recent collection 20% discount, sizes from 42/44 to
48/50. Silk blouses, seconds for W € 37,50, samples, second tier collection 60%
discount.

Postacchini Stock

Via Carbonesi, 6 - 40123 Bologna (BO)   051 269847
9.15-12.45/15.30-19.30   C.C.:All Major

Clothing, accessories
DISCOUNTS

*In the historical center of Bologna, a limited traffic zone, autobus 20 from Piazza
Maggiore or the train station.*

The remainder collection of the Postacchini store in Via Farini 11 is sold here.
For thirty+ woman in search of clothes by Byblos, Ferré, Valentino, Cerruti and
other staples of the Made in Italy look, all in great quality but with a 50% off
price tag all year round.

Vitaliano Pancaldi

Via dei Lipidari, 15 - 40129 Bologna (BO)   051 323220
9.00-12.30/13.30-17.00. Saturday closed. Closed in August   C.C.:All Major

Ties
FACTORY OUTLET

*Take the Tangenziale to San Lazzaro, exit no. 5, Lama and turn right to Castel
Maggiore. At the 1st or 2nd traffic light turn right to Via dei Terraioli, follow the street
to the end and turn right into Via dei Lipidari.*

Specialized sales of ties, ascots, scarves, waistcoats, foulard in silk, all elegant and
sophisticated. This is also the kind of place where one can find silk handkerchiefs, just the thing for a luxurious present.

WP Lavori in Corso

Via Don Bedetti, 18 - 40126 Bologna (BO)   051 4161411
17.30-19.30. Sat. 11.00-19.00. Only Wedn., Thurs. & Frid.   C.C.:All Major

Clothing, accessories
FACTORY OUTLET

From the Tangenziale of Bologna take exit Castelmaggiore for Zona Corticella.

Remainders, unsold, end of series, irregular sizes of Woolrich, John Rich and
Bros., W.P. and others of all the WP Lavori in Corso shops in Italy. Casual clothing, a bit English country in style also for children. Many items for the house
and garden. They reopen towards the end of September.

Lipparini

Via G. di Vittorio, 6 - 40056 Crespellano (BO) 051 969417
9.00-12.00/15.00-19.30 C.C.:All Major
In July open only on Mon.,Thurs., Sat.

Furniture, various
FACTORY OUTLET

From Bologna take the road to Casalecchio and Vignola/Marabello. In Crespellano turn right at the roundabout and immediately right again.

Lipparini produces furniture in bronze, copper and iron alloys and in cast iron. Large choice of bed stands, lamps, coffee tables, consoles reduced 40% if shown during furniture fairs or used for catalogs. The bed stands in cast iron are just the thing for country houses.

SPW Company

Via Cavour, 91 - 40014 Crevalcore (BO) 051 980933
8.45-12.45/15.30-19.30
Thursday 8.45 - 12.45 Closed in August C.C.:All Major

Clothing, casual, jeans
FACTORY OUTLET

Autostrada A1, exit Modena Nord. Take the road for Ferrara, the outlet is behind the church of Crevalcore.

Sportswear, casual wear, all young, smart and well designed by C.P. Company, Fendissime, Repubblica Italiana. It's always worthwhile to visit this outlet, even though they might lack the more popular sizes and colors. Good offer in pea coats, car coats and stylish sweat shirts.

G.P.V. Palladium

Via Martini, 7b - 40019 Finale Emilia (BO) 0535 93074
16.30-20.00. Wed. & Sat. 10.30 - 13.00 Thursd. closed C.C.:All Major

Clothing, shirts
FACTORY OUTLET

From Bologna take the S.S. 568 to S. Giovanni Persiceto and the S.S. 255 to Bevilacqua and Finale Emilia. Via Martini is the main street. At the bridge turn right, down the ramp to the left then first right.

Modern blouses and shirts in crinkly shocking pink, curvy dresses in stretch, two piece suits in high-tech fabrics, jackets ecc. They are specialised in linen '120%' suits. Sizes for W from 38 to 48 and for M from S to XXL. For men one finds mostly shirts, for women a complete range of attractive, insouciant clothing.

Calzature Tarcio

Via Galliliera, 119 - 40050 Funo di Argelato (BO) 051 861303
8.00-12.00/14.00-18.30. Sat. 8.00-12.00 C.C.: None

Shoes
ARTISAN'S WORKSHOP

Take the autostrada A13 to Padova, exit Interport. Funo di Argelato is another 2 km. and Calzature Tarcio is in the center of the village.

They only make Alta Moda shoes for very special occasions and only work to order. There are prototypes to choose from and the price per pair starts at around € 150,00 and up depending on the type of leather used and the work-manship required.

Maglificio Adèle

Via Malatesta, 4 Z.I. Pasquala - 40026 Imola (BO)   0542 669511
8.30-12.30/15.00-19.00   C.C.:All Major

Knitwear, cashmere
FACTORY OUTLET

The industrial zone of Pasquala is north of Imola and towards the A14 to Ravenna and Massa Lombarda. It is near Maglificio Briciola and Camster/Via 1° Maggio.

This is one of the largest producers of knitwear in the area, churning out tons of tight zebra striped tops, small bits of ribbed cotton with oriental letters that just about cover the upper torso or wool melangé sweaters for M, rather sporty in neon colours. It's all funny and amusing and definitely for the young. Tables full of seconds at € 6,00 a sweater are worth a look, very good quality price level.

Maglificio Briciola

Via Malatesta, 17 Z.I. Pasquala - 40026 Imola (BO)   0542 641011
8.00-12.00/14.30-19.30. Sat. closed   C.C.:None

Knitwear, cashmere
FACTORY OUTLET

The industrial zone of Pasquala is north of Imola and towards the A14 to Ravenna and Massa Lombarda. Maglificio Briciola is near Maglificio Adele and Camster/Via 1° Maggio.

A small outlet bordered by flowers and plants. They produce highly specialized knitwear for M/W and work for some major designers. A two toned cardigan € 50,00, twinsets € 50,00, a fringed poncho straight from the 70's € 100,00. Short, sassy dresses in woolen jersey à la Prada € 150,00. They work to order and their showroom collection goes on sale in October.

Bruna Bondanelli

Via Sandro Pertini, 1-3 - 40062 Molinella (BO)   051 882725/936
8.00-12.30/13.30-18.00   C.C.: None

Knitwear, cashmere
FACTORY OUTLET

Autostrada A13, exit Bologna Interporto to Molinella. Bondanelli is in the Zona Artigianale.

From September onwards they organize special sales of the winter collection with fabulous offers in cashmere. In summer there are always plenty of tops and cardigans to choose from either in viscosa and silk or long tunics in linen/viscosa. Their designs are contemporary classics and 'Alta Moda'.

Rossi 1924

Via Nazionale, 99 - 40065 Pianoro (BO)   051 770255
12.30-14.00/16.00-19.00. Sat. 9.30-12.30. Closed Monday   C.C.: None

Handbags, leathergoods, suitcases
FACTORY OUTLET

Autostrada A1, exit Sasso Marconi. From Bologna S.S. 65. The entrance to the outlet is in the back in Via dell' Artigiano.

They produce purses for some very well known Made in Italy names like Borbonese & Redwall and in their outlet sell off only end of series or unsold items of the last couple of years. These handbags are always good buys, because they are practically handcrafted in classical, lasting styles, like the tapiro bags by Borbonese or the striking shopping bags by Redwall. Prices, though not low, are very reasonable considering the first-rate quality.

Calzaturificio Bolognese

Via Badini, 10 - 40057 Quarto Inferiore (BO)   051 767004
8.00-12.00/13.30-19.00. Sat. 8.00-12.00   C.C.:All Major

Shoes
ARTISAN'S WORKSHOP

Take the Tangenziale around Bologna, exit no. 9, S. Donato. Turn to the left, in the direction of S.Donato/Granarolo for circa 3 km to the Zona Industriale.

Shoes for M/W handmade by artisans with a contemporary flair in a casual city style. Sample sizes for men 42, for women 37, other sizes available. There tends to be more choice in men's shoes, especially mocassins in various types of leather, even in snakeskin and lizard skins or in soft butterscotch suede.

Centro Silver

Via B. Buozzi, 9 - 40067 Rastignano (BO)   051 742069
9.00-12.30/14.00-18.00. Sat. 9.00-12.30. Closed in August   C.C.: None

Silverware/Pewter
FACTORY OUTLET

Autostrada A1, near Bologna take the tangenziale in the direction of Ancona and exit 11/bis. Follow the S.S. 65 della Futa to the left till Rastignano. It's the first street on the left immediately after the Rastignano city sign. Follow the street up till the sign 'bomboniere' on the left.

Ideal for gifts in silver or silverplate, serving dishes, table centers, frames, foldable holders for pyrex dishes, lamps, cutlery, carafes, accessories for the table in silver or silver and crystal/china, all with brand name Centro Silver. There is a corner with seconds, specials and samples. They work to order and do repairs on antique silver. Multilingual personnel.

Sutor Mantellassi

Via Morandi, 10/12 - 40018 San Pietro in Casale (BO)   051 810451
9.00-12.00/15.00-18.30. Sat. 9.00-12.00   C.C.:All Major

Shoes
FACTORY OUTLET

From Bologna take the Autostrada A13, exit Altedo. Turn right, then continue for 6/7 km, at the intersection go straight to the Zona Artigianale, second street on the left.

Shoes by Sutor Mantelassi are well known for their fearless elegance, a bit English in stile but with lots of flair. The winter showroom collection is for sale after the middle of September, sample size 37 for W and 42 for M, and all discounted 50% compared to shop price. In July sales of the summer collection.

Mandorlamara

Via dell'Industria, 20 - 40037 Sasso Marconi (BO)   051 6750800
9.00-13.00/14.00-17.00. Phone first   C.C.:None

Clothing, beachwear
FACTORY OUTLET

Autostrada A1, exit Sasso Marconi, take the S.S. 64 for circa 10 km.

An authentic factory outlet that sells only second choice and end of series. Utterly up to the minute wet look blouses, knitwear in white tight fitting lycra, with glitter, plunging necklines, pareos for for the disco all by brandname Mandorlamara. Lots of accessories like fake fur scarves, computer print or optical suits, all very feminine. Sizes till 46, and a small 46 at that.

Confezioni Maribel

Via Bertini, 83 - 47100 Forlì (FO)
8.30-12.30/15.00-19.30

0543 795998
C.C.: None

Clothing, beachwear
FACTORY OUTLET

Autostrada A14, exit Forlì, turn right, at the intersection turn left, after 250m. turn left. Follow a wide street, past the Palazzetto dello Sport, for 350 m. circa. After the 3rd traffic light the outlet is on the right. Parking is not easy.

Beachwear and bathing costumes, gym clothing for M/W, casual shorts, exercise sweats, tanks and T-shirts by brandname Maribel. All sizes available from size 40 to size 56, but the showroom size is 44. The bikinis can be bought in different sizes for top and bottom, in 4 colors and three different types, (either with underwire bras, in a triangular shape etc).

E.G.O. Project

Via Colombo, 9/11 - 47100 Forlì (FO)
9.00-13.00/16.00-19.30

054 335373
C.C.:All Major

Shoes
FACTORY OUTLET

In the center of Forlì, Via Colombo takes you to the central train station.

Very nice looking sandals in pink suede with a plastic heel and long ankle straps, duck toed ballerina slippers in three colours, two tone stiletto boots and pumps, all highly original, brandname Materia Prima by Goffredo Fantini. Sample size for W 37, for M 41.

Calzaturificio Pollini

Via Erbosa, 2/B - 47030 Gatteo (FO)
9.30-12.00/15.00-19.00

0541 816311
C.C.:All Major

Shoes, handbags, leather goods
FACTORY OUTLET

Autostrada A14, exit Rimini Nord to Savignano sul Rubicone and Gatteo. After the center take the road to Sala/Cesenàtico and the industrial zone. The Pollini factory is very large and visible from afar.

A very large outlet full of distinctive shoes, handbags and small leatherware, all in impeccable taste. Only samples and remainders are for sale but there is a great quantity of shoes to choose from! Showroom size for W 37 € 80,00, for M 42 € 100,00. All other shoes and boots are € 100,00 - € 160.00. Original evening bags made of ostrich feathers or a shopping bag in boiled wool with leather trim. Brand name Pollini, Studio Pollini & Who's.

Confezioni Simona - La Perla

Via del Molino, 18 - 47026 S.Piero in Bagno (FO)
9.00-19.00. Closed Monday

0543 900811
C.C.:All Major

Lingerie, underwear
FACTORY OUTLET

Between Cesena and Arezzo, exit S.Piero in Bagno. Go through the village and in front of the cemetery take the road leading down to the left.

Two large rooms with remainders, seconds and special offers by La Perla, Grigio Perla, their men's line and Malizia, Joelle, Occhiverdi for women's lingerie. La Perla bathing costumes € 40,00, a linen bathrobe by Grigio Perla, 2nds, € 37,50, a Malizia body suit € 37,50, Joelle, Occhiverdi bras and slips in bins, enormous choice, all sizes and lots of special offers.

Baldinini

Via Rio Salto, 1 - 47030 San Mauro Pascoli (FO)
8.00-12.00/14.00-19.00. Sat. 9.00-12.00/15.00-19.00

0541 932898
C.C.:All Major

Shoes, leatherwear
FACTORY OUTLET

Autostrada A14, exit Rimini Nord, follow the road signs to San Mauro Pascoli and Baldinini. In the Industrial Zone.

The outlet is on the first floor. Mountains of boxes with shoes and accessories are for sale: leather and suede shoes for M/W. Sample size for M is 42, € 90,00, for W 37 € 85,00 for quitessentially Italian, well made shoes. Shoes for M, brandname Barker in English leather, only size 42, were a steal at € 139,00 versus a normal price of € 350,00. They have another shop in the San Marino Factory outlet center.

Alea Outlet Store

Via Emilia Ovest, 83 - 47039 Savignano sul Rubicone (FO)
9.30-12.00/15.30-19.00. Closed Wed. morning

0541 945481
C.C.:All Major

Shirts
FACTORY OUTLET

Autostrada A14, exit Rimini Nord, turn left to S.Vito and continue to Savignano. At Savignano the outlet is after the third traffic light on the left opposite Sergio Rossi.

A traditional shirtmaker now also offering polo shirts, knitwear and ties in their ground floor outlet. There is a large choice of fabrics and shirt collars to choose from, button down, French collar, floppy 3 button style etc. Their striped shirts are very handsome, especially with a pure white collar.

Dibrera Calzaturificio

Via Circonvallazione, 51 - 47039 Savignano sul Rubicone (FO)
14.30-19.30. After 15/9 also open in the morning

0541 941470
C.C.:All Major

Shoes
FACTORY OUTLET

Autostrada A14, exit Rimini Nord. In Savignano sul Rubicone after the second traffic light on the right.

Short pink snakeskin booties with stiletto heels, red metallic open toed wedgies, cobalt blue pumps with silver strips and ankle straps, all eye catching, not for shrinking violets, medium quality shoes, sample size 37, but all sizes available. Brand name 'Dibrera by Paolo Zanoli'.

Sergio Rossi

Via Emilia Ovest, 86/90 - 47039 Savignano sul Rubicone (FO)
9.30-12.00/15.30-19.00. Closed Thursday

0541 942580
C.C.:All Major

Shoes
FACTORY OUTLET

Autostrada A14, exit Rimini Nord to S.Arcangelo and Savignano. After the third traffic light on the right, opposite Alea shirts.

Worth the trip for fans of Sergio Rossi's beautiful shoes and boots. Last year's collection starts at € 100,00, same price for the showroom collection, size 37 for W and 42 for M, brand names Sergio Rossi, Miss Rossi, Sergio Rossi Uomo, Eco, and Le Tini. Prices for second tier line are € 70,00 circa. They also sell W. handbags, gloves, belts and speak English.

Vicini Outlet

Via Oslo, 13 - 47039 Savignano sul Rubicone (FO) 0541 938270
9.00-12.30/15.30-19.00 C.C.:All Major

Shoes
FACTORY OUTLET

Autostrada A14, exit Rimini Nord to S.S. 9 and Savignano. Continue to S. Mauro Mare, just before on the left, a small shopping center.

Luxury ladies shoes, very fashionable and fun; 'queenies' from the fifties in black and white or round toed pumps in patent leather. Good choice, either in end of line or sample pairs (size 37) at € 69,50 circa. Other sizes sell at € 139,00 for a pair of rainbow-hued sandals with stiletto heels. All shoes are very striking and amusing, and will stand out in any crowd anywhere. They work for major designers.

Frarica - DinoErre

Via Anna Frank, 6/a - 41012 Carpi (MO) 059 687056
15.30-19.30. Sat. 10.00-12.00/15.30-19.30 C.C.:None

Shirts
FACTORY OUTLET

Tangenziale Bruno Losi, to the right for Via Guastalla, Via Manzoni, left for Via Frank.

A small outlet, the walls covered with boxes all containing shirts: button-down, French collar, Italian style collar, double cuffs, striped, Oxford, you name it, they have it. Prices circa € 30,00. There is also a good selection in silk ties € 15,00.

Italo Confezioni

Via Lama di Quartirolo, 48/B - 41012 Carpi (MO) 059 643191
8.30-12.00/14.30-19.00. Sat. 9.00-12.00. Closed in August C.C.:All Major

Knitwear, cashmere
FACTORY OUTLET

At the beginning of Carpi and before the tangenziale Bruno Losi at the roundabout to the right, Via Cattani Ovest and Est, at the traffic light straight, Via Lama, at the end of the road to the right, a new building next to a lila coloured house.

Knitwear by Susan Brooks N.Y., I Righi Knitwear. Recommended for those who like to dress in classical Italian city style or boldly striped USA flag colours. Sharp tops and twinsets in 60% wool/40% cashmere, cotton/viscose knitted jackets with zip € 88,00. Their regular collection is discounted circa 20%. The winter collection is sold after September 20th.

Maglierie Effepi

V.le del Commercio, 32 - 41012 Carpi (MO) 059 697690
16.00-19.30. Saturday 9.30-12.00. Closed Monday C.C.:All Major

Knitwear
FACTORY OUTLET

From the Tangenziale Bruno Losi turn left at the crossing with Via Nuova Ponente. At the end of Viale Commercio, on the right.

This is an authentic outlet selling basic sweatshirts, T-shirts, jogging pants, polo's and knitwear with brandnames like Free Pride, EffePi and Martin City for M/W/Ch at very low prices in very acceptable quality. They have a special room with samples, knitted shirts for M by Setball di Gabriella Frattini € 3,00, cotton polo shirts by Martin City in excellent quality. All sizes with more choice in either XS or XXL.

Maglificio Rosmarie

S.S. Romana Sud, 78 - 41012 Carpi (MO)   059 663925
8.00-12.00/14.00-18.00. Saturday closed   C.C.: None

Knitwear, cashmere
FACTORY OUTLET

On the S.S. 413 between Modena and Carpi. Ring the bell.

A small outlet next to the factory. They produce knitwear for the German market, brand name Zucchero. Jerseys and tops that follow fashion trends, colorful and well finished € 30,00 circa. More elegant are the summer dresses in viscosa with a voile spencer, seconds, (but instantly repaired).

Migor Camicerie

Via C. Colombo, 5 - 41012 Carpi (MO)   059 694222
9.30-12.30/15.30-19.00. Closed Monday   C.C.:All Major

Shirts
FACTORY OUTLET

From Modena and the S.S. 413 follow Via Marx, after the stadium (Stadio) turn left, then 4th street to the left.

A well known outlet for men's shirts. Tremendous choice in shirts by Rocco Barocco, Navigare, Lotto, € 35,00 - € 45.00, Stefano, Gandolfi, Philo Vance € 30,00 circa. Special offers and seconds at € 9,00 - € 16,00 in all sizes. Silk ties € 23,00. Worthwhile address to find shirts at a good price, very attentive personnel.

Parrot

Via Cattani Ovest, 77 - 41012 Carpi (MO)   059 695044
9.30-12.30/15.30-19.00. Closed in January   C.C.:All Major

Clothing
FACTORY OUTLET

At the beginning of Carpi and before the tangenziale Bruno Losi at the rotonda to the right, Via Cattani Ovest, at the beginning, a secondary road on the right.

Delightful clothes by brand name Parrot, Miss Blumarine, Iceberg, Lu-Ma and Byblos for babies and toddlers to teeanagers, from 0 to 16 years old. Creative little girl babydoll dresses € 25,00 with matching tights, amusing T-shirts € 15,00 or small blazers in pure Oxford style make this a must for parents on a shopping spree for their offspring. The most recent collection of Blumarine is discounted 20%.

Tac Ceramiche

Viale del Commercio, 21/B (Z. I.) - 41012 Carpi (MO)   059 695969
8.30-12.30/14.30-18.30   C.C.:All Major

Ceramics, terracotta, porcelain
FACTORY OUTLET

Autostrada A22, exit Carpi for Tangenziale Bruno Losi and Via Nuova Ponente to the left for the Industrial Zone. Ring the bell if there is no one around.

Recommended as a good source for gifts. Colorful, cheery pie-dishes with covers in the shape of vegetables € 13.50 (+ VAT), apple pie dishes with a sliced apple cover, ceramic olives on olivepicks € 2,00, vases designed for Missoni € 44,00, tiger printed ashtrays made for Blumarine, ice cream scoops with cone shaped ceramic handles € 9,00, some end of series and seconds. They speak English and French.

Intima Moda

Via G. Campagna, 46 - 41010 Cognento (MO)   059 2924911
16.00-19.00. Sat. 9.00-12.00. Only Tues. & Thurs. aft.   C.C.:All Major

Lingerie, underwear
FACTORY OUTLET

Tangenziale Modena, exit no. 17. Via Campagna is immediately on the right. Just before the overpass turn left, the outlet is at the end of the narrow street with a parking in front. Look for a sign PIN. (Past the K.B.P. Group and opposite Rotondi T.R.S. Evolution).

On the first floor, very busy. Night shirts in white lacy S. Gallen cotton € 19,00, also seconds, peignoir and kimono € 25,00, all sizes up to48/50. Sets of bra/panty in lace, unusual colours, up to size 4, tiger striped bodysuits and lace stockings, satin culottes € 2,00, by brandname Verde Veronica, Verdissima Light. Very buys outlet.

K.B.P. Group

Via Campagna, 72 - 41010 Cognento (MO)   059 358920
15.00-19.00. Sat. 9.00-13.00/15.00-19.00   C.C.:All Major

Knitwear, cashmere
FACTORY OUTLET

Tangenziale Modena, exit no. 17. Via Campagna is immediately there, on the right. The outlet is on the corner on the left.

K.B.P. Group is specially known for the Irish fisherman type sweaters, called Hangfish, cotton inside and wool outside in basic colours like navy, natural, grey, black € 65,00. (they can be dried on a coat hanger and will not loose their shape). Other sweaters for M by Kerryblue Le Maglie, Brownell and Zinco start at € 20,00. For W XXL sweaters € 25,00 - € 35,00 in pastel/flowery designs for the over-50.

T.R.S Evolution

Via Campagna, 12 - 41010 Cognento (MO)   059 421556
15.00-20.00. Sat. 10.00-20.00   C.C.:None

Clothing, sportswear, casual, jeans
FACTORY OUTLET

Autostrada A1, exit Modena Nord, Tangenziale Modena, exit no. 17. Via Campagna is immediately on the right. Just before the overpass turn left to park, the outlet is on the right. (Past the K.B.P. Group and opposite Intima Moda).

Production of jeans and casual clothing for Trussardi Jeans and Trussardi Sport in very good quality. Various types of jeans in denim fabric of 10, 12 and 14 ounces, either straight legged or hip styled jeans, all colours from indigo to white, so popular now to wear in winter with a tweed or leather jacket. Discounts of circa 20% but prices remain high, there are no seconds or special offers.

Joseph Baby

Via Rovere, 31 - 41034 Finale Emilia (MO)   0535 91108
Telephone for opening hours   C.C.:All Major

Clothing
FACTORY OUTLET

In Finale Emilia take the direction of Sermide, one can't miss the factory. The best time to go is just before Easter and the beginning of October. Phone for the right dates.

A large outlet with clothing for children from 0 - 8 years old, brand name Joseph Boy, Joseph Girl and Joseph Baby. Little pants and dresses that are not only original in their design but also cheerful and well made. Overalls in jeans with embroidery or small pearls € 25,00, small T-shirts with slogans € 7,50, matching dresses and jackets. A corner for 1 year olds offers jeans at € 5,00.

Messori Productions

Via Sacco e Vanzetti, 1 - 41042 Fiorano Modenese (MO)   0536 910316
16.00-20.00. Sat. 10.00-13.00/15.00-20.00   C.C.:All Major

Clothing, casual, jeans
FACTORY OUTLET

Between Sassuolo and Maranello, in the Industrial Zone, from Sassuolo at the roundabout turn left.

A very well appointed outlet with more choice for men than for women (only some jackets and skirts). Well made suits for M in a chic casual/city style that has great wearability, in mixtures of wool and silk € 225,00, with or without waistcoat. Shirts, French collar, button down, € 37,50 - € 75,00, colored jeans € 37,50, English style classical blazers € 268,00. Special sales and they speak English.

M.G.S. Maria Grazia Severi

Via Divisione Acqui, 1 fraz. Casinalbo - 41041 Formigine (MO)   059 551707
14.30-19.00. Saturday 9.00-12.00/14.00-18.30   C.C.:All Major

Clothing
FACTORY OUTLET

Autostrada A1, exit Modena Nord to Baggiovara and Casinalbo. At the level of the Banca Pop. Emiliana (Red/white) turn right to Sassuolo. Straight and first to the left, first to the right, an industrial zone.

Party dresses for the more mature by brand name Maria Grazia Severi, very fashionable suits in bright colours. Charleston dresses in strass, floating skirts in voile, an embroidered top € 177,00, a suit in jewel tone tweed € 350,00. All sizes and one rack with showroom size 42 at special prices.

Muratori

Via Trento Trieste, 119 - 41043 Formigine (MO)   059 573320
8.00-12.00/14.00-19.00. Sat. 9.00-12.30/15.30-19.30   C.C.:All Major

Knitwear, cashmere
FACTORY OUTLET

From Modena, Muratori is at the beginning of Formigine. On the right, an old villa in a large garden.

Knitwear in wool, cotton, skirts, tunics, jackets, high quality and definitely for the over 40/50 set. Their designs are elegant, very wearable, dresses in a fantasy print € 70,00, golf, T-shirts with glitter € 25,00. Sizes from 42 to 56. Large corner with special offers and seconds, all kinds of tricot by Renato Balestra, Raniero Gattinoni, Maluf, Giusi Slaviero, Antonella Tricot.

M.B.M. Confezioni

Via Nicolo Biondo, 272 - 41100 Modena (MO)   059 827086
14.00-19.00. Sat 9.00-12.00/15.00-18.30   C.C.:All Major

Clothing
FACTORY OUTLET

Autostrada A1, exit Modena Nord to Modena Ovest, take the tangenziale exit Ponte Alto, Parco Ferrari.

Production of women's suits in a very feminine style with details like fur trimmed collars in lighter shades or velvet trimmed pockets on a bouclé suit, silk inserts on long sleeves, they work for Pierre Cardin. All sizes available, from 40 to 52, but few XXL sizes. They don't sell knitwear.

Simint Ind. - Emporio Armani

Via Naz. Gardini 1324/Via Monte Cuccoli   059 584411
41100 Modena - Baggiovara (MO)   C.C.:All Major
10.00-19.00. Closed Monday

Clothing, sportswear, casual, jeans
FACTORY OUTLET

Autostrada A1, exit Modena Nord, take the tangenziale exit Baggiovara. After the overpass to the left, at the 2nd traffic light to the left, first dirt track to the left.

Simint produces the Emporio Armani casual line, from T-shirts, sweatshirts, jeans to bermudas in linen, little sun dresses and capris for the holidays. Large space with separate areas for M/W & Ch.(from 4 years up), dizzying selection, but mostly smallish sizes and sort of okay prices. Lovely knitwear by Lawrence Steel starting at € 59,00 (bargains, bargains!), equally stunning T's with paillettes by Gai Mattioli from € 49,00 and up.

Griffes Diffusion

Via Regina Pacis, 92-100 - 41049 Sassuolo (MO)   0536 808413
10.00-12.00/14.00-19.00. Saturday 10.00-12.00   C.C.:All Major

Clothing, shoes
FACTORY OUTLET

In Sassuolo take the main road to Fiorano.

This is one of the outlets for the Mariella Burani Fashion group. Nice classy clothing for men, also casuals and accessories. Dresses and suits, supple spring jackets in bright rainbow colors for W. an ample choice of leatherwear, all sizes available. There is something for everybody from the 15 brandnames (Mila Schon, Mariella Burani, Gai Mattioli, Revedi) that make up this fashion group, at reasonable prices.

Coccapani Sicem

Via Modena-Carpi, 290, Loc. Appalto - 41019 Soliera (MO)   059 5690308
10.00-12.30/15.30-20.00   C.C.:All Major

Clothing
FACTORY OUTLET

From Modena take the S.S. 413 to Carpi. The outlet for G.B. Pedrini and Marchese Coccapani has been moved to the shopping center Le Gallerie on the left of the Sicem factory, past the road split in the direction of Carpi.

There are two shops, one with the current collection at slight discounts and the 2nd with last year's (and the year before) remnants and seconds. On the left of the entrance there is a separate room with super discounts: a wrap skirt in black cotton by em.bai.si € 10,00, embroidered tops € 5,00, jackets € 20,00. Last year's collection is sold at -50%, attractive party dresses and suits, contemporary flair, worth a visit.

Confezioni Marilyn

Via Carpi-Ravarino, 62/66 - 41010 Soliera Limidi di (MO)   059 561623
15.30-18.30. Sat. 9.00-12.00   C.C.:None

Clothing, maternity clothes
FACTORY OUTLET

From Carpi to Limidi/Sorbara, on the right before Limidi.

Confezioni Marilyn produces various lines: maternity wear with swinging suits, dresses and T-shirts starting at € 20,00, an XXL line with over sizes up to 57 and rather flowery dresses for the older generation and a third collection of sporty suits at € 70,00, practical skirts € 35,00, all very wearable.

Confezioni Raffaella

Strada Statale 12, 32-34 - 41030 Sorbara (MO)　　　　059 902106
9.30-12.00/15.30-19.30　　　　　　　　　　　　　　C.C.:All Major

Clothing
FACTORY OUTLET

S.S.12 Modena-Verona.

The right place for over 50 ladies in search of classically styled, well made suits in sizes that will happily go up to 56 and beyond. A pair of pants plus matching tunic blouse in linen € 65,00, bermudas € 28,00, brand name Antonietta Bulgarelli. Colours are bright and catchy and if the right size is not there they will find it in their warehouse.

Aceto Balsamico del Duca

Via Medicina, 2340 - 41057 Spilamberto San Vito (MO)　　059 469471
8.00-12.00/14.00-18.00 Saturday closed　　　　　　　　C.C.:All Major

Food, vinegar, olive oil
FACTORY OUTLET

Autostrada A1, exit Modena Sud to Modena. After an overpass to the left, follow a sign for Ristorante La Bussa. Another 150 m. to the right.

The Modena area is famous for the production of balsamic vinegar. The aceto balsamico del Duca is well known and their outlet also provides excellent olive oil from nearby producers. Gourmet cooks looking to buy small and large bottles of aceto balsamico del Duca will enjoy the variety on offer, the oldest bottle has been aged for over 30 years!

Agrinascente

Via S. Michele Campagna, 22 - 43036 Fidenza (PR)　　　0524 522334
7.30-20.30　　　　　　　　　　　　　　　　　　　　C.C.:All Major

Food, local products
GOOD PRICES

Autostrada A1, exit Fidenza/Salsomaggiore, 600 meters towards Fidenza. Be sure to find the name Agrinascente on the shop.

A large outlet, ideal for travellers in a hurry, who can stock up on Parmesan cheese and butter per kilo, Felino salami at € 10,50 per kilo, boiled ham on the bone € 9,00 p.kilo and so on. They like to sell in quantity, a leg of raw ham, a meter of salami, rather than by the 100 grams, and offer wine at 3 for the price of two.

Bormioli Rocco & Figlio

Viale Martiri della Libertà, 1 - 45036 Fidenza (PR)　　　0524 511200
15.00-19.00. Saturday closed　　　　　　　　　　　　C.C.:All Major

Crystal, glassware
FACTORY OUTLET

Autostrada A1, exit Fidenza to the center. After the train station in Piazza Garibaldi to the left. Via Berenini turns into Via Martiri della Libertà and the S.S. 9 Via Emilia. From Parma at the traffic light towards the center.

Next to the factory there is an outlet for the Bormioli products. They sell their entire series of glass ware for the home or for restaurants at very competitive prices. Very useful for buying champagne, wine and water glasses in 3 or 6-packs, dessert bowls, vases, storage jars from their 'Linea Frigo', candlesticks, a large salad bowl € 2.13. Worthwhile.

Fidenza Village
Via S. Michele Campagna, Loc. Chiusa Fernanda   0524 335511
43036 Fidenza (PR)
10.00-19.00. Sat.& Dom. 10.00-20.00   C.C.:All Major

Clothing, household linen
OUTLET CENTER

Autostrada A1, exit Fidenza, after 50 m on the left and well indicated. Large parking.

A fairly recent outlet center with an Egyptian theme. Circa 32 shops: Versace, Trussardi Jeans, Golden Lady (good deals), Bassetti, Stefanel, Samsonite, Reebock, Bodum, Mantellassi, Blunauta, Triumph, Bodum, a restaurant, bar, playground for kids, all very clean. Prices are circa 20 - 30 % lower.

Cerve
Via Paradigna, 16/a - 43100 Parma (PR)   0521 2786
9.00-12.30/14.30-19.00   C.C.:None

Crystal, glassware
FACTORY OUTLET

Autostrada A1, exit Parma, after a double set of traffic lights take the Tangenziale to Reggio, after 50 m turn right.

Cerve produces more than 3000 different articles in glass per year and exports to over 54 countries. Coloured glass objects or the Milennio collection of flutes, the Romeo collection of wine glasses, or sturdy tumblers in light blue, green, pink, decanters and jars. There are lots of useful and enjoyable things to buy, ideal for presents.

Unico Outlet Store
Strada Traversante Pedrignano 26 - 43100 Parma (PR)   0521 663224
15.00-19.00. Saturday 8.30-12.30/15.00-19.00
Thurs. & Frid. 8.30-12.30   C.C.:All Major

Furniture, various
FACTORY OUTLET

Autostrada A1, exit Parma Centro, to Colorno/Mantova. Below the overpass, after 300 m and on the right is an area for artisans. Turn right till the end, then right again, a further 500 m and look for a large factory hall on the left.

An eclectic collection of furniture that has been used for fairs, exhibitions, photo-sessions and catalogues, all discounted circa 40%. They sell cupboards by Mazzali and mostly modern furniture, but nothing for kitchens or bathrooms. They do have some rustic tables and beds in cast iron but very few sofas. Shipping has to be arranged by the client.

Distillerie Faled
Via Tolarolo, 6 - 43010 Roccabianca (PR)   0521 374004/6
8.00-11.30/14.00-17.45   C.C.: None

Wine, liqueurs
FACTORY OUTLET

Autostrada A1, exit Fidenza, take the road to Soragna. Roccabianca is about 30 km from Parma and about 25 km from Cremona.

They produce tipically Italian liqueurs like 'Nocino' or fruit based grappas. Large showroom with an assortment of distilled spirits and jars with whole pears in syrup next to their office. Also vodkas, amaro bitters, fortified wines. Prices are ok.

Creazioni Ermes

Via Galeotti, 2 - 43038 Sala Baganza (PR)   0521 834080
15.00-19.30   C.C.: None

Handbags, leather goods
ARTISAN'S WORKSHOP

On the provincial road from Sala Baganza to Stradella on the right. Parking.

The Ermes outlet has some very trendy bags for sale. Snake-skin hobo bags € 195,00, a small lizard-skin rucksack € 300,00. Prices, though not exactly low, are reasonable for the quality offered. Smaller bags in kid leather, lizard or nappa were equally appealing. They work for some well known Alta Moda brand names.

Kallisté

Via Emilia Ovest, 26 - 29010 Alseno (PC)   0523 945041
9.00-12.30/15.00-19.30. Thursday 15.00-19.30 C.C.:All Major

Shoes
FACTORY OUTLET

Autostrada A1, exit Piacenza Sud to the S.S. 9 for Parma. The outlet is in the center of Alseno, on the main throughfare on the left and next to a pharmacy.

Shoes for the highly fashion conscious, stylish but with a dose of humour. For sale are samples and showroom models by Kallisté, KTé and Daniela Jasoni. Afrodite sandals, clogs covered in glitzy paillettes or pony, stilettos in snakeskin, mocassins in a Scottish clan fabric. Sample size 37 start at € 50,00, other sizes € 75,00 up to € 150,00 for a pair of boots in faux crocodile. In September they sell their winter collection, 2nds € 50,00.

System Silvia Charrel

Via G. Marconi, 2 - 29010 Alseno (PC)   0523 949994
9.00-12.30/15.30-19.30. Open on Sunday   C.C.:All Major

Clothing
FACTORY OUTLET

Autostrada A1, exit Piacenza Sud to the S.S. 9 for Parma. At the beginning of the village, on the left.

2 large showrooms with a sporty and a more elegant collection, modern fabrics, subdued, practical colours, ideal for travelling or the office, it's all very wearable. Suits € 90,00, tops € 20,00. Large choice also in stretch trousers and mini jackets with zip and mandarin collars. The winter collection goes on sale around the end of August.

Jolly Junior

Via XXI Aprile, 1 - 29010 Pontenure (PC)   0523 510627
9.00-12.00/15.00-19.00. Saturday 15.00-19.00 C.C.:All Major

Knitwear, cashmere
FACTORY OUTLET

Autostrada A1, exit Piacenza Sud to the S.S. 9 in the direction of Parma. At the beginning of Pontenure on the right and well indicated, parking.

An authentic outlet that produces knitwear for some major 'Made in Italy' brand names, well known for their wearability and smart city style. Twinset in viscose € 75,00, short sleeved cashmere tops € 50,00, short dress with cap sleeves in wool € 55,00, on offer. They organize a special sale of cashmere in the first week of September, phone for the right dates.

G.F.M. Ter et Bantine

Via Zanzi, 16 - 48019 Granarolo Faentina (RA) 0546 641521
9.00-12.30/15.30-18.00. Saturday 10.00-18.00. Monday open all day C.C.:All Major

Clothing
FACTORY OUTLET

Autostrada A14, exit Faenza, to the left for Granarolo, continue for a couple of kilometers. Follow the road to the center of Granarolo and take the last residential street to the right. Enter the gate on the left into a large factory complex.

This is the Ter et Bantine, Hache and Items outlet, all well known French brandnames. Very modern surroundings, large choice, sizes up to 46 (but a smallish 46). The prices on the label are to be discounted 40%-70%. Two piece suits € 220,00 - € 330,00, leather skirts € 345,00, jeans skirts € 50,00. Also belts, knitwear, shirts, all in innovative fabrics and with a genuine, avantgarde slant.

Emporio Minardi

S.S. San Vitale, 1/b - 48020 Lugo - S. Agata sul Santerno (RA) 054 545282
9.00-12.00/15.00-19.00. Sat. phone first C.C.:All Major

Clothing, household linen
FACTORY OUTLET

Aitostrada A14 dir. exit Lugo Cottignola to Lugo and S. Agata sul Santerno. Follow the indications for the industrial zone.

Large outlet of eiderdowns, sleeping bags, pillows, bed covers in a sophisticated palette of colours, all made on the premises in siberian eiderdown. The bed covers have names like Dundee, Kilt, Ascot or Monaco, from € 34,00 - € 335.00 depending on size. The quilted or eiderdown coats and jackets are equally well made with labels by some prestigious brand names: a Husky € 113,00, a long coat € 99,00, special offers. From August onwards new arrivals, also seconds.

Punto Pelle

S.S. 16, Z.A.n. 26 - 48020 Sàvio di Ravenna (RA) 0544 928249
9.00-12.30/15.00-19.00. Closed in summer and Thurs. aft. C.C.:All Major

Clothing, leatherwear
FACTORY OUTLET

From Ravenna to Sàvio on the S.S. 16. At the beginning of the village, on the left in a small industrial zone.

Punto Pelle has two shops in Ravenna and Milano Marittima but in Sàvio they sell the end of line and showroom models, brandname Zen. Ample choice and good offers in suede and leather jackets, long skirts and leather jeans in neon colours. For men blazers and bombers in black leather, sheepskins and leather jeans in western style. Competitive prices for very good quality. The new sample collection is for sale after September 1.

Cristina Maglierie

Via Vitt. Emanuele, 86/a Fraz. Cassellina. - 42020 Albinea (RE) 0522 347441
9.00-12.00/15.00-18.30 C.C.:All Major

Knitwear, cashmere
FACTORY OUTLET

Autostrada A1, exit Reggio Emilia and the S.S. 63 to Albinea. At Puianello turn left and left again for Cassellina. Look out for a small industrial zone and Cristina Maglieria.

Only knitwear for W up to size 52 in wool, cotton or cashmere from € 35,00 - € 75,00 for a cardigan, spencer, or sweater or € 9,00 - € 20,00 for seconds and showroom samples. They really produce some supremely elegant woollies in winterwhite with a black bow knitted in front, Chanel style, or a top in pinkish wool with beautiful peekaboo embroidery in lila, dropdead chic, small sizes only. They speak English.

Bolgheri
Via Goleto, 13 - 42022 Boretto (RE)   0522 963124
9.00-12.30/15.00-19.30. Sat. 9.00-19.30   C.C.:All Major

Clothing
FACTORY OUTLET

Autostrada A1, exit Parma Centro, take the Tangenziale to Mantova, Sorbolo in the direction of Guastalla. In Boretto Bolgheri is opposite the Diffusione Tessile outlet, on the right.

Bolgheri is known for its snazzy men's fashions. Jackets by Ermenegildo Zegna, Les Copains and Givenchy in summer wool or wool/cashmere € 175,00. Also raincoats, windbreakers, anoraks. Ties by Aquascutum, Church's, Memphis € 20,00, 2nds € 10.00. Ties by Leonard de Paris € 40,00 regular, € 20,00, 2nds. Lots of cashmere. Sales in January & July at -50%.

Diffusione Tessile
Via Goleto, 13/B - 42022 Boretto (RE)   0522 964415
9.00-12.30/15.00-19.00. Sat. 9.00-19.30   C.C.:All Major

Clothing
FACTORY OUTLET

Autostrada A1, exit Parma Centro and the Tangenziale to Mantova, Sorbolo in the direction of Guastalla. In Boretto Diffusione Tessile is opposite the Bolgheri outlet.

This is the Max Mara outlet selling off last years collection (minus the Max Mara labels) and a special line of clothing for their outlets. Casual and elegant clothes also in Marina Rinaldi styles (but no labels) all discounted 30% - 50%. There is a corner with leatherwear, a lot of handbags (€ 40,00 and up) and shoes (€ 50,00 and up). Sizes from 38 to 50 plus XXL over sizes up to 60.

Spacci Bassetti
Via Goleto, 13/d - 42022 Boretto (RE)   0522 481021
9.30-13.00/15.00-19.30. Sat. 9.30-19.30   C.C.: None

Household Linen
FACTORY OUTLET

S.S.62 Parma-Mantova, in Boretto follow the indications for the Bassetti outlet.

Household linens with small defects called 'Primetta' that are only sold in their 12 outlets all over Italy at low prices. Ample choice of last year's remainders like terrytowel robes, sheets, slipcovers, quilted bedspreads, duvets & duvet covers, Gran Foulard and end of line blankets, all discounted 30/40%.

Griffes Diffusion
Via Marzabotto, 15/17/19 - 42016 Guastalla (RE)   0522 835136
9.00-13.00/15.30-19.30. Thursday 9.00-13.00   C.C.:All Major

Clothing, accessories
FACTORY OUTLET

Autostrada A22, exit Reggiolo to Guastalla. Via Marzabotto is at the beginning of Guastalla.

This is one of the outlets of the Mariella Burani Fashion group. Nice classy clothing for men, also casuals and accessories. Dresses and suits, supple spring jackets in bright rainbow colors for W. an ample choice of leatherwear, all sizes available. There is something for everybody from the 15 brandnames (Mila Schon, Valentino, Mariella Burani, Gai Mattioli, Revedi) that make up this fashion group, at reasonable prices. They speak English and have another outlet in Reggio Emilia, Via F.lli Cervi, 312.

SIMA Fashion
Via F. Menotti, 39 - 42030 Quattro Castella Puianello(RE)   0522 245256
9.30-12.30/15.00-19.30   C.C.:All Major

Knitwear, cashmere
FACTORY OUTLET

From Reggio Emilia take the S.S. 63. In the center of the village in front of the Eden Cinema and the 'lavanderia' and near Piazza Gramsci. Large parking.

Mainly knitwear for men by Fiume, Giunco, Nani Bon. Sweaters and T's in excellent quality, in an African style with a worn look € 25,00 or cable knits ready for a game of tennis. Also sporty, jaquard or classical sweaters € 37,50, a cotton polo shirt € 20,00, shirts € 23,00. There is corner with samples and seconds. For women clothing by Sevres and Julia Garnett at practically normal shop price.

Diffusione Tessile
Via S. Carlo, 8/B - 42100 Reggio Emilia (RE)   0522 437861
9.00-12.30/15.30-19.00.
In summer only open in the morning   C.C.:All Major

Fabrics
FACTORY OUTLET

Autostrada A1, exit Reggio Emilia to the center. Via S. Carlo is a parallel street to Via Toschi, in the Zona Mercato or Market area.

Sales of fabric remnants by the Max Mara fashion group. Superior quality silks, woollens, mohair, linen, camelhair for coats, laces, stretchy fabrics with paillettes. Their sales of winter fabrics starts after August 26. There are always special offers and promotions, this outlet is a must for the able seamstress.

Gin Fizz
Via Mameli, 15 - 42100 Reggio Emilia (RE)   0522 283599
9.00-13.00/16.00-20.00.   C.C.:All Major

Clothing, casual, jeans
BARGAIN BASEMENT

Via Mameli crosses the ringroad around Reggio Emilia.

There are three sales areas, one for M or W and one for jeans and casuals for both M/W. The more famous 'Made in Italy' brand names like Dolce & Gabbana, Burani, Versace, Valentino, Max Mara, ErreUno, Kookai, Martins, Antonio Fusco are well represented. A men's suit in viscosa € 175,00, colored jeans € 20,00, they sell larger sizes too (up to 56 for men).

Cemar
Via G. di Vittoria, 10/a - 42046 Reggiolo (RE)   0522 971221
9.00-12.30/15.00-19.00   C.C.:All Major

Clothing,
FACTORY OUTLET

Autostrada A22, exit Rolo/Reggiolo. At the roundabout and by-pass to the left for 2 km in the direction of Reggello. In the Gorna industrial zone next to the Profiltubo factory.

Two very large rooms, on the right their current collection discounted 20% and last year's at -50%, by the Maska brandname. A good source for attractive tailleurs, long party dresses, jackets and skirts in all sizes, also over sizes, in good quality, traditional but stylish. On the left super discounts of up to 60/70% offering real bargains in sweaters (also for men) suits and jeansy dresses in sizes 38 - 54. Worth a look for the true bargain hunter.

Maglieria Loma

Via G. Galilei, 49 Z.I. Rame - 42046 Reggiolo (RE)   0522 973708
15.00-19.00. Sat. 9.00-12.00/15.00-19.00. Closed Monday   C.C.:All Major

Knitwear, cashmere
FACTORY OUTLET

Autostrada A22, exit Reggiolo to the 'Rame' industrial zone in the direction of Moglia, to the left for Bondino and Z.I. Rame. The outlet is circa 50 m after the factory on the left.

Woollies by 'Giorgia for me' and 'per esteso', young, modern and trendy, at reasonable prices. Tops, gilets, cardigans, sweatshirts in cotton or viscose in summer and in wool or cashmere in winter circa € 35,00 - € 59,00. Baskets with seconds € 10,00-€ 20,00. The new winter collection is for sale as of September. Not bad at all.

Milar

V.le Magellano 6/8 (Z. I. Ranaro) - 42100 Reggiolo (RE)   0522 211132
10.00-12.00/15.30-19.30. Closed Wednesday morning   C.C.:All Major

Knitwear, cashmere
FACTORY OUTLET

Autostrada A22, exit Reggiolo, turn left to the Industrial Zone of Ranaro, at the roundabout take the parallel road to Rolo. Via Magellana is the first street to the left in the industrial zone.

Knitwear and shirts in good quality and competitive prices. They open from February 1 to May 1 to sell off their summer collection and from October 1 to January 1 for their winter collection. Tops, T-shirts in wool/cotton/viscose mixtures with brand name 'Donna Si' and 'Gazebo' € 15,00 and up, blouses in viscose € 17,50. Lots of choice for W, less so for M.

Miss Deanna

Via del Corno, 29 - 42018 S. Martino in Rio (RE)   0522 698842
10.00-13.00/15.00-19.00. Closed Monday   C.C.:All Major

Knitwear, cashmere
FACTORY OUTLET

Autostrada A22, exit Campogalliano to S.Martino in Rio and the industrial zone close to the center of S. Martino.

A large new outlet with a very varied choice of flawless avantgarde or sexy sweaters and dresses with labels by Trussardi, Louis London, Krizia, Miss Deanne, Joseph Tricot and Lawrence Steele. Best time to go for their showroom collections in size 42: March and September, phone for the right dates.

Maska

Via Contarella, 20 - 42019 Scandiano (RE)   0522 766211
9.00-12.30/15.00-19.00. Sat. 9.00-19.00   C.C.:All Major

Clothing
FACTORY OUTLET

Take the S.S. 467 below Reggio Emilia to Scandiano and follow the signs for Hotel Sirio. Maska is on the right in an industrial zone and well indicated.

Large-scale outlet with attractive fashions by 'MK', Maska, Elekta, Balajò for young and busy women looking for casual/elegant clothes. Linen skirts € 42,50, suits € 232,00, dresses € 92,50 and up. Also great assortment in chic silk suits: € 332,00. Racks and racks with seconds and remnants, some quite smashing. All sizes, also over sizes (at -70%) but more choice in 42 (at -60%). The winter showroom collection goes on sale in September. Phone for the right dates.

Calzaturificio Valleverde

Via Piane, 78 - 47853 Coriano di Rimini (RN)　　　　0541 656289
9.00-12.30/15.00-19.30. Open on Sunday　　　　　　C.C.:All Major

Shoes
FACTORY OUTLET

Autostrada A14, exit Riccione to Coriano. The factory is in a valley just before Coriano and well indicated. The outlet is in the back of the complex. There is a large parking and a playground for children.

Valleverde is a well known brandname for comfortable shoes for older feet in medium quality. They also produce a regular collection. There are two large areas for M/W&Ch. Their current collection is sold at shop price but their stock for M is sold at € 65,00 - € 120,00 a pair, for Ch € 25,00 - € 65,00, and for W € 49,00 - € 99,00. Special offers, 3 pairs at an extra 20%, all shoes are classical, no surprises, no sexy stilettos.

Stock Moda

Via Ausa, 173 - 47853 Coriano di Rimini (RN)　　　　0541 756264
9.30-13.00/15.30-20.00 Sunday 9.30-19.30. Closed Monday　C.C.:All Major

Clothing, bridal wear and formal
FACTORY OUTLET

Along the main road from San Marino to Rimini, on the right.

A large outlet of 370 sq.m. with an ample choice of good quality clothes for everyday use or for formal occasions and weddings. Dresses, jackets, skirts, suits, shirts, ties, accessories, either classical or elegant by some major brandnames for M/W in all sizes, also XXL and oversizes. Discounts of 50%-60% and up on the showroom collection, seconds or end of line. Worth a visit for the more mature.

Spaccio Massimo Rebecchi

Via Raibano, 37 - 47036 Riccione (RN)　　　　　0541 658103
9.00-12.30/15.30-19.30. Sun.15.30-19.30　　　　　C.C.:All Major

Clothing
FACTORY OUTLET

Autostrada A14, exit Riccione. Take the street to the 'Zona Artigianale', passing in front of 'ACI', following the road and the sign 'Virginia'. The outlet is in the first factory building.

All the Virginia brand names are present: Via Maggio, Terra di Maremma, Massimo Rebecchi, which means casual/city/country clothes, very relaxed, for the young professional. Showroom size 42 for W and 48 for M are well represented. Fabrics are modern mixtures: microfiber, fleece, wool/acrylic, nylon, linen/cotton. Sales and extra discounts in July, their winter collection goes on sale at the end of August.

Calzaturificio Pollini

Viale Vespucci, 83 - 47037 Rimini (RN)　　　　　0541 391724
9.30-12.30/15.30-19.30. Open on Sunday　　　　　C.C.:All Major

Shoes
FACTORY OUTLET

Autostrada A14, exit Rimini Sud to the center and the Lungomare di Rimini. The Pollini outlet is in front of the Hotel Continental at the level of 'Bagno 31'.

Lots of distinctive shoes, handbags and small leatherware, all in impeccable taste. Samples and remainders are for sale next to current models, which means quantities of shoes to choose from! Showroom size for W 37 € 80,00, for M 42 € 100,00. All other shoes and boots are € 100,00 - € 160,00. Nice evening bags made of ostrich feathers or a shopping bag in boiled wool and leather trim. Brand name Pollini, Studio Pollini & Who's.

Gilmar Outlet

Via delle Rose, 15 - 47842 S. Giovanni in Marignano (RN) 0541 959186
10.30-19.30. Tues. and Sun. 15.30-19.30 C.C.:All Major

Clothing, casual, jeans
FACTORY OUTLET

Autostrada A14, exit Cattolica to S. Giovanni Marignano, at the roundabout to the left for 300 m.

Large outlet of 300 sq.m., the place to go for fans of knitwear and clothing by Gilmar, Iceberg, Gerani, Block 60, Victo Alfaro, History. They sell samples, seconds, end of line and last year's collections, mostly in size 42, but there is a lot of 44/46 available. Unusual, original and fun designs. A lot of goodlooking jeans by Iceberg € 60,00 size 44/46 for W and 48/50 for M. Eye-catching, spirited suits for W € 320,00.

Bruno Magli Outlet Store

Via al Mare, 180 - 47003 S. Giov. in Marignano (RN) 0541 825168
10.00-19.30. Monday 14.00 - 19.30 C.C.:All Major

Shoes
FACTORY OUTLET

Autostrada A14, exit Cattolica, to the left for S.Giovanni, 500 m. on the left. Close to Gilmar and next to Diffusione Tessile.

A well appointed outlet for those famous Magli shoes. All sizes are available from 34 to 42 for women and from 39 to 45 for men in a great variety of shapes and colours. Sample size for W is 37, for M 42. They also sell handbags, small leather goods, clothing in leather and suede and other accessories like belts and tennis bags.

Diffusione Tessile

Via al Mare, 180 - 47842 S. Giov. in Marignano (RN) 0541 827164
9.30-12.30/15.00-19.00 C.C.:All Major

Clothing, shoes
FACTORY OUTLET

Autostrada A14, exit Cattolica, to the left for S.Giovanni, 500 m. on the left. Close to Gilmar and next to Bruno Magli.

This is a large Max Mara outlet selling last years collection (minus the Max Mara labels) and the series designed for their outlets. Casual and elegant clothes also in Marina Rinaldi styles (but no labels) all discounted 30% - 50%. There is a corner with leatherwear, a lot of handbags (€ 40,00 and up) and shoes (€ 50,00 and up). Sizes from 38 to 50 plus XXL sizes up to 60.

San Marino Factory Outlet

Via III Settembre, 3 - 47031 Serravalle (RN) 0549 904014
9.00-19.00 C.C.:All Major

Clothing, sports accessories
FACTORY OUTLET CENTER

Autostrada A14, exit Rimini Sud to San Marino. After Dogana on the right, a bright balloon indicates the entrance to the outlet center.

A large outlet center full of tourists in the summer. There are 27 shops selling brand names like La Perla, Calvin Klein, Mariella Burani, Valentino, Superga, Vestebene, Ferré, Les Copains and others. All collections (last season or end of line) are discounted 50%, in July there are sales that last for at least 5 weeks with discount of 70% to 80%.

Calzaturificio Pratesi

Via Dante Alighieri, 83 S.S. 540 - 52020 Ambra (AR)
9.00-12.30/15.00-19.00

055 996820
C.C.:All Major

Shoes
ARTISAN'S WORKSHOP

Autostrada A1, exit Valdarno, follow the directions for Bucine - Ambra. From Siena and Valdarno, Pratesi is on the S.S. 540 along the ring road around Ambra.

An artisans workshop producing shoes in the heart of Tuscany. Classical, well made shoes for M/W, sandals with comfortable inlays in classical or more fashionable styles. Showroom size 36/37 for W at € 30,00, for M size 41/42 at € 40,00. They can make XXS/XXL, extra-wide or half sizes to order and even produce shoes according to the client's model at very reasonable prices.

La Porcellana Bianca

Via Garibaldi, 53 (Casenuove di Ceciliano 166)
52100 Arezzo (AR)
9.00-12.00/15.00-18.00. Sat. 9.00-12.30

0575 320793
C.C.:All Major

Ceramics, terracotta, porcelain
FACTORY OUTLET

Autostrada A1, exit Arezzo, take the Casentino road to Poppi, Stia. The factory is behind the furniture manufacturer Emmelunga.

La Porcellana Bianca has a string of shops all over Italy. They produce white china in simple, classical designs that resist rough handling, dishwashers and daily use. In their outlet only second choice and end of series are sold at a 20% to 40% discount, plus various gift objects in forged iron, cutlery, wine glasses ideal for country homes.

Marzotto Factory Store

Via Galileo Ferraris, 20 - 52100 Capolona (AR)   0575 333002
9.30-13.00/15.00-19.00. Sat. 9.30-13.30/15.00-19.30   C.C.:All Major

Clothing
FACTORY OUTLET

Autostrada A1, exit Arezzo, turn left for the center, after 3/4 km after the turn of for the Pratacci I. Z. and near the Hotel Trucialini turn right and follow the indications for 'Spaccio Aziendale'.

A large factory hall with the Marzotto showroom collection at 50% off. Parkas, bomber jackets, jeans with the Marlborough label, dresses (also larger sizes), children's jeans in bright colors. Also baskets with special offers in household linen, blankets by Lanerossi, bed covers at 30/40% discount. Sales in January-March and July-September. Special discounts and fidelity cards.

Unoaerre

Via Fiorentina, 550 - 52100 Arezzo (AR)   0575 925862
9.00-18.00. Sat. 8.00-13.00   C.C.:All Major

Jewelry
FACTORY OUTLET

Autostrada A1, exit Arezzo, take the ringroad till the last exit, at the traffic light go straight under the bridge, after two more traffic lights turn left, continue towards a roundabout (Ipercoop) and follow the indications for Via Fiorentina, circa 3 km.

One of the largest producers of jewelry in Italy, they recently created an outlet for end of series and last years collections inside their factory building. Massive quantities of bracelets, brooches, necklaces, earrings, ankle bracelets and rings in solid gold or silver, classical or modern design, with or without precious stones or diamonds are on view. The price of gold depends on the market price but one saves about 25% on the finished piece of jewelry.

Calzaturificio Soldini

Via Vittorio Veneto, 55 - 52010 Capolona (AR)   0575 42811
9.00-13.00/15.30-19.30. Sun. 10.00-13.00/15.30-19.30   C.C.:All Major

Shoes
FACTORY OUTLET

On the local road S.S. 71 north of Arezzo in the center of Capolona opposite the factory.

A very busy place, ideal to find shoes for the whole family at very reasonable prices and in very good quality. Best buys are the famous 'Stonehaven' mocassins in very soft leather and in a wide range of colors and sizes. Also sporty shoes and sneakers and shoes for older feet, handbags, belts. Worthwhile.

Textura Vendita Diretta

Via Vecchia Aretina, Z.I. - 52029 Castiglion Fibocchi (AR)   0575 479223
10.00-14.00/15.00-19.00   C.C.:All Major
Monday closed. Sat. 9.00-13.00/15.00-19.00

Clothing
FACTORY OUTLET

Autostrada A1, exit Valdarno coming from Florence, to Loro Ciuffenna, Castiglion F. From Rome exit Arezzo to Castiglion F. Parking.

The Textura Group produces well cut, utterly up-to-the-minute suits for men: mandarin style, in clotted cream linen € 150,00, in double breasted grey flannel, English style € 112,50, bermudas in linen/cotton. Labels by City Time, Sartoria Tai e Ceasar. For W. there is less choice, classical suits and coats. Sales in July at 30%.

Camiceria L.I.B.A.

Loc. Renzino, 130/a - 52045 Foiano della Chiana (AR)   0575 648705
8.30-12.30/14.30-18.30. Sat. closed   C.C.:None

Shirts
FACTORY OUTLET

Autostrada A1, exit Val di Chiana. Coming from Arezzo, immediately after the sign Foiano della Chiana, circa 50 m., there is a narrow track on the left leading to the L.I.B.A. outlet.

L.I.B.A. produces shirts for well known national and international fashion names (but only with the L.I.B.A. label). Choice is limited, but prices are reallly OK! € 20,00 for seconds, € 42,00 for regular merchandise with all sizes available for men's shirts. For W there is limited choice, very classical blouses € 20,00 - € 30,00.

Frantoio Corrado Maddi

Via 2 Giugno, 17 - 52025 Levane (AR)   055 9789321
9.00-13.00/15.30-19.30. Open on Sunday   C.C.:All Major

Food, olive oil
FACTORY OUTLET

On the local road Montevarchi-Levane, before the bridge on the right. Parking in front of the entrance.

Delicious and very fragrant X-virgin olive oil in tins of 2, 3 or 5 liters or in presentation boxes: 1.5 liter in a round fiasco type bottle packaged in a wooden box € 20,00 or smaller amphora or tub-shaped containers with wooden cover. One can try the various oils, either locally grown or from the Puglia area, on a piece of bread. They ship all over the world.

Calzaturificio CAM

Viale Diaz, 131 - 52025 Montevarchi (AR)   055 900702
9.30-12.30/15.00-19.00. Sat. 9.00-12.30   C.C.:All Major

Shoes
FACTORY OUTLET

Autostrada A1, exit Valdarno. In the center of Montevarchi, after Hotel Delta on the left. We suggest you phone first.

The first floor showroom offers a large collection of classical shoes for M, made in top-quality leather, the kind of shoes to be comfortable in. Men's shoes € 60,00 and up, women's € 50,00 and up. Very nice summer sandals in strips of colored leather adorned with a leather flower or butterfly, € 37,50. Men's leather travel slippers € 37,50. They also work for Pierre Cardin.

Prada - I Pellettieri d'Italia

Località Levanella, S.S. 69 - 52025 Montevarchi Levanella (AR)   055 91901
9.30-19.00. Sun. 14.00-19.00   C.C.:All Major

Handbags, clothing, shoes
FACTORY OUTLET

Autostrada A1, exit Valdarno, S.S. 69 Montevarchi-Levane. After Levanella turn left into the Zona Industriale.

This is one busy outlet! Pullman buses with Japanese frantic to buy handbags by Prada at € 225,00 and up but also gorgeous clothes: waiflike dresses by MiuMiu € 165,00, small sizes. Men's jackets € 295,00, ties € 30,00. Shoes start at € 75,00. Don't count on finding the latest fashion hits and they do make you wait when there are too many clients but it's worth a visit if only to people watch.

Bazaar

Via Roma, 83/81 - 52013 Ponte a Poppi (AR)   0575 529704
9.00-13.00/16.00-20.00. Open on Sunday and in August   C.C.:All Major

Clothing
BARGAIN BASEMENT

From Florence take the Consuma Pass. From Autostrada A1, exit Arezzo and the S.S. 71 to Casentino, Bibbiena-Poppi. Poppi is a delightful village perched on a hill.

A new shop in the central square of Ponte a Poppi. They sell off showroom models of Renato Balestra, Nicoletta Ruggiero, Gerani, Iceberg, Cotton Belt, M. Rebecchi, CentoxCento, Swish, Ferré women's collection. For men there are nice casuals for sale by Chevignon, Pelle Baggies, Vespa. They start selling the winter collection already in August.

Gianfranco Ballerini

Via di Camaldoli, 4 - 52010 Poppi Moggiona (AR)   0575 556092
8.30-13.00/14.30-19.00. Sat. phone first   C.C.:None

Ceramics, terracotta, porcelain
ARTISAN'S WORKSHOP

From Florence via the Consuma Pass. From Autostrada A1, exit Arezzo and the S.S. 71 to Casentino (Bibbiena - Poppi). Moggiona is above Poppi.

Ceramics in a country style, simple clean lines in blue and white, very decorative and ideal for furnishing a country house. Plates, bowls, cups, all coordinated and cheerful.

Spaccio Gallorini

Loc. Rigutino Est, C.C. Planet - 52100 Rigutino (AR)   0575 979597
9.00-12.30/16.00-19.30. Sat. 9.00 -12.30   C.C.:All Major

Shoes
FACTORY OUTLET

Autostrada A1, exit Arezzo for Perugia/Cortona. Rigutino is about 12/13 km from Arezzo.

Shoes only for women, all sizes and all types of shoes in a medium price/quality range. There are casual shoes, mocassins or lace-ups, but most of their collection is geared towards the more elegant pumps, true stilettos with pointed or rounded toes, sandals or mules decorated with pailettes or flowers.

IVV

Lungarno Guido Reni, 60 - 52027 S. Giovanni Valdarno (AR)   055 942619
9.00-13.00/16.00-20.00   C.C.:All Major

Crystal, glassware
FACTORY OUTLET

Autostrada A1, exit S.Giovanni Valdarno, the IVV factory is on the left upon entering S. Giovanni Valdarno.

Beautiful colored glass vases, tableware, small objects in modern or ethnic designs. Discounts of circa 40% on their export collection. There are no seconds for sale but at lot of end of line items like flower vases, plates and platters, all in clean, modern styles. Good for presents and they ship. They speak English.

Fabio Inghiramo

Via M. Inghirami, 1/3 - 52037 Sansepolcro (AR) 0575 7811
9.30-13.00/16,00-19.30 C.C.:All Major
Sat. 9.00-13.00, closed 27/7-21/8

Clothing
FACTORY OUTLET

From Arezzo continue towards S. Sepolcro. The outlet is in the Zona Industriale Trieste.

A major producer of men's and women's clothing in classical but modern styles.
For men sizes go up to 60, for women up to 50. Prices are really more than all
right for a well made product: a tailleur for W € 125,00, a suit for M € 160,00.
Made to measure shirts by Ingram are ready in a week.

Laps

Via Petrarca, 15 - 52017 Stia (AR) 0575 504343
9.00-12.00/14.00-18.00. Sat. closed C.C.:None

Clothing, leatherwear
FACTORY OUTLET

*Autostrada A1, exit Firenze Sud to Bagno a Ripoli/Pontassieve, take the Consuma Pass
to Stia. From Arezzo take the local road 310 to Subbiano, Poppi and Stia.*

Leather clothing for M/W in sizes up to 60 for M and up to 48 for W. They use
prime quality skins, so prices are on the level but lower than in the city. There
is a good choice of jackets, coats, sheepskins, blazers but they do not stock trousers or skirts.

T.A.C.S.

Via Sanarelli, 49 - 52017 Stia (AR) 0575 583 659
8.00-12.30/14.00-18.30. Open on Sunday C.C.:All Major

Fabrics, clothing
FACTORY OUTLET

*Autostrada A1, exit Firenze Sud to Bagno a Ripoli/Pontassieve and the Consuma Pass
to Stia. From Arezzo take the local road 310 to Subbiano, Poppi and Stia.*

Production of the original Casentino fabrics per meter or made into blankets,
plaids, jackets and coats. Casentino woollen fabrics are very soft with a nubby
texture and muted colors. A woman's coat € 175,00, a wide cape € 40,00.

Tessilnova

Via Sartori, 2/4 - 52017 Stia (AR) 0575 582685
9.00-13.00/15.00-19.30 C.C.:All Major

Clothing, fabrics
FACTORY OUTLET

*Autostrada A1, exit Firenze Sud to Bagno a Ripoli/Pontassieve and the Consuma Pass
to Stia. From Arezzo take the S.P.310 to Subbiano, Poppi, and Stia.*

Production of Casentino fabrics in 100% wool, cashmere or wool and cashmere. They make nice coats in this nubby textured material at € 250,00 for W and
€ 325,00 for M. In cashmere € 350,00 - € 400,00. Jackets € 140,00. The fabrics
start at € 25,00 per meter, 150 cm wide.

Lori, Clara e Lorenzo

S.S. 70 - 52100 Strada in Casentino (AR)   0575 500190
9.00-13.00/15.00-19.30. Wednesday 15.00 - 19.30   C.C.:All Major

Clothing, accessories
BARGAIN BASEMENT

Autostrada A1, exit Firenze Sud, towards Pontassieve-Poppi. Lori is indicated by a red sign and on the local road, 3 km before Poppi.

Mostly women's clothing: Max Mara, I Blues, Prisma. The winter collection arrives in the middle of July and even at summer temperatures it is worth a look. They have sheepskin coats and leather and suede skirts and pants for sale and stock a good selection of party dresses. Sizes from 40 to 48, but a lot of 42, the sample size. Sales in January and July. They have another shop in Florence.

Calzaturificio ElleModa

Via Aretina, 201/203 - 52040 Tegoleto (AR)   0575 410051
15.30-19.30   C.C.:All Major

Shoes
FACTORY OUTLET

Below Arezzo, on the S.S. 73 from Arezzo to Siena. The entrance is on the left of the factory. Ring bell.

Beautiful shoes by brand names Gastone Lucioli and ElleModa, very fashionable, with an enormous assortment in all sizes € 60,00 and up. Their showroom collection size 36/36.5 sells at € 40,00. In winter boots with stiletto heels in black with silver ankle straps, femme fatale style. They also sell some handbags, but not much.

Cantarelli & C.

S.S. 71, Terontola - 52044 Terontola (AR)   057 567901
10.00-12.30/15.00-19.00. Closed Mond. and Tues.   C.C.:All Major

Clothing
FACTORY OUTLET

Autostrada A1, exit Val di Chiana, take the superstrada to Perugia, exit Castiglione d. Lago, to the right for Arezzo, continue for another 500 meters to the factory.

Jackets and suits in great style, made of superior fabrics. All sizes are available and though a large part of the collection is last year's production, Cantarelli produces the kind of traditional but trendy looks that will last. For men there are also shirts and ties for sale, with the Cantarelli label but made elsewhere. Worth a visit.

Hermion Cosmetici

Via Provinciale Settore Sud-Est   055 9737717
52028 Terranuova Bracciolini (AR)   C.C.:All Major

Beautycare, perfumes
ARTISAN'S WORKSHOP

Autostrada A1, exit Valdarno, to Montevarchi. After the bridge to the left to Levane, follow the Hermion signs. The outlet is in a small industrial zone close to the autostrada.

For natural cosmetics made according to age-old herbal recipes: 250 ml anti-cellulite cream € 15,00, creams based on royal jelly, turtle oil, propolis. Creams for tired feet, dry skin, shampoos, gels, all very effective! They do mail-order.

Mabel Moda Mare

Via dell'Olmo, 78 - 52028 Terranuova Bracciolini (AR)   055 9199666
8.30-12.30/14.30-18.30. Open from April to July   C.C.:All Major

Clothing, beachwear
FACTORY OUTLET

*Autostrada A1, exit Valdarno, continue towards Valdarno, turn left to Bucine Levane. The
shop is near 'Centro Scarpe' and the Volkswagen car dealer.*

Bathing costumes, bikinis, bermudas, ponchos by Linea Mabell, Moai and Berné for
M/W/Ch in sizes from 42 to 52 and at prices between € 15,00 - € 45,00. Good
choice also in beach apparel like pareos, kimonos, Hawai shirts, bandanas.

Gheriluce

Via Pisana, 36 Loc. Ponte Spada - 50021 Barberino Val d'Elsa (FI)   055 8078328
9.30-13.00/16.00-20.00. Sun. 16.30-19.30. Closed in Aug.   C.C.:All Major

Lamps
ARTISAN'S WORKSHOP

*Autostrada A1, exit Firenze Certosa to the Siena Superstrada, exit Poggibonsi Nord.
Follow the signs for Epson, 3 roundabouts, on the right, a small industrial zone.*

Modern designer lights, wall lights in Murano glass, table lamps, standing lights.
They also sell lamps by Artemide, Murano and other well known designers at a
discounts of 10% to 25%. Their own designs have nice clean lines. There is a
corner with special offers.

Gori Tessuti

Via Vitt. Emanuele, 9 - 50041 Calenzano (FI)   055 8876321
8.30-12.30/14.30-18.30. Sat. closed. Closed in Aug.   C.C.:None

Fabrics, home furnishings, household linen
WHOLESALER

*Autostrada A1, exit Calenzano/Prato, turn left for Sesto F. after 200 m. circa, on the left
and next to a Agip service station. From Florence, Piazza Stazione and Bus 28C.*

3 very large factory halls, 5000mq of fabrics mostly remnants from the clothing
industry but also some furnishing material. A mind boggling and totally confu-
sing quantity of rolls of linen, acrylics, cottons, woollens in every conceivable
colour or weight, all piled on top of each other. One can buy 3 m. or 3.000 m.
but with VAT added, since they are wholesalers. Scottish tartans in heavy wool
€ 5,00, 150 cm wide. They speak English, French and German.

Manetti & Roberts

Via Baldanzese, 177 - 50127 Calenzano (FI)   055 88351
9.00-11.30/14.00-16.00. Saturday closed   C.C.:None

Beauty care, perfumes
FACTORY OUTLET

*Autostrada A1, exit Prato-Calenzano. At the roundabout turn left, at the next rounda-
bout turn right, the factory is immediately after the railway bridge on the left.*

Borotalco, talcum powder in a distinct green packaging and Acqua alle Rose in an equally
distinct deep blue bottle are well known products of this 'Italo-Brittanica society'. They
also produce soaps, creams, shampoos, shower gels with either the Borotalco or the
Roberts or Rogé Cavaille logo. Special offers, discounts, 3 for the price of 2 offers, refills.

Conte of Florence

Via dei Limite, 170 - 50013 Campi Bisenzio (FI)   055 8969484
10.30-19.30. Closed Monday   C.C.:All Major

Clothing, sportswear, casual, jeans
FACTORY OUTLET

Autostrada A11, exit Prato Est to Campi Bisenzio and the Z. I. Pantano, keep going straight past Il Giglio Shopping Center, towards Florence till the traffic light at Via Allende. Turn right and before the autostrada bridge left into Via Limite. From Autostrada A1 take the Calenzano exit for Campi Bisenzio

A large outlet selling casual and sporty clothing for golfers, sailers and tennis players. There is ample choice of regular, irregular and seconds. W. pants in linen/acetate € 28,00, polos for M with the Conte of Florence golf logo, 2nds, € 10,00, irregular € 20,00 and regular € 30,00. Long dresses for W in mesh cotton € 49,00, irregular € 25,00, sizes from 42 to 50. They speak English.

MALO Cashmere

Via di Limite, 164 - 50013 Campi Bisenzio (FI)   055 8731990
10.30-19.00. Closed Monday   C.C.:All Major

Knitwear, cashmere
FACTORY OUTLET

Autostrada A1, exit Firenze Nord. The outlet is next to the Autostrada church. Autostrada A11, exit Prato Est to Campi Bisenzio and the Z. I. Pantano, going straight past Il Giglio Shopping Center, to Florence till Via Allende. Right, before the autostrada bridge left.

This is a relaxed but elegant outlet selling casual/chic cashmere knitwear by Malo. The new winter collection and the showroom samples are already for sale in August, (they only close the 3rd week of August). In summer they sell cotton tops and lots of special offers in wool/cashmere. Prices are discounted, yes, but still in the luxury category. In January and July sales at 50%. They speak English.

Wilker

Via Mugellese, 4 - 50013 Campi Bisenzio (FI)   055 8974483
10.00-13.00/15.00-20.00. Sat. 10.00-20.00   C.C.:All Major
Sunday 10.00-13.00/15.00-20.00. Monday closed

Clothing, sportswear, casual
FACTORY OUTLET

From Calenzano to Campi Bisenzio, in the area if the 'I Gigli' shopping center, going towards the Star Hotel Vespucci. 50 meters up the road, on the left and after the Black Sheep store.

A large factory hall full of casual clothing but much more original than the usual T-shirts, sweatshirts and jeans. The Wilker style is pure 'Made in USA' and prices are very competitive. A separate section for children offers some very amusing bits and pieces for toddlers, children up till 14 years old, the kind that can be thrown in the washing machine and comes out looking better, though prices are not low.

Black Sheep Store - Clark Jeans

Via S. Quirico, 199/b - 50010 Campi Bisenzio - Capalle (FI)   055 8974518
Closed Sat. aft. in summer   C.C.:All Major

Clothing, casual, jeans
FACTORY OUTLET

From Calenzano to Campi Bisenzio, in the area if the 'I Gigli' shopping center, going towards the Star Hotel Vespucci. 50 m. up the road, on the left, next to Toys. Close to the Wilker outlet.

Large outlet, very interesting prices for basic workstyle jeans, cargo pants, T's and sweatshirts with the Clark, Seapant or 40Weft brandname. There is a corner with even steeper discount € 5,00 - € 20,00 for a pair of indestructible canvas trousers. The cargo pants by Seapant with water resistent pockets and zippers to transform them in bermudas were a find.

Chiarugi

Via Ugolini, 5 - 50051 Castelfiorentino (FI)
16.00-20.00. Sat. 9.00-13.00/16.00-20.00

0571 628042
C.C.:None

Lingerie, underwear
FACTORY OUTLET

On the S.S. 428 between Empoli and Poggibonsi. In Castelfiorentino go past the station and the Duomo, another 400 m., on the left.

The recently opened outlet of Chiarugi, producers of beachwear, sleepwear and lingerie in a very attractive and sophisticated style. The beach collection of costumes, bikinis, bermudas and pareos is sold only in spring and summer. They reopen towards the end of September selling pyamas, nightshirts, corsets and other bits of lingerie plus underwear for men by Guess.

Enny Borse

Via Piave, 169/171 - 50050 Cerreto Guidi (FI)
9.00-13.00/15.00-19.00. Closed in August

0571 55144
C.C.:All Major

Handbags, leather goods
FACTORY OUTLET

Autostrada A11, exit Montecatini, S.S. 436 Fucecchio. At Ponte di Masino take the road to Cerreto Guidi. Enny borse is at the beginning of Cerreto, on the right. The outlet is on the left of the entrance behind large cacti. From Florence take the superstrada to Livorno, 2nd Empoli exit for Cerreto/Ponte di Masino.

A very good choice of supple handbags in soft nappa, the kind they are justly famous for and sell at competitive prices. A large office shoulder bag that even holds a pc € 90,00, spring bags in apple green € 72,00. Large part of their collection is in black, navy and cognac but also striking colors like fire red, yellow and emerald. All kinds of shapes, slingbags, satchels, hobo bags, shopping bags. They speak English, French and German, sales in february.

Facimp

Via G. Cecchi, 12 - 50053 Empoli (FI)
9.00-12.30/15.00-19.00

0571 72056
C.C.:None

Clothing, leatherwear
FACTORY OUTLET

In the center of Empoli, near the central railway station.

Tremendous choice in suede jackets, sheepskin and shearling coats, leather coats in very good quality. The long shearling coats, very light in weight and soft, € 300,00 - € 500,00, shirts in kid skin € 150,00 - € 200,00, also rain coats lined in detachable fur in classical models.

Nuova Cev

Via Val d'Elsa, 47/49 - 50057 Empoli Ponte a Elsa (FI)
8.30-13.00/14.30-19.00. Sat. 14.30-19.00

0571 931593
C.C.:All Major

Crystal, glassware
FACTORY OUTLET

S.S. 429 from Empoli to Siena. After the Autostrada bridge the outlet is on the right next to the factory.

A fairly recent selling point of hand blown crystal with more than 24% lead made on the premises. There are carafes and vases with a very thick diameter, brilliant reflections and deep incisions. Crystal glasses start at € 8,00, a chess set and board in crystal € 390,00.

Modyva G.I.C.

Via 1° Maggio, 31 - 50053 Empoli - Terrafino Z.I. (FI)　　　0571 950246
9.30-13.00/15.30-19.00. Sat. 9.30-13.00　　　　　　　　　　C.C.:None

Clothing
FACTORY OUTLET

From Florence and the Autostrada A1 take the Firenze Signa exit and the Superstrada Florence-Livorno. Take the second Empoli exit, follow the curve then go straight. At the first crossing, turn left, continue till the traffic lights and turn right. The outlet is opposite 'Tutt'auto'.

A good place to visit for business and/or dressy clothes in very wearable designs with the Modyva, Privilegio and Delia Ferrari brand names. The Modyva sizes run from 42 to 48, Privilegio from 40 till 46. The Delia Ferrari line carries XXL over sizes, (misure calibrate) for the fuller figure. Count on spending € 125,00 - € 215,00 for a dress or two-piece suit fit for any kind of social event.

Giap Confezioni

Via Renai, 11a - 50050 Empoli Vitolini (FI)　　　　　　　　0571 584000
8.30-12.30/14.30-18.30. Open on Saturday after1/9.　　　　C.C.:All Major

Clothing, leatherwear
FACTORY OUTLET

Autostrada A11, exit Pistoia to Empoli. At Vinci follow the indications for Vitolini. Giap is at the beginning of the village, on the right (Ellebi). From Florence take the Superstrada to Livorno and the 1st Empoli exit to Vinci.

Special sales in their warehouse, enormous choice of scratch resistant leather bombers, jackets in antiqued leather, blazers in nappa, sheepskins with fur collars etc. with labels by Daniel Hechter and Pierre Cardin. A black leather blazer for M € 230,00, a kid skin suede shirt for W € 180,00 in nice honey or brandy colors. All sizes, trendy styles.

Beltrami

Via dei Panzani ,11r - 50123 Firenze (FI)　　　　　　　　　055 212661
9.30-13.00/15.30-19.30. Open all Mon. and Aug.　　　　　　C.C.:All Major

Shoes
BARGAIN BASEMENT

Near Piazza della Stazione and Piazza di S. Maria Novella.

Good deals can be found: boots in glove-soft leather € 80,00 and up, evening sandals € 65,00, leather and suede clothing, lovely quality but sometimes in need of cleaning, handbags in raspberry or egg yellow, evening bags encrusted with crystals. Men might also do well here, since there are masses of classical very well made shoes to choose from. Sales in July and August.

Boa Mazzanti

Via R. Giulliani, 144 (int.) - 50141 Firenze (FI)　　　　　　055 431752
Phone first　　　　　　　　　　　　　　　　　　　　　　C.C.:None

Accessories, various
ARTISAN'S WORKSHOP

Autostrada Firenze Nord towards the airport, to the left for Castello. Follow the directions to the Rifredi station. They are circa 200 m further up the road.

An atelier specializing in fancy feather, marabou or ostrich boa's in a wide range of colours. For those looking for a particular colour they do the dyeing in their own workshop. They also work with artificial flowers. We suggest to phone first for an appointment.

Calzaturificio Buccioni

Via Aretina, 403d - 50136 Firenze (FI)   055 690013
8.30-12.30/15.00-19.00   C.C.:All Major

Shoes
ARTISAN'S WORKSHOP

Circa 1.5 km on foot from Piazza Alberti (Bus 14) and not that far from the 'Lori' outlet.

Highly recommended for busy feet in need of classical, well-made shoes that will last. Women's shoes € 60,00, lace-ups, mocassins, booties and mid heel pumps in mainly black, brown and cognac. For men a 'Church' type shoe € 145,00, a loafer type € 90,00, also in classical shapes and colors. Worthwhile.

Daisy Maglierie

Via Guglielmo Pepe, 47 - 50133 Firenze (FI)   055 577251/2
9.00-19.00. Sat. closed   C.C.:All Major

Knitwear, cashmere
FACTORY OUTLET

Firenze Zona Cure, near the stadium. Autobus 1, 3, 7 or a taxi because parking is quite impossible.

The Laura Moretti outlet. Very nice knitwear, modern, for M/W. Short jersey dresses in wool € 30,00, polos for men in silk € 30,00; large cable knit sweaters for M in cashmere € 135,00. Large choice of samples, all in the latest colors, small sizes, in linen/silk or viscosa/cotton at low prices, seconds and sales. They speak English and French.

Horserie

Via Baracca, 15g - 50123 Firenze (FI)   055 350763
10.00-14.00/15.30-19.30. Sat. 10.00-14.00   C.C.:All Major

Fabrics, home furnishings, household linen
BARGAIN BASEMENT

From the Autostrada take the Firenze Aeroporto outlet to Florence center along Viale Guidoni. At the first overpass turn right and follow the signs for Via Baracca. Horserie is in front of the parking exit of the Esselunga Supermarket.

Fabrics for soft furnishings at low prices. Exceptional offers of remnants and samples in unusual designs to furnish a house, from heavy, imposing jacquards to light silks, from fresh, flowery cotton chintzes to crushed linen velvets in subdued colors. Prices from € 5.50 to € 37,00 per meter. Upholstered sofas € 830,00 for a two seater to € 1.000,00 for three. Also carpets and wall paper. In October and November promotional sales with discounts of up to 70%.

Il Guardaroba

Borgo Albizi, 85/87 - 50122 Firenze (FI)   055 2340271
9.00-19.30   C.C.:All Major

Clothing, casual, jeans
BARGAIN BASEMENT

In the center of Florence. Borgo Albizzi is a narrow street that leads to P.zza Santa Croce.

Great collection for the young and trendy on a budget. Jackets, sweaters, ties, shirts by Alpi, Henry Cottons, Armani, Best Company (felpe € 27,50). For women smaller selection: snazzy dresses by Ferretti, a row of mini/maxi skirts, nice tops in summer. There are 2 other shops in Via dei Castellani 26r and Via Verdi 28r.

Li-puma

Via Baracca, 33 - 50127 Firenze (FI)   055 419758
8.30-12.30/14.30-18.30. Sat. 8.30-12.30   C.C.:All Major

Lamps
ARTISAN'S WORKSHOP

From the Autostrada take the Firenze Aeroporto exit to Florence center along Viale Guidoni. At the first overpass turn right and follow the signs for Via Baracca. Li-Puma is on the right.

Gold sprayed ceiling appliques € 35,00 and up, carriage lights, tasselled umbrella stands, flower trimmed mirrors, lamps fit for rococo palaces, all made by hand, all in gold or bronze colors, one can see them made on the premises, quite fascinating.

Lori, Clara e Lorenzo

Via Enrico de Nicola, 15 - 50136 Firenze (FI)   055 6503204
9.00-13.00/15.00-20.00   C.C.:All Major

Clothing
BARGAIN BASEMENT

Follow the Arno to the statale for Pontassieve. At the level of the Varlungo bridge, the 4th after Ponte Vecchio, to the left. Or Autostrada A1, exit Firenze Sud.

Showroom models, end of series by Prisma, I Blues, Federica, Max Mara, Cardin, Valentino and others. Sheepskins in mad colors, rain jackets and jeans jackets lined in faux mink, little black cocktail dresses by the hundreds. Phone to find out the dates for new arrivals. This place is always busy but amusing. There is a sister store in Strada in Casentino (FI).

Mulas Riciclo

Via Marsuppini, 4 - 50100 Firenze (FI)   055 6800487
9.30-12.30/15.00-19.00. Saturday 9.30-13.00   C.C.:All Major

Clothing
FACTORY OUTLET

Near Piazzale Michelangelo and Piazza Ferrucci.

At Mulas Riciclo one can find unsold items of the two Mulas shops in Via Panzani. Brandname clothing, chic casuals, some shoes or slippers and lots of jeans and T-shirts by Diesel. Also dresses and shirts by John Richmond, all extremely fashionable and up to date even though they weren't immediately sold.

On the Stocks

Via Il Prato, 63/R - 50123 Firenze (FI)   055 2399170
9.00-13.00/16.00-19.30. Sat. 9.30-13.00   C.C.:All Major

Clothing, shoes
BARGAIN BASEMENT

Autostrada A1, exit Firenze Centro. From the Porta al Prato to the center.

A rather large shop with a great deal of clothing on show, occasionally one can find children's clothes or shoes. At the moment of visiting there was a lot of casual/city clothing by Massimo Rebecchi for sale, discounted circa 50%.

Calzaturificio Baracchino (SAX)

Via della Querciola, 4 - 50054 Fucécchio (FI)   0571 24721
16.00-19.30. Sat. 9.30-13.00/16.30-19.30   C.C.:All Major

Shoes
FACTORY OUTLET

Autostrada A11, exit Altopascio, from the Superstrada Firenze-Pisa-Livorno take the San Miniato o S. Croce exit. At Fucécchio take the direction of Ponte a Cappiano. The outlet is on the right after the traffic light.

A large showroom with row upon row of shoes, sorted by size, brand name SAX. Sporty shoes for M: boat shoes, mocassins or tennis shoes in leather or canvas € 30,00 - € 45,00. Biker jackets in hammered leather € 225,00. For W Indian-type sandals € 60,00, cow hide sandals, mocassins. Special offer of Husky golf shoes, water repellent for M/W or shoes by Utility with wavy rubber soles.

Calzoleria Harris

Viale Colombo, 92 - 50054 Fucécchio (FI)   0571 261508
15.30-19.30. Sat. 10.00-12.30. Closed 1/7 - 1/9   C.C.:None

Shoes
FACTORY OUTLET

Autostrada A11, exit Altopascio, from the Superstrada Firenze-Pisa-Livorno take the San Miniato o S. Croce exit. At Fucécchio take the direction of Ponte a Cappiano. The outlet is on the right after the traffic light and close to SAX.

A small first floor outlet. Men's shoes in absolutely eye catching styles. Square toed, hand stitched with light thread, in ox blood red or midnight blue leather, unusual and ready for any kind of super trendy event, € 115,00 a pair. For W. less choice, high heeled booties or slippers in pink or violet snake skin, Texas style, € 150.

Marianelli

Via Pistoiese, 51 - 50054 Fucécchio - Loc. Le Botteghe (FI)   0571 261602
8.30-12.00/14.30-18.00. Saturday closed   C.C.:All Major

Handbags, leather goods
FACTORY OUTLET

Autostrada A1, exit Montecatini to S.S.436 Fucécchio. Just before Loc. Le Botteghe on the right. It's a dark building with bronze sculptures in front. From Florence take the Superstrada to Livorno, exit San Miniato to Montecatini.

Abundant choice in bags, leather goods, belts by famous brand names like Les Copains, Blumarine, Fiorucci and of course Marianelli at 'light' discounts. Handbags in leather and fabric, bright colors € 122,00, evening bags by Blumarine printed with rambling roses € 162,50, in fake snake € 212.50. For men there are some attaché cases and belts for sale.

Dolce & Gabbana Industria

Loc. S. M. Maddal. Pian dell'Isola - 50066 Incisa Val d'Arno (FI)   055 833 1300
9.00-19.00   C.C.:All Major

Clothing, accessories
FACTORY OUTLET

Autostrada A1, exit Incisa, turn right in the direction of Florence. After 4 km at the bridge and a sign Pian dell'Isola turn left.

Last year's Dolce & Gabbana collection, samples and some seconds (but not much). For men sizes run from 44 to 56, sample size 48 is well represented, for women size 38 to 48 with far more choice in 40/42, less so in 46/48. A two piece suit, very noticeable € 250,00, for men € 200,00 circa. (At sales everything is discounted 20-40%). They speak English, German, French and Japanese.

The Mall - Gucci

Via Europa, 8 - 50060 Leccio Reggello (FI)   055 8657775
10.00-19.00. Sun. 15.00-19.00 but closed in August   C.C.:All Major

Clothing, accessories
OUTLET CENTER

Autostrada A1, exit Incisa in Val d'Arno, take the S.S. 69 Pontassieve/Firenze. After 6/7 km to the right after the Fina service station, follow directions. For info on the shuttle bus between Florernce and the Mall tel. 055 8657775.

The Mall was opened on August 4, 2001 and now houses outlets by Bottega Veneta, Giorgio Armani, Gucci, Loro Piana, Sergio Rossi, Yves Saint Laurent, Fendi, I Pinco Pallino e Marni. Large, luxurious, just like a store in the city, busy, busy, a lot of buses in the tourist season, very helpful personnel. There is a new coffeeshop and restaurant named Dot.Com on the premises.

Calzaturificio Taccetti

Via Castelucci, 8 - 50056 Montelupo Fiorentino (FI)   0571 91471
14.30-19.00. Sat. 9.30-13.300/15.00-19.00   C.C.:All Major

Shoes
FACTORY OUTLET

Superstrada Firenze-Pisa, exit Montelupo Fiorentina towards Sammontana. After 100 meters turn right into the Zona Industriale.

Very well made and up-to-date shoes. There is less choice for men, to find the right size it is better to visit at the beginning of the season. For W. there are ballerinas in silver, celeste or with paillettes, either with round Donald Duck or pointed toes. Also elegant sandals in every color possible. Showroom size 37 € 30,00, other sizes € 70,00 - € 80,00.

Corradini, C. & G.

Via T. Romagnola Nord, 8a Loc. Camaioni   0571 910130
50056 Montelupo Fiorentino (FI)   C.C.:All Major
8.00-12.00/13.30-19.00

Ceramics, terracotta, porcelain
ARTISAN'S WORKSHOP

S.P. 67 from Empoli to Lastra. Loc. Camaioni is quite far from Montelupo Fiorentino, Corradini is on the main road, on the right at the beginning of the village.

The Corradini factory produces authentic terracotta vases, columns, busts and cachepots that have not been glazed or unduly embellished but remain their simple, original selves. Garden vases or corner vases (€ 32,50) and large strawberry pots with hand made pockets, leaping rabbits, shell shaped containers. Most of the production is still handmade.

Terrecotte Fiorentine

Via del Lavoro, 1/3 Z.A - 50056 Montelupo Fiorentino (FI)   0571 542224
8.30-12.00/14.00-18.00. Sat. 9.00-12.00   C.C.:None

Ceramics, terracotta, porcelain
ARTISAN'S WORKSHOP

Superstrada Firenze - Pisa - Livorno, exit Montelupo Fiorentino to S.S. 67 Empoli. Turn right into a new Zona Artigianale. On the left and clearly visible.

Terracotta in Florentine styles, all the age old designs with 'putti' winding around belly shaped pots, corner pots and anforas. New are the labrador dogs in terracotta € 35,00 or dachshunds and boxers, cats and rabbits that can hold plants. The very large and beautiful Puglia olive jars are € 400,00. All their wares are frost resistant.

Bellini Più

Via Virginio, 150 Loc. Baccaiano - 50025 Montespertoli (FI)   0571 671145
9.00-18.00   C.C.:All Major

Ceramics, terracotta, porcelain
FACTORY OUTLET

Autostrada A1, exit Firenze Signa to the Superstrada Firenze/Livorno, exit Ginestra Fiorentina, S.P. 80 to Montespertoli for circa 5 km. The factory is between Montespertoli and San Casciano Val di Pesa, circa 20 minutes from Florence and 40 min. from Siena.

Hand painted ceramics, plates, mugs, jugs, platters, umbrella stands, bases for lights, all useful and decorative items in a modern floral style. Special offers from € 5,00. Since 1950 they export all over the world to clients like John Lewis in the U.K., Printemps in Paris, Heine in Germany and Sacks, Neiman Marcus and Bloomingdale in the U.S.

Ceramiche Leona

Via Virginio, 524 Loc. Anselmo - 50025 Montespertoli (FI)   0571 671918
8.00-12.00/13.30-17.30. Saturday closed   C.C.:All Major

Ceramics, terracotta, porcelain
FACTORY OUTLET

Autostrada A1, exit Firenze Signa to the Superstrada Firenze/Livorno, exit Ginestra Fiorentina, S.P. 80 to Montespertoli for circa 7 km. On the right.

Traditional Florentine ceramics, bases for lamps, vases, containers for herbs, pharmacy pots, plates in all sizes, jars, table center pieces, Della Robbia placques, all very well made with lots of charm. There is a corner with seconds that start at € 5,00.

Tau

Via di Poppiano, 38 Loc. Poppiano - 50025 Montespertoli (FI)   055 82359
9.00-13.00/14.30-18.30   C.C.:All Major

Clothing, sportswear, casual
FACTORY OUTLET

Superstrada Pisa-Livorno, exit Ginestra Fiorentina. Before arriving in Montespertoli turn left to Poppiano. Follow the road to Poppiano passing the castle, a narrow cobbled road till a small parking area, Tau is on the right, a covered walkway.

Apparel for super active sportsmen: pullovers, T-shirts, sweatshirts in cotton in classical or neon colours, with or without logos, in alll sizes, from S to XXL and in very good quality. Waxed anoraks for sailing, thermal underwear, accessories. Special offers at € 6,00 in a vaulted, frescoed room. Web specials at www.tausport.it. They speak English and French.

Cotton Belt

Via Provinciale Lucchese, 181 - 50019 Osmannoro (FI)   055 3022542
13.00-19.00. Sat. 10.00-18.00   C.C.:All Major

Clothing, casual, jeans
FACTORY OUTLET

From Osmannoro to Campi Bisenzio, after the building of the Motorizzazione Civile on the right, the first gate on the left. A factory complex ex Lunginotti (Vicini Tubi).

Cotton Belt, Guess jeans in a nicely laid out store. All the jeans and jeansy dresses and jackets had a worn look, no seams, but all in a patch work of textures and faded colours, tyedye T-shirts. Clothing for the very young at fairly high prices. Sizes from 38 up to 46.

Roberto Cavalli

Via Volturno, 3 - 50019 Osmannoro Sesto Fiorentino (FI)   055 317754
10.00-19.00   C.C.:All Major

Clothing, accessories
FACTORY OUTLET

Autostrada A1, exit Firenze Nord to Sesto Fiorentino and Florence, follow the directions for Ikea. After the bridge and the Osmannoro sign turn right and follow the directions for Metro Cash & Carry. The outlet is on the first floor above Aldo Giardi.

All the wildlife and glam outfits Roberto Cavalli is famous for, jeans in techno-colour, fur lined accessories, tartan miniskirts and voile tiger striped maxi skirts, leather and metal studded biker jackets. Only end of line or items specially made for their outlet. Prices are still stratospheric, even during their twice yearly outlet sales: men's T-shirt € 200,00, a top in viscose for W € 250,00.

Confezioni 2002

V.le Hanoi, 35 - 50065 Pontassieve (FI)   055 8368508
9.00-12.00/14.00-19.30   C.C.:None

Clothing, leatherwear
ARTISAN'S WORKSHOP

From Florence S.S.69 at the beginning of Pontassieve follow the signs for the Zona Industriale. After the round-about 'Confezioni 2002' is on the left. Parking.

The choice depends a bit on the season. In spring some nice suede shirts made in soft and supple kid skin, well finished were € 200,00. Good buys too were the blazers in black nappa or the bomber jackets in honey coloured suede. They also make to measure and will show sheep skin coats when asked, even at 35°Celsius in summer.

Cuoieria Fiorentina

Via dei Ciliegi, 25 - 50064 Reggello (FI)   055 8662191
9.30-19.30   C.C.:All Major

Handbags, leather goods
GOOD PRICES

Autostrada A1, exit Incisa Val d'Arno to Reggello. On the local road going south, on the right.

Handbags and travel bags in scratch resistant nappa, in classical models like Kelly bags and Birkins or Bugatti bags but also mini Kellys, carpet bags, totes, foldable wardrobe bags, hold alls and leather suitcases, in a rainbow of colors. Kelly type bag € 110,00, a small Bugatti type € 60,00.

Ennio Sottili

Via A. Costa, 9 - 50066 Reggello (FI)   055 868374
8.30-12.30/15.00-19.30   C.C.:All Major

Gifts, local products
ARTISAN'S WORKSHOP

Autostrada A1, exit Incisa in Val d'Arno to Reggello. Follow the indications for San Donato in Fronzano. Two large lions guard the entrance to the shop.

A very interesting place to visit. They make mantel pieces, bases for large or small tables, sculptures in travertine or marble. A marble column in Corinthian style € 600,00, a simple Greek column in travertine € 325,00. Also good for small objects, a small obelisk in green marble € 12,00. (or funerary articles). They work to order and speak English, German and Spanish.

Desmo

Via Matteotti, 22/d - 50060 Reggello S.Donato in Fronzano (FI)   055 8652311
8.00-12.00/13.30-17.30 or by appointment. Sat. closed   C.C.:All Major

Handbags, leather goods
FACTORY OUTLET

Autostrada A1, exit Incisa in Val d'Arno towards Reggello. Once there follow the pretty road to S. Donato in Fronzano. In the center of the village turn right. The Desmo outlet is left of the factory.

They only sell their current or last season's showroom samples. Large choice, bags in scratch resistant leather € 125,00, or in ostrich € 380,00 an average saving of circa 50% on regular shop price. Fashionable colours and styles for wrist bags or clutch bags in lizard, pleated nappa, kid skin, the summit of elegance and style. Classical or unusual colors and unbeatable quality. For men there is little, some attaché cases and small leather goods like wallets or some shoes, € 110,00. Super.

Fendi Outlet

Via Pian dell'Isola, 66/33 - 50067 Rignano sull'Arno (FI)   055 834981
10.00-19.00. Sun. 15.00-19.00   C.C.:All Major

Clothing, accessories
FACTORY OUTLET

Autostrada A1, exit Incisa. Take the S.S.69 and follow the signs for Fendi and Rignano sull'Arno.

Not only luxury clothing but also hand bags, belts, scarves and other delectable fashion items. They sell off remnants, last year's unsold and over production. Prices are circa 30% less than shop price but still at luxury levels. This is also a good place to stock up on gifts. The Celine outlet is in the same building.

Pelletteria Emmetiesse

Via G.Marconi, 2/4/6 Z. I. Scopeti - 50068 Rufina (FI)   055 8397102
8.00-12.00/13.30-17.30. Sat. closed   C.C.:All Major

Handbags, travel bags
FACTORY OUTLET

From Florence towards Pontassieve, Borgo S. Lorenzo, Forli, circa 25 km. From the Autostrada A1, exit Incisa in Val d'Arno, direction of Pontassieve, Forli.

For sale are handbags in leather, or leather trimmed fabric, evening bags, travel bags, umbrellas, belts and small leather goods in a feminine, colorful style. Modern or classical colours like cognac or light beige, it's all very wearable. Good price/quality level. They work for some major Italian prêt à porter brand names. Multilingual personnel.

Mazzini Moda

Via Benvenuto Cellini, 74 - 50020 Sambuca Val di Pesa (FI)   055 8397102
15.30-19.30. Closed on Monday   C.C.:All Major

Handbags, leather goods
FACTORY OUTLET

Superstrada Firenze-Siena, exit Tavarnelle to Sambuca, turn right into the industrial zone. Continue till just before the Carapelli Olive Oil factory, on the left.

A new and very modern outlet with handsome handbags and fun beach and shopping bags. Large hold-alls for travelling in leather trimmed canvas, P.C. bags in bordeaux, silver or gold beach bags. Small leather goods and sunglasses with their brandname € 20,00. Prices are not exactly low but acceptable for an innovative, high quality product.

La Rosa - Calzaturificio L.G.R.

Z.A. Bardella, Via Cigliano, 8 - 50026 S.Casciano Val di Pesa (FI)   055 8228468
8.00-12.30/114.00-17.30. Saturday phone first   C.C.:None

Shoes
ARTISAN'S WORKSHOP

Autostrada A1, exit Certosa. Take the Superstrada Firenze/Siena. The first exit is S. Casciano N., follow the road to Empoli and the Cantina Antinori on the right. The outlet is in the Zona Industriale Bardella, a factory hall with a canopy.

They only produce good quality shoes for women in a classical style, the kind of shoe that is supremely comfortable and never goes out of fashion, be it a loafer, moccasin or pump. They work for major American & French designers. Showroom sizes are 36 and sell at € 60,00 and up. They can come up with personalized shoes or boots in unusual sizes or made up to client's specifications and need about 15 to 20 days. They charge circa € 70,00 per pair or more depending on the leather used.

Signoria di Firenze

Via di Luciano, Area Ponte Rotto   0558292334
50026 San Casciano Val di Pesa (FI)   C.C.:None
Phone first

Household linen, various
FACTORY OUTLET

From S. Casciano take the road to Siena, after the Agip service station turn right to Certaldo.

Very distinctive and striking linens with unusual colour combinations and sophisticated workmanship. There are table linen, cushion covers, throws, sheets and bed covers for sale plus fabrics for home furnishing. The choice depends very much on the time of year one is visiting. For information tel. 800528252.

Spaccio Italpel

Via Charta 77, 34 - 50018 Scandicci Z.I. (FI)   055 721570
10.00-19.00. Sat. 10.00-13.00 only from 1/9-1/7. Closed in Aug.   C.C.:All Major

Handbags, leather goods
FACTORY OUTLET

Autostrada A1, exit Firenze Signa. At the roundabout to the left, at the traffic light to the left, first road to the right. Italpel is at the end of the street on the right.

Handbags in snakeskin, baguettes in pink lizard. A shopping bag in ostrich printed nappa € 95,00, in trueblue anaconda € 240,00, a small backpack in printed snakeskin € 90,00. Large choice, there is something for everybody. For M wallets and belts in nappa, crocodile, snakeskin, also agendas, keyholders, beautycases. The winter showroom models go on sale in July.

Berti Coltellerie

Via Roma, 43 - 50038 Scarperia (FI)   055 8469903
10.00-12.30/16.30-19.30. Sat. closed   C.C.:All Major

Household goods, various
ARTISAN'S WORKSHOP

Autostrada A1, exit Barberina del Mugello (from Bologna it's the exit before Firenze), continue to Scarperia.

Scarperia is known as an age-old production center for fine hunting knives, pocket knives, table knives etc. Gift sets of hunting or wedding knives with horn handles or inlaid with walnut or other fine woods, highly specialized, beautiful workmanship. They produce 3 different series of cutlery for which one can choose various types of handles. Minimum price per piece €13,00 up to € 25,00. They only work to order but some ready-made cutlery is for sale.

Coltellerie Conaz

Via Roma, 8 - 50038 Scarperia (FI)   055 8430270
10.00-12.30/16.00-19.30   C.C.:All Major

Accessories, various
ARTISAN'S WORKSHOP

Take the S.P. 65 above Florence. In the old center, at the beginning.

Scarperia is known as an age-old production center for fine hunting knives, pocket knives, table knives etc. Gift sets of hunting or wedding knives with horn handles or inlaid with walnut or other fine woods, highly specialized, beautiful workmanship. One can order the 'Antico Salitano' or 'd'Amore' (dating back to 1600-1800) in horn, ebony, silver or bronze with a personal dedication € 550,00. A 'Isabellina' or a 'Navajo' € 575,00. Also unique cutlery, handmade, highly unusual original pieces.

Botteguccia Richard Ginori

Viale G. Cesare, 19 - 50019 Sesto Fiorentino (FI)   055 4210472
9.00-13.00/15.00-19.00. Closed Monday   C.C.:All Major

Ceramics, terracotta, porcelain
FACTORY OUTLET

Autostrada A1 exit no. 19 Sesto/Calenzano. Towards the center of Sesto and the train station. A factory hall, entrance and parking in the back, Sesto Fiorentino is about 20 minutes away from Florence.

Totally renewed outlet, large and spacious but we missed the dusty but promising bargains in seconds and end of series that were once so plentiful and low-priced. China statuettes, oven dishes, hexagonal plates, microwave proof serving dishes, close-outs in gold rimmed cake plates and coffee mugs, china dinner sets, tea or coffee pots, mocca cups all discounted circa 30%. The company ships all purchases. The Richard-Ginori museum nearby is interesting to visit.

Calzaturificio Doni Silvio

Viale Ariosto 490 c/d - 50019 Sesto Fiorentino (FI)   055 4217082
9.00-11.00/14.00-18.00. Saturday 10.00-12.30   C.C.:All Major

Shoes
FACTORY OUTLET

Autostrada A1 exit no. 19 Sesto/Calenzano. Towards the center of Sesto and the train station and not far from Richard Ginori. From Viale Ariosto look for the Lidl parking, the shop is on the right of the super market.

Doni produces boots and shoes since 1962 in Tuscan cowboy or chic but casual city styles. Canvas and leather boots € 135,00, shoes, sandals in sturdy leather M/W € 75,00. Sizes for W up to 42. They work for a major USA designer known for his embellished country looks. They also produce leather saddle bags, clutch bags, wrist bags, all very genuine.

La Tessitura Toscana Telerie

Via Mazzini, 161 - 50019 Sesto Fiorentino (FI)   055 4210754
9.00-12.30/16.00-19.30. Saturday closed   C.C.:All Major

Household linen, various
FACTORY OUTLET

Autostrada A1 exit no. 19 Sesto/Calenzano. Towards the center of Sesto and the train station. Sesto Fiorentino is about 20 minutes away from Florence.

Rather refined household linen, sheets, bedspreads, table clothes, embroidered, quilted, with contrasting borders and chic colour combinations. Design is basically classical but done with a light hand and a savvy mix of styles. Prices are very competitive for the quality offered.

BP Studio

P.zza Marconi, 1 - 50019 Sesto Fiorentino Osmannoro (FI)　　055 3236370
11.00-18.30. Closed on Mon. and Aug. Sun. phone first　　C.C.:All Major

Knitwear, cashmere
FACTORY OUTLET

Autostrada 11, exit Sesto Fiorentino, go straight, at the major traffic light turn left at the level of Ingrosmarket, Via Fermi, (percorso obbligato), follow the signs for Ikea.

Knitwear in first class quality and luxurious yarns, sold at major shops throughout Italy. Prices start at € 10,00 for a T-shirt to € 35,00 for knits in merinos. Cashmere sweaters start at € 75,00 for simple designs. They make a special series of tops, vests and cardigans for their outlet and sell seconds and remnants. Sizes from S to XL. Sales in January and July, the new collection goes on sale after September 15. They speak English.

Etienne Aigner

Via Indicatorio, 71 - 50058 Signa (FI)　　055 8997651
14.00-17.00. Saturday closed　　C.C.:None

Handbags, leather goods
FACTORY OUTLET

Autostrada A1, exit Signa, continue towards Campi Bisenzio. The factory is on the left on the main road, a grey building, towards San Mauro a Signa. Parking in front, ring office bell.

Small Kelly type bags € 50,00, large € 92,50 - € 122,50, all showroom models or seconds, classical, well made in calf's skin, the type of leather that doesn't scratch easily. For men ties in super classical designs € 17,50, scarves € 32,50, also bathing costumes, other bits and pieces, to be checked carefully. A good address for handbags and small leathergoods.

Confezioni Rentor

Via F.lli Rosselli, 7 - 50059 Sovigliana - Vinci (FI)　　0571 508352
9.30-12.45/15.00-19.00. Closed in August　　C.C.:All Major

Clothing, leatherwear
ARTISAN'S WORKSHOP

Autostrada A1, exit Firenze Signa, superstrada to Pisa/Livorno for 30 km, exit Empoli Ovest, for the center and direction of Vinci.

Leatherwear, shearlings and furs, either ready made or made to measure. Sizes for men go up to 58 for women up to 50. For children they only work on special order. Jackets in nappa € 225,00 - € 500,00, coats € 360,00, 3/4 length in suede € 300,00. Pants, skirts, vests are only made to measure, they need 1 to 2 weeks.

Calzaturificio "Buttero"

Via della Repubblica 99/101 Z.I.　　0571 586633
50050 Stabbia-Cerreto Guidi (FI)　　C.C.:All Major
15.00-19.30. Saturday 9.30-13.00

Shoes
FACTORY OUTLET

Autostrada A11, exit Montecatini Terme to Fucècchio. Well before Fucècchio follow the road to Stabbia and the Industrial Zone and follow the signs for Buttero.

Casual and sporty shoes for M/W all with rubber soles, but also boots in Tuscan Texan style, in printed snake skin, or slippers in suede € 70,00. The showroom size for W is 37 at € 50,00, same price for M but in size 42. Sales from January 1 - 15 February, and from July 1 to 10 September. They speak English.

Calzaturificio Victor

Via della Repubblica, 36 - 50050 Stabbia - Cerreto Guidi (FI) 0571 586396
8.00-12.00/14.00-18.00 C.C.:None

Shoes
FACTORY OUTLET

Autostrada A11, exit Montecatini Terme to Fucècchio. Well before Fucècchio follow the road to Stabbia and the Industrial Zone and look out for a sign 'Vendita Diretta'. Victor is just before Buttero, but on the right.

Authentic outlet inside the factory and a good place to stock up on wellmade but inexpensive shoes at € 40,00 circa a pair. Men especially should have a good look around to snap up Oxfords or summer moccasins made for important shops in England or Germany like Mansfield, John Varvatos and Sioux. For W the choice is a bit more eclectic but still worthwhile.

Ermanno Daelli

Via Benvenuto Cellini 161, Z.I.Sambuca Val di Pesa 0558070183
50028 Tavarnelle Val di Pesa (FI) C.C.:All Major
Phone first

Clothing, leatherwear
FACTORY OUTLET

From Florence take the Superstrada to Sienna, exit Tavernelle Val di Pesa, before the center turn into the industrial zone Sambuca Val di Pesa.

They reopen around the first of October and we suggest you phone first to make sure they have some stock to show. They produce very dizzying, rainbow hued and etheral chiffon clothing to be worn in layers on top of a pair of jeans, with satin cargo pants or short 'Vintage' coats by brandname Ermanno Daelli. They have a shop in Florence in Via Roma.

Il Manichino Margutta

Piazza Guerrazzi, 4/7 - 57100 Livorno (LI) 0586 887267
9.00-13.00/15.30-19.30. Open first Sunday from 1/9-1/5 C.C.:All Major

Clothing
BARGAIN BASEMENT

In the center of Livorno, at the end of Via Grande.

A popular stockhouse, always busy, with a large choice of clothing for M/W. They have a quick turn over of inventory, impossible to name all the brand names that are for sale but there is somethhing for everybody. They speak English.

Casablanca Outlet

Via dei Sandroni, 24 - 55011 Altopascio (LU) 0583 216465
9.00-19.30. Sat. 9.30-12.30/15.30-19.30 C.C.:All Major
In June and July closed on Saturday

Household goods, various
FACTORY OUTLET

Autostrada A12, exit Altopascio, turn left, at the crossing left and follow the street till the Ceramica Manciolli factory on the left. Ring bell, parking inside the gate.

A large factory hall with a number of amusing and/or usefull items for the house and garden all either discontinued or close-outs. Cutlery by Gotthingen, original English stoneware, crystal glasses, cake plates or pizza plates, bases for lamps, coffeetables in cast iron, oven dishes, jugs, silverplate picture frames, trolleys etc., all in good taste and even better prices.

Le Firme Stock House

Via Italica / Via Cimabue - 55043 Lido di Camaiore (LI)
9.00-13.00/15.30-19.30

0584 611384
C.C.:All Major

Clothing, shoes
BARGAIN BASEMENT

Autostrada A12, exit Viareggio, follow the sign for Lido di Camaiore, second roundabout on the right, another 100 m on the right.

Clothing, accessories, either end of series or samples for M/W by some of the more famous brand names like Versace, Ferré, Dolce & Gabbana, Jean Paul Gaultier, Gai Mattioli. Busy, busy with clients in search of two piece suits, skirts, dresses and cargo pants, all discounted 50%. They speak English and French.

Calzaturificio Fiorina

Loc. Piaggione Di Gello, 2 - 55064 Pescaglia Diecimo (LU)
8.30-12.00/14.00-17.00. Closed Saturday

0583 359431 - 94
C.C.:None

Shoes
FACTORY OUTLET

From Lucca take the S.S.12 to Borgo Mozzano. A Diecimo turn left to Pescaglia for circa 5.5/6 km. The factory is on the left next to a carpenter, in a white building.

A small showroom with their own production of boots and slippers, sandals and clogs, brand name Fiorina. Cowboy booties in ostrich, afrodite in lizard, sandals in straw, it is all amusing and fashionable. Very cute (and comfortable) Scholl's type sandals but in bright, shiny colours and with strass buckles € 30,00. They work for the U.K., Germany and the U.S.A. and speak English.

Maglificio Manu'

Maglificio Manu' - 55016 Porcari (LU)
16.00-19.30. Sat. open after 1/9

0583 211030
C.C.:None

Knitwear, cashmere
FACTORY OUTLET

From Lucca take the main road to Porcari. Manu' is in the center, look for a small placque of a lightblue madonna, turn left and follow the street going up. Manù is on the right, parking in front.

Their own production of knitwear with brandname Offshore, Backer Street and two major Italian and English designers known for their punky style. Some sweaters sported handpainted stripes, some were done in faded vintage cotton, all quite original and a touch mad. All sizes though they onlly sell prototypes and remainders minus the famous labels. Offers of knitwear at € 10,00 and up.

Minimalia Outlet

Via Giacomo Puccini, 2/E - 55016 Porcari (LU)
9.00-13.00/15.30-19.30

0583 210686
C.C.:All Major

Knitwear, cashmere
FACTORY OUTLET

From Lucca to Porcari, before the center at the roundabout look for the Esselunga shopping center. Minimalia is on the right of the supermarket complex.

A modern shop that used to be named Gruppo Del Carlo. Large quantities of quality knitwear: twinsets in merinos wool, bouclé sweaters, tops in mixed wool/acrylic, cotton, viscose, amusing and at good prices, brand name Moda mia e tua, Lady A and Paola Collection. Offers at € 5,00, T-shirts € 8,00 - € 14,00, cardigan for M with zip in cotton €14,00, there are really lots of bargains in good quality.

D'Avenza

Via Aurelia, 22 - 54031 Avenza (MS)   0585 857265
9.00-12.30/14.30-18.00. Sat. 9.00-12.30   C.C.:All Major

Clothing
FACTORY OUTLET

Autostrada A12, exit Carrara to the left for the S.S. 1 Aurelia. D'Avenza is about 1 km further on the left.

Very classy menswear, definitely Alta Moda. Super elegant men's suits, fit for the board room, € 650,00 - € 1100.00, hand finished in all sizes, from 48 to 60, trousers € 180,00. Coats in cashmere or camelhair € 1,000,00. Their showroom models are made in size 50 and are certainly worth checking out. They stock some things for women but in a super classical style. Worth a visit for M.

Ciompi

Via Tosco Romagnola, 75 - 56025 Fornacette (PI)   0587 420137
8.00-12.00/14.00-18.00   C.C.:None

Umbrellas
FACTORY OUTLET

Superstrada Firenze-Pisa, exit Pontedera Ovest, then S.P. to Fornacette Calcinaia.

Umbrellas in every possible shape and size, against the sun, against the rain, for golfers, for brides, for managers. With handles in bamboo, walnut, plastic, tremendous choice. They work for Lancetti, Renato Balestro, Beverly Hills Polo Club and Ponte Vecchio.

Maria Sartini Cashmere Italia

Via Novecchio 27, Z.A. Ovest - 56014 Pisa Ospedaletto (PI)   050 985393
9.00-13.00/15.00-19.00. Sat. closed   C.C.:All Major

Knitwear, cashmere
FACTORY OUTLET

Superstrada Firenze - Pisa exit Pisa SudEst, direction Livorno. Follow the indications for the Zona Artigianale Ovest and take the 2nd street on the right, then 2nd street on the right again, first on the left. Follow signs 'Cashmere'.

A large first floor showroom selling knitwear in Mongolia cashmere by Marina Sartini and Old Tower in lovely colors. Exceptional workmanship, reversible models, two-ply to 6-ply cashmere cardigans. In summer tops in linen weave € 50,00, very stylish twinsets in cool linen € 164,00, special offers of short cashmere twinsets € 100,00 in all sizes.

Calzaturificio Marros Tremp

Via Ayrton Senna, 3 - 56028 San Miniato Basso (PI)   0571 417060
16.00-19.00. Sat. 10.00-12.30   C.C.:All Major

Shoes
FACTORY OUTLET

Near the Stilnuovo outlet but slightly further ahead, turn left at the Madonna, after the bridge and next to 'Pitti'.

Shoes and boots in the absolutely latest casual styles, loafers in suede or shiny black, ankle boots in natural cow-hide for men, in nappa with shiny buckles for W. Riding boots that look used in a Tuscan/Texas style with lots of small buckles on the side, also biker boots with steel toe caps. Sample size for W is 37, for M 42, all at € 60,00.

Emilio Cavallini Stilnovo

Via A. Volta, 13/15 - 56028 San Miniato Basso (PI)
9.00-12.00/14.00-18.00. Closed in Aug. & Sept.

0571 400827
C.C.:All Major

Lingerie, underwear
FACTORY OUTLET

From Florence take the Superstrada towards Pisa, exit San Miniato. The outlet is on the road to the San Miniato Basso train station, after the overpass/bridge turn left.

Stilnovo reopens near the end of September and sells high quality T-shirts in micro fiber € 20.00 - € 30.00, bodysuits, stockings, pantyhose € 12,50 and kneehighs € 3,00, socks € 2,50 in all the colours of the rainbow and contemporary or traditional designs. Good offers in remnants, brandname Emilio Cavallini.

Calzaturificio Gemini

Via G. Marconi, 28-32, Z.I. - 56020 S. Maria a Monte (PI)
14.00-19.00. Sat. 8.00-12.00

0587 709149
C.C.:None

Shoes
FACTORY OUTLET

From Fucecchio take the Strada Provinciale to S. Maria a Monte, than follow the signs for Z.I. di Ponticelli and the indications for Gemini.

A luminous space with a large choice in shoes by Gianna Meliani and Anne Klein USA. Very stylish models, elegant sandals with stiletto heels, summer clogs in raffia, embroidered slippers and rather mad high heels in pink suede. All sizes available, count on spending € 55,00 - € 75,00 for any pair of shoes. Their showroom size is 37 at € 55,00. The winter collection goes on sale after 15/9.

Ghelarducci Stock House

V.le del Tirreno 24/M - 56018 Tirrenia (PI)
10.00-13.00/16.00-20.00. Monday closed

050 32708
C.C.:All Major

Clothing, accessories
BARGAIN BASEMENT

Superstrada Florence - Pisa. The shops are in the center of Tirrenia, about 10 meters past the Telecom Italia building.

Two shops, one for kids from 0 to 18 years old and the other for M/W selling clothing with important Made in Italy labels at half price. New stock arrives every 15 days so it's quite impossible to cite any specific label since their merchandise changes all the time. Sales from 15/7 and 20/1 with further reductions. Remodelling service and English/French speaking personnel.

Soc. Coop. Artieri Alabastro

Piazza dei Priori, 5 - 56048 Volterra(PI)
8.30-12.30/15.30-18.30

0588 87590
C.C.:All Major

Gifts, local products
ARTISAN'S WORKSHOP

Piazza dei Priori is the central square in Volterra.

The Società Cooperativo Artieri Alabastro sells alabaster articles in good quality and at reasonable prices. There are statues, columns, small tables, book ends, boxes and of course quantities of alabaster eggs in all colours.

Pratesi Shop

Via Montalbano, 41 - 51034 Casalguidi (PT)   0573 526462
9.30-12.30/14.30-19.00Household linen, various   C.C.:All Major

Household linen, various
FACTORY OUTLET

Autostrada A11, exit Pistoia, take the local road to Vinci. After the sign Ponte Stella turn left into the Pratesi grounds. The factory is an anonymous looking building with the entrance to their outlet on the left and parking in front.

All their grandly luxurious sheets are seconds with a discount of circa 50%. Beach towels € 90,00 - € 122,50, terrytowel bathrobes € 55,00 - € 90,00, small baskets for the bathroom with the Pratesi emblem € 32,50. Cute perfumed shoe-forms in terrytowel € 15,00 a pair, lots of small presents to bring back, all sumptuous.

Alberto Gozzi

Via della Lama, 31-31A, Z.I.   0572 480011
51013 Chiesina Uzzanese (PT)   C.C.:All Major
15.00-19.00. Sat. 9.00-12.00

Shoes
FACTORY OUTLET

Autostrada A11, exit Chiesina Uzzanese. To the left in the direction of the IperCoop Montecatini shopping center. After the bridge to the left, turn right at the level of Parmalat.

Very fashionable women's shoes brand name 'Designed by Luciano Padovan', and 'esKo'. Elegant stilettos, sandals, slippers, ballerinas, Mary Poppins booties. Their sample size is 37 at € 60,00, high heels covered in paillettes € 80,00, in snakeskin € 100,00. Other sizes are circa € 102,50. Fun beach bags with amusing decorations € 50,00. A very busy outlet.

Calzaturificio Pamar

Via Cerbaia, 321 - 51035 Lamporecchio (PT)   0573 82935
8.00-12.00/14.00-18.00. Sat. 8.00-12.00   C.C.:None

Shoes
ARTISAN'S WORKSHOP

Autostrada A11, exit Montecatini Terme to the S.S.436, to the left for Lamporecchio. From Florence take the Superstrada to Pisa, 1st exit for Empoli, Vinci and Lamporecchio.

M/W shoes produced in first class luxury leather like farmbred crocodile, ostrich, lizard or snakeskin, combined with unusual materials and in mad colours like a pair of mocassins for M in strawberry coloured crocodile, or lace ups in butterscotch English leather, stilettos in snakeskin. The showroom size for M is 42 for W 37 and they stock some pretty eyecatching shoes and boots.

Intershoe - Via Spiga

Via Lucania, 22-24 - 56016 Montecatini Terme (PI)   057292781
9.00-12.30/14.30-19.00   C.C.:All Major

Shoes
FACTORY OUTLET

Autostrada A11, exit Montecatini. After the autostrada exit turn right, cross the busy intersection to the left, keep going straight, at the traffic light turn left. Before the roundabout turn right, past Carlos Carozzeria, look for a new, all blue glass building on the right.

Large modern outlet, very well laid out, offering contemporary shoes in impeccable taste. There are pumps with round or pointed toes, stiletto sandals, two-tone queenies with laces, platform- and carshoes in red suede or orange patent leather together with a matching clutch bag at € 100.00-€ 130.00. For men rubber soled moccasins, sandals € 30,00, Oxfords € 130,00, all beautifully made but less of a choice. Showroom size 36 for W at € 50,00 like the sales shoes on the left.

Confezioni Alba

Via Statale Fiorentina, 265 - 51038 Olmi (PT)
9.30-13.00/15.30-19.30

0573 718822
C.C.:All Major

Lingerie, underwear
FACTORY OUTLET

From Florence take the S.S. 66, Alba is on the right, well indicated. Parking.

Large showroom selling their own production of sleepwear by brand names Adely, Stefany, Alba, I Cuoriccini, Alba Bargiacchi. Very chic night gowns in silk and lace € 135,00, a silk baby doll € 36,00, a presentation set of nightshirt and gown € 100,00. Baskets with offers in cotton pyjamas at € 17,00, bathing costumes, T-shirts. They also sell the Fila underwear collection and Matignon hosiery at normal shop price.

Coralba

Via delle Melocche, 43 - 51038 Olmi (PT)
9.00-12.30/14.30-19.00. Saturday phone first

0573 717121
C.C.:None

Household linen, various
FACTORY OUTLET

Take the S.S. 66 from Florence to Pistoia, near Quarrata. The Coralba outlet for lingerie and sleepwear is on the corner of the main road and for household linen at the end of the dead-end street.

Very high level of workmanship for night gowns and pyjamas, sheets and quilted bed spreads, table linen and towels. The designs are floral or classical, in very classy jacquard, all made to last forever like the charming kitchen towels and table mats. Very luxurious sheets bordered in lace or satin, with matching towels and robes. Savings around 30%. They speak English and French.

Balducci

Via del Melo, 1a - 51018 Pieve a Nievole (PT)
10.00-12.30/16.00-19.00

0572 95661
C.C.:None

Shoes
FACTORY OUTLET

Autostrada A11, exit Montecatini Terme, turn right and follow the bypass and the signs for Balducci.

The Balducci shoes for children are very famous in Italy. In their outlet they sell shoes for kids from 0 to 14 years, sneakers, tennis, basket booties, all kinds of styles, last year's unsold, samples and irregular sizes at very competitive prices.

Freeport

Via Roma, 41 - 51015 Pieve a Nievole (PT)
9.00-13.00/15.30-19.30. Open on Sun. Closed on Mon.

0572 71134
C.C.:All Major

Clothing, casual, jeans
GOOD PRICES

Autostrada A11, exit Montecatini Terme. Take the exit to the right for Pieve a Nievole, at the intersection turn left, a wide street with trees, before the service station to the left.

All the remainders of the Ralph Lauren casuals collection end up at the Freeport stores. Tennis- and boat shoes, sweatshirts USA, bermudas and T-shirts in red, blue and white, jeansy dresses and cotton sweaters with the famous polo logo, RLPolo shirts € 60,00, belts € 10,00, jeans € 55,00. There is a limited choice, sizes are a bit erratic, fidelity card, sales and they speak English.

Incom - G.B. Pedrini

Via Roma, 47 - 51018 Pieve a Nievole (PT)
10.00-12.30/15.30-19.30. Closed Monday

0572 777405
C.C.:All Major

Clothing
FACTORY OUTLET

Autostrada A11, exit Montecatini Terme. Take the exit to the right for Pieve a Nievole, at the intersection turn left, a wide street with trees, before the service station to the left. Next door to Freeport and John Ashford.

A large, airconditioned shop where one can browse with ease amidst the many special offers by INCOM and Pedrini in medium quality. Sizes start at 42 to 46 for W and from 46 to 54 for M. Long floaty dresses € 39,00, pants for M € 22,50, T-shirts € 10,00, suits € 65,00. There is nothing that will make your heart skip a beat, but it's all acceptable and wearable.

John Ashfield Factory Store

Via Roma, 41 - 51018 Pieve a Nievole (PT)
10.00-13.00/14.00-20.00

0572 73499
C.C.:All Major

Clothing, casual, jeans
FACTORY OUTLET

Autostrada A11, exit Montecatini Terme. Take the exit to the right for Pieve a Nievole, at the intersection turn left, a wide street with trees, before the service station to the left. Next door to Freeport and near Incom.

The English flag with Rule Britannia atmosphere next to the stars and stripes of the Freeport outlet. Blazers and flowery teagowns, long white trousers € 80,00 and polos all ready for afternoon tea or a game of cricket. A striped linen blazer € 220,00, long floaty skirts in voile with a cabbage rose print € 50,00, all bcbg but updated and adapted to the 21st century.

DubinSport

Via Lucchese, 105 - 51010 S. Allucio di Uzzano (PT)
9.30-12.30/15.00-19.30

0572 441220
C.C.:All Major

Clothing, sportswear, casual, jeans
FACTORY OUTLET

Autostrada A11, exit Chiesina Uzzanese. Take the road to Péscia. At the first traffic light to the right, after the bridge to the left, go straight, at the Stop sign to the right.

A large and well ordered outlet with all sizes for both M/W well represented. Specialized clothing for skiing, swimming, trekking etc. in attractive colors and 'high tech' fabrics that will resist intensive use and last forever. A polo High Tech € 37,00, a down filled coat for W € 300,00. Large corner with 2ds and remnants at -50%.

Gruppo Osvaldo Bruni

Via Galcianese, 67/69 - 50047 Prato (PO)
9.00-13.00/15.30-19.30

0574 607591
C.C.:All Major

Knitwear, cashmere
FACTORY OUTLET

Autostrada A11, exit Prato Est. Follow the road to Pistoia, then turn right to the Zona il Pino e i pompieri(= fire station). Parking.

Large outlet selling knitwear for the young, active and fearlessly trendy. Latest fashion colors and styles in medium high quality. A cotton polo shirt for men € 30,00, a large sweater in cotton inlaid with the American flag € 67,00. Tops for W in viscosa, polyamide, cotton € 30,00 - € 60,00, sizes tend to be small.

Marangoni Davide

S.S. 146 Km 7.400 loc. Querce al Pino - 53043 Chiusi (SI)
8.00-13.00/14.00-17.00. Saturday phone first

0578 274015
C.C.:None

Ceramics, terracotta, porcelain
ARTISAN'S WORKSHOP

Autostrada A1, exit Chiusi to Chianciano Terme. After 800 m. on the S.S. 146 on the right.

Production and sales of industrial or handmade terracotta vases and amphoras, strawberry pots in all sizes. All the terracotta products will withstand freezing temperatures. One can order special formats or shapes and they will ship.

Cristalleria La Moleria

Via Roma, 20 - 53034 Colle Val d'Elsa (SI)
9.00-13.00/15.30-20.00. Open on Sunday

0577 922175
C.C.:All Major

Crystal, glassware
FACTORY OUTLET

In the center of Colle Val d'Elsa.

Lovely objects for presents: small perfume bottles in crystal can be bought for as little as € 6,50, whiskey decanters € 22,50, engraved grappa bottles € 40,00, cut crystal flower vases, very impressive, quite heavy and priced according to size. Large choice.

Cristalleria Laica

Loc. S. Marziale - 53034 Colle Val d'Elsa (SI)
9.00-13.00/15.00-19.30

0577 928720
C.C.:All Major

Crystal, glassware
FACTORY OUTLET

From Colle Val d'Elsa take the local road to Grosseto to arrive at the Zona Industriale of San Marziale.

The Laica showroom abounds in small crystal objects, ideal for gifts. A small cut crystal bowl for chocolates € 5,00, a whiskey decanter circa € 17,50. Also vases, glasses, plates, animal figurines etc.

Cristalleria Vilca

V. F.lli Bandiera, 53 Loc.Gracciano
53034 Colle Val d'Elsa (SI)
8.30-12.00/14.00-17.30. Sat. closed

0577 929188
C.C.:All Major

Crystal, glassware
FACTORY OUTLET

On the local road S.S. 541 from Colle Val d'Elsa to Grosseto, on the right.

Extremely well-stocked with crystal stemware, complete sets of goblets with Greek names like Atene, Circe or Tebe can be ordered and will cost around € 15,00 per glass. Modern centerpieces, crystal chess-set at € 330,00, it's all very contemporary and striking!

Cristallerie L. Grassini

Via di Spugna, 124 - 53034 Colle Val d'Elsa (SI)
9.00-13.00/15.30-20.00

0577 922739
C.C.:All Major

Crystal, glassware
ARTISAN'S WORKSHOP

At the beginning of Colle Val d'Elsa, from Poggibonsi on the right.

Loreno Grassini is a crystal engraver with more than 30 years experience and can personalize crystal glasses with intials or a family coat of arms. The cost per 2 letters € 2,00, for a heraldic design prices start at € 4,50. The workshop is specialized in wedding lists and small gifts. They ship everywhere.

Cristallerie Mezzetti

Via Oberdan, 13 - 53034 Colle Val d'Elsa (SI)
9.00-13.00/15.30-20.00

0577 920395
C.C.:All Major

Crystal, glassware
FACTORY OUTLET

From Florence take the superstrada to Siena, exit Colle Val d'Elsa Nord. The factory outlet of Cristalleria Calp is in the center of Colle Val d'Elsa, near Piazza Arnolfo.

Beautiful crystal objects, all in 24% lead crystal, vases, platters, bottles, small animals, the choice is overwhelming. Sets of 12 or 24 glasses, special items for the house, made by Calp or personalized, also in glass. Objects by RCR Royal Crystal Rock, Primavera di cristallo e DaVinci Crystal. A 'design' perfume bottle by Dior € 46,00, similar but nameless € 8.00.

Compagnia del Cristallo

Loc. Pian dell'Olmino
53034 Colle Val d'Elsa Mensanello (SI)
15.00-18.00. Saturday closed

0577 928279
C.C.:All Major

Crystal, glassware
FACTORY OUTLET

From Colle Val d'Elsa take the old provincial road S.P.541 to Siena. At the intersection with Mensanello keep going straight for circa 100 m., the factory is on the left.

A wide choice of small and large objects in crystal by Arnolfo di Cambio at very good prices. There are wine glasses, flutes, whiskey decanters, small perfume bottles, crystal frames and chess pieces, vases and byoux.

Ellepiemme Piastrelle

Via P. Nenni,16 Loc. Badesse - 53035 Monteriggioni (SI)
9.00-12.30/15.00-19.30. Sat. closed

0577 309058
C.C.:All Major

Ceramics, terracotta, porcelain
GOOD PRICES

Superstrada Firenze-Siena, exit Badesse to the center. Follow the indications for Ellepiemme piastrelle.

They claim to have the lowest prices in Italy for tiles, either regular, second or third choice. In their warehouse there are large quantities to choose from, rather pretty and well made, ideal for a bathroom or kitchen. For large quantities one needs to order and they need 10 days before the consignment is ready to take away.

Cantine Melini

Loc. Gaggiano - 53036 Poggibonsi (SI)
8.00-12.00/13.30-17.30

0577 998511
C.C.:None

Wine, liqueurs
GOOD PRICES

From Poggibonsi take the road to Castellina in Chianti, after 7 km on the right.

An enormous wharehouse and winery where one can buy all the wines the Cantina Melini produces, like a Vernaccia di S. Gimignano € 3,70, per bottle or Isassi a Chianti classico 'gallo nero', a dry red that's a little bit tannic € 5,500. They also ship everywhere.

Distillerie Bonollo

Via Trav. Valdigiana, 2/4 - 53049 Torrita di Siena (SI)
8.00-12.00/14.00-18.00. Ring bell

0577 685210
C.C.:None

Wine, liqueurs
FACTORY OUTLET

Autostrada A1, exit Sinalunga to the road for Betolle and Torrita di Siena.

The Bonollo distillery is an important producer of grappa, brandy and 15 different types of liqueurs. Here in their factory outlet one can sample their wares, buy in quantity and visit the factory.

U M B R I A

....

San Rufino

Via San Rufino, 43/a - 06081 Assisi (PG)
7.30-13.00/16.30-20.00. Thursday 7.30 - 13.00

075 812866
C.C.:None

Food, meat
GOOD PRICES

Near the San Rufino Basilica.

A tiny sales point of typical Umbrian sausages and other meats like capocollo, dried sausage, with truffles, with red peppers, with fennel seeds, clauscolo, guanciale rustego, cojoni di mulo. Wild boar salami € 21,00 al kilo. They ship.

....

Hemmond Socrea

Via del Lavoro, 9 - 06083 Bastia Umbra (PG)
9.30-13.00/15.30-19.30

075 8012103
C.C.: All Major

Knitwear, cashmere
FACTORY OUTLET

From Perugia take the E45, 2nd exit to Bastia Z.I., to the left, pass I.S.A., after the road curve Hemmond is on the left.

Large outlet selling clothing, knitwear, jeans by Hemmond, Valentino, and Romeo Gigli. All sizes are available from S to XXL, there is a corner with special cashmere sales, and lots of casual country clothing, polos in silk, tweed jackets, cord pants all very attractive and at good prices.

RI.GA
Strada delle Fratte - 06100 Castel del Piano Perugia (PG)
16.00-20.00. Saturday 9.00-13.00/15.00-20.00

075 5270187
C.C.: None

Clothing, leatherwear
FACTORY OUTLET

Superstrada Firenze-Perugia, exit Corciano, turn right, then straight towards the Nestlé Perugina factory. In front of the Coop S.Sisto to the right, then to the left. RI.GA is on the left. Ample parking.

A small outlet worth a visit for those looking for leather clothing. In summer prices are considerably lower, not only because of the summer season and sales but they also sell their showroom models for W in size 42, in size 50 for M at low prices. A Saharienne € 140,00, skirts € 60,00, pants € 100,00. Friendly and helpful personnel.

Bassini
Via Treves, 23 Cerbara - 06011 Città di Castello (PG)
9.00-12.30/16.00-19.30

075 851721
C.C.: All Major

Handbags, leather goods, suitcases
FACTORY OUTLET

From Perugia take the Superstrada to Città di Castello, at the second exit turn right to the main road for circa 2 km. At Cerbara in front of the bar 'Il Coccodrillo' turn left, continue and follow the indications for Bassini.

Belts, bags, travel bags, beauty cases, suitcases by El Campero, all in sturdy cow hide, in fact the style is Italian cowboy from the Maremma area. Some items from their more recent collection are on show but they mostly sell off samples, end of series and last year's unsold.

Camicieria Etrusca
Vle. Romagna, 73 - 06011 Città di Castello (PG)
9.00-13.00/15.00-20.00

075 8518087
C.C.: All Major

Shirts
FACTORY OUTLET

From Perugia and the Superstrada take the second exit for Città del Castello, keep to the right, at the Stop sign turn left, continue for 2/3 km. On the left there is a large, yellow building with a sign Etrusca.

An elegant outlet with a vast array of shirts for the whole family. There are quantities of striped shirts with white or lightblue collars with triple buttons, buttondown in Oxford cotton or classy French collars. All the shirts are ready made they do not work to order, but they can adjust anything, longer or shorter sleeves, different buttons, larger collars etc.

Ciarabelli
Via Piemonte Z.I. - 06012 Città di Castello (PG)
8.00-12.00/14.00-18.30. Sat. 9.00-12.30

075 8511595
C.C.: All Major

Shirts
FACTORY OUTLET

From Perugia take the Superstrada, exit Città di Castello, keep left to take the main road in the direction of S.Sepolcro, continue till the Ciarabelli factory on the right.

Well made shirts in various models, button-down, French collar in sizes from 38/44 for M/W, either short-sleeved or long-sleeved. This is all their own production and prices are very reasonable for the quality offered, € 20,00 up to € 40,00 and beyond for silk or hand finished shirts.

Bolle di Sapone

Via Ponchielli, 35 - 06073 Corciano Ellera (PG)
9.30-13.00/15.30-19.30. Open in August

075 5179641
C.C.: All Major

Clothing
FACTORY OUTLET

Superstrada Perugia-Firenze, exit Corciano, follow the signs for Bolle di Sapone. There is a large parking and a playground for children.

A good address for large families. Quantities of knitwear, jeans, coats and jackets, skirts, jodhpurs, cargo pants and coveralls for children from 0-14 years old. Little dresses for girls € 25,00, special offers and sales from 10/1 and 10/7. They speak English, French and German.

Ellesse

Via Turati, 19 - 06073 Corciano Ellera (PG)
9.00-13.00/16.00-20.00

075 5171523
C.C.: All Major

Clothing, sportswear, casual
FACTORY OUTLET

Superstrada Perugia-Florence, exit Corciano. It is difficult to miss the factory which is right near the exit and the entrance of the outlet, once through the gates, is in the back, up two floors. Large parking.

Sportswear for the active skier, tennis player, swimmer and hiker and anything for other sport one can think of. Ellesse sportswear, Valentino and Chervo parkas and wind breakers, boots and fishing waders: regular merchandise 41% discount, 2nds 55%, 3rd choice 65%, plus special offers. Large & busy.

Maglificio Bilc

Via Ponchielli, 17 - 06073 Corciano Ellera (PG)
9.00-13.00/15.00-19.00

075 5170639
C.C.: All Major

Knitwear, cashmere
FACTORY OUTLET

Superstrada Perugia-Firenze, exit Corciano, follow the signs for Maglificio Bilc.

Small outlet selling polo and cowl neck knit tops, ideal to wear under jackets. Most of their collection is classical with a few items for the young and slim. Their knitwear is made in wool, wool/silk and cashmere/silk mixtures and sold at reasonable prices with an extra discount of 20% at the end of January and in August.

Spaccio Aziendale Primigi

Via Juri Gagarin, 6 - 06074 Corciano Ellera (PG)
9.30-13.00/15.00-19.30

075 50281
C.C.: All Major

Shoes
FACTORY OUTLET

Superstrada Firenze - Perugia, exit Corciano to Ellera on the right.

1000mq of shoes with one shop dedicated to samples, special offers and last year's unsold at low prices by brandname Igi and Primigi, well made in quintessentially Italian styles. There are really some excellent deals as long as one finds the proper size! The other shop sells their recent collection with discounts, yes, but prices are definitely much higher.

Camiceria Massucci

Via Palazzeschi, 28 - 06073 Corciano Taverne (PG)
9.00-13.00/15.30-19.30

075 6978266
C.C.: All Major

Shirts
FACTORY OUTLET

From Perugia take the Superstrada for Firenze and the exit for the Industrial Zone of Taverne di Corciano.

A quite breathtaking collection of shirts for men, in every type of weight, colour, design, in cotton or silk. A shirt with short sleeves € 27,50, long sleeves € 30,00 and up. In linen € 32,50 either button-down or French collar. Some very bright ties in silk € 12,00 and a few blouses for women, all classical.

Bettini Germano

Via Tiberina Sud, 320/322 - 06053 Deruta (PG)
9.00-13.00/15.00-19.00. Sunday 15.00-19.00

075 9710550
C.C.: All Major

Ceramics, terracotta, porcelain
ARTISAN'S WORKSHOP

Take the S.S. 3/b to the center of Deruta, on the left.

A big yard with a great variety of terracotta pots and vases on show in very original and appealing shapes. 'Putti' angels wind their way around a curved vase, garlands decorate an amphora. Inside, an 'ecological' collection of white or flowers-on-white platters and plates, ideal for country houses.

La Bottega del Vasaio

Via Tiberina, 119 - 06053 Deruta (PG)
8.00-12.00/15.00-19.00

075 9711284
C.C.: All Major

Ceramics, terracotta, porcelain
ARTISAN'S WORKSHOP

Via Tiberina is the main street of Deruta.

Well-known for very striking maiolica plates with heraldic designs, coat of arms, based on original plates dating back to the 15th century. Very reasonable prices, they work to order.

U. Grazia Maioliche

Via Tiberina, 181 - 06053 Deruta (PG)
9.00-13.00/14.30-18.30. Saturday 9.00-13.00

075 9710201
C.C.: All Major

Ceramics, terracotta, porcelain
ARTISAN'S WORKSHOP

On the main street traversing Deruta.

A lot of traditional maiolica wares; the blue and white rooster salt and pepper sets, apothecary jars (very pretty), handpainted plates with initials or names, made to order, initials € 12,50, a heraldic motif € 15,00 and up. Mad, modern California-style coffee mugs were interesting and fun. They export to the USA: Bergdorf Goodman, Henry Bendel, Saks, Tiffany.

Cinelli

Viale Umbria, 33 - 06063 Magione (PG)   075 8472050
9.30-12.30/15.30-19.00. Saturday closed   C.C.: None

Clothing
FACTORY OUTLET

From Perugia take the superstrada, exit Magione, to Chiusi on the right.

For large sizes and mature ladies only. Clothing in very good quality but definitely very classical. Brand names Ann Weinberg, Ruffo, Rosante. Average price for
a wool- or cotton jersey dress € 65,00. Silk blouses were low-priced as were
the trousers for men in summer wool. All sizes avaiilable.

Uni Euro

Z.I. Bacanella - 06063 Magione (PG)   075 8474011
9.00-13.00/15.30-20.00   C.C.:All Major

Knitwear, cashmere
FACTORY OUTLET

*From Perugia take the superstrada to Florence, exit Magione. Take a U-turn towards
Perugia, the outlet is 1.5 km further on, to the right.*

Located in a camphor scented warehouse, but this is the place to buy cable-knit
sweaters or clever twinsets made for trendy Burberry, original and fun, in up to
date colours, with the famous Burberry tartan and at prices that are really
worth the detour. However, keep in mind that the Burberry label will be cut out
after your purchase.

Sposini Tessuti Umbri

Strada Marscianese/S. Valentino della Collina   075 8784134
06100 Marsciano (PG)   C.C.:All Major
9.00-13.00/15.30-19.30

Fabrics, home furnishings, household linen
ARTISAN'S WORKSHOP

*Autostrada A1, exit Orvieto to Todi, after Todi to the left to S.P. 397 Marscianese. The
Tessuti Umbri outlet is after Masciano in S. Valentino della Collina, on the left.*

Traditional handprinted tablecloths, bedspreads, fabrics, towels in natural fibers
at competitive prices. The distinctive designs according to age-old Umbrian
custom are very handsome and striking in a quality that will last for years.

RucoLine

Via Rapallo 32 - 06063 Mugnano (PG)   075 695836
10.00-13.00/15.30-19.30   C.C.:All Major

Shoes
FACTORY OUTLET

*From Perugia take the S.P.220 in the direction of Città del Pieve. Pass La Perugina, con-
tinue for circa 10 km and take the overpass for Mugnano. Rucoline is in front of the
'Campo Sportivo'.*

Rucoline makes very nifty shoes, contemporary, stylish with the latest high-tech
materials for M/W and lots of accessories like bags, belts, agendas, wallets. Their
shoes are in soft but water resistent leather with the initial R of Rucoline, rubber molded soles, extremely comfortable. Showroom size for W is 37, for M 42.

Luisa Spagnoli

Loc. S. Lucia Sobborghi - 06100 Perugia (PG)
9.00-13.00/16.00-19.30

075 4591
C.C.: All Major

Clothing
FACTORY OUTLET

Superstrada Firenze - Perugia, to Perugia and exit Mandonna Alta. Continue to the stadium and the village of S. Lucia.

Luisa Spagnoli is well known in Europe for their wide selection of clothing in a style that always looks attractive and will suit most sizes. In their warehouse samples, end of line and last year's unsold are for sale at half shop price. Sizing tends to be on the M, L to XXL level for dresses in woollen jersey or cotton in classical but updated colors. Around November they bring out a series of formal/cocktail dresses and suits.

Sterne Int. Lorena Antoniazzi

Z. I. S. Andrea delle Fratte, Via Manna 75 - 06132 Perugia (PG)
9.00-13.00/15.30-19.30

075 5289810
C.C.: All Major

Knitwear, cashmere
FACTORY OUTLET

Superstrada Firenze-Perugia, exit Val di Chiana, continue to Perugia and take the Corzano exit, turn right, straight ahead and pass La Perugina. Follow the signs to Sterne.

A very good address to stock up on woollen jerseys in a variety of styles. They sell heavy woollen knits for winter, cotton long sleeved T's, tops to wear under jackets, twinsets and cardigans in a cable knit. Good offers too in cashmere, classical styling and an exceptional choice of colours and sizes. Brand name Lorena Antoniazzi.

Galassia

Via Edison, 1 Z.I. Molinaccio
06087 Perugia - Ponte S. Giovanni (PG)
15.30-19.30. Closed from 1/6-15/9

075 5996932

C.C.: All Major

Knitwear, cashmere
FACTORY OUTLET

From Perugia/Rome/Florence take the second exit for Ponte S. Giovanni. From the Park Hotel it's circa 300 m to Balanzano. From the superstrada E45 take the Torgiano-Ponte San Giovanni exit.

Sweaters, cardigans, skirts by brandname Pashmere. For M. jackets, ribbed sweaters, for W. stylish knits in cashmere in a rainbow of colours and in excellent quality all discounted circa 30%. They have a corner with end of line, super offers and remnants at low prices and sales in January and July.

Balmoral

Via G. Dottori, 72 - 06100 Perugia S.Sisto (PG)
9.30-13.00/15.30-19.30

075 5271308
C.C.: All Major

Clothing
ARTISAN'S WORKSHOP

Superstrada exit Corciano, turn right passing the Quattro Torre shopping center, keep going straight in the direction of Nestlé Perugina. The Sartoria Balmoral is in front of the super market entrance on the right (gommista).

A large and elegant atelier showing a vast collection of suits made with fabrics by Loro Piana, Zegna. A men's suit € 150,00, a dress for W in linen € 90,00, a tailleur € 170,00, ideal for the more mature customer. Their staff is very helpful, they make to measure and offer extra discounts and a fidelity card to their clients.

Maglificio La Perugina

Via dei Mille, 8 - 06050 Ripa Bianca - Deruta (PG)   075 972871
9.00-12.00/15.00-19.00   C.C.:All Major

Knitwear, cashmere
FACTORY OUTLET

Autostrada A45 to Rome, exit Casalina, go through the village, after 1 km to the right there is a large factory hall with La Perugina written on it.

Knitwear in cashmere, cashmere/silk and viscose. Large choice of mostly classical models for M/W, rib knit or cable knit cardigans, polos, jackets with zip, V-neck sweaters. Prices are very reasonable and they give an extra discount of 50% on their winter collection in January and on the summer collection in July.

Legnomagia Outlet

Via Settevalli km 11,5 - 06070 S. Biagio della Valle Perugia (PG)   075 972871
8.30-13.00/14.00-17.30. Sat. closed   C.C.:None

Household goods, various
FACTORY OUTLET

From Perugia take the road to Pila. After the traffic light continue for circa 3 km. After the intersection look for a warehouse on the left.

Household items, decorative objects for the table, kitchen, bathroom, all in wood or other natural materials like glass, felt, cork. Cutting boards, boxes for cutlery, small containers for salt (also sold on-line). They only discount their end of series or seconds and only here in their outlet. They speak English and German.

Brunello Cucinelli

Piazza Alberto della Chiesa, 6 - 06070 Solomeo (PG)   075 5293121
9.00-12.30/15.30-18.30. Saturday 9.00-12.30   C.C.:All Major

Knitwear, cashmere
FACTORY OUTLET

Superstrada Firenze-Perugia, exit Corciano, per Solomeo. Cucinelli is on the main square of Solomeo.

The right address for cashmere fanatics. Although prices have increased a bit, this remains a busy and popular outlet to buy the famous cashmere knitwear by Brunello Cucinelli in superb colors, fashionable designs and excellent quality. In summer their opening hours are rather flexible, we suggest to phone first.

Gunex

Via dell'Industria, 5 - 06070 Solomeo (PG)   075 529491
9.00-12.30/15.30-18.30. Sat. 9.00-12.30   C.C.:All Major

Clothing
FACTORY OUTLET

From Perugia take the superstrada to Florence, exit Corciano and follow the signs for Solomeo. Before the ascent to Solomeo look for a new yellow building, a large complex with a garden.

Lovely pants and skirts in modern fabrics. Long skirts in linen with a bit of nylon to give it a nubby texture € 65,00, the same fabric but in wide sailor pants € 80,00. Tey sell remnants to make a gilet or jacket in the same material. Striking and original designs, brand name Gunex and Timeo.

Rivamonti

Via dell'Industria, 5 - 06070 Solomeo (PG)
9.00-12.30/15.30-18.30. Sat. 9.00-12.00

075 697071
C.C.:All Major

Knitwear, cashmere
FACTORY OUTLET

From Perugia take the Superstrada to Florence, exit at Corciano and follow the sign for Solomeo. Before the ascent to Solomeo look for a new yellow building, quite large, with a garden.

Rivamonti/Gunex are part of the Smail-Cuccinelli Group. Faultless knitwear in silk, silk/viscose, or linen/viscose, twin-set € 120,00, T-shirts in a silk-knit € 60,00. Also some seconds in baskets but not much. In winter tweedy jerseys in brown wool with black-edged button holes, it's all in contemporary taste. In June & July they give an additional 20% discount.

Mastro Raphael

Loc.S.Chiodo 161, Z.I. - 06049 Spoleto (PG)
9.00-12.30/14.00-19.00
Monday closed, Saturday 9.00-18.30

0743 230859
C.C.:All Major

Household linen, various
FACTORY OUTLET

In Spoleto take the direction of Acquasparta.

The bed linen collection by Mastro Raphael is well known for the intricacy of the designs and the elaborate combinations of material and colors for sheets, bedspreads, towels. They sell remnants of terrytowel fabric, silks and cottons. Stock changes all the time, it's all in very good quality and rich, fantasy designs.

Nazareno Gabrielli

Via dell'Artigianato - 06089 Torgiano (PG)
9.00-12.30/15.00-19.30. Closed on Monday

075 985468
C.C.:All Major

Clothing, leatherwear
FACTORY OUTLET

From Perugia go through all the various tunnels, exit Torgiano S. Martino in Campo. After Torgiano continue to Bastia, After the traffic light, 200 m ahead, there is an orange coloured building, well indicated.

Discounts of 25% to 50% on their whole inventory. Skirts and sleeveless dresses in nabuck, a large quantity of travelbags to choose from, small leatherware, shoes, silks, watches. Classics but with a youngish feel, for the over 30. The new collection is for sale in March for the summer- and in July for the winter collection.

Seta & Cashmere Group

Z.I. Madonna del Moro - 06019 Umbertide (PG)
9.00-13.00/15.30-19.30

075 9417554
C.C.:All Major

Knitwear, cashmere
ARTISAN'S WORKSHOP

From Perugia take the exit for Zona Industriale Madonna del Moro and look for the 'Aero Confezioni' building.

There is always someone around in the workshop to show their knitwear collection. They produce very nicely styled knits in cashmere, cashmere/silk, viscosa and merino wool either classical or in the latest fashion trends and colours, it all depends on the time of the year. For men there is less choice.

Az. Agric. Dubini Locatelli

Località Rocca Ripesena, 68 - 05019 Orvieto (TR)   0763 344921
8.00-13.00/14.00-17.00. Sat. closed   C.C.:All Major

Wine, liqueurs
GOOD PRICES

Autostrada A1, exit Orvieto, follow the indications for Castelgiorgio. Pass Serracavallo, after 2.5 km at the intersection take the road to Palazzone.

Their own production of Orvieto Classico: Muffa Nobile, Grechetto, Terre Vineate. One can taste the various wines and they do ship. The Palazzone wines are served in the best restaurants all over the world.

Gruppo Italiano Vini Bigi

Loc. Ponte Giulio, 3 - 05018 Orvieto (TR)   0763 316224
8.00-12.00/13.00-17.00. Saturday closed. Friday open till 13.00   C.C.:None

Wine, liqueurs
GOOD PRICES

Autostrada A1, exit Orvieto per Serracavallo. One can see the Bigi industrial complex from the autostrada. After Serracavallo continue for circa 4km till the sign Gruppo Italiano Vini Bigi.

An enormous winery with an extensive choice of all the local wines, even spumanti and sparkling wines. One can not buy wine per liter but only in packs of 3 to 6 bottles of 0.75 lt, 1.5 lt or 3 lt. Good prices for a wine that is distributed everywhere and can be found in all the large shopping centers.

Il Borgo e la Città

Via 4 Novembre, 55 - 05100 Piediluco - Terni (TR)   0744 407027
17.30-24.00. Open on Sundays.
Open from 1/7-15/9, closed Mondays   C.C.:None

Gifts, local products
GOOD PRICES

From Terni take the road to Rieti.

Handmade, unusual objects sold in an original shop, even the opening hours are different. All year round they open on Sundays and holidays and between 15/6-15/9 also in the evening. They sell ceramics of the 'Graziella' series, mugs, plates, jugs (seen in Porto Cervo at double the price), prints and fabrics.

Astancolli

Via del Rivo,126/130 - 05100 Terni (TR)   0744 300179
9.30-13.00/16.00-20.00   C.C.:None

Clothing
FACTORY OUTLET

From Orte it's the second exit. Go towards the zona Il Tulipano and Via del Rivo, on the left.

Smocked dresses and flannel blazers with velvet collars for special occasions. A little Chanel jacket, rimmed in velvet € 50,00, Vyella shirts € 14,00, plus First Communion dresses in the best of traditional good taste at various prices. They also produce practical things not afraid of the washing machine, all very pretty.

Ellesse

Via del Sersimone, 2 - 05100 Terni (TR)
8.30-12.30/15.30-19.30

0744 300088
C.C.:All Major

Clothing, sportswear, casual
FACTORY OUTLET

Autostrada A1, exit Orte to the Superstrada for Terni and exit Terni Ovest. The factory outlet is on the right.

Basically the same merchandise as in their main outlet near Perugia. Depending on the condition of the article, take 41%, 55% or 65% off the label price. Ellesse ski-fuseaux, Valentino parkas, Ouragan things for kids. Enormous choice in sportswear, casuals, weekend wear.

Space

Via Luigi Albertini, 12 Z.I. Baraccola - 60131 Ancona (AN)
10.00-19.00. Sunday 15.00-19.00

071 8717264
C.C.:All Major

Clothing, accessories
FACTORY OUTLET

Autostrada A14, exit Ancona Sud to Ancona. After circa 1 km turn into the Q8 service station, the new outlet is next to it.

Large place, starkly modern, selling not only Genny but also Byblos, Prada and MiuMiu. Genny suits € 375,00, (in sizes that go happily up to a 48). Myriad racks of pants/skirts € 95,00 - € 220,00, silk scarves € 45,00. There is an average choice of Prada, MiuMiu clothes, mostly casuals in smaller sizes and not many handbags, but there are some bags and accessories by Genny and Byblos. Phone for the date of new arrivals!

La Stockeria

Via Aspio, 24, S.S. 16 - 60021 Aspio Terme (AN)
10.00-12.30/16.30-19.30

071 959402
C.C.:All Major

Clothing, shoes
BARGAIN BASEMENT

Autostrada A14, exit Ancona Sud, on the S.S. 16, from Ancona on the right and in front of the Hotel Concorde and the market. From Pescara it is 800 mt from the autostrada exit.

Large choice of super trendy brands like Prada, Cristian Fissore, Versace, Ikam, Wolford, Polo RL, Ferré and many others. Sizes tend to be smallish 42-46 for W and 48-52 for M. Shoes are € 50.00 circa, the dresses and men's suits were very nice and discounted 50%. They speak English and Russian and have a sister shop in Corridonia (MC).

Danilo Dolci

Via Abbadia, 10 - 60021 Camerano (AN)
9.30-12.30/16.15-19.00. Saturday 9.30-12.30
Only Thurs/Sat morning, only Wed/Fri afternoon

071 730021
C.C.:All Major

Handbags, leather goods
FACTORY OUTLET

Autostrada A14, exit Ancona Sud to Camerano. At the level of the 'Cucine Gatto' building follow the signs for Danilo Dolci.

Super sales of their showroom collection of handbags by Gerardhini, Byblos and Mary Read, only for W and at competitive prices. Occasionally there are also some jeans and shoes by Mary Read for sale mostly in sample sizes: 42 for the jeans, 37 for the shoes. For M. there is far less choice, really only some belts and wallets.

Giorgio Grati

Via de Gasperi, 32 - 60021 Camerano (AN)
Phone for opening hours

071 732440
C.C.:All Major

Clothing
FACTORY OUTLET

Autostrada A14, exit Ancona Nord to Camerano.

This outlet is fairly new and opens towards the end of September. Glitterati looks, jeans with strass, dresses in technicolour prints, fantasy prints, evening tops with jais edges, byoux like traffic lights, tiger printed ponchos, glammy tweed jackets and multi coloured shoes, all by brand name Precious, very aptly named!

Fly 3 Factory Store

Via del Lavoro, 1 - 60120 Falconara (AN)
9.00-12.30/16.00-20.00

071 918117
C.C.:All Major

Clothing, casual, jeans
FACTORY OUTLET

Autostrada A14, exit Ancona Nord to Falconara. After the Q8 service station, on the left on the corner of Via del Lavoro.

There are two shops, one with their current collection of relaxed casuals by Gente di Mare, all in impeccable taste. The shop on the right is packed with seconds and old stock that can hold some surprising bargains. Woollies or cotton sweaters for M/W, bermudas, trousers, short cotton polo dresses, parkas and dress shirts, all discounted 40%-50%, in a vaguely nautical style. One can browse for hours!

Gulliver Look

Via Tornazzano, 3 - 60024 Filottrano (AN)
9.00-12.30/15.30-17.30

071 7221227
C.C.:All Major

Clothing
FACTORY OUTLET

Autostrada A14, exit Ancona Sud or Loreto, take the road to Osimo and Filottrano. S.S. Jesine. At the beginning on the right.

Luxury clothing on the level of the best prêt à porter/Alta Moda in refined fabrics (Tasmania by Loro Piana) by well-known brandname Lardini. Average price of a suit for W € 135,00, for men € 165,00 and up. Lots of very smart and luxurious coats in camelhair or tweedy jackets and pinstriped suits. They also work for some major international brand names. This is a worthwhile address to stock up on basics that will last. Sales at 30%.

Industria Confezioni Maschili

Via Villanova 1/a - 60024 Filottrano (AN)
9.00-12.30/15.30-19.30

071 7223601
C.C.:None

Clothing
FACTORY OUTLET

Autostrada A 14, exit Ancona Sud to Filottrano. Before the center turn right to the Villanova industrial zone in the direction of Osimo. Next to the Bar/Pizzeria King.

Another address for buying some seriously well taylored suits for both M/W in the best fabrics form the U.K. or the Biella area near Turin. Men's suits, well cut in a classical/faultless style € 180,00 - € 200.00. For those in need of a frac, they work to order at a cost of circa € 550,00. For W far less choice, some very british looking suits € 150,00.

Simonetta

Via Belardinelli, 6/8 - 60035 Jesi (AN)
8.30-12.00/15.30-19.00

0731 205125
C.C.:All Major

Clothing
FACTORY OUTLET

Autostrada A14, exit Ancona Nord to the S.S. 76, exit Jesi-Est. Follow the signs for the zona Zipa.

Kids' clothes from 2 years old up to size 44. Skirts, pants and knitwear from last year's collection, in an insouciant, wacky style, very colourful, brandname 'Angels' by Roberto Cavalli. Not all sizes and colors are available but there is plenty of choice. They sell off their summer collection towards the end of June.

Samsonite Outlet Center

Via Alfieri, 3 - 60027 Osimo fraz. San Biagio (AN)
9.00-12.30/16.00-20.00

0717 108675
C.C.:All Major

Handbags, leather goods, suitcases
FACTORY OUTLET

Autostrada A14, exit Ancona Sud to Osimo, circa 7/8 km. Before the village, on the right.

On sale are mostly travelbags and suitcases made out of sturdy material, but also hard shell Oyster suitcases, Samsonite shoes, attaché cases all seconds at 35% less than shop price. Defects are of the 'hardly noticeable' kind. Definitely worthwhile for the frequent traveler and fans of the Samsonite brandname.

Meg

Z.I. Campolungo - 63100 Ascoli Piceno (AP)
8.30-12.30/15.30-19.30

0736 403340
C.C.:None

Clothing, bridal wear and formal
FACTORY OUTLET

Autostrada A14, exit Benedetto del Tronto, follow the superstrada to Ascoli, exit Castel di Lama. Take a wide road on the left, after 1 km in front of the Autolellia dealer and on the left, look for a building with shiny glass windows.

3 different series of bridal gowns are made here at a minimum price of € 600,00 for a smashing bridal confection. They also make to measure and work (among others) for Lancetti. One can find the proper morning dress for men, dresses and suits for bridesmaids or the mother of the bride. The new collection is ready in November.

Alice Calzaturificio

Via Curiel, 123 - 63011 Casette d'Ete (AP)
9.00-13.00/15.00-19.30

0734 871326
C.C.:All Major

Shoes
FACTORY OUTLET

Autostrada A14, exit Civitanova Marche, follow the superstrada to Tolentino in the direction of Macerata. Exit at Monte Cosaro Scalo, the 2nd exit, and continue to Casette d'Ete. In the center at the intersection turn left - Civitanove M.- and take the last street to the left before leaving the town.

Production of shoes for children from 0 to 14 years old and in sizes 18 to 40 in medium high quality. Sample size are 20, 24, 31 sold at € 15,00. Pretty little winter shoes are sold at € 25,00 - € 35,00. It's a small outlet but full of brand names and there is a good chance to find a genuine bargain.

Araba Fenix

Via Teano, 26 - 63011 Casette d'Ete (AP)
9.00-12.00/14.30-20.00. Sat.. 9.00-12.00/15.30-20.00

0734 871631
C.C.:None

Shoes
FACTORY OUTLET

Autostrada A14, exit Civitanova Marche. Follow the superstrada for Tolentino, exit Montecosaro Scala (the 2nd exit) and continue to Casette d'Ete. After the church, 150 mt. on the left on the main street.

This is quite a small outlet and only for serious shoe addicts looking for unusual very well made shoes in avantgarde styles, brandname Pane e Tulipani. One can personalize the shoes by choosing a different type of leather or colour, they will send them by mail. Prices start at € 60,00 and up and their sample size is 37. The new winter collection arrives at the end of September.

Calzaturificio Gian Ros

Via E. Fermi, 204 - 63011 Casette d'Ete (AP)
9.00-13.00/14.00-19.00. Open in August

0734 871606
C.C.:All Major

Shoes
FACTORY OUTLET

Autostrada A14, exit Civitanova Marche, follow the superstrada to Tolentino in the direction of Macerata. Exit at Montecosaro Scalo, the 2nd exit, and continue to Casette d'Ete. At the industrial zone turn left immediately after the Q8 service station.

Very well made rubber soled or rubber cleated shoes and mocassins made famous by another local shoe manufacturer. Casual shoes for M/W start at € 45,00 and up in various colors. Modern looking lace-ups, ankle booties in water resistant suede for M/W. Remnants and discontinued shoes at very low prices. They speak English, French, Spanish and German and ship.

Calzaturificio Kid's Heaven

Z.I. Brancadoro, Via L. da Vinci, 10 - 63011 Casette d'Ete (AP)
8.00-12.30/14.00-19.00. Sat. 9.30-12.30/14.00-19.30

0734 871030
C.C.:All Major

Shoes
FACTORY OUTLET

Autostrada A14, exit Civitanova Marche, follow the superstrada to Tolentino in the direction of Macerata. Exit at Montecosaro Scalo, the 2nd exit, and continue to Casette d'Ete. In the industrial zone, (Zona Industriale), after the servicestation to the left.

This shoe manufacturer is specialized in children's shoes, brand name Bimbi Belli, Guys & Girls. Very charming designs at circa € 35,00 a pair, occasionaly their prototypes can be bought at very low prices. Also booties and sneakers up to 16 years, less choice but good prices.

Della Valle - Tod's

Corso Garibaldi, 134 - 63019 Casette d'Ete (AP)
10.00-19.00. Monday 15.00-19.00

0734 871671
C.C.:All Major

Shoes
FACTORY OUTLET

Autostrada A14, exit Civitanova Marche, follow the superstrada to Tolentino in the direction of Macerata. Exit at Montecosaro Scalo, the 2nd exit, and continue to Casette d'Ete.

Large, busy outlet, great choice. The famous Tod's handmade mocassins from € 95,00 and up, Diego della Valle elegant evening shoes € 70,00, also Deva shoes for older feet € 65,00, Koss sandals, current € 70,00, Hogan sporty shoes € 75,00 and up. Nice comfy styles in hand bags but nice prices too! There is not much sales personnel, we suggest self service.

Ikam Italia

Via P. Nenni, 72 - 63011 Casette d'Ete (AP)
9.30-12.30/15.30-20.00

0734 871313
C.C.:All Major

Shoes
FACTORY OUTLET

Autostrada A14, exit Civitanova Marche, take the superstrada to Tolentino, exit Montecosaro Scalo (the 2nd exit) and continue towards Casette d'Ete. In the center of Casette d'Ete.

A small outlet of classical shoes for men, for women there is far less choice. Boat shoes can be found next to classical Oxfords or Italian mocassins in soft leather, American pennyloafers at € 70,00 circa, boots and heavy soled Church's type shoes are € 98,00. In summer they also stock shoes in white leather, very modern, but no sample sizes or end of series.

Kast

Via A. Volta, 60 - 63019 Casette d'Ete (AP)
10.00-12.30/16.00-20.00

0734 861254
C.C.:All Major

Clothing, shoes
DISCOUNTS

Autostrada A14, exit Civitanova Marche, follow the superstrada to Tolentino in the direction of Macerata. Exit at Montecosaro Scalo, the 2nd exit, and continue to Casette d'Ete. In the industrial zone, (Zona Industriale), after the Q8 servicestation to the left.

A modern, airconditioned shop in the industrial zone of Casette d'Ete specialized in sporty and casual shoes of bestselling brand names like Nike, Adidas, Reebok, Levi's, Asics, Diadora etc. One can look around and snap up T-shirts by Fila € 10,00, M. shirts € 15,00, sweatshirts € 12,50, Adidas sneakers € 55,00, mocassins for W by Biagiotti Roma € 50,00.

Pelletteria Torresi Lucio

Via Ferruccio Parri, 143 - 63011 Casette d'Ete (AP)
9.00-12.00/15.00-19.00

0734 871244
C.C.:None

Handbags, leather goods
FACTORY OUTLET

Autostrada A14, exit Civitanova Marche to the superstrada for Tolentino, exit Montecosaro to S. Elpidio. This outlet is in a garage and well indicated. Go through Casette and turn right, before the bridge. Ring their bell if the place looks closed.

Torresi works for major international brand names. Handbags start at € 50,00 and up, depending on size and type of leather. You'll find attaché cases, travel bags in scratch resistant calf's leather, ideal for everyday use or travelling, and very well made in international, prestigious styles. Some small leathergoods make stylish presents. All year round they sell handbags with tiny defects at very low prices.

Moda Clan Riel Fiorangelo

Via Molino Vecchio, 1/E - 63022 Falerone (AP)
9.30-12.30/14.00-19.30. Sat. 8.30-12.30/15.30-19.30

0734 750225
C.C.:All Major

Clothing
FACTORY OUTLET

Autostrada A14, exit Porta S.Giorgio towards the Ippodromo S.Paolo/Piane M.Giorgio, continue to the industrial zone (Zona Produttivo) of Piane Falerone. A pink building, well indicated.

All kinds of shoes for W. only, in medium and medium high quality: boots, booties with platform soles, sporty lace-ups, gold sandals in Marilyn style in size 35 up to 41 by brandname Fiorangelo at a medium price of € 65,00. Their showroom size is 37 at € 32,00. Ballerinas by L. Biagiotti € 62,00, also handbags in many colours. They hand out discount cards of 10%-30% and speak English and Russian.

Lagostina

Via Piano Selva, 2 - 63040 Maltignano (AP)
9.30-12.30/16.00-19.00. Closed Monday

0736 304140
C.C.:All Major

Household goods
FACTORY OUTLET

Autostrada A14, exit S.Benedetto del Tronto for the superstrada to Ascoli Piceno, exit Maltignano. Drive through the village, the Lagostina factory is at the last corner after the bridge on the right.

Large offer of the Lagostina production of pots and pans in stainless steel. Pressure cookers according to the latest European standards, those very practical pasta pans, Teflon coated frying pans, the various series of kitchenware for brides-to-be, cutlery, it's all discounted. They also have special offers in 2nds and end-of-series and will supply missing covers or handles.

Montefiore Manifatture

Viale Abruzzi, 26 - 63040 Maltignano (AP)
8.30-12.00/14.30-19.00. Sat. 8.30-12.00

0736 402620
C.C.:All Major

Clothing
FACTORY OUTLET

Take the Superstrada to Ascoli Piceno, exit Maltignano.

Production of children's clothes, brand names Baby & Kid and Baby Line. Apart from their regular collection they have good offers in 2nds at low prices. This place is always very busy especially just before Easter when the new spring and summer collection has arrived.

Calzaturificio Sandro Mori

Contrada San Pietro, 60 - 63010 Massignano (AP)
15.30-19.30. Saturday 7.00-13.00

0735 72422
C.C.:All Major

Shoes
FACTORY OUTLET

Autostrada A14, exit Pedaso for the S.S.16. In the area of Cupra Marittima in front of Mobili Lucidi, take the road to Massignano for about 6 km.

Shoes, either classical, sporty, casual for all age groups, though for Ch. there is less choice. There are ankle boots in leather, sandals, clogs and 'super comfort' lace ups for the more mature. For W. even some super extravagant stilettos can be found. Prices are reasonable.

Chaday Complit

Via S. Giorgio, 2B - 63020 Montappone (AP)
Saturday by appointment. In August tel. 0734 760970

0734 760712
C.C.:None

Hats
FACTORY OUTLET

Autostrada A14, exit Civitanova Marche, take the superstrada to Tolentino, exit Sforzacosta to Petriolo and Montappone. In the center after the square, a road going up.

The region of Montappone is well known for the production of hats. Chaday sells hats for M/W/Ch mostly classical and a smaller collection of sporty models, all made on the premises. Prices are competitive, € 10,00 for an alpino type to € 20,00 for a fedora (a soft felt hat with the crown creased lengthwise) or a classical Borsalino type hat to € 30,00 for a large woven straw 'Mother of the bride' type or a small sixties pillbox. Brandname Graziella.

Calzaturificio A. Giannini - Donna Serena

Via Montegrappa, 1 - 63015 Monte Urano (AP)
16.00-20.00. Saturday 9.00-13.00

0734 842393
C.C.:All Major

Shoes
FACTORY OUTLET

Autostrada A14, exit Civitanova Marche, take the superstrada to Macerata, exit Montecosaro to S.Elpidio Mare/Monte Urano. In the center of town, look out for the Banca Popolare di Ancona. Parking is difficult.

The ideal outlet for older feet. Comfortable shoes, lined for support and softness, brand name Lady Italia and Donna Serena. Prices start at € 50,00 up to € 100,00. Their showroom models are made in size 37. There is a good choice in seconds, very worthwhile and a large choice in handbags.

Calzaturifico Marilungo

Via Manzoni, 51 - 63014 Montegranaro (AP)
8.30-12.30/15.30-19.30. In August phone first

0734 891570
C.C.:All Major

Shoes
FACTORY OUTLET

From the Autostrada A14, exit Civitanova Marche take the superstrada for Tolentino, exit Montegranaro. In the center, S.Liborio area, near the church.

Production of M/W shoes, with a rather limited selection for women. Sample size for M 41/42, for W size 37/38 all discounted 50%-60%. Large selection of hospital shoes and clogs for professionals € 20,00 and up. Their corner of seconds and special offers at € 25,00 is worth checking out, also for the small leather goods. They speak English.

Calzaturificio Monna Lisa

Via Veregrense, 183/185 - 63014 Montegranaro (AP)
9.00-12.30/16.00-19.30

0734 891077
C.C.:All Major

Shoes
FACTORY OUTLET

From Montegranaro towards Casette d'Ete, at the roundabout to the left. The factory is on the left. The outlet is inside the gate at the end of the track on the first floor.

2 rooms with well made, original shoes for W at € 55.00 circa. Their 'Linea Ospedale' (shoes for medical personnel), has a more original approach to the the basic white clog, they managed to make them look attractive (at € 30,00). Their showroom size 37 is sold in their wharehouse at € 20,00, very good deals indeed. In winter there is a large collection of furlined boots and booties with anti-slip soles (they export to Russia).

Calzaturificio Novecento

Via Fermana Sud, 403 - 63014 Montegranaro (AP)
15.30-19.30. Sat. 9.00-13.00/15.30-19.30. Closed in Aug.

0734 892643
C.C.:All Major

Shoes
FACTORY OUTLET

Autostrada A14, exit Civitanova Marche. Superstrada per Tolentino, exit per Montegranaro. Cross the village and take the street to Fermo.

Only shoes and boots for women, brand name Mariagrazia Ripari and Ripari Collection in medium high and high quality. There are elegant high heeled sandals, unusual combinations of leather, platform shoes, stiletto boots in black patent leather and so on. Sizes from 35 - 40, sample size is 37. Prices start at € 75,00 up to € 150,00 for a pair of boots, either in leather or suede/sheepskin or snakeskin. Sales in Jan./July and they speak English.

Calzaturificio R.D.B. Dino Bigioni

Via Veregrense, 310 - 63014 Montegranaro (AP)
9.00-12.00/14.30-18.00. Sat. 8.30-12.00

0734 891259
C.C.:All Major

Shoes
FACTORY OUTLET

From the Autostrada A14, exit Civitanova Marche take the superstrada for Tolentino, exit Montegranaro. In Montegranaro take the circular road, at the roundabout turn left to the industrial zone in the direction of Casette d'Ete. On the left.

For well-made men's shoes, rubber soled, perforated uppers, English wingtips, € 80,00, or smart looking 'Harley Davidson' type boots € 60,00. For women, classical models, Oxford styles € 65,00, leather tennis shoes, lined and washable € 30,00, brand name Dino Bigioni Uomo. This is also a good place to find ankle boots at competitive prices.

Calzaturificio Zeis Excelsa

Via Elpidiense Sud, 195 - 63014 Montegranaro (AP)
10.00-13.00/16.00-20.00. Sat. 9.00-13.00/16.00-20.00
Closed Monday

0734 891435
C.C.:All Major

Shoes
FACTORY OUTLET

From the Autostrada A14, exit Civitanova Marche take the superstrada for Tolentino, exit Montegranaro.

Calzaturificio Zeis produces Docksteps, sporty shoes and boots. This is a very large outlet geared to the young and selling brand names Docksteps, Cult, Cultdynamic Sonora Boots, Miss D, Barten & Sons, Harley Davidson, Merrell, Armando d'Alessandro. The recent collection is discounted 20%, 2nds start at € 25,00, sneakers € 10,00. They also sell T's, tops and 2nds in jeans € 10,00 circa.

Outlet Alberto Guardiani

Viale Zaccagnini, 138 - 63014 Montegranaro (AP)
15.30-19.30. Sat. 9.30-12.30/15.30-19.30

0734 889009
C.C.:All Major

Shoes
FACTORY OUTLET

Autostrada A14, exit Civitanova Marche to Montegranaro. The outlet is in the center of Montegranaro, look for the signs Spaccio Aziendale and Banca Toscana.

M/W shoes are for sale starting at circa € 60,00 and up. Classical dress shoes, brogues, casual loafers but also more trendy models with round or pointed toes, saddle stitching or anklestraps. One can find all sizes, for summer or winter, all well made. Showroom sizes for W 37 for M. 42, Sales in July and January, sales corner all year round at € 40,00. They export all over the world.

Premiata
Via Veregrense, 68 - 63014 Montegranaro (AP)   0734 891197
9.00-12.00/15.00-19.00   C.C.:All Major

Shoes
FACTORY OUTLET

In Montegranaro towards Casette d'Ete, at the roundabout, immediately to the right. Look for the sign Mazza.

A high-tech showroom with shoes by Prada Sport, MiuMiu and Trussardi plus two rows of dresses and suits in severe black, white or cream. W. shoes by MiuMiu, early 60ish style queenies in draped leather with a rococo heel € 100,00, a Luna Rossa sneaker by Prada Sport € 70,00, samples in size 37 at € 50,00, for M size 42. Lots of white shoes for both M/W.

Space
Via Alpi, 97 Z.I. - 63014 Montegranaro (AP)   0734 8978272
10.00-13.00/15.30-19.30   C.C.:All Major

Clothing, shoes
FACTORY OUTLET

From Montegranaro follow the signs forthe autostrada for circa 2 km. At the bridge to the left to the industrial zone of Montegranaro, follow the road till the factory of Silvano Mazza. 'Space' is right there.

Similar to the Space outlet in Ancona but much easier to reach. Starkly modern outlet of clothing/shoes/sporty bags by Prada and Helmut Lang. Lots of space indeed, some travel bags at the entrance, two rows of miniskirts, tops and tight little dresses, stretchy shirts by Luna Rossa € 120,00, knitwear in cashmere and silk, M. shirts, all impeccably stylish.

Rodrigo Outlet
Via Piave, 72 - 63039 Porto d'Ascoli (AP)   0735 757564
9.30-13.00/16.30-20.30   C.C.:All Major

Clothing
FACTORY OUTLET

Autostrada A14, exit S.Benedetto del Tronto/Ascoli Piceno. Take the S.S.16 to Ancona, after circa 2km along this road.

A revamped outlet that offers a total look for M/W in classical or sporty style. There are quantities of suits, shirts and sweaters to choose from at low to medium prices starting at € 20,00. They sell their showroom collections in July and January, offer an alteration service and a fidelity card with further discounts of 20%.

Giorgio Fabiani
Viale Cavallotti, 139 - 63023 Porto S. Giorgio (AP)   0734 671369
18.15-20.00. Saturday 8.00-12.00   C.C.:All Major

Shoes
FACTORY OUTLET

Autostrada A14, exit Porto S. Giorgio, follow the dir. for the center and the railway station.

Shoes with matching handbags of their own production in lovely quality. High heeled ankle boots in black patent with a matching hand bag in Fendi style or suede cow-girl boots and matching suede fringed backpack. Sizes from 34 up to 41.5, also half sizes. Sample sizes only in 37. Every pair of shoes is priced around € 100,00 and they export all over the world.

Calzaturificio L'Idea
Via Mar Egeo, 101/103 - 63018 Porto Sant'Elpidio (AP)
8.30-12.30/15.30-20.00. Sat. 9.00-12.00/16.00-20.00

0734 909790
C.C.:All Major

Shoes
FACTORY OUTLET

Autostrada A14, exit Civitanova Marche for the S.S.16.

Mad shoes in the latest designs! A must for young girls who look good in granny booties with pointed toes, high heels in crumpled fabric or in raffia. Brandnames Ixi, Vivien Lee, Tony Montana and Gianna Barbato. Sample pairs in size 37 only, € 60,00, others € 90,00 and up. (Nordstrom USA sells their shoes).

Ixos - Gilò
Via del Progresso, 2 - 63108 Porto Sant'Elpidio (AP)
10.00-13.00/15.30-20.00

0734 909051
C.C.:All Major

Clothing, shoes
FACTORY OUTLET

Autostrada A14, exit Civitanova Marche and the S,S.16. Go through Porto S.Elpidio, this is quite long and boring, till the last traffic light, turn right, go straight, pass the autostrada bridge, turn right and take the last street on the left.

Ixos and Malloni Gilò are wellknown brandnames for avantgarde shoes and clothing. This outlet is a good source for updating one's wardrobe with contemporary, up to the minute and very stylish essentials like sharply cut suits in stretchy black, two-toned   ankle boots, high-heeled open toe Oxfords and myriad other fashion must haves.

Norma J. Baker
Via Adriatica, 28 - 63018 Porto Sant'.Elpidio (AP)
8.00-12.00/14.00-18.30. Sat. closed

0734 992015
C.C.:None

Shoes
FACTORY OUTLET

Autostrada A14, exit Civitanova Marche. Take the S.S.16 road to Porto S. Elpidio and cross the Chienti river. The outlet is circa 2 km further on, on the right along the road.

Very elegant and unusual shoes, only for women, brand name Norma J.Baker. There are high-heeled pumps, low-heeled city styles, lace-ups with or without heels. Sizes from 35 to 41, sample size 37. Prices start at € 50,00 and up to € 95,00. They export to the USA.

Calzaturificio Nando Muzi
Via Falieriense, 2103 - 63019 S. Elpidio a Mare (AP)
8.00-12.00/14.00-19.00. Sat. 9.30-12.30/15.00-19.00

0734 810234
C.C.:None

Shoes
FACTORY OUTLET

In the center of Porto S.Elpidio follow the road for Fermo-Amandola, Via Faleriense is on the right.

Beautiful shoes with dashing details in high quality leather. Shoes for M/W start at € 65,00, matching handbags € 60,00 and up. Boots start at € 100,00, ankle boots € 65,00, for men € 90,00. Their samples sell for € 45,00. Phone first for the right opening hours and days. They export shoes all over the world.

Miandro Calzature

Via Porta Romana, 39 - 63019 S. Elpidio a Mare (AP)
8.00-12.00/14.00-20.00

0734 810221
C.C.:None

Shoes
ARTISAN'S WORKSHOP

Autostrada A14, exit Civitanova Marche, towards Porto S.Elpidio.

Shoes for women in various styles at € 65,00. The proprietor, an experienced podiatrist, can advice on the best shoes for one's feet or if necessary can make a pair specially at an average cost of € 85,00. The shop is on the first floor above the workshop.

Cantina Saladini Pilastri

Via Saladini, 5 - 63030 Spinetoli (AP)
9.30-12.30/15.00-19.00. Open in August

0735 753462
C.C.:None

Wine, liqueurs
GOOD PRICES

The Saladini Pilastri winery is on the main road between Porto d'Ascoli and San Benedetto del Tronto.

Their own production of red and fizzy wines, grappas and olive oil. Rosso Piceno superiore 1993 € 3,00 a bottle, a fizzy wine called Parnara or Falerio € 3,00, white grappa € 15,75, lt 0.70, aged grappa € 20,75 lt 0.50. Some rather fruity olive oil in packs of 6 or 12 bottles.

Ceramiche F.lli Testa

Via Borgo Santa Croce, 33 - 62010 Appignano (MC)
8.00-12.00/14.00-18.00

0733 57484
C.C.:None

Ceramics, terracotta, porcelain
ARTISAN'S WORKSHOP

Autostrada A14, exit Loreto to the S.S. 77 or from Macerata on the main road to Appignano.

Worth the detour in order to stock up on hand-painted platters and plates, coffee mugs, jugs and vases, ideal to decorate country houses or to buy original presents. The style is rustic and prices are very convenient indeed, especially for second choice items with tiny defects.

Manifattura Paoloni

Via E. Fermi, 17 (Z.I.) - 62010 Appignano (MC)
16.00-20.00. Sat. 9.30-12.30/16.00-20.00

0733 400711
C.C.:All Major

Clothing
FACTORY OUTLET

Autostrada A14, exit Loreto to the S.S. 77 or from Macerata take the road to Appignano and the industrial zone, turn right.

Classical clothing in medium high quality in wool, linen and cotton, brand name Berry & Brian. A suit in linen € 105,00 and up, men's suits in summer wool start at € 95,00 and up. They also produce skirts and pants at € 40,00 but don't work in silk. There are other sales points in Filottrano, Via Schiavoni 14, and Colonnella (TE) in Via S. Giovanni, 98.

Falc

Contr. S. Domenico, 24 Z.I. B - 63013 Civitanova Alta (MC)
8.30-12.00/14.00-19.30

0733 79091
C.C.:None

Shoes
FACTORY OUTLET

Autostrada A14, exit Civitanova Marche, turn right and right again at the roundabout, at the traffic light turn left for Civitanova Alta/Ospedale and continue for circa 1 km towards Contrada S. Domenico, Zona Industriale B.

Shoes for 0- 14 years old and up to no. 34 by brand names Moschino, Naturino, Logos and Rasker, brandnames one can find all over Europe. Sample sizes no. 20 & 21. Shoes in Goretex or in soft leather at half price, yes, but not all sizes are available. Very, very busy during sales time.

Tartufoli e Tartufoli, King

Via Contrada S. Domenico, 20
62012 Civitanova Alta (MC)
17.00-19.00. Saturday closed

0733 890586
C.C.:None

Shoes
FACTORY OUTLET

'Autostrada A14, exit Civitanova Marche. Take the road to Civitanova Alta. Before getting there look for the Zona Industriale.

Their own production of shoes for women in very good quality and in the absolute latest styles. Shoes with half size heels € 50,00 and up, boots € 75,00 and up, ankle boots in the latest colors. Lots and lots of high heels in sorbet colours or two-tone queenies. Sizes start at 35 up to 41, sample size 37. Brand names King, Sofia Tartufoli by King.

Calzaturificio Strategia

Via Calatafimi, 60 - 62012 Civitanova Marche (MC)
16.00-19.00. Sat. 16.00-20.00

0733 813626
C.C.:None

Shoes
FACTORY OUTLET

Autostrada A14, exit Civitanova Marche. Via Calatafimi is a parallel street to Via M. di Belfiore that leads to the S.S.16, the Industrial Zone and the Superstrada to Foligno.

Production of highly fashionable, luxury shoes for women, brand name Strategia by Graziano Iachini and JFK. Very trendy, 10 cm high heels, ankle straps, sandals with touches of the 'forties' platforms and wedgies, prices start at € 75,00. Their sample size 36.5 € 55,00. The latest in well-made shoes in sophisticated or wacky styles.

Cesare Catini

Via Martiri di Belfiore, 167 - 62012 Civitanova Marche (MC)
9.00-12.00/16.00-19.00

0733 772527
C.C.:All Major

Shoes
FACTORY OUTLET

Autostrada A14, exit Civitanova Marche. Take the main road south, the outlet is on the right. Large parking.

This is a large warehouse with all shoes placed on racks in a rather anonymous atmosphere. Boots start at € 115,00 and up, sandals by Byblos with high heels € 80,00 and up, mules by Byblos € 60,00, lots of sexy high heeled sandals in shiny fantasy leather and rounded toes designed by Luciano Padovan. Prices are very much in line with the expensive brand names.

Cesare Paciotti

Zona Industriale B. - 62013 Civitanova Marche (MC) 0733 890427
10.00-12.00/15.00-19.30 C.C.:All Major

Shoes
FACTORY OUTLET

Autostrada A14, exit Civitanova, turn right, at the intersection take the S.S.16 to the left till the first traffic light, then right to Zona Industriale B. The outlet is on the right.

Small selling point of highly unusual, striking and luxurious shoes and leather-wear for M/W. Small leather goods start at € 75,00, a leather waistcoat at € 125,00. Shoes for M/W, very original and noticeable from € 140,00 and up up for a pair of high-heeled boots in bordeaux or stilettos in striped snakeskin. Brand names Cesare Piaciotti, Heroes, Versus. Sample size for men 42, for women 37 all cost € 60,00. The winter collection arrives in September.

GPM Product

Via Giarrocchi, 18/20 - 62012 Civitanova Marche (MC) 0733 892300
15.30-19.00. Saturday 9.30-12.30 C.C.:None

Shoes
FACTORY OUTLET

Autostrada A14, exit Civitanova Marche, continue to Civitanova Alta, the outlet is in the industrial zone B.

Their own production of shoes for M/W for brand name Xenos and WILP. Elegant mules with a black sole and beige uppers, very striking, suede ballerinas in the softest of leather, ankle boots with high heels or hussar style boots in shiny black patent. Sizes for W 35/41, for M 39/46. Prices start at € 70,00, their sample sizes are 37 and 41.

Les Tropeziennes - Ercoli

Via Frat. Bandiera, 89 - 62012 Civitanova Marche (MC) 0733 802001
10.30-12.30/15.30-20.00
Sat. 11.00-13.00/14.30-20.00. Wed. morn. closed C.C.:All Major

Shoes
FACTORY OUTLET

Autostrada A14, exit Civitanova Marche, to the right, first overpass to the right, straight and to the right for Via Frat. Bandiera on the left.

Very charming, original and well made shoes for women, elegant and casual, in suede, gold-toned nappa, snakeskin or lizard. They also produce some pretty handbags and clutch bags. Shoe sizes from 35 to 41, brandname Les Tropeziennes Couture, sample size 37. Sales in July and February and their fidelity card is good for another nice discount.

M.A.

Via L. Einaudi, 166 - 62012 Civitanova Marche (MC) 0733 829564
9.30-12.30/15.30-18.30. Sat. 9.00-12.30/16.00-20.00 C.C.:All Major

Clothing
FACTORY OUTLET

Autostrada A14, exit Civitanova Marche, turn right till the sign for Pennesi (Centro Commerciale Aurora) comes into view.

An elegant environment for elegant clothes: two-piece suits for W € 145,00 and up, a top in silk jersey € 51,00, a light summer overcoat € 106,00. For men a suit in linen € 190,00, in a woollen fabric by Loro Piana € 280,00 and up. This address becomes really worthwhile during their sales, 7/7-7/9 and 8/1-1/3, fantastic deals for the true blue bargain hunter. Fidelity card of 10% and they speak English and French.

Calzaturificio Novarese

Via L. Lotto, I - 62014 Corridonia (MC)
0733 433631
8.00-12.00/14.00-20.00. Sat. 10.00-12.00. Closed 3/8-16/8
C.C.:None

Shoes
FACTORY OUTLET

Autostrada A14, exit Civitanova Marche. Take the Superstrada to Corridonia, at the exit turn left. In the center of Corridonia.

Shoes from classical to sporty only for men with brand names like Novarese, Rizzente, Magli, Cavalli, Samsonite. Sizes from 39/44, for larger sizes they can also make to measure, count on circa two weeks. Prices depend a bit on the type of shoe one is looking for, summer loafers start at € 60,00 in very supple leather, with or without rubber soles. For winter they produce double or triple soled Church type shoes, € 150,00 circa and comfy booties.

La Stockeria

V.le dell'Ind., 182 Palazzo Zenit - 62014 Corridonia (MC)
0733288163
9.00-12.30/16.00-19.45. Open in August
C.C.:All Major

Clothing
BARGAIN BASEMENT

Superstrada Civitanova Marche - Tolentino, exit Corridonia, in the building in front of the intersection, a bit on the right.

Large choice of super trendy brands like Prada, Cristian Fissore, Versace, Ikam, Wolford, Polo RL, Ferré and many others. Sizes tend to be smallish 42-46 for W and 48-52 for M. Shoes are € 50.00 circa, the dresses and men's suits were very with it and discounted 50%. They speak English and Russian and have a sister shop in Aspio Terme (AN).

Outlet Paciotti

Via Enrico Mattei 7/9, Z.I. - 62012 Corridonia (MC)
0733 283512
10.00-12.00/15.00-19.00. Sat. 15.00-19.00
C.C.:All Major

Shoes
FACTORY OUTLET

From the Superstrada Civitanova Marche - Tolentino take the Corridonia exit and turn to the left. Continue till the directions for this outlet appear on the right.

New, spacious outlet with a large exhibition of modern and casual shoes for the whole family by brandname Paciotti. Prices are around € 50,00 a pair for sporty casuals to € 100,00 for some elegant evening sandals. Sample sizes for W 37 and for M 40/41 are sold at € 80,00. The men's showroom collection offers some very 'camp' models in gold or lila and red, highly noticeable, but most of the shoes are sporty.

Santoni

Via E. Mattei, 59 Z.I. - 62014 Corridonia (MC)
0733 281904
9.30-12.30/15.30-19.30. Sat. 9.00-12.30/15.30-19.30
C.C.:All Major

Shoes
FACTORY OUTLET

Superstrada Civitanova Marche - Tolentino. Circa 200 m from the Corridonia exit, turn left and right again to the industrial zone. Close to Outlet Paciotti.

A new showroom on the 1st floor. Very luxurious shoes in English style for men and women from € 120,00 € 295,00. Showroom for men size 42 € 120,00, for women size 37 € 100,00. Mocassins € 167,00, travel bags in canvas with leather trimmings € 264,00 to € 350,00, all very snazzy.

Valentino Orlandi

Via Enrico Mattei, 25 Z. I. - 62014 Corridonia (MC)
8.00-12.00/14.00-19.00. Sat. 8.00-12.00

0733 283090
C.C.:None

Handbags, leather goods
FACTORY OUTLET

Superstrada Civitanova Marche - Tolentino. Circa 200 m from the Corridonia exit, turn left and right again to the industrial zone. Close to Outlet Paciotti.

On the ground floor of the building, a large showroom with rows and rows of bags, in very pretty and soft leather € 80,00 - € 140,00. Also carrier bags made of fabric with leather trim for beach or travel. The Kelly bag with a painted scene of Venice was quite something, most of the handbags on view were of the flashy type, fur bordered, lizard patchwork, gold trim etc. Their leather goods, agendas, belts in fake croccodile were well made and well priced.

Armani Factory Store

Via Merloni, 10 - 62024 Matelica (MC)
9.00-12.30/15.00-19.30. Closed Monday

0737 782352
C.C.:All Major

Clothing
FACTORY OUTLET

From Ancona take the S.S.76 till the intersection with Matelica. At the city-sign for Matelica the factory is circa 600 m further on on the right. There is a sign 'Confezioni di Matélica - Factory Store'. From Castelraimondo go to Fabriano.

They sell both their Armani and Emporio Armani line, casuals next to Armani underwear, T-shirts and jeans, elegant tailleurs and evening skirts and blouses, glittery tops and satin slip dresses. Embroidered evening scarves € 38,00, jeans € 52,00, shoes from € 25,00 for W to € 119,00 for M. For M there are the famous Armani jackets and suits, also in seconds and end of series. For children there is little of interest.

Calzaturificio Lepi

Via del Lavoro - 62015 Monte San Giusto (MC)
8.30-12.00/14.00-19.00. Saturday closed

0733 539039
C.C.:None

Shoes
FACTORY OUTLET

Autostrada A14, exit Civitanova Marche, take the superstrada to Morrovalle and follow the indications for Monte S. Giusto. The outlet is in the I. Z. before the center of town.

There are many factories for children's shoes in the Monte San Giusto area and they all produce more or less the same kind of collection: water resistent sneakers, basket and tennis shoes, sturdy booties in leather or suede. The Lepi outlet is worth a visit because the shoes are made in sizes 18 - 40 and prices are reasonable: € 25,00 for the smaller sizes to € 40,00 for the larger, adult sizes.

Fabi

Via G. Rossa, 49 - 62015 Monte San Giusto (MC)
9.30-12.30/14.30-19.30. Sat. 9.00-12.30/16.00-19.30

0733 83921
C.C.:All Major

Shoes
FACTORY OUTLET

Autostrada A14, Macerata-Civitanova M. Superstrada Tolentino, 2nd exit Morrovalle, left towards Monte S. Giusto and the Industrial Zone, it's the last building.

Fabi produces shoes since 1965 and in their showroom there are many classical shoes to choose from. For W rainbow coloured mocassins with high or low heels at circa € 70,00. More choice for men, rubber-soled, all-weather shoes that will last € 90,00 brand name Nazareno Gabrielli Uomo or leather soled loafers by Fabi. After the middle of February their new summer collection arrives.

Petris

Via Martin L. King, 10 - 62015 Monte San Giusto (MC)
15.00-19.30

0733 539446/7
C.C.:All Major

Shoes
FACTORY OUTLET

Autostrada A14, exit Civitanova Marche, take the superstrada to Macerata, exit Morrovalle, turn left for 2/3 km to the industrial zone of Monte S. Giusto. The outlet is near the Fiat dealer.

High-tech shoes with an airboost system, brand name Blackstone Skap, Heich, Blackstone Wots. These super ventilated, good-looking and super comfortable shoes start at size 39 - 46 for men, 35 - 39 for women. Prices are around € 50,00 but are lower for their sample sizes 36 for W and 40 for M.

Calzaturificio Manas

Via Roma, 12 - 62010 Montecosaro Scalo (MC)
17.00-19.30. Sat. 9.30-12.30/17.00-19.30

0733 866386
C.C.:None

Shoes
FACTORY OUTLET

Take the Superstrada, exit Montecosaro, the outlet is in the Industrial Zone.

They produce only shoes for women, brandname Lea Foscati and also work for Missoni. There are summer sandals, winter boots and mocassins and their samples are for sale in September in size 37 at circa € 45,00. Other sizes are € 55.00. There is also quite a collection of comfy slippers for sale for M/W/Ch, brandname Alfiere.

Eurolook - Hi-Look

Via del Donatore, 6 Z.I. Beldiletto
62010 Montefano (MC)
9.00-12.00/14.00-19.00

0733 850341
C.C.:All Major

Clothing, sportswear, casual
FACTORY OUTLET

Autostrada A14, exit Ancona Sud, follow the S.S. 77 in the direction of Macerata. After Osimo and Passatempo one reaches Montefano and the industrial zone of Beldiletto.

This is a large outlet with ample choice of well made clothing and sportswear in a faintly equestrian style. They work for some well known brand names and offer an interesting range of quilted Husky type jackets € 49,00 and up, with an anti-piling, anti-allergic and anti-moth lining. Their outlet on the 1st floor offers very good deals. Quilted jackets in Stewart or Blackwatch tartans € 15,00, bermudas in linen € 5,00, very cute tartan childrens jackets € 10,00.

Spaccio C.Cam

Via A. de Gasperi, 12 - 62010 Montelupone (MC)
8.00-12.00/15.00-18.30. Saturday 9.00-12.00

0733 226200
C.C.:All Major

Clothing
FACTORY OUTLET

Autostrada A14, exit Loreto, take the Statale Regina and follow the signs for Montelupone driving circa 10 km to the town of Montelupone and follow the signs for the Ambrosini spaccio.

Medium high quality clothes of their own production, discreet, not loud, for the more mature woman who likes classical styles with a faint nod to current trends. Woollen skirts €45,00 and up, coats €180,00 and up, silk blouses, long sleeved €70,00. Brandname Carla Brosi and Deanna Baroni. 20% extra discount during the sales period and they speak English.

Calzaturificio Galizio Torresi

Via Romagna, 19 - 62010 Morrovalle (MC)
8.00-12.00/14.00-20.00. Sat. 8.00-12.30. Closed 7/8 - 21/8

0733 222333
C.C.:All Major

Shoes
FACTORY OUTLET

From Macerata take the S.S. Jesine 362.

A spacious outlet selling quality shoes, very elegant models, for men at € 110,00 and up. For women large offer of mocassins at € 60,00. Also shoes made by hand in luxury materials like ostrich, snakeskin, kid skin. The more economical line for men starts at € 80,00. This outlet is recommended for their excellent quality/price level.

Calzaturificio Vittorio Spernanzoni

Via F.lli Cervi, 65 - 62010 Morrovalle Scalo (MC)
9.00-12.30/15.00-19.30. Closed 1/8-15/8

0733 865149
C.C.:All Major

Shoes
FACTORY OUTLET

From Civitanova Marche take the Superstrada to Tolentino, exit Morrovalle to Montelupone, on the right, follow the signs. The outlet is in a small villa with a garden.

Great choice of men's shoes, brandname Il Gergo, classical English style, with water resistent soles that will withstand any kind of weather. They work for some well known North-European brand names and their speciality are the mocassins for M and it shows. The double soled lace-ups are € 90,00 and up, mocassins € 50,00, the ankle boots € 120,00 and up. Sample size for M 42, for W 37. Worthwhile to find shoes that are made to last.

Calzaturificio Ruggeri & Pagnanini

Via Alvata, 131 S.S.16 - 62018 Porto Potenza Picena (MC)
9.00-12.00/16.00-19.00

0733 888211
C.C.:None

Shoes
FACTORY OUTLET

Autostrada A14, from Loreto or from Civitanova M. take the S.S. 16. From Civitanova the outlet is before Porto Potenza Picena, on the right and well indicated, in front of the Eurospin supermarket.

A very large outlet selling classical shoes, handbags and small leather goods by 'Ruggeri Uomo' and highly original shoes for men by Manufacture d'Essai. For women mocassin type shoes but with a medium heel or the absolute latest in stilettos by 'Wannabe by Patrick Cox' or 'Velluto'. Prices start at € 60,00 and will go well up. Sample sizes no. 41 for men and no. 37 for women, all very fashionable. Sales at 20%.

Clementoni

Z.I. Fontenoce - 62019 Recanati (MC)
17.00-20.00

071 7581238
C.C.:All Major

Toys
FACTORY OUTLET

Autostrada A14, exit Loreto, take the S.S. 77 for circa 15 km. The outlet is on the right of the factory.

Clementoni manufactures educational toys, eletronic games, puzzles, and family board games in the style of Monopoly or Trivial Pursuit. They also make those cubes one has to put back together (usually with great difficulty). Their outlet is very large and they have a lot of special offers and corners with remainders.

Fratelli Guzzini

Crt. Mattonata, 60 - 62019 Recanati (MC) 071 9891
9.00-12.30/14.00-18.00. Closed Saturday C.C.:None

Household goods, various
DISCOUNTS

Autostrada A14, exit Loreto/Porto Recanati, take the main road to Porto Recanati and to Macerata, continue and at the intersection turn right for Recanati.

They don't have an outlet but give out a discount card. This card can be used in the household shops in Recanati when buying Guzzini articles: objects in plastic for the kitchen, garden or camping or small appliances in plastic like cheese graters, grills, toasters etc. All shops will give a 30% discount on list price.

Arena Italia

Contrada Cisterna, 84/85 - 62029 Tolentino (MC) 0733 956264
10.00-13.00/15.00-20.00. Mon. & Tues. only 15.00-20.00 C.C.:All Major

Clothing, beachwear
FACTORY OUTLET

Autostrada A4, exit Civitanova Marche, superstrada per Foligno, exit Tolentino Ovest and circa 1 km to the industrial zone. Just before ' Poltrona Frau' turn right, 200 m., go under the overpass, after two bends in the road look out for a building with mirror windows, entrance through the second gate.

Arena Italia is a well known brandname for beachwear and gym wear. For the super athletic, stretch bodysuits, ribbed kneehighs, sweatshirts, hairbands and whatever else helps to keep one looking smart while doing kneebends. Beachwear is available at the beginning of the season, T-shirts € 17,50, M. bermudas € 12,00, bathing costumes from € 15,00 size 40-56, it's all in supersporty designs.

Creazioni CM

Via C.A. Dalla Chiesa, 1 - 62029 Tolentino (MC) 0733 968083
9.00-12.30/15.00-19.30 C.C.:All Major

Clothing, bridal wear and formal
FACTORY OUTLET

Autostrada A14, exit Civitanova Marche to the Super strada, exit Tolentino Ovest.

An elegant environment for future brides, brandname Juliet. One can find everything necessary for a stylish wedding: hats, gowns, stoles, dresses for bridesmaids, wedding gowns made to measure and so on. Prices run the whole gamut of inexpensive to prohibitive, but their corner with samples is worth checking out because of the very low prices.

Laipe

Via Walter Tobagi, 2 (Z.I. le Grazie) 0733 967480
62029 Tolentino (MC) C.C.:None
15.00-18.30

Handbags, leather goods
FACTORY OUTLET

Autostrada A14, superstrada to Tolentino. At the end of Tolentino to the right for the Industrial Zone, Z.I.

Laipe works for some major Made in Italy names. They produce leather bags for Krizia and, only for men, very snazzy leather clothing in vivid colors and a razor sharp cut, very much in line with the sex bomb style of the brand name they work for. This outlet is for young spenders. Phone first to find out what, if anything, is for sale.

Nazareno Gabrielli Multifirme

Viale Repubblica, 14 - 62029 Tolentino (MC)   0733 960800
9.00-12.30/16.00-20.00. Closed Monday   C.C.:All Major

Clothing, accessories
FACTORY OUTLET

Autostrada A14, exit Civitanova Marche, superstrada to Tolentino. The Nazareno Gabrielli Multifirme outlet is in the center.

Discounts of 25-50% on all merchandise. 3-piece suit in summer tweed € 160,00, nabuck leather skirts € 75,00, linen dresses € 80,00, large offer of leather bags and shoes, all classical in style for the 40+ group looking for contemporary comfort. The best time to buy is from 1/3-1/5 and 1/7-1/9 when the new collections arrive.

Tombolini Area. T

C.d.A. Rancia, 8 - 61029 Tolentino (MC)   0733 961735
10.00-20.00. Closed Monday   C.C.:All Major

Clothing
FACTORY OUTLET

From Civitanova Marche take the superstrada, exit Pollenza to Tolentino. The outlet is nearby, follow the sign.

In this new outlet both the recent and last year's collection by Urbis di Tombolini is for sale. Beautifully made, classical but distinctive jackets and suits, dresses and coats with fabrics by Loro Piana and Cerruti, Men's suits € 197,50 and up, for women € 165,00 and up. Downstairs there is a permanent special sales area, either remnants, end of line or seconds and definitely worth a look.

Claudio Orciani

Via dell' Industria, 3 - 61032 Fano (PU)   0721 814011
9.30-12.30/15.00-19.00   C.C.:All Major

Handbags, belts
FACTORY OUTLET

Autostrada A14, exit Fano to Fano center, then follow the indications for Torrette - Marotta. Pass the Ford car dealer and turn immediately to the right.

Well known as a producer of fancy belts in leather, lizard, ostrich, strass, fabric, all luxurious and in the latest colors, both for M/W. They also sell handbags, the party and fantasy kind, a baguette type in red pony, a satchel in all white or an embroidered clutch bags for the evening. For men rather smart attaché cases and small leather goods plus totally trendy sandals in summer.

Gruppo Gabriella Frattini

Via Flaminia, 128 - 61032 Fano Rosciano (PS)   0721 864322
15.00-19.00. Sat. 15.00-19.00. Closed Wed.   C.C.:All Major

Knitwear, cashmere
FACTORY OUTLET

Autostrada A14, exit Fano, immediately after Pesaro. Fano is situated between Rimini and Ancona.

Knitwear for women, brand name 'Gabriella Frattini' and for men by 'Setball' and 'Sport Project' in medium high quality. Interesting prices for an interesting product: super classical knitwear in merinos but also the latest trends for a younger clientele. They offer a total look for women, dresses with matching cardigans, gloves and knitted hats.

Valentino
Via dei Tigli, 48 - 61016 Pennabilli (PS)
9.00-12.00/15.00-19.00

0541 928465
C.C.:All Major

Clothing, leatherwear
FACTORY OUTLET

Autostrada A14, exit Santarcangelo di Romagna, go over the railway bridge and turn right, continue on the S.S. 258 to S. Sepolcro.

They specialize in leather clothing for the whole family, for men in size 48/60, for women in size 40/50 and for children in size 34/40. The entire collection is made on the premises and they also make to measure. One can find suede vests, blazers in nappa, skirts in nabuck, long trench coats and short bomber jackets. A men's jacket is circa € 200,00.

PGH Piero Guidi
Via Provinciale, 185 - 61020 Schieti di Urbino (PS)
9.30-12.00/14.30-18.30. Saturday closed

0722 59086
C.C.:All Major

Handbags, leather goods, clothing
FACTORY OUTLET

Autostrada A14, exit Pesaro. Take the local road 423, per Carpegna and after circa 35 km follow the indications for Ca'Gallo. Turn left for Urbino, after 2km the factory, a very colorful building, is in the middle of the countryside on the left.

All the famous Piero Guidi bags are for sale: handbags, rucksacks, travel bags in plastified fabrics with leather or combinations of fabric, leather and metal strips. The famous Magic Circus travel bags are absolute status symbols as is the series 'Linea Fiori' or 'Bold': black attache/computer cases in very modern combinations of fabric, leather and heavy metal trimmings. Also clothes and accessories in the same upbeat spirit.

L A Z I O

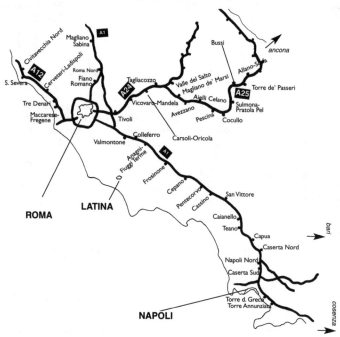

Abbazia Casamari
Fraz. di Casamari - 03020 Veroli (FR)
9.00-12.30/15.30-18.30. Open on Sunday

0775 282371
C.C.: None

Food, olive oil, honey
GOOD PRICES

Autostrada A1, exit Frosinone, S.S. 214 till the second intersection for Boville Ernica, Casamari, circa 15 km from Frosinone.

The Cistercian monks produce honey, olive oil, chocolate and natural cosmetics, all genuine products sold at low prices. Honey € 3,00 for 500 gr., amaro liqueur € 6,50 for 1 liter, chocolates € 3,50 a kilo. In the house next to the abbey one can buy books printed in their printshop.

Cravattificio Gino Pompei
Via Olivastro Spaventola - 04023 Formia (LT)
8.00-19.00

0771 321094
C.C.:All Major

Ties
FACTORY OUTLET

From Gatea to Formia, follow the indications for Mercato Nuovo. From the Superstrada take the road to the right before entering Formia.

Production of men's ties in silk or acrylics in various qualities, printed, striped, in wool and silk, jacquard, polyester produced for Tierack, J.C. Penney and other important brand names, The second choice ties are sold at very competitive prices. There are also foulards, scarves, ascots and stoles for sale.

Pascuzzi

Via G. Garibaldi 13/15 - 00062 Bracciano (RM)
9.00-13.00/15.30-18.30
Sunday phone first. Closed Thursday afternoon

06 99802371
C.C.:None

Clothing
ARTISAN'S WORKSHOP

In the historical center of Bracciano near the train station, there is a parking nearby.

A small company run by the same family since 1961. Pietro Pascuzzi has worked for Osvaldo Testi and for Brioni and produces suits for the best Roman shops. Classic and chic 2-piece suits for M start at € 450,00, a frac € 1,000,00. Bridal gowns € 1,000,00 - € 1,500,00. Men's shirts € 38,00, a tailleur for W € 140,00 in fabrics by Valentino or Ungaro.

McArthurGlen Outlet Center

Via Ponte di Piscina Cupa, 64 - 00128 Castel Romano (LT)
10.00-22.00. Open 7 days a week

06 5050050
C.C.:All Major

Clothing, household linen
OUTLET CENTER

From Rome: EUR Via C. Colombo-Via Pontina (SS148), exit Castel Romano
EUR Via Laurentina-Via di Trigoria-Castel Romano
Da Pomezia: Latina Via Pontina, dir.Roma - exit Castel Romano
From the GRA, exit 26 - Via Pontina- dir. Pomezia-exit Castel Romano

This is the 2nd designer outlet center of McArthurGlen in Italy with more than 90 shops:Lagostina, O'Neill, Mariella Burani, Mandarina Duck, Moreschi, La Perla, D&G, Luca Barbieri, Stefanel, Viceversa, Rifle, North Sails, Golden Lady, Sutor Mantelassi, Etro and many others. The best brandnames in clothing, textiles, accessories, household goods, either first choice, stock, overproduction. Large parking, bars and restaurants and a play area for children.

Diffusione Tessile

S.S. Pontina - 00040 Pomézia (RM)
10.00-19.30

06 9105673
C.C.:All Major

Clothing
FACTORY OUTLET

From Rome, before entering Pomezia, on the left and well indicated.

This is the Max Mara outlet selling off last year's collection (minus the Max Mara labels) and a special line of clothing for their outlets. Casual and elegant clothes also in Marina Rinaldi styles (but no labels) all discounted 30% - 50%. There is a corner with leatherwear, a lot of handbags (€ 40,00 and up) and shoes (€ 50,00 and up). Sizes from 38 to 50 plus XXL sizes up to 60.

Timberland Outlet Factory Store

Centro Arcom,Via Orvieto, 36 - 00040 Pomézia (RM)
9.00-13.00/16.00-20.00. Open in August

06 91602237
C.C.:All Major

Clothing, shoes
FACTORY OUTLET

From Rome take the Via Pontina to Pomezia Nord in the direction of Albano. After 500 meters on the left.

Filled to the brim with Timberland clothes, shoes, boots and bags. End of series, samples and seconds. The Timberland shoes are well represented, from kid's tennis shoes at € 25,00 to € 70,00 for a men's trekking boot. A shirt in lamb skin, special offers in duffel bags in canvas and leather € 90,00, bermudas, samples and jeans in every possible shape and size.

Balloon Stock

Via Terenzio, 12/14 - 00193 Roma (RM)   06 68806404
10.00-20.00. Open on Sunday   C.C.:All Major

Silks
BARGAIN BASEMENT

Metro A. exit Lepanto.

'Made in China' clothes at very low prices. Balloon Stock sells all the remainders from the Balloon shops all over Italy right here. It's always very busy with many tourists from all over the world trying on silk blouses at € 2.00 - € 35,00 or 3 sweaters for the price of 2, even the (Chinese) cashmere is deeply discounted. There is another Balloon Stock shop in Largo del Pallaro 19/a.

Bottega dell'Artigiano di Lucidi

Via L. Settembrini, 41-43 - 00195 Roma (RM)   06 3217446
9.30-13.00/15.30-19.30   C.C.:All Major

Shirts
ARTISAN'S WORKSHOP

Metro A, exit Lepanto, near Piazza Mazzini.

Made to measure shirts for the discerning male. One can order extra collars and cuffs, button down, French collar, stripes, Oxford cotton, initials etc. Prices from € 25,00 for ready-made to € 40,00 and up on order. Large choice of fabrics and colors. There are no sales but they do speak English.

Botteguccia Richard Ginori 2000

Via Rapagnano, 18 Galleria A.Sordi - 00100 Roma (RM)   06 8815558
10.00-19.00. Mon. 15.30 - 19.00. Closed in Aug.   C.C.:All Major/Taxfree

Ceramics, terracotta, porcelain
FACTORY OUTLET

Circonvallazione Via Salaria or Autostrada A1, exit Settebagni.

The Bottegucce Richard Ginori is part of a small chain of outlets selling end of series, 2nds and remnants in china. For sale are tea and coffee sets, complete dinner sets, oven dishes, small gift objects espcially around Christmas, statues etc. The 2nds especially are good value, a tiny black dot is enough to make a soup bowl irregular. Other outlets in Settimo Fiorentino (FI) and Milano (MI).

Bulgari

Via Aurelia, 1052 - 00166 Roma (RM)   06 6617071
10.00-18.00. Sat. closed. Phone first for groups   C.C.:All Major

Jewelry, ceramics, gifts
FACTORY OUTLET

From Rome take the Via Aurelia, S.S. 1 out of Rome, pass the G.R.A. in the direction of Civitavecchia (ring road), on the right there is a wall and a hill with a large Citroen sign. Turn into the semi-circular shopping plaza with Conbipel on the ground floor. Bulgari is on the first floor, no sign but ring the bell.

A perfect place to find a special gift since this outlet carries all the end of series and unsold items from Bulgari shops around the world. Worthwhile to find handbags, home furnishings, scarves, sun glasses, modern silver, all with the Bulgari logo. Also jewelry for which Bulgari has been famous for over 100 years. Ties € 75,00, men's billfold € 180,00 - € 250,00, crocodile handbags € 1.750,00, all to be discounted 30%.

Cafilan

Via Biancamano, 7 - 00185 Roma (RM)
9.00-13.00/16.00-19.00. Sat. 9.00-13.00

06 7000503
C.C.:All Major

Knitting wool, fabrics, notions
DISCOUNTS

Metro Linea A, San Giovanni.

The best of the 'wool for knitting' shops in Rome. Kid mohair, lambswool, merino, cashmere in all the colors of the rainbow. Friendly service, they take their time advising the client and are always busy.

Carpe Diem

Via Leonardo Bufalini, 32 - 00176 Roma (RM)
9.30-13.00/16.00-19.30

06 2427841
C.C.:All Major

Clothing
BARGAIN BASEMENT

A cross road of Via Casilina, going towards the center turn right.

There is a large choice of clothing by Laura Biagiotti, Armani, D&G, Moschino and knitwear and lingerie by Missoni, Verri Sport and Basile. All sizes are available, also large and extra large. The whole collection is discounted 50% all year round. They speak English.

Casa dello Stock

Via Giulio Cesare, 165/167 - 00192 Roma (RM)
9.00-13.00/16.30-19.30

06 39740324
C.C.:None

Clothing, casual, jeans
BARGAIN BASEMENT

Close to the Metro Ottaviano exit. There is a second shop, J.Stockino in Via Ottaviano, 67. Parking is difficult.

2 Floors of jackets and suits for the over 40 discerning male looking for quality at good prices. Casual pants € 29,00, suits in 'fresco di lana' or summer wool € 165,00, shirts start at € 19,00. There is a vast choice of contemporary classics, helpful personnel and they speak English.

D.A. Dress Agency

Via del Vantaggio, 1/b, - 00186 Roma (RM)
10.30-12.00/16.30-19.00. Monday 16.00-19.30

06 3210898
C.C.:All Major

Clothing, shoes
VINTAGE

Near the Piazza del Popolo. Parking Lungotevere.

Luxurious and elegant clothing, maybe gently worn a couple of times before being taken to the Dress Agency to make room. One can find capacious handbags by Ferragamo at € 100,00, fashionable dresses by Prada or D&G at € 130,00, sunglasses by Chanel € 70,00, shoes by Ungaro € 55,00, sandals by Sergio Rossi and lots of trendy accessories to create an instantly updated deluxe look. There is another shop in Via Piana, 5.

Decathlon

Via Schiavonetti, 325 loc. La Romanina - 00173 Roma (RM)　　06 724681
9.00-20.00. Sun. 10.00-20.00　　C.C.:All Major

Sports articles, clothing
DISCOUNTS

Exit G.R.A. 20, La Romanina, follow the indictaions for Decathlon Tor Vergata. Parking.

A very large warehouse filled with whatever one needs to practice over 63 different sports divvied up in sections dedicated to cycling, mountaineering etc. with brandnames like Adidas, Nike, Arena, Tecnica, Speedo. They also sell clothing with their own brandname (M. shirts € 14,50) and offer a library, internet access, technical assitence, they speak English and prices are low.

Divani & Divani Outlet

Viale P. Togliatti, 1545 - 00175 Roma (RM)　　06 4060300
10.00-13.00/16.00-20.00.　　C.C.:All Major
Open on Sun. Thurs. Fri. & Sat. 10.00-20.00

Furniture, various
FACTORY OUTLET

Near Ponte Mammola, corner of Via F. Santi.

Divani & Divani is known for their leather sofas and have shops all over Italy. This is their only outlet where they sell remainders, uncollected stock, leasing furniture, last year's models. Discounts vary from a minimum of 20% to 50% for their showroom collection to over 70% for sofas or easy chairs that have slight scratches or look a touch used.

Faress Italia

Via A. Carruccio, 37 - 00134 Roma (RM)　　06 71350124
9.30-13.00/15.30-19.30　　C.C.:All Major

Sports accessories
FACTORY OUTLET

G.R.A. exit 24 Adreatina, Via Adreatina at 23 km. Parking. There is a 2nd address in Via Tor Cervara 10, 00155 Roma, corner of Via Tiburtina, GRA exit 13.

Three floors with sports accessories for home fitness, (an Exercycle at circa 30% less then elsewhere) camping, tennis, football, atlethics, trekking and mountain climbing. Also games and furniture for schools and kindergarten, spas. All the items necesary for a baseball court or football field. There is a corner with books about fitness, vitamins. Worth a visit for the serious health fanatic.

Firmastock

Via delle Carrozze, 18 - 00187 Roma (RM)　　06 69200371
10.30-19.30. Open on Sunday　　C.C.:All Major

Clothing, shoes
BARGAIN BASEMENT

Metro Spagna, Via delle Carrozze is a cross road of Via del Corso.

Two large rooms selling up-to-date casuals for M/W of the more popular current brandnames for the young and not so young, sizes from 38 to 56. D&G pumps in black patent € 110,00, suits by Pal Zileri € 280,00, a wind breaker by Murphy & Nye € 98,00, Pirelli shoes for M/W € 87,00, Armani T-shirts € 25,00, trousers by Marella € 129,00. Samples and sales and friendly personnel, they speak English.

Gran Bazaar

Via Germanico, 136 - 00192 Roma (RM)
9.00-13.00/15.30-19.30

06 39732946
C.C.:All Major

Clothing, sportswear, casual
DISCOUNTS

Metro Ottaviano, near the Vatican. Difficult parking.

Very large shop on two floors. One can find any kind of sports clothes or sports article for tennis, skiing, skating, foot ball etc. All the better known brands are well represented: Belfe, Nordica, Think Pink, Lotto. A separate department sells off remainders and special offers at heavily discounted prices, which makes it easy to find real bargains. Young, friendly sales help and they speak English.

Il Discount delle Firme

Via dei Serviti, 27 - 00187 Roma (RM)
9.30-13.30/15.30-19.30

06 4827790
C.C.:All Major

Clothing, accessories
BARGAIN BASEMENT

Traforo - Via Nazionale - Viale Tritone.

Clothing, handbags, shoes and perfume at discounted prices. Gucci handbags € 100,00 and up, Versace shoes at € 80,00, Trussardi at 40% off, Prada or Fendi at 50-60% less. Valentino, Ungaro, Krizia, G.M. Venturi, Missoni ties, umbrellas, scarves. They speak English and French and offer a special customer card with a flexible extra discount.

La Fonte del Risparmio - Fai da te

Via Monte San Savino, 10 - 00138 Roma (RM)
9.30-13.00/16.00-19.30

06 8818157
C.C.: None

Various
BARGAIN BASEMENT

Just after GRA exit 9 Bel Poggio, Borgo Fidene. Near Via Salaria.

For the true lover of bargain basements. La Fonte del Risparmio sells merchandise originating from bankrupcy, public auctions, customs etc. and their prices certainly indicate this, there are goods either 'ready for the bin' and others at 'superb value for money'. At the time of visiting there was clothing by Ellesse, Energie, Princessa lingerie, Trussardi jeans, perfume Giorgio Beverley Hills, bermudas Sergio Tacchini.

La Murrina - Murano

GRA   4687 Appia Tuscolana - 00173 Roma (RM)
9.30-13.00/16.00-19.30

06 7235389
C.C.:All Major

Crystal, glassware
FACTORY OUTLET

G.R.A. 4687, tratto Appia Tuscolana. On the last floor.

Wall lights, chandeliers, candlesticks, vases in colourful Murano glass. Wine or whiskey glasses in crystal, tea and coffee cups, it's a good address for finding wedding presents or bits and pieces for the house. Lights, various decorative objects in crystal, vases, there is even a collection of German china, all discounted between 30% and 70%.

Marzotto Factory Store

Via E. Carnevale, 74 (loc. La Romanina)- 00173 Roma (RM) 06 72630021
10.00 - 19.00 C.C.:All Major

Clothing
FACTORY OUTLET

Exit G.R.A. 20 La Romanina: follow the indications for the Romanina C.C. shopping center and Carrefour. The warehouse is close to the Ipermercato Carrefour, in front of the Giotto shop. Parking.

Clothing for M/W, last year's collection with discounts of 30-40%. Some important brand names for W: Missoni, Borgofiori, Gianfranco Ferré Studio, GFFForma, Arezia, Made in Marzotto, Sonia Lazaroff, Versione. They also stock XL and XXL sizes, cocktail and evening dresses and nice handbags. For M they stock Marlborough Classic, Marzotto, Uomo Lebole and shoes. A sales corner at 70% is worth checking out.

Penetta

Via Dandolo, 2/A - 00153 Roma (RM) 06 5896648
8.30-19.30. Sat. 8.30-13.00/16.00-19.00 C.C.:All Major

Electric appliances, cd, photo, video
DISCOUNTS

In Trastevere, easy to get to by public transport or by car, there is even a parking area.

A corner shop with young sales assistants patiently taking their time to figure out what is wanted. They have the best assortment and best prices in Rome for photography buffs. Loads of special offers on new models (but they do not sell old cameras or anything that's discontinued).

Pulp

Via del Boschetto, 140 - 00184 Roma (RM) 06 485511
10.00-13.00/16.00-19.00. Monday closed C.C.:All Major

Clothing, accessories
VINTAGE

Metro Republica, at the end of Via Nazionale - on the left

Accessories and dresses from Southern Italy, hippy trash from the 60's and 70's and pulp from the 80's. Fantasy print dresses for W € 16.00-€ 22.00, raincoats from the 70's € 40,00, leather and suede jackets from 60's-70's € 50,00. Sandals, bags, byoux. They speak English.

Quadrifoglio Outlet

Via delle Colonnelle, 10 - 00186 Roma (RM) 06 6784917
10.00-19.30 C.C.:All Major

Clothing
BARGAIN BASEMENT

Metro-autobus 116-64-8-46-30-70-44-75-63-80. Behind the Pantheon and between Piazza della Magdalena and Piazza Capranica.

Clothing for newborns and kids up to 10 years old but in classical styles. Everything is practically hand-made in good quality fabrics. Smocked dresses, little blazers with gold toned buttons, bathrobes and velvet pants. There is no casual clothing for sale. They also work to order and speak English and French.

Sergio Tacchini Stock House

Via Tiburtina, 1115 - 00173 Roma (RM)　　　　06 41205558
9.00-21.00　　　　C.C.:All Major

Clothing, shoes
FACTORY OUTLET

Metro B, Ponte Mammolo, Autobus 040/041.

Remainders, unsold, seconds in sweatshirts, jeans, T-shirts, polo's and tennis shoes. Large baskets with special offers 3 for the price of 2 in sneakers or sweats, not always in all sizes but it is certainly cheap and cheerful!

Soprani

Via del Mascherino, 80 - 00193 Roma (RM)　　　　06 68801404
　　　　C.C.:All Major

Various
DISCOUNTS

The shop is next to the Basilica San Pietro. Autobus 64, (pickpockets!), Piazza del Risorgimento or the Metro, exit Ottaviano, a ten minute walk. No parking, except inside the Vatican grounds for those with a special pass.

Soprani is the place to buy rosaries, religious articles, inexpensive guides in many languages, souvenir items, postcards at prices that are 50% cheaper than in other areas of Rome. A must for all religious tourists and extremely crowded with tour groups: Polish nuns purchasing a year's supply of postcards of the pope, African friars in search of colorful rosaries. Extra discount for religious orders.

Stock House

Piazza Monte d'Oro, 91-92 - 00186 Roma (RM)　　　　06 6876353
9.00-13.00/15.30-19.30　　　　C.C.:All Major

Fabrics, home furnishings, household linen
BARGAIN BASEMENT

From Piazza di Spagna take Via Condotti, go straight towards Lungotevere and turn right to Via Monte d'Oro.

Two rooms packed with furnishing material: damask, velvets, cottons, chintzes in various weights and quality. A good choice of fabrics at reasonable prices, on average € 15,00 circa p.m. and up. There are country cottons and heavy velvets for city appartments. Service is slow but it's worth a trip.

Tonel

Porta Cavalleggeri, 15-19 - 00165 Roma (RM)　　　　06 632896
9.30-13.00/15.30-19.30　　　　C.C.:All Major

Electric appliances, cd, photo, video
GOOD PRICES

In the Città del Vaticano area.

Tonel is considered the best-stocked shop in Rome offering the lowest prices for electronics. Their assortment is vast, also of videos and hi-fi. However, since the place is always busy, they don't spend much time on giving advice; one is supposed to know what one wants and get on with it.

www.fashionstock-house.it

Via Anastasio II, 146 - 00165 Roma (RM)
06 6380520
9.30-13.00/16.30-19.00
C.C.:All Major

Clothing, shoes
BARGAIN BASEMENT

From Piazza Pio XI at the back of the McDonalds franchise to Cipro and Vatican Museums. Parking Gregorio IV and proceed to Prenatal.

A shop on two levels, recently opened, for 40+ ladies looking for medium high quality clothing, bon chic bon genre or casual chic by brandname Marella or Penny Black. Suits € 200,00, summer tops € 40.00. longish skirts € 60,00. For M sneakers by Reebok € 30,00. They can also make up evening dresses at € 90,00 circa.

Fashion District Valmontone

Loc. Pascolaro - 00038 Valmontone (RM)
06 9599491
10.00-20.00
C.C.:All Major

Clothing, accessories
OUTLET CENTER

From Rome, take the A1 south, exit Valmontone.

A fairly recent outlet center with around 100 shops, parking for 2000 cars, a bar and restaurant, a fast food, congress center and children's play area. There are both Italian and foreign brandnames: Mariella Burani, Just Cavalli, Gianfranco Ferré, Corneliani, Extè, Bassetti, Rosenthal, Villeroy & Boch and many others.

Oleificio Bulcento

S.S. Castrense Km 17 - 01011 Canino (VT)
0761 437366
8.00-13.00/15.00-20.00
C.C.:All Major

Food, olive oil
GOOD PRICES

Between the lake of Bolsena and the sea, S.P. 312.

The regions of Canino and Vetralla are known for the high quality of the olive oil, since it has a very low level of acidity and a fruity taste. The price per litre depends a bit on the time of buying, € 5,00 circa per litre for Xvergin oil. They also sell tins of 5 liters or even damigiani.

F.lli Aquilani

S.S. Cassia km 62.200 - 01013 Cura di Vetralla (VT)
0761 461644
8.30-13.00/16.00-19.00. Sat. 8.30-13.00
C.C.:All Major

Furniture, various
FACTORY OUTLET

From Rome, before Cura di Vetralla, on the right.

The Vetralla region is known for the production of garden furniture and the F.lli Aquilani produce their share. Excellent value in their remainders section, wooden bookcases € 49,00, small sidetables € 17,00, plus wooden benches and various garden furniture. Good buys are their Ecobrics for open fires and grills, which they ship.

Gae's - Scuderi

S.S.Cassia, 38 - 01013 Cura di Vetralla (VT)   0761 483464
9.00-13.00/16.30-19.30. Thurs. & Sat. 9.00-13.00   C.C.:All Major

Clothing
FACTORY OUTLET

In the center of Cura di Vetralla on the Cassia, one can't miss. Large outlet with a parking lot next to the factory.

Classic men suits, blazers, at factory prices, the best buys are the Scuderi suits at € 99,00 to € 250,00 in fabrics by Loro Piana, Cerruti and Moessmer. Men's cord pants by Zegna € 64,50, by Scuderi € 35,00. For women classical clothes by Escada, Versace, Penny Black at normal shop prices except for the sales in January and August with discounts of 30-50%.

Tiffani Boutique

Località Quartaccio - 01030 Fabrica di Roma (VT)   0761 598144
9.00-13.00/15.00-17.30. Saturday closed   C.C.:All Major

Ceramics, terracotta, porcelain
FACTORY OUTLET

Next to the Aldero hotel.

A part of this large warehouse is filled to the brim with seconds or end of line china discounted up to 60%. Up to 50% discount on dinnerware, decorative objects, lamps, mugs, vases made for USA companies like Williams Sonoma, Pier I Imports, Pottery Barn. Tiffani is known for their classical style: scallopped, flowery or lace patterned plates.

Cantina di Montefiascone

Via Grilli, 2 - 01027 Montefiascone (VT)   0761 826148
8.00-13.00/15.00-18.30   C.C.:All Major

Wine, liqueurs
GOOD PRICES

The cantina is on the Viterbo side of Montefiascone, on the main road on the left, impossible to miss.

Home of the famous Est!Est!!Est!!! white wine. They sell by the bottle or by damigiana. A good white Est!Est!!Est!!! can be had for as little as € 1,50 and up a bottle, and the same amount will buy an equally nice red wine named Rufus.

Idea Luce Lampadari

Loc. Mazzocchio Basso - 01019 Vetralla (VT)   0761 461920
9.00-13.00/16.00-20.00. Closed in August   C.C.: None

Lamps
ARTISAN'S WORKSHOP

From Rome, on the Via Cassia 67th km. go just past Cura di Vetralla, take a left turn to Mazzocchio, pass the modern Istituto Tecnico and a small roundabout. The Idea Luce laboratory is next to Orsolini building supplies.

A sprawling factory hall with hundreds of lamps hanging from the ceiling, set on shelves and floors, all very disorganized. They will repair, rebuild and help invent lamps: a Roman amphorae fitted out with a matching shade. Missing parts, glass globes for antique lamps can be found here too. There is also a section of hard-to-find lamp shades in parchment.

Brands Store Factory Outlet

Via Vico Squarano, 34/9 - 01100 Viterbo (VT)
9.00-13.00/15.00-20.00

0761 326569
C.C.:All Major

Clothing, accessories
BARGAIN BASEMENT

Autostrada A1, exit Orte for Viterbo. Near the rotary of the Tuscia Centro Commerciale, well marked, a large stone factory building that can be seen from a distance.

Well organized, rack after rack of jeans, (only tiny sizes) & last year's fashion musts for teens. For larger ladies Elena Miro and Marina Rinaldi. Serious suits for W, Arezia brand, evening dresses at 50%, € 250,00 circa, also W.Versace suits, Ralph Lauren polos € 30,00, coats, underwear, bags, belts, shoes in wild styles. For Ch. Disney sweaters, Fiorucci T-shirts € 15,00, Trussardi. New shipments every week, loud music, unobtrusive service.

Ginevra Poleggi

S.S. Cassia Sud, 52/A, Loc. Ponte di Cetti - 01100 Viterbo (VT)
9.00-13.00/16.00-20.00

0761 263211
C.C.: None

Antiques
GOOD PRICES

Ponte di Cetti is below Viterbo on the way to Vetralla, and Poleggi is just off the Cassia on the left, coming from Viterbo, opposite ristorante da Oliviera.

A big yard full of ancient and medieval stone doorways, headless statues, stone troughs for at least 20 cows, fountains, pillars, benches and great quantities of handmade bricks and Roman tiles. This is just the place for doing up an old castle or manor house. Prices considering provenance are reasonable. Poleggi ships to all parts of the globe.

A B R U Z Z O

S. Benedetto del Tronto
Teramo-Giulianova
Teramo · Roseto
Val Vomano · Atri · Pesccara Nord.
Basciano
Assergi · S. Gabriele · Pesccara Villanova · Chieti
L' Aquila · Allano-Scafa · Pescara
Tagliacozzo · Valle del Salto · Bussi
Magliano de' Marsi · Torre de' Passeri
Carsoli-Oricola · Aielli Celano
Tivoli · Vicovaro-Mandela · A25 · Sulmona-Pratola Pel
Pescina · Cocullo
Colleferro
Valmontone · Anagni-Fiuggi Terme · A1
Frosinone

Ceramiche Bontempo

V.le Nettuno, 114 - 66023 Francavilla al Mare (CH)   085 817475
9.30-12.30/16.30-20.30   C.C.:All Major

Ceramica, terracotta, porcelain
ARTISAN'S WORKSHOP

Autostrada A14, exit Pescara Sud. Bontempo is quite close to the Francavilla train station, (circa 200 meters).

Rather than go to the factory, which is quite far inland, we suggest a visit to the Bontempo shop. Ceramics from the Abruzzi region are authentic and pleasingly rustic. There is a vast array to choose from: platters and plates, vases, small objects, mugs and jugs with an average saving of circa 20%, more if it's end of series or 2nd choice.

Italiangriffe

Contrada da Tamarete - 66026 Ortona (CH)   085 905141
9.00-12.30/14.00-17.30. Sat. 9.00-12.30   C.C.:None

Clothing, sportswear, casual
FACTORY OUTLET

Autostrada A14, exit Ortona, 200 meters to the right after the autostrada exit, continue towards Contrada da Tamarete.

Special sales twice a year, 10 days before Easter until everything is sold and another one by the middle of September, we suggest you phone first for the exact dates. They produce sporty clothes, brand name Betsy and also golf bags by Laura Biagiotti. Very cute sporty/casuals for girls, brand name Piccola Betsy, up to 16 years old. High quality products, also in 2nds.

Di Cicco Liquori

Piazza Marconi - 66047 Villa S. Maria (CH)   0872 944554
8.00-13.00/14.30-17.30. Saturday closed   C.C.:None

Wine, liqueurs
FACTORY OUTLET

Autostrada A14, exit Val di Sangro. Follow the 'Strada Sangritana', no. 652. This area is known for the school for professional cooks nearby.

Production of liqueurs and bitters. The 'Abruzzese' amaro has a sweet but strong taste, € 7,00 a bottle of 0.75 l. The limoncello is sold in 0.50 and 0.75 l. bottles, at € 6,00. They ship everywhere. Ring the bell at the private house of Di Cicco if there is no one there.

Liberti

Via Tiburtina km 68.750 - 67061 Carsoli (AQ)   0863 997193
9.00-13.00/15.30-19.30. Closed Thu. afternoon   C.C.:All Major

Lingerie, underwear
FACTORY OUTLET

From Rome take the A24, exit Carsoli. Immediately after the exit to the left towards Carsoli, circa I km on the right.

Lingerie in the latest colors is discounted an average 20%. Panty+bra in cotton € 11,50. For men pyjamas in cotton satin € 30,00, also shorts and singlets on special offer. They sell larger sizes in bras, no. 5-7, and also in petticoats. Vast choice of night shirts and robes, seconds, at € 15,00.

Confetti Pelino

Via Introdacqua, 55 - 67039 Sulmona (AQ)   0864 210047
8.00-12.30/15.00-18.30   C.C.:All Major

Food, biscuits, sweets
GOOD PRICES

From Rome, Autostrada A25, exit Cocullo to Sulmona, in the direction of Scanno.

The Pelino factory was founded in 1783 and has received many special prizes for their famous pralines based on almonds. In Italy their confetti is given at weddings and on other special occasions. One can buy in quantity here and we highly recommend a visit to the nearby Pelino museum.

Murphy & Nye Outlet

Via 22 Maggio 1944, 10/12/14 - 65100 Città S. Angelo (PE)   085 950312
10.00-20.00. Sun. 16.00-20.00. Open on Mond. morning   C.C.:All Major

Clothing, sportswear, casual
FACTORY OUTLET

Autostrada exit S.Angelo, the outlet is right there.

Sporty, nautical styles for M/D: fleece jackets € 35,00, bermuda's € 20,00, long pants € 25,00, cotton fishing vests € 30,00, cotton tanks € 20,00, also parka's, peacoats, boatshoes, coveralls, all water resistant and ready for some sailing. They have another outlet in Serravalle (AL).

Italbest Factory Outlet

Contrada Congiunti s.n. - 65010 Collecorvino (PE)   085 4471817
8.30-13.00/15.30-19.00. Sat. 8.30-13.00   C.C.:All Major

Clothing
FACTORY OUTLET

Autostrada A14, exit Città S.Angelo to the S.S. 16/b and 151.

Quality clothing, either end of season or samples and showroom models.
Classical shapes but perfect for an active life style. All suits are made with superior fabrics, also the jackets, trousers, shirts and ties are practically all made on
the premises. There is a special department with clothing made by other designers. They speak English.

Diffusione Tessile Max Mara

Corso Umberto, 434 - 65016 Montesilvano (PE)   085834610
9.30-13.00/15.30-20.00. Sat. 9.30-12.30   C.C.:All Major

Clothing
DISCOUNTS

*From Pescara take the circular road and then the main road to Montesilvano. In front
of the BMW dealer and the Esso service station, on the left.*

This is the Max Mara outlet selling off last years collection (minus the Max Mara
labels) and the special series designed for their outlets. Casual and elegant clothes also in Marina Rinaldi styles (but no labels) all discounted 30% - 50%. There
is a corner with leatherwear, a lot of handbags (€ 40,00 and up) and shoes (€
50,00 and up). Sizes from 38 to 50 plus XXL sizes up to 60.

Miss Sixty

Corso Umberto, 395 - 65016 Montesilvano (PE)   085 4458703
10.00-20.00   C.C.:All Major

Clothing
FACTORY OUTLET

Take the exit for Città S. Angelo and the main road along the sea, on the right.

Miss Sixty is a very popular brandname for the 'under 20': mini T-shirts, mini
skirts, mini dresses in stretchy tartan, with strass, rumpled shirts and jeans with
elephant legs, with strategic holes, faded, hip pants and so on. They sell last years
collection, samples, prototypes, seconds and remnants at half shop price.

Comp. del Cucito - Muffin

Via Bonifica Tronto, km 14.900 (Z.I.) - 64010 Ancarano (TE)   0861 870931
9.00-12.30/15.00-19.30   C.C.:None

Clothing
FACTORY OUTLET

*Autostrada A14, superstrada to Ascoli Piceno, exit Ancorano to the Zona Industriale.
From the S.S. 16 take the Bonifica till the sign on the left 'Compagnie del Cucito'.*

Sporty and casual clothing for children from 2 - 16 years old. Lots of sweatshirts, t-shirts, coveralls, denim jackets and jeans, brand name Muffin. Overalls at
€ 15,00, summer dresses from € 10,00 and up. There is a small playground for
children on the premises.

Melchiorre

Bivio Villa Rossi, - 64041 Castelli (TE)　　　　　0861 974957
8.00-12.00/13.30-19.00.　　　　　　　　　　　C.C.:All Major
Sat. 14.00-19.00. Open on Sun. and in Aug.

Ceramics, terracotta, porcelain
ARTISAN'S WORKSHOP

Autostrada A24, exit San Gabriele. After Isola Gran Sasso continue to Castelli, on the right.

This is an interesting place to visit in order to buy old style bathroom ceramics, sinks, soap dishes, tubs, often with an antique finish. Prices depend very much on the amount of time involved. They work to order and ship.

Simonetti

Villaggio Artigiano - 64041 Castelli (TE)　　　　0861 979493
8.00-12.00/14.00-18.00　　　　　　　　　　　C.C.:All Major

Ceramics, terracotta, porcelain
ARTISAN'S WORKSHOP

Autostrada A24, exit Colledara, circa 15 km. After Isola del Gran Sasso continue to Castelli, pass the Villaggio Artigiano, Simonetti is in the last building.

Various furnishing objects in ceramics: umbrella holders, plates, table tops, apothecary vases, tiles for kitchen and bathroom, all decorated by hand. Simonetti is well known also outside of Italy and they ship anywhere in the world. There is another shop with their complete collection at factory prices in Castelli, in Piazza Marconi. They speak English and French.

Maglificio F.lli Giovannini

C. da S. Eurosia, 12 - 64010 Civitella del Tronto (TE)　　0861 910373
8.00-12.00/14.00-18.00. Sat. closed　　　　　　　C.C.:None

Knitwear, cashmere
FACTORY OUTLET

From the main road between Tortoreto and Giulianove take the parallel street going up and keep going straight. The outlet is circa 8 km before Civitella on the right.

Winter knits from € 30,00 and up in mixed cashmere. Tops to wear with a tailleur € 25,00, polos in wool € 21,00. A two piece outfit in woollen jersey € 40,00 and up. Worth a visit because of their excellent quality/price level.

Manifattura Paoloni

Via S. Giovanni, 98 S.P. Bonifica - 64010 Colonnella (TE)　　0861 749007
14.00-20.00. Sat. 9.30-12.30/16.00-20.00　　　　　C.C.:None

Clothing
FACTORY OUTLET

Autostrada A14, exit Ascoli Piceno per S.S. 16 and Martinsicuro, to the right.

A worthwhile address for finding practical yet elegant suits for M and tailleurs for W, ideal for the office or for travelling. Summer suits in linen € 105,00, pants € 35,00. All sizes available, even some XXL. Sales in July and January/February. They have other sales points in Appignano and Filottrano (AP).

Az. Agr. Montori

Piane Tronto, 82 - 64010 Controguerra (TE) 0861 809900
8.00-12.00/14.00-17.30. Sat. closed C.C.:All Major

Wine, liqueurs
GOOD PRICES

Autostrada A14, exit Porto d'Ascoli, take the main road between Martinsicuro and Porto d'Ascoli, then the 'strada Bonifica'. Continue till the company sign on the left and turn immediately left again.

A well known producer of wine, the famous Montori, but also olive oil and fruit, spumante and grappas. A bottle of Montepulciano d'Abruzzo DOC € 3,00 - € 5,00, X-virgin olive oil € 6,00 per liter. The fruit in season is sold at a minimum of 10 kilos. They ship.

Saca Ceramiche

Contrada da Tembrietta - 64045 Isola Gran Sasso (TE) 0861 975941
8.00-12.30/14.00-18.00. Sat. 8.00-12.00. Open on Sun. C.C.:None

Ceramics, terracotta, porcelain
ARTISAN'S WORKSHOP

Autostrada A24, exit S. Gabriele. After Isola Gran Sasso continue to Bivio Castelli on the right.

Saca produces high level ceramics seen in magazines like AD. Lamps, table tops, gift items all done in an antique style and known as maiolica d'arte. Prices are not exactly low but here at their outlet at least lower than elsewhere.

Confezioni Boschi 80

Via Roma, 409 - 64014 Martinsicuro (TE) 0861 797393
8.00-13.00/14.30-19.30 C.C.:All Major

Clothing
FACTORY OUTLET

Autostrada A14, exit San Benedetto del Tronto to S.S. 16 and Martinsicuro.

Clothing for W in wool, cotton, linen and şilk/viscose. A two piece suit for W € 100,00, in silk € 80,00, a car coat in wool € 90,00, shirts € 25,00 like the skirts, jackets € 75,00. This is the kind of place one has to visit often to find well made outfits to be bought immediately because next day they are gone!

Ni.Ma di Costantini

Via Toscana, 26 - 64014 Martinsicuro (TE) 0861 796419
8.30-12.30/14.00-20.00 C.C.:All Major

Clothing
ARTISAN'S WORKSHOP

Autostrada A14, exit S. Benedetto del Tronto to S.S. 16 and Martinsicuro. Via Toscana is a crossroad near the center.

They only produce suits made to measure in fine fabrics by Zegna and Cerruti, like the suits in summer wool or 'grisaglia' at circa € 175,00. Pants in cotton/wool or in summer wool € 35,00, jackets in linen or cotton € 75,00, a coat € 150,00, a montgomery € 125,00. This place is known for its excellent 'value for money' and superior workmanship.

Oleificio M.G.M.

S.S. Adriatica 16 km 392 - 64014 Martinsicuro (TE)   0861 796618
8.30-13.00/14.00-20.00 ring bell   C.C.:None

Food, olive oil, honey
GOOD PRICES

*Autostrada A14, exit Ascoli Piceno. Take the S.S. 16 to Martinsicuro. The oleificio is befo-
re the village, on the right. If it looks closed ring the bell at 'Marioni'.*

This is an interesting spot to visit in order to see the original stone milling pres-
ses used for centuries to extract the olive oil. Olive oil € 6,00 per liter, unfiltered
honey € 5,00, special oils for diabetics, the weak or ill, € 6,00 and up. Olive oil
with lemon or chilies € 3,50 0.50 liter. They also sell very nice pecorino (goat)
cheese from the nearby Gran Sasso meadows and green olives in pots. They ship.

Lab. Riuniti delle Farmacie

Contr. Trinità Z. I. - 64046 Montorio al Vomano (TE)   0861 590446
9.30-13.00/15.00-18.00. Closed Sat.   C.C.:All Major

Beauty care, perfumes
FACTORY OUTLET

*From Rome or Teramo take the A24, exit Basciano, direction of Motorio al Vomano,
after 4.5 km, go right to the Zona Industriale of Montorio. From the S.S. 150, (Roseto
- Montorio al Vomano) follow the signs for Z.I. Trinità, circa 8 km from Montorio.*

Bioapta produces cosmetics for the face or body, soaps, detergents either in small
tubes and bottles or in containers of 1 to 5 kilos. These are very good products at
fantastic prices and only sold in pharmacies. There are creams for various skin types,
anti-stretch marks, for hands and feet, cellulite, sun creams and after sun creams, too
much to name all. Best prices for quantity buying. They speak English.

Quartermaster

Via 1° Maggio, - 64023 Mosciano (TE)   085 8072650/551
10.00-12.30/15.30-19.30. Sat. 9.00-13.00/15.30-19.30   C.C.:None

Clothing, sportswear, casual
FACTORY OUTLET

*From the S.S. Teramo Giulianove take the street to Mosciano S. Angelo-Zona Artigianale
Rigoli, Via de Filippo (which crosses the Viale I Maggio). Large parking*

Casuals and jeans for the whole family, sizes from S to XL, for jeans sizes 25 - 40,
for children sizes from 11 years and up. Brand names Indian, Motocycle, Indian
Rose, Bombay, Be-bob. Woollen tops € 15,00, T-shirts long sleeves, jeans jackets,
jeans, shirts. Sample pairs in jeans € 5,00 up to € 50,00 for regular. There are
seconds and XXXL sizes, one has to browse a bit but bargains can be found.

Antica Ditta Migliorati

Via Gramsci, 1 - 64015 Nereto (TE)   0861 82229
8.30-12.30/15.00-19.00. Sat. 8.30-12.30. In Aug. 16.00-19.30   C.C.:All Major

Household linen, various
ARTISAN'S WORKSHOP

Autostrada A14, exit Val Vibrata, 8 km. In the center of Nereto.

Household linen, fabric and upholstery materials are for sale at good prices.
Made to measure table linen in jacquard linen cotton, very elegant, table clothes
plus 12 napkins € 125,00, for 6 persons € 25,00 - € 50,00. White canvas € 5,00
- € 17.50. Also bed linen made to measure, sheets, bed spreads. They stock
rustic looking articles, typical of the Abruzzi area, ideal for country homes.

Fegi Manifatture Wampum

Largo Brodolini, 10 (Z.I) - 64015 Nereto (TE)   0861 80621
8.00-12.00/14.00-19.00   C.C.:All Major

Clothing, sportswear, casual
FACTORY OUTLET

From Alba Adriatica take the S.S. 259 to Nereto and turn left before the traffic lights.

For sale are jeans by brand name Wampum, quite famous in Italy, at € 17,50, jeans jackets M/W € 40,00 - € 65,00, shorts € 15,00 - € 30,00, jeans shirts M € 20,00, jeans for Ch € 15,00 and up. Occasionally there are 2nds and there is always a good offer of denim remnants at low prices.

Spaccio Zucchi

S.S. 150 del Volmano Km. 11.300 - 64024 Notaresco (TE)   085 898882
9.30-12.30/16.00-20.00. Sat. 9.00-12.30/15.30-20.00   C.C.:None

Household linen, various
FACTORY OUTLET

Autostrada A14, exit Roseto degli Abruzzi, towards L'Aquila for 5 km. circa. The outlet is on the main road on the left.

Coupons in linen/cotton, seconds in sheets (unfinished), guest towels by Valentino sold by weight, all seconds. Bermudas, beachwear by Zeta Zuki, polo Jantzen, slipcovers. Great place to stock up on Grand Foulard, duvet covers, blankets, slipcovers, all last year's collection or seconds, all discounted 30-40%.

Az. Agr. Di Nicola

Via Nazionale, 7 - 64026 Roseto degli Abruzzi (TE)   3332898802
8.00-12.30/15.00-19.30. Sunday open   C.C.:None

Wine, liqueurs
GOOD PRICES

Autostrada A14, exit Roseto, autostrada A24, exit Valvomano/Roseto. The vineyard is on the main road S.S. 16 at km. 147. Their sales point is inside the main house.

Known for their excellent spumanti or fizzy wines : Spumante Dunatill, traditional champenois method € 6,50 a bottle, grappa of Chardonnay grapes € 11,00 for 0.50 l., X-virgin olive oil € 4,80 a liter, plus olive oil with lemon, with red peppers, also very good red wines. They ship everywhere in the world and speak English.

Biffin Maglieria

Viale Marconi, 12 - 64016 S. Egidio alla Vibrata (TE)   0861 840432
9.00-12.30/16.00-19.30. Open on Monday   C.C.:All Major

Knitwear, cashmere
FACTORY OUTLET

Autostrada A14, exit Ascoli Piceno and S. Egidio. Near Maglificio Gran Sasso.

Biffin has a small chain of outlets but this is their main one. They sell knitwear in good quality, but no sweatshirts or T's. Prices are low, from € 7,50 and up for remainders and end of line to € 22,50 - € 100,00 for their cable knit sweaters or twinsets in cashmere/merinos. During sales time they give an extra discount of 30 to 50%.

Confezioni Laurenzi

Via Archimede, 10 - 64016 S. Egidio alla Vibrata (TE)   0861 840165
14.30-18.00. Saturday closed   C.C.:All Major

Clothing, lingerie, underwear
FACTORY OUTLET

After S. Egidio continue to the right.

Nightwear in good quality: pyjamas, night shirts, flannel, cotton, wool, silk or fleece robes. Pyjamas € 30,00 and up, robes € 27,50 and up. A silk night gown €
75,00, a matching silk robe € 80,00. Cotton night shirts € 25,00. The right place
to buy matching sets of sleep wear in all sizes.

Maglificio Gran Sasso

C.so Adriatico, 155 - 64016 S. Egidio alla Vibrata (TE)   0861 8460
10.00-12.30/15.00-18.30. Monday closed   C.C.:All Major

Knitwear, cashmere
FACTORY OUTLET

Autostrada A14, exit Ascoli Piceno and S. Egidio. The outlet is inside the factory building.

Classical and trendy knitwear, medium-high quality, polos, turtlenecks, V's, cardigans at € 40,00, a long sleeved polo in pure wool € 35,00, in silk/wool € 32,50.
The collection is varied, sexy little numbers in the latest colours next to serious
tunics in merinos for the over 50's with sizes up to XXL. They sell remnants at
€ 5,00 and cotton knitting wool at € 12,50 per kilo.

New Men - Men's Club

Via Metella Nuova, 68   Z.I. - 64027 S.Omero (TE)   0861 81231
8.30-12.00/14.30-18.00. Sat. 15.00-18.00   C.C.:All Major

Shirts
FACTORY OUTLET

*Autostrada A14, exit Teramo, take the S.S. 262 to Sant' Omero. The outlet is circa 500
meters after the intersection for the hospital of Sant' Omero.*

This is a well known and busy outlet for men's shirts only. Shirts in cotton, long
sleeves, € 22,00 - € 32,50, in silk long sleeves € 47,00, in viscose, short sleeves,
€ 27,50 - € 40,00. Occasionally they sell off their 2nds at € 12,50 an excellent
bargain. The best time to visit is early in the afternoon.

Italian Clothing

Via Metela Nuova, 315 - 64016 S.Omero Garutto (TE)   0861 81271
8.00-12.00/14.00-18.00. Saturday 8.00-12.00   C.C.:None

Clothing, casual, jeans
FACTORY OUTLET

*Autostrada A14, exit Porto d'Ascoli and the superstrada Ascoli Piceno, exit Val Vinrata,
continue to S. Egidio till reaching Sant' Omero and Garutto.*

Mostly jeans and casual clothing by Cover, Cover Young & Cover Kids (Linea
Casucci) for M/W/Ch. Jeans sizes for W from 26/36, for men 28/40, from 6 to
14 years for children. There is ample choice in trendy jeans, not only in indigo
but also in all the colours of the rainbow as befits the Cover style. Prices are
between € 20,00 - € 50,00 a pair.

Gruppo Produzione Moda GPM

Via Nazionale Adriatica - 64019 Tortoreto Lido (TE)   0861 77201 83701
8.30-12.30/15.00-19.00   C.C.:All Major

Clothing, shirts
FACTORY OUTLET

On the S.S. 16 after the super market.

Enormous choice in men's shirts and shirts for small boys, 8 years and up. A classic buttondown shirt for men, long sleeves € 20,00, short sleeves € 17,50. Also many T-shirts for men and lightweight jackets and vests that don't fear the washing machine like the sweatshirts, also for women, at € 20,00.

Ripani Italiana Pelletterie

Via Nazionale Adriatica, 112/B - 64019 Tortoreto Lido (TE)   0861 788128
9.00-12.00/15.00-19.00. Sat. 9.00-12.00   C.C.:All Major

Handbags, leather goods
FACTORY OUTLET

Autostrada A14, exit Val Vibrata. S.S. 16 towards the end of Tortoreto Lido. On the right is a large sign indicating the right direction.

A well known producer of small leather goods, travel bags, hand bags and attache cases, shoes and gloves in leather or combinations of leather, nylon or canvas. These are luxury products for every age group and the outlet is large and well stocked. Nice handbags start at € 50,00, all in the latest trends. There are various series: 'Young', 'Fashion', 'Flower' and the more classical 'Cocco', or 'Pitone'. Ask for the fidelity card for an extra 10% discount.

M O L I S E

G.T.M.

Z.I. ctr Cannivieri - 86036 Montenero di Bisaccia (CB)   0875 95931
9.00-12.30/16.00-19.30   C.C.: All Major

Clothing, sportswear, casual
FACTORY OUTLET

Autostrada A14, exit Vasto Sud/Montenero di Bisaccia, continue to Montenero but remain on the outer circle road to Mafalda.

Casual jackets, jeans, travel shirts, blouses in cotton, shirt dresses in colorful designs, brand name Holiday. Sizes range from 40-54 for women and up to 60 for men, which is a hefty XXL. Prices are reasonable, circa € 35,00 for casual jackets, € 20,00 for shirts and blouses.

GTR Group

S.S.85 - 86075 Monteroduni (IS)   0865 4541
10.00-13.00/16.00-19.30   C.C.: All Major

Clothing
FACTORY OUTLET

Autostrada A1, exit San Vittore and the S.S.85 to Isernia. After Monteroduni on the left, a large building. Coming from Isernia before Monteroduni on the right, after a tunnel.

They sell their current collection together with some end of season & discounted merchandise at -40%. There are no seconds or special offers but there are a lot of famous brand names floating around, also for men, since they work for a lot of different companies. A shirt in silk velvet € 49,50, a pair of pants in suede € 195,00, knitwear in silk or cashmmere € 55,00 and up, a coat in cashhmere € 400,00.

HDM Factory Store

S.S. 85 km 33.800 - 86075 Monteroduni (IS)
10.00-13.00/16.00-20.00

0865 494225
C.C.: All Major

Clothing, casual, jeans
FACTORY OUTLET

From Pescara or Autostrada A14, exit Vasto Sud and take the S.S. 85.

A new outlet with brandname clothing, shoes and small leather goods, jeans and perfumes. They also sell jeans and T-shirts with the Soviet brand name, the selection for men is larger, though their sample size for jeans is 28. A corner with seconds and end of series is worth checking out. They offer a special discount card of 20% and speak English.

Fashion Design Ittierre

Z.I. - 80170 Pettoranello di Molise (IS)
10.00-14.00/16.00-20.00. Closed Monday

0865 460456
C.C.: All Major

Clothing
FACTORY OUTLET

Autostrada A1, exit San Vittore, continue to Isernia, Campobasso until the exit for the Zona Industriale Pettoranella.

Very wide assortment of clothing for M/W, casual & sporty, all their own production in small to medium sizes. One can find floaty dresses by Romeo Gigli, together with accessories, handbags, shoes, jackets. A women's suit for as little as € 100,00 was really good value. For W sizes from 40/46 and up to 50/52 for men.

CAMPANIA

Alois Raffaele Tessitura Serica

Via Quercione, 40 - 81100 Caserta Briano (CE)   0823 301153
9.00-12.00/13.00-19.00. Sat.closed   C.C.:None

Fabrics, home furnishings
FACTORY OUTLET

Autostrada A1, exit Caserta Nord to San Leucio. Follow the signs.

This area is well known for the production of silk upholstery fabrics made according to age-old traditions and all done by hand. It is possible to view the collection of samples and then order, though there is a minimum quantity per order.

Antico Opif. Serico De Negri

Piazza d. Seta, 1 - 81020 Caserta San Leucio (CE)   0823 361290
9.00-12.00/15.00-19.00. Saturday 9.00-12.00   C.C.:All Major

Fabrics, home furnishings
FACTORY OUTLET

Autostrada A1, exit Caserta Nord, immediately after the exit turn left, continue for 10 minutes to S. Leucio. In the center of S. Leucio follow a wide street to a large central square. The outlet is behind the fountain.

Curtain fabrics in silk, really very intricate and particular, made according to very old techniques. The minimum quantity to buy is 50 cm or more but only those available in their showroom. For requests for other colors or different designs there is a minimum order of 240 meters, enough for a lot of curtains!

Marzotto Factory Outlet

Via S. Maria La Nova, C.C. Le Porte di Napoli
80021 Afragola (NA)   081 5453105
9.00-21.00   C.C.:All Major

Clothing
FACTORY OUTLET

From Napoli take the Autostrada A1, exit Afragola after circa 5 km. Follow the signs for Ipercoop and C.C. Le porte di Napoli. Marzotto is next to the Maxi Cinema.

Marlborough sportswear, two-piece suits by Borgofiori in wool or cotton up to size 52 and discounted circa 35%, bridal party dresses, tweedy jackets for office wear, chic grey pin stripe suits by Ferré for elegant men but also special offers in men's suits. Racks with samples, dresses in size 42 for W, discounted 40%. Large offer of blankets by Lanerossi. Impossible not to find something.

Antica Manifattura Capodimonte

Via Remo de Feo, 2 - 80022 Arzano (NA)   081 7318341
8.00-17.00. Saturday closed   C.C.: None

Ceramics, terracotta, porcelain
FACTORY OUTLET

Autostrada A1, Afragola-Assemdiano till exit Arzano Zona ASI, first to the right, second cross road to the left, last gate on the right.

One of the original factories that produced the famous Capodimonte porcelain. China roses, vases, lamps, statuettes in an elaborate and classical style. Excellent for gifts representative of this area. Phone first to make sure they are open.

Calzaturificio Campanile

Via Napoli, 244 - 80022 Arzano (NA)   081 5734833
9.00-13.00/14.00-19.30   C.C.:All Major

Shoes
FACTORY OUTLET

Autostrada A3 Napoli-Salerno, exit Afragola to Arzano. In the center, Via Napoli is the main street from Naples to Grumo Nevada. Near the Starlet outlet. Parking difficult, we suggest a taxi.

Campanile makes very handsome shoes for men, you'll find them only in the best shoes shops. Their classical series are circa € 120,00 all sizes, large choice of colors. The sample size for men is 42.5 and at € 95,00 a good buy. The sporty line 'Brian Cress' offers boat shoes at € 85,00. For women there is little, some two-tone ballerinas, sample size 37 at € 65,00.

Calzaturificio Starlet

Via Sette Re - 80022 Arzano (NA)   081 5733064
9.00-13.30/16.00-20.00. Sat. aft. closed in summer   C.C.:All Major

Shoes
FACTORY OUTLET

Autostrada A3 Napoli-Salerno, exit Afragola to Arzano. From the center to the Zona Industriale, not that far from Campanile, at the end of Via Sette Re to the left, a fenced in compound with parking.

Large choice of shoes for M/W starting at € 60,00 for a pair of well made and original shoes. They export to the US and produce femme fatale stilettos in red lizard or fifties style queenies, usually showroom models. The Starlet Linea Comfort line of shoes is aimed at mature feet, more classical in style, with a soft leather lining inside, all sizes available.

Calzaturificio Melluso

Viale della Resistenza, 181 - 80012 Calvizzano (NA)   081 7130944
8.30-18.30   C.C.:All Major

Shoes
FACTORY OUTLET

Calvizzano is in the industrial suburbs of Napoli on the provincial road from Marano - Qualiano. The factory is surrounded by a garden, with parking inside.

Melluso is a wellknown brandname and this is an excellent address for older feet. In their large outlet all shoes are neatly shown on racks and sorted by size at prices of € 50,00 - € 90,00, sometimes discounted an additional 30% at the cashiers. Samples for W, size 37, € 60,00, mocassins like Tod's or sandals by Sanagens € 22,50 and up. For men too there is ample choice € 55,00 - € 90,00, showroom size 41.

Kadoa Uomo

Via L. da Vinci, 12 - 80028 Grumo Nevano (NA)   081 8333076
8.00-13.00/14.00-19.00. Sat. 8.30-13.00   C.C.:All Major

Clothing
FACTORY OUTLET

Autostrada A1, exit Napoli, on the circular road at the second intersection continue to Melito, exit Grumo Nevano.

Only for men and ideal for those looking for a complete change of wardrobe. Classical coats, jackets, knitwear, ties, belts, shoes and whatever else the well dressed men needs, like the suits in summer wool, linen or linen/cotton, ideal for spring and summer at very competitive prices.

Prénatal Outlet

Via Egiziaca, 8/10 - 80132 Napoli (NA)   0815 635825
9.30-13.30/16.00-19.30. Sab. 9.30-13.30. Mon. closed   C.C.:All Major

Clothing, maternity clothes
DISCOUNTS

Autostrada A1, exit Napoli Centro, follow the signs to Piazza Garibaldi and - 100 m on the right - C.so Umberto I. They are below the Annunciata hospital, near Piazza Garibaldi.

Circa 200 m of maternity clothes and articles for new borns at a 30% discount. Pre-maman bathing costumes, prams and strollers, beds, clothing from 0-11 years. Large baskets with special offers, all at rockbottom prices.

The Sisters Gloves

Via Sanità, 89 - 80136 Napoli (NA)   081 5447993
8.00-18.00   C.C.:All Major

Gloves
FACTORY OUTLET

In the center towards Capodimonte, near the S. Camillo hospital.

Gloves of high quality, all kinds of styles, car gloves, long evening gloves, with dashing details in classical kid skin, nappa or sheepskin, in suede, embroidered or sporty, lined with silk or fur. All sizes available.

Tenuta Vannulo

Contrada Vannulo - 84040 Capaccio Scalo (SA)   0828 724765
9.30-17.00. Saturday closed   C.C.:None

Food, milk products
GOOD PRICES

From Paestum take the S.S. 18 to Capaccio Scalo, before the village, on the right.

This address is off the beaten track but worth the detour because of the excellent quality of their mozzarellas at a very reasonable price. All cheeses are biologically sound, produced with milk from buffalos of the Campania area. Apart from mozzarella di bufala they sell cheeses made from cow's milk, burrita, goat cheeses, smoked cheese etc. They can ship and have special travel packs.

Ceramica F.lli Solimene

Via Madonna degli Angeli, 7 - 84019 Vietri sul Mare (SA) 089 210243
8.00-19.00. Sat. 8.00-13.30/16.30-19.30   C.C.:All Major

Ceramics, terracotta, porcelain
FACTORY OUTLET

Autostrada A3, exit Vietri, S.S. 18 to Salerno. Circa 100 meters on the left after the intersection of the main road. The building is very noticeable since it is covered with maiolica tiles and ceramics. From Salerno it takes 10 minutes by bus.

The ceramics that are for sale everywhere in Positano and Amalfi can be bought here at circa 20 % less, or up to 40% for seconds. Plates and platters € 5,00 and up, coffee mugs and teapots, decorated in an innocent, very charming country style with rabbits, sheep, roosters, cows, all hand painted. Mugs with flowery motifs by Tricia Guild. The building itself can be visited, they do work to order, ship and speak English.

P U G L I A

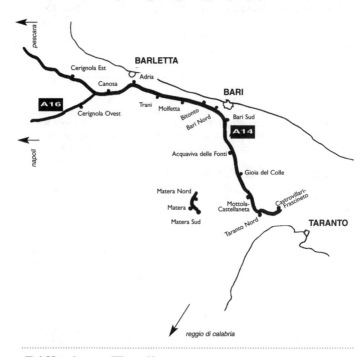

Diffusione Tessile

Via Zippitelli, 16 - 70123 Bari (BA)   080 5662068
9.30-13.00/16.00-20.30. Open Mon. morn. closed Tues. morn.   C.C.: All Major

Clothing
FACTORY OUTLET

Autostrada A14, exit Bari Nord and the circular road to Brindisi, exit 7, follow the indications for Diffusione Tessile.

This is the Max Mara outlet selling off last years collection (minus the Max Mara labels) and a special line of clothing made for their outlets. Casual and elegant clothes also in Marina Rinaldi styles (but no labels) all discounted 30% - 50%. There is a corner with leatherwear, a lot of handbags (€ 40,00 and up) and shoes (€ 50,00 and up). Sizes from 38 to 50 plus XXL oversizes up to 60.

Scarparium

Via Calefati, 196 - 70122 Bari (BA)   080 5282016
9.00-13.00/16.30-20.00   C.C.: All Major

Shoes
BARGAIN BASEMENT

In the center of Bari, a cross road of Via Sparano, the main street.

A large shop stocked to the ceiling with shoes, boots, booties, sandals and clogs by a variety of more or less well known brandnames, either in leather, canvas, or combinations thereof. One can browse in peace, some of the more popular sizes might be missing but there are plenty of bargains at € 19,00, maybe next to a pair of stiletto boots in lizard at €200,00. They also sell handbags, clothing, accessories.

Superga Outlet

Viale Europa, 3/A - 70100 Bari (BA)　　　　　080 5348669
10.00-14.00/16.00-20.00　　　　　　　　　　C.C.: All Major

Shoes, clothing
FACTORY OUTLET

Autostrada A14, exit Bari for the tangenziale/circular road, exit no. 5, the outlet is immediately there. Parking.

Remainders, unsold, first and second choice quality shoes and sneakers by Superga. Tennis in bright colours, all sizes. Outerwear by K-way, quilted jackets, cotton polos with Superga logo, jackets or skirts in suede. Sales at 20-50% less, lots of special offers.

Business

Via Imbriani, 416 - 70052 Biscieglie (BA)　　　0803 953907
9.00-13.00/17.00-21.00　　　　　　　　　　　C.C.: None

Clothing
BARGAIN BASEMENT

On the outskirts south of Biscieglie, a town circa 30 km north of Bari on the S.S.16. Parking.

A very large warehouse of 1000 sq. meters selling clothing at bargain prices. They have an enormous assortment of Made in Italy brand names for M/W/Ch, one can happily spend a morning here going through the racks. The label price on every garment has to be discounted 50%.

Austerity Calzature

Via de Robertis, 86-88 - 70059 Trani (BA)　　　0883 506368
9.30-13.00/17.00-21.00　　　　　　　　　　　C.C.: All Major

Shoes
BARGAIN BASEMENT

A large shop of 250 sq.m. near the center of the town and the train station.

Only brand name shoes, nicely on show, priced between € 30,00 and €100,00 by Casadei, Campanile, Colette, Cardin, GMV, Clark's, Dodoni and others, sizes from 34 to 41 for women and from 39 to 46 for men. Sales in July/August and January/February.

Cravatteria Silene

Via Gonfalone, Z.PIP - 73031 Alessano (LE)　　0833 782528
9.00-13.00/16.30-20.30. Saturday closed　　　　C.C.: None

Ties
FACTORY OUTLET

From Lecce take the S.S. 275. In Alessano look out for the Gum supermarket on the left, turn left after Gum, Silene is well indicated and at the end of the street on the right.

An outlet for ties, mostly in silk but also a good choice in polyester, all year round. There are ties with or without famous griffe in a thousand different designs or colours. Also butterfly, ascot, evening scarves, shawls. They work for major national and international brandnames.

Fratelli Coli

Zona Artigianale - 73020 Cutrofiano (LE)
9.00-12.30/16.00-20.30

0836 544383
C.C.: All Major

Ceramics, terracotta, porcelain
GOOD PRICES

From Lecce take the road to Màglie, turn to Corigliano and coninue to Cutrofiano. On this road on the right is the factory and outlet.

Very large showroom inside and outside in the courtyard, of terracotta, maiolica and ceramics, typical of the Puglia area, very often made or painted by hand. Ideal place to find original decorating items for the house and garden.

Adelchi Calzaturificio

Via provinciale per Montesano - 73039 Tricase (LE)
9.30-13.00/16.00-20.00

0833 526111
C.C.:None

Shoes
FACTORY OUTLET

From Méglie to Montesano on the S.P. 275, after the village to Alessano.

This area is quite well known for the production of shoes in medium to medium high quality. Adelchi is a large factory outlet with classical or sporty shoes for M/W/Ch. in all sizes, even American half sizes at sharp reductions. For M size 39 - 46, for W 36 - 42.

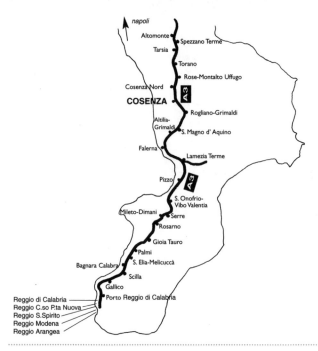

napoli
Altomonte
Spezzano Terme
Tarsia
Torano
Rose-Montalto Uffugo
Cosenza Nord
COSENZA
A3
Rogliano-Grimaldi
Altilia-Grimaldi
S. Magno d' Aquino
Falerna
Lamezia Terme
Pizzo
A3
S. Onofrio-Vibo Valentia
Mileto-Dimani
Serre
Rosarno
Gioia Tauro
Palmi
S. Elia-Melicuccà
Bagnara Calabra
Scilla
Gallico
Porto Reggio di Calabria
Reggio di Calabria
Reggio C.so P.ta Nuova
Reggio S.Spirito
Reggio Modena
Reggio Arangea

Garritano 1908

Corso Vittorio Emanuele, 13 - 87100 Cosenza (CS)   0984 71393
8.30-13.00/15.30-19.30   C.C.:None

Food, local products
GOOD PRICES

In the center of Cosenza.

They are specialized in the production of dried figs, sterilized in the oven and
then filled with walnuts, almonds, pistacchio, rum, chocolate, 350 grams € 6,00
and all produced without artifical color. It's a local speciality, quite delicious. They
also ship.

Calzaturficio Di Luzzi

C/da Gidora 46 - 87040 Luzzi (CS)   0984 543947
9.00-13.00/15.00-18.30. Sat. 9.00-13.00   C.C.:All Major

Shoes
FACTORY OUTLET

Autostrada A3 Salerno-Reggio Calabria, exit Torano Castello. Turn right towards Cosenza,
at the intersection turn left crossing the bridge over the river Crati, keep going straight
for 200 m. and turn right. Go straight till the Campo Sportivo, the outlet is next to it.

Shoes by Linea Cesare Firrao, sewn by hand and only for men, at a maximum
price of € 250,00. All sizes up to 46/48. This place is worth a visit to find good
looking, hand made shoes at reasonable prices.

Bottega Sartoriale Valentini

Contrada Pantoni - 87046 Montalto Uffugo (CS)
14.30-19.30. Sat. closed

0984 939804
C.C.:None

Clothing
FACTORY OUTLET

Autostrada A3, exit Rose - Montalto Uffugo, the factory is immediately to the right.

Valentini is specialized in the production of hand finished trousers for men. They are a well-known brandname in the USA were a pair of Valentini corduroy pants can cost € 250,00. Here in their outlet prices are definitily a lot lower.

Marzotto Factory Store

Via della Repubblica, 85 - 87028 Praia a Mare (CS)
9.00-13.00/16.00-20.00

0985 72725
C.C.:All Major

Clothing
FACTORY OUTLET

Outside of Praia a Mare in the North Litoranean area. The outlet is next to the Marlane factory building.

Marlborough sportswear, two-piece suits by Borgofiori in wool or cotton up to size 52 and discounted circa 35%, bridal party dresses, tweedy jackets for office wear, chic grey pin stripe suits by Ferré for elegant men but also special offers in men's suits. Racks with samples, dresses in size 42 for W, discounted 40%. Large offer of blankets by Lanerossi. Impossible not to find something.

Torronificio Taverna

Piazza Italia, 8 - 89029 Taurianova (RC)
9.00-13.00/16.00-19.00

0966 611106
C.C.:None

Food, local products
GOOD PRICES

Autostrada A3, exit Gioia Tàuro to Taurianova.

They make nougat, a sweet very much appreciated in Italy and particularly good in this area. The Taverna nougat is considered one of the best and made with fresh almonds from Avola, honey, candied fruit, chocolate, very delicious. They also sell susumelle, a local speciality and small cakes. One can buy in quantity or per 100 grams, friendly service.

S I C I L Y

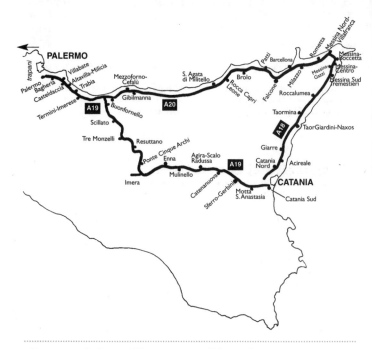

Ceramiche Giacomo Alessi

Via P. Amadeo, 9 - 95041 Caltagirone (CT)
9.00-13.00/15.30-20.00

093 321967
C.C.: All Major

Ceramics, terracotta, porcelain
ARTISAN'S WORKSHOP

In the center of Caltagirone.

Large choice of maiolica in traditonal styles, shelves and tables in a local stone
called pietra lavica, platters and plates decorated by hand and quantities of small
objects that will make nice presents.

Prénatal

Via Aldo Moro, 12 - 95045 Misterbianco (CT)
9.30-13.00/16.00-20.00

0957 557002
C.C.: All Major

Clothing, maternity clothes
FACTORY OUTLET

*Autostrada Messina - Catania, exit Misterbianco - Paternò, going straight. Just before
McDonalds, in the commercial area before the town. Parking inside.*

Circa 200 m of maternity clothes and articles for new borns at a 30% discount.
Pre-maman bathing costumes, prams and strollers, beds, clothing from 0-11
years. Large baskets with special offers, all at rockbottom prices.

ISCA
Piazza del Popolo, 3 - 94019 Valguarnera (EN)
15.00-18.00. Sat. 9.00-12.00. Phone first

0935 959044
C.C.: None

Clothing
FACTORY OUTLET

Autostrada A9, exit Mulinello to the S.S. 117b.

Men's suits in a very elegant, international style, ready for any kind of social event anywhere. All sizes available. Brand names Isca, Renato Barbero and G.V. Arena. Worth a look but we suggest to phone first and find out if they are open.

Ceramiche Caleca
Via Giovanni XXIII - 98060 Marina di Patti (ME)
9.30-12.30/15.30-19.30. Open on Sunday and in August

0941 3631
C.C.: All Major

Ceramics, terracotta, porcelain
ARTISAN'S WORKSHOP

Autostrada A20, Messina - Palermo, exit Patti and continue to Marina di Patti.

Italian ceramics, decorated by hand in bright Sicilian colors but in a rustic, modern style. There are bowls, mugs, plates, cups, pots, sauce boats, serving dishes and complete table sets € 420,00 for 12 settings. They give discounts and export a lot of their wares to the USA.

Vini Corvo
Via Nazionale S.S. 113 - 90014 Casteldaccia (PA)
9.00-13.00/16.00-20.00

091 945111
C.C.: All Major

Wine, liqueurs
GOOD PRICES

Autostrada A19, exit Casteldaccia to the S.S. 113.

A visit to this winery is interesting for those who are in the area. One can sample the famous Corvo wines of the Duca di Salaparuta and have them shipped.

Nicolò Giuliano
Via Circonvallazione, 25 - 90046 Monreale (PA)
8.30-13.00/15.00-19.30. Sat. 8.30-13.00

091 6404393
C.C.: All Major

Ceramics, terracotta, porcelain
ARTISAN'S WORKSHOP

From Palermo take the S.S. 186 to Monreale.

A well known laboratory of terracotta vases and ceramics practically made by hand. Garden vases decorated with garlands of lemons and oranges, in a style that has its roots in the Sicilian baroque art of the 15th and 16th century. A large assortment of bases for lamps is also on show. One can order by mail and they ship.

Angela Tripi

Via Vittorio Emanuele, 450/452 - 90134 Palermo (PA)   091 6512787
8.30-13.00/15.30-19.30   C.C.: All Major

Gifts, local products
ARTISAN'S WORKSHOP

On the 'circonvallazione', the ring road of Palermo, take the Corso Calatafini towards the cathedral.

Small statues for nativity scenes, folklore products from Sicily, Sicilian souvenirs and maiolica. The factory next to the shop is open all day from 8.30 - 18.30, go there in case the shop is closed.

De Simone Margherita

Via G. Lanza di Scalea, 698 - 90100 Palermo (PA)   091 6711005
8.00-13.00/14.00-18.00. Sat. 10.00-13.00. Closed in Aug.   C.C.: All Major

Ceramics, terracotta, porcelain
FACTORY OUTLET

In front of the Velodromo, a well-known reference point in Palermo.

Modern ceramics, typical of Sicily, in vivacious colors, yellow, red, bright blue. Their products can be found in expensive decorating shops! Here at their factory showroom the regular collection is on show plus tiles that can be specially ordered and a corner with seconds and special offers. Prices are circa 30% less.

Antica Dolceria Bonaiuto

Corso Umberto I, 159 - 97015 Modica (RG)   093 2941225
9.30-13.30/16.00-20.30. Monday closed   C.C.: None

Food, local products
GOOD PRICES

Modica is below Ragusa on the S.S. 115 from Siracusa to Gela. Bonaiuto is in front of the San Pietro church.

Modica is the chocolate mecca of Sicily and the chocolatier Franco Ruta makes chocolate and marzipan also in summer without adding vegetable fats. Other typical local specialities like the biscuits from Modica and the nucatoli of almonds and honey are equally tempting.

S A R D I N I A

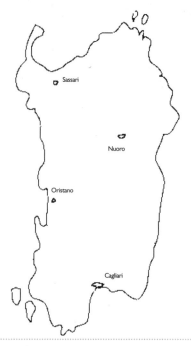

Chocolateria Sperandri

Zona Industriale - 08010 Suni (NU)
9.00-17.00. Closed on Sat.

0785339021
C.C.:None

Food, chocolate
GOOD PRICES

In the Suni industrial zone, a pink building.

A well known producer of chocolats, praline and fruit dragees of a very high quality. It pays to buy in quantity but they also sell per 100 grams. Nice gift packaging and friendly service.

Sella & Mosca

Località I Piani - 07041 Alghero (SS)
8.30-12.30/15.00-19.30

079 997700
C.C.: All Major

Wine, liqueurs
GOOD PRICES

From Sassari take the S.S. 291 to I Piani and Alghero.

Famous producers of the Sella & Mosca wines, appreciated all over the world. Here it is possible to buy in quantity at competitive prices and have the wine shipped.

Loris Abate Outlet
Piazza Azurra - 07020 Porto Cervo (SS)
10.00-12.30/17.00-20.00   C.C.:All Major

Clothing, accessories
DISCOUNTS

Near the Yachting Club and the Marina Nuova.

A shop front with two windows. Clothing made to very high standards for M/W in classical styles. Unsold items from their boutique in Milan but also a series of coats and jackets specially made for their outlets. Important discounts on evening dresses € 200,00, jackets and tailleurs in silk € 200,00, a silk sweater € 60,00. For men suits € 260,00, linen jackets € 200,00, cashmere sweaters € 160,00, ties € 15,00, also handbags and byoux.

Mercato settimanale

Piazza Cav. di Vittorio Veneto - **Aosta** (AO)   0165 235343
8.00-14.00 Every Tuesday

Autostrada exit Aosta Est. Near the covered market and the train station. Very large, of interest are the wooden utensils, cheese molds, scoops, sieves and the various products by local artisans.

Mercato settimanale

Fraz. Dolon - **Courmayeur** (AO)   0165 842060
8.00-12.30 Every Wednesday

Autostrada exit Courmayer, Mont Blanc, Chamonix. In the Dolon area. Mainly for food, especially local cheese like fontina, toma, fonduta. Some very interesting stalls with remnants in knitwear, also cashmere and mountain boots.

Fiera dell' Antiquariato di S. Margherita

Nel centro - **Entreves** (AO)   0165 842060
9.00-17.00 Only mondays in August till September 15th

In the center of Entreves which is part of Courmayeur. Among the bric-a-brac or antiques one can find some interesting products made by local craftsmen.

Mercatino dell'Occasione e dello scambio

Centro storico - **Verres** (AO)   0125 929550
9.00-18.00 1st Sunday from May to September

In the town center, 'centro storico'. Some interesting local utensils and instruments: scales, watches, barometers. Wooden sculptures, tools to cut wood, knives, old hunting gear.

Officina delle Memorie

Centro storico - **Alessandria** (AL)   013140035
9.00-13.00 Every 1st Sunday of the month

It's very pleasant to stroll through the town center with it various stalls showing comic books, linens and old lace, ribbons and old hats, books, prints and small objects of uncertain vintage.

Mercatino Antiquariato

Piazza Castello - **Casale Monferrato** (AL)   0142 454757
Every 2nd Saturday and Sunday

In Piazza Castello, under the covered market, 'il mercato Pavia'. For over 30 years it attracts buyers from all over Piedmont. More than 200 stalls selling bric-a-brac and small antiques, furniture, books and old records.

Novantico

Centro Storico, Via Marconi - **Novi Ligure** (AL)   0143 72585
9.00-19.00 4th Saturday of the month

In Via Marconi in the historical center of Novi Ligure. Small antiques, furniture, bric-a-brac, glasses, music stands and wooden sewing boxes. Also some stands with furniture and objects from the fifties and sixties.

Mercatino dell'Antiquariato e Usato

Centro storico - **Ovada** (AL)   0143 821043
Phone first

At the first dawn till dusk more than 200 exhibitors crowd the streets and squares in the center showing jewelry, stamps, books, furniture, small objects. Also modern items from the 60's and 70's.

Mercatino Antiquario di Asti
Piazza San Secondo - **Asti** (AT)   0141 399461
9.00-19.00 Every 4th Sunday of the month (except in August)

Circa 200 stalls nicely grouped in Piazza S. Secondo. An impressive offer of ceramics, even hungarian porcelain and glass collection pieces. Rustic utensils, lamps in hammered copper, bronze and forged iron.

Mercato di Antiquariato
Piazza Garibaldi - **Nizza Monferrato** (AT)   0141 530357
9.00-18.00 3rd Sunday of the month

In the central square of Nizza Monferrato. This market offers good opportunities for those in search of furniture, coins, stamps, toys and other curiosities.

Mercato delle Pulci
Piazza Ellerio - **Mondovì** (CN)   0174 40389
9.00-13.00 2nd and 4th Sunday of the month

A classical flea market with a great choice of small bric-a-brac, knickknacks and lots of simply old bits and pieces, clothing. It is also held on the fifth Sunday of the month, if there is a fifth sunday.

Mercato d'Ivrea
Piazza del Mercato - **Ivrea** (TO)   0125 618131
9.00-15.00 Tuesday and Friday

The ring road of Ivrea and Piazza del Mercato. A weekly market, (on Tuesday only food) with a large offer of clothing for children. Also shoes, accessories, knitwear.

Mercato Libri Usati & Antiquariato
Piazza Carlo Felice - **Moncalieri** (TO)   011 535181
9.00-13.00 1st Sunday of the month

A very large fair for antiques and old books on Piazza Carlo Felice. There is also a smaller market in Santena.

Rivoli Mercato Antichità
Via Fratelli Piol - **Rivoli** (TO)   011 9513300
9.00-18.00 3rd Sunday of the month

In the center of Rivoli. A large quantity of stalls selling everything under the sun from old records to ancient english pocket books to vintage clothing.

Mercato C.so Racconighi
C.so Racconighi / Via Mongirevio - **Torino** (TO)   011 535181
9.00-13.00 Every day. Saturday 9.00-19.00

Towards Corso Peschiera. This is a general market which has good shoe stalls selling shoes by YSL, Trussardi, Sergio Rossi, Guido Pasquali, Pancaldi, Madras, Ugo Rossetti and other good quality shoes at low prices. Also men's shoes.

Mercato P.zza Benefica
Via Principe d'Acaja/Via Duchessa Jolanda - **Torino** (TO)   011 535181
9.00-13.00 Every day, Saturday 9.00-19.00

Near the Porta Susa Station, or bus 55, 56 and 65. This is a general market. Thursday is the best day to visit, but on Wednesday and Friday you'll find Natta shoes, and on Saturday the Crazy shoe stall plus a good clothes stall on the corner of Via Palmieri and Via Susa.

Mercato Porta Palazzo
Porta Palazzo - **Torino** (TO)   011 535181
9.00-13.00 Every day, Saturday 9.00-19.00

A large general market with very fresh and varied offers of fish and vegetables. On Saturday there is a flea market Balon in Via Borgo Dora and the 2nd Sunday of the month the antique market Gran Balon which is quite famous and worth a visit.

Mercato settimanale
Lungolago - **Stresa** (VB)   0323 30416
8.30-13.30 Every Friday

A general market along the lake shore with food stalls, clothing and shoes. A pleasant walk with a beautiful lake view. For info about the antque market phone 0323 30150.

Mercato di Desenzano sul Garda
Lungolago - **Desenzano sul Garda** (BS)   0309141510
9.00-13.00 Every Tuesday

In the center of town, along the lake front, a general market that sells mostly food, but also known as a good place to buy shoes, knitwear and handbags. Busy with lots of German tourists in the summer.

Mercato di Antiquariato e Brocante
Piazza San Fedele - **Como** (CO)   031 3300111
9.00-19.00 1st Saturday of the month

One of the few bric-a-brac markets that actually become more lively in July and August, thanks to an influx of tourists. You'll find a bit of everything here, small furniture, books, collectibles.

Mercato settimanale
Viale Cesare Battisti - **Como** (CO)   031 3300111
9.00-13.00 Tuesdays & Thursdays, Saturday 9.00-19.00

Along the walls of the old Como city center, lots of stalls selling ceramics, handbags, lingerie, small leather items and of course silk scarves and ties. All the food stalls are in Via Metana.

Mercatino antiquariato e brocante
P.zza Carlo Marx - **Bollate** (MI)
9.00-13.00 Every Sunday

Over 300 participants offering furniture, silver and flatware, watches, and other collectionables. Very popular with the Milanese and a nice outing for the Sunday morning.

Al Mercatino
Via Marcora, 8 - **Milano** (MI)   02 29011279
8.30-12.30/15.00-19.00

MM3 Repubblica. Indoor market, 700 mq, selling old and not so old cupboards, benches and chairs, sofas and tables, books, watches and small china objects.

Il Borsino del Cordusio
Via e Galleria Cordusio - **Milano** (MI)   02 725421
9.00-13.00 Every Sunday

In the center of Milan near the Duomo. Well known and interesting for collectors of small items like stamps, coins, medals, visiting cards, post cards etc.

Mercato Città Studi

Via Moretto da Brescia - **Milano** (MI)   02 725421
9.00-12.30 Every Monday

This general market starts on the corner of Viale Romagna, Via Moretto da Brescia to Piazzale Gorini. Mostly clothes, shoes, secondhand fur hats (a black mink hat at € 10,00), cosmetics, knitwear, stockings and socks, sleepwear. Busy and plenty of good buys.

Mercato di Viale Papiniano

Viale Papiniano - **Milano** (MI)   02 725421
9.00-12.30 Tuesday & Saturday

MM2 exit S. Agostino. One of Milan's more popular general markets, offering clothes, shoes, fabrics, household goods, and of course food. Possible to find Alta Moda remnants, brand name cashmere, sample pairs in shoes and boots, jeans also used or seconds, kids clothes and vintage lingerie.

Mercato Piazzale Martini

Piazzale Martini - **Milano** (MI)   02 725421
9.00-12.30 Every Wednesday

A weekly general market on the outskirts of Milan. Useful to find good quality shoes, byoux, accessories, knitwear, lingerie, fabrics and old linen. Always very busy.

Fiera dell'Antico e Brocantage

Parco Esposizione di Novegro - **Novegro** (MI)   02 466916
Phone for the right dates

About once or twice a month an antique and brocante fair either open to the general public or only to antique dealers, near Linate Airport. It's a covered market, plus an open air section, with merchandise spilling out of the back of a car or truck. The fairs are usually held with a 'theme': medical instruments of the 18th century, old books, radios, garden furniture and statues etc.

Mercato pulci

Capolinea MM3 - **San Donato Milanese** (MI)   02 725421
Every Sunday morning

At the end of MM3. A flea market with more than a 100 stalls, a large part selling etnic articles, secondhand clothing, old cd's and cell phones, ceramics, shoes, accessories.

Mercato Fiera del Cardinale

Piazza Garibaldi - **Castiglione Olona** (VA)   0331 824801
9.00-19.00 1st Sunday of the month

Castiglione Olona is a delightful village, perched on a hill not far from Varese, Como and Milano. To stroll along the stalls of the antique market in the winding streets of its 15th century centre is quite a treat. The best time to visit is in the morning.

Mercato del Sabato

Piazza Centrale - **Bolzano** (BZ)
8.00-14.00 Every Saturday

A large, well known and busy market selling local food products like dried herbs, honey and speck or knitwear and jackets in boiled wool, Tyrolean dresses, mountain boots, knitting wool.

Mercato di Merano

Piazza della Stazione - **Merano** (BZ)
8.00-14.00 Only Fridays

On Piazza della Stazione and nearby streets. The Merano market dates back hundreds of years and offers a rich and varied choice of local products with over 320 stalls. Tyrolean clothing, knitting wool, leather accessories, religious statuettes in hand carved and painted wood. Near Via Laurin speck, cheeses, honey, herbs and spices.

Mercato settimanale Fiera di Primiero

Via M. Grappa - **Primiero** (TN)
8.00-12.30 Only Mondays

A rather charming market near the Hotel Mirabello, not that large, selling mountain honey, bundles of fresh herbs for curative or culinary purposes, mountain boots, Birkenstock type clogs and sandals, copper pudding forms and woven baskets plus a fair offer of Tyrolean clothing, new and used, at very interesting prices.

Mercatino dei Gaudenti

Piazza Garzetti - **Trento** (TN)   0461 235062
8.00-17.30 2nd Saturday except January

The market is open to vendors without a license and offers used items, byoux, books, comics, cd's, handmade objects, collectors items like coins and medals, ceramics, etc.

Mercatino di antiquariato

Centro storico - **Villalagarina** (TN)   0464 494222
9.00-19.00 Every 4th Saturday from 1/1 -1/6 and 1/9-1/1

A very pleasant market in the old center of Villalagarina offering used objects, bric-a-brac and some antiques.

Mercatino Cose di Vecchie Case

Centro storico - **Belluno** (BL)   0437913509
9.00-19.30 4th Sunday from 1/6-30/9

In the center of Belluno, a summer market where one can find antiques next to brocante next to old or used items all mixed together.

Mercatino dell'Antico e dell'Usato

Villa Roma, 90 - **Brugine** (PD)   049 5806768
1st Sunday of the month

Along the main street of Brugine in the Villa Roberti Bozzolati. There are various sectors for antiques or bric-a-brac but also more modern or simply used furniture, china, a bit of everything.

Mercatino dell'antiquariato

Prato della Valle - **Padova** (PD)   049 8205856
9.00-18.30 3rd Sunday of the month

A well known market where one can find antiques next to brocante next to old or used objeccts all mixed together. Also many collectors items like stamps, coins and medals.

Mostra Mercato dell'Antiquariato e Cose d'altri tempi

Piazza centrale - **Piazzola sul Brenta** (PD)   049 9601019
9.00-18.00 Last sunday of the month

In the center of Piazzola on the large square in front of Villa Contarini with more than 300 exhibitors offering furniture, vases from Murano, plates, copper pots and pans etc. at reasonable prices in a beautiful setting.

Mercatino dei Portici

Centro - **Piove di Sacco** (PD)   0495840705
9.00-18.00 2nd Sunday of the month

In the center of Piove di Sacco, a market where one can find antiques next to brocante next to old or used objeccts all mixed together. Also many collectors items like stamps, coins and medals.

Mercatino dell'usato
C.C.Via Eridania - **Rovigo** (RO)   049 8205856
9.00-18.00 4th Sunday of the month

In the shopping center in Via Eridania. A market of bric-a-brac and knickknacks next to old or used items all mixed together. Also minor collector's items like postcards, stamps, old books and prints.

Mercatino dell'Antiquariato
Centro Storico - **Asolo** (TV)   0423 55967
9.00-18.00 2nd Saturday afternoon and all Sunday except 1/7-1/9

In the center of Asolo, a very popular market, where one can find important antiques next to byoux from the seventies.

Mercatino dell'Antiquariato
Centro Storico - **Portobuffolè** (TV)   0422850075
9.00-18.00 2nd Sunday of every month

A charming little market with a mixed offer of old or nearly old furniture and collectables.

Mercatino dell'Antiquariato e dell'hobbistica
Piazza Flaminio - **Vittorio Veneto Serravalle** (TV)   0438551400
9.00-18.00 1st Sunday of the month

Mostly small items for collectors, but also some furniture, decorating objects in copper or rustic tools, ceramics and wall hangings.

Mostra Mercato dei Trovarobe
Piazza XX Settembre - **Noale** (VE)   041440805
9.00-17.00 2nd Sunday of the month

Minor antiques and bric-a-brac, old and used items, some furniture, fabrics, household wares, appliques and glass vases.

Mercatino dei Miracoli
Venezia (VE)   041 5230399
Phone for location & opening hours

This market becomes very lively during the summer thanks to the presence of tourists from all over the world. One finds mostly used items from the forties and fifties.

Mercato Settimanale del Paese
Piazzetta del Donatore di Sangue - **Salizzole** (VR)   0457100013
8.00-12.00 Every Friday

A general market, not large but with some interesting stalls selling sportswear, shoes and more elegant brand name clothing at half price.

Mercato dell'Antiquariato
Centro Paese - **Valeggio sul Mincio** (VR)   045 7951880
9.00-18.00 4th Sunday of the month

This is a popular Sunday market with a very varied offer of objects for the house and lots of old prints and books.

Mercato Domenicale
Centro Paese - **Camisano** (VI)   0444419911
8.00-12.30 Every Sunday

In the center of town, a very old and busy market selling food, clothing and some bric-a-brac.

Mercatino dell'Antiquariato
Piazza del Castello - **Marostica** (VI)   0424 72127
9.00-19.00 1st Sunday of the month

On the Piazza del Castello where in September a game of chess is played by people in period costumes. About 100 stalls with the usual mixture of old and not so old, antiques next to used items.

Mercatino Cose Vecchie e Usate
Piazza IV Novembre e Portici - **Noventa Vicentina** (VI)   0444788511
8.00-12.30 1st Sunday of the month

A classical flea market, a bit of everything.

Mercatino dell'Antiquariato e del Collezionismo
Piazza dei Signori - **Vicenza** (VI)   0444 323863
8.30-18.00 2nd Sunday of the month

In the center of Vicenza in a striking setting a very decorative market selling paintings, books, flat ware, silver frames, stamps, coins and military objects.

Mercatino d'Antiquariato
Centro storico - **Trieste** (TS)
9.00-19.00 3rd Sunday of the month

An interesting market in the old part of Trieste offering dolls, lamps, jewelry and byoux, ceramics and some small furniture.

Mercatino d'Antiquariato
Piazza Matteotti - **Udine** (UD)
9.00-19.00 1st Sunday of the month

A bit of everything: furniture, decorating items, paintings, porcelain and silver or flatware.

Mostra Mercato dell'Antiquariato
Via Martiri della Liberazione - **Chiavari** (GE)   0185 3095588
9.00-19.00 2nd Saturday and Sunday

In the historical center of Chiavari, this market is considered one of the best open air antique fairs in Liguria. There are all kinds of thing for sale, but it is especially known for byoux from the USA, pearl necklaces, watches or utensils for wood fires, copper pots, massive iron keys.

Mercatino d'Antiquariato
Piazza Ducale - **Genova** (GE)   010 588735
9.00-19.00 1st Saturday & Sunday

In the center of Genova, under the arcade and in the courtyard. The usual mixture of furniture, old books and ceramic objects but also jewelry and silver cutlery.

Collezionismo sotto ai portici
Centro storico - **Taggia** (GE)   0184 476222
9.00-20.00 3rd Saturday and Sunday

This is an interesting fair for collectors and it is a pleasure to browse among the many stalls that often remain open well into the evening. On Saturday it takes place in Arma di Taggia, Viale delle Palme and on Sunday in Taggia, in the center, circa 3 km. away.

Mercato di Sanremo
Piazza del Mercato - **Sanremo** (IM)   018459059
8.00-13.00 Tuesday and Saturday

A general market where one can find fake Vuittons next to fruit and vegetables, underwear, shoes, olive oil and knitwear. Very popular with many day visitors from France.

Mercato
Lungo i giardini e passeggiati a mare - **Ventimiglia** (IM)   0184 351183
8.30-13.30 Every Friday

Along the sea front, gardens and promenade. An important market offering a very mixed bag of goods from Italy and France. Parking in P.zle del Comune or near the shopping center.

La Soffitta nella Strada
Centro - **Sarzana** (IM)   0187 718997
From 5 to 20 August

This market has been around for more than 30 years, from early evening till midnight. It is held at the same time as the Mostra Nazionale dell'Antiquariato. Good quality bric-a-brac at fair prices.

Mercatino dell'Antiquariato e dell'Artigianato
Piazza San Nicolò - **Pietra Ligure** (SV)   019 629003
9.00-19.00 Last Sunday of the month

There are circa 50 stalls, about half showing products made by local artisans. A market that offers a good chance to find interesting gift items at low prices.

Mercato dell'Antiquariato
Piazza Santa Stefano - **Bologna** (BO)   051 246541
9.00-19.00 2nd weekend of every month

Any kind of old or antique object can be found here: furniture, small objects for home decorating, paintings and prints, china and ceramics, silver and flatware.

Mercato della Piazzola
Piazza 8 Agosto/Via Irnerio - **Bologna** (BO)   051 246541
8.30-18.30 Friday all day, Saturday till 13.00

This is a very popular general market. The more interesting stalls are on the side of Via Irnerio and the Montagnola park. Mountains of knitwear in cashmere/wool, down ski jackets by Ferré, 2ndhand Tyrolean jackets in boiled wool, granny lingerie, slipcovers, seconds in ceramics. Fun!

Mercatino dell'Antiquariato & Modernariato
Piazza Centrale - **Pieve di Cento** (BO)   051974593
9.00-19.00 Every 4th Sunday of the month

On the central square of Pieve di Cento, there are antique, old, used and fairly modern objects and furniture plus some stalls dedicated to collectors of stamps, books, coins.

Mercato settimanale Cesena
Piazza Centrale - **Cesena** (FC)
8.00-14.00 Every Wednesday

A large and colourful weekly market with great offers in sportswear and underwear. O'Neill swimming costumes, Max Mara skirts, T-shirts by Missoni, sweatshirts, sample shoes. The Bertozzi stall sells hand printed table linnen in rustic Romagnola designs, very pretty.

Mercatino dell'Antiquariato
Rocca San Vitale - **Fontanellato** (PR)   0521 829055
8.30-19.00 Every 3rd Sunday except in january

Around the Rocca San Vitale. Among the minor antiques there is some furniture of the 19th century, lots of ceramics and lace.

Mercatino dell'Antiquariato

Via d'Azeglio - **Parma** (PR)   0521 386329
8.30-18.30 Every Thursday

Under the arcade of Via d'Azeglio, a small market with circa 20 stalls offering a bit of everything.

Mercatino di Caorsa

Via Roma - **Caorsa** (PC)   0523 329324
9.00-19.00 Every 4th Sunday except in December

About 100 stalls by professionals and collectors. The speciality of this market are the old type writers and other office machines for sale and the rustic locks and various decorative metal pieces/utensils.

Mostra Mercato di Antiquariato e Artigianato

Piazza del Popolo, centro storico - **Ravenna** (RA)   0544 482111
9.00-19.00 3rd Saturday and Sunday

In the historical center of Ravenna. A popular market offering quality objects at interesting prices, old dolls, lamps, jewelry, cutlery. One area is entirely dedicated to products by local artisans.

Fiera Antiquaria

Piazza Grande - **Arezzo** (AR)   0575 21869
9.00-19.00 1st Sunday of the month

This was one of the first outdoor antique fairs in Italy and also the most famous one with circa 600 exhibitors. The center of Piazza Grande is taken up by furniture: cupboards, night tables, chairs and wooden benches. Under the arcades there are stalls with smaller objects: silver, jewelry, ceramics, old prints.

Mercato d. Cascine

Piazzale Vittorio Veneto/Viale degli Olmi - **Firenze** (AR)   055 23320
9.00-14.00 Only Tuesday

Florence's largest general market is worth a visit if only to experience a hefty dose of 'local color'. Mortadella, live chickens, extra virgin olive oil, stalls with copper bowls, authentic bees wax, secondhand clothing, Benetton sweaters & other treasures at low prices.

Mercato d. Pulci

Piazza dei Ciompi - **Firenze** (AR)   055 23320
9.00-19.00 Last Sunday of the month

2 small 'village style' streets filled with objects and furniture of uncertain date and provenance. Most of it looks unwanted, unneeded and unloved, yet... you might be lucky!

Mercato Santo Spirito

Piazza S. Spirito - **Firenze** (AR)
8.30-12.30

Not far from Piazza Pitti. A general market, fresh vegetables near the church, the rest of the stalls sell jackets, shoes and household supplies at low prices. One can also bargain. On the 3rd Sunday from 9am - 7 pm the Fierucolina is held here, agricultural produce: local chestnuts made into castagnaccio, olive oil, lambswool vests, fleecelined jackets, bio-dynamic food. Each fair is dedicated to a theme and a saint.

Maremma Antiquaria mercato

Lungomare - **Marina di Grosseto** (GR)   0572478269
9.00-19.00 3rd Sunday of the month

Along the sea front, in summer it remains open till late at night. Small objects, collectables.

Mercato Americano
Piazza XX Settembre/Fortezza Nuova - **Livorno** (LI)
9.00-12.30/15.30-19.30 Every day and 1st Sunday

After the 2nd world war one could find cigarettes and other contraband from the American army base nearby. Today it still is a good source for military clothing, used jeans, vintage Ray Bans, Zippo lighters but mostly one finds fake brandname clothing and handbags.

Mercato Settimanale
Piazza Marconi - **Forte dei Marmi** (LU)
8.00-13.00 Every Wednesday

A general market known for high quality products and the many stands with shoes, pots and pans and ceramics. Look out for embroidered shirts for kids, household linen and cashmere sweaters. The 2nd weekend of every month from May to October an antique fair is held here from 9.00 - 19.30.

Mercato Antiquariato
Piazza San Martino, Via dei Bacchettoni - **Lucca** (LU)   0584 962350
9.00-19.00 3rd Saturday and Sunday

There is something about Lucca that makes a visit to this market unforgettable even though prices for the antiques and bric-a-brac on show are not exactly low.

Mercato dell'Antiquariato
Piazza d'Azeglio - **Viareggio** (LU)   0584 962350
9.00-19.00 4th Saturday and Sunday of the month

Fairly large with an ample choice of furnishing objects for the house and lots of old books and prints to choose from. In Piazza Cavour there is a large daily market from 8.00-20.00.

Mercato dell'Antiquariato
Piazza Cavalieri - **Pisa** (PI)   0584 962350
9.00-19.00 2nd Saturday and Sunday of the month

In the historical center, a fairly varied choice of small furniture, also more modern pieces and silver and jewelry, ceramics, books and prints.

Mercato settimanale
Piazza Duomo - **Pistoia** (PT)   057321622
9.00-13.00 Wednesday and Saturday

A general market in the center of Pistoia where one can find everything except furs, live animals or fabrics by the meter. This is an autentic market, ideal for people watching.

Mercato Settimanale
Piazza Mercato su Viale Galilea - **Prato** (PO)
8.30-12.30 Every Monday

Worth a visit for those in search of inexpensive, fashion accessories, shoes, bijoux, fabrics, silks, flowers and a good place to stock up on inexpensive gifts to take home. Open on monday morning when other shops are closed.

Mercatino delle Quattro Stagioni
Centro città - **Bastia Umbra** (PG)   075 812450
9.00-19.00 2nd Sunday of the month

Between Perugia and Assisi, in a very good position for visitors to Umbria. There is a very large choice of small items like prints, glasses, coins, small furniture.

Antiqcarta

Centro storico - **Città della Pieve** (PG) 075 8409366
9.00-19.00 2nd weekend of the month

This fair is entirely dedicated to collectors of items made of paper, all very specialized: there are geographical maps, postcards, playing cards, calendars, books and prints, paper money etc.

Fiera dell'Antiquariato, dell'Usato e del Collezionismo

Lungo la vecchia Flaminia 0743 521048
Pasignano di Campiello sul Clitunno (PG)
8.00-19.00 Every 1st Sunday of the month

Along the old Flaminia road. There are true bargains to be found early in the morning and prices are reasonable. This is also a good spot to find furniture in need of restoration.

....

Mercato

Corso Mazzini - **Ancona** (AN)
9.00-19.30 Every day

A daily, general market along Corso Mazzini, circa 300 meter from the port of Ancona and the ferry for Greece. Excellent market to stock up on shoes from the nearby Marche region, either showroom models, end of series and remainders at low prices. Mink coats (used) can be found for a pittance!

Mercato dell' Antiquariato e Collezionismo

Chiostra Maggiore - **Ascoli Piceno** (AP) 0735 592237
9.00-19.00 3rd Saturday 13.00-19.00 and Sunday

Circa 70 exhibitors of furniture and small collectables in the splendid cloister of the San Francesco church.

Mostra Mercato dell'Antiquariato e Artigianato

Piazza del Popolo - **Fermo** (AP) 0734 284282
17.00-24.00 Only Thursday in July & August

An evening market selling small bric-a-brac, various knickknacks and a lot of local products like wine, honey and olives.

Mercato dell'Antiquariato

Piazza Maruzzi - **Tolentino** (MC) 0733 972937
9.00-19.00 4th Saturday and Sunday

Inside the Sala San Giacomo are the stands with serious antiques, furniture, wall hangings, silver candle holders. Outside are the usual stalls with small bric-a-brac.

Fiera Mercato dell'Antiquariato

Nelle vie del centro - **Fano** (PU) 0721 8871
8.00-19.00 2nd Saturday and Sunday

In the center of Fano. The market has been divided in two areas, inside the church all the paintings, furniture and other precious objects and outside in the streets of Fano small knickknacks and collectables.

XXV Mostra Mercato Naz. di Antiquariato

Centro storico - **Pennabilli** (PU) 0541 928578
Phone for the right dates

This is one of the more important antique fairs in Italy showing both rare and unusual furniture, silver, jewelry and paintings and smaller bric-a-brac at lower prices.

Sulle orme del passato

Centro storico - **Albano Laziale** (RM)   06 9323162
9.00-19.00 2nd Sunday of the month

Near the Terme di Cellomaio. Antiques, general knickknacks, collectables like playing cards and old records, paintings, prints and crystal glasses, a bit of everything.

Mercato di Antiquariato, Rigatteria, Modernariato

Nel borgo medioevale - **Bracciano** (RM)   06-9043374
9.00-19.00 2nd Sunday of the month

A very old market in a medieval city, well-known and very valid to find not only bric-a-brac or small antiques but also products by local artisans.

CAR

Via Tenuta del Cavaliere, 1 - **Guidonia Montecello** (RM)   0733 972937
8.00-12.00 Only Saturday morning

East of Rome, just off the A24 Roma- L'Aquila autostrada but well before the tollgate. Three tunnel shaped halls, two with fruit and vegetables and one only fish plus a cash and carry hall with prepackaged food. Only open on Saturday morning to the public. Good place to buy organic food. Enormous choice, set up in line with EU criteria.

Mercato

Via Pepe - **Roma** (RM)   06 36004399
9.00-14.00 Every day, closed Sunday

One shops here for food, especially exotic herbs and spices like cilantro or various currys, Thai rice, cured meats. Shopping stands run paralell to all four sides of this oversized square. Though basically a food market one can find some bargain priced shoes and sweaters. From Via Napoleone III to Via Principe Eugenio vegetables, fruit, eggs and kosher/islamic butchers, the northeast corner is crammed with fishmongers, cheese and cured meats and the southwest side has less interesting clothing stalls.

Mercato Porta Portese

P.za I. Nievo, Via Portuense/Bargoni/Bezzi - **Roma** (RM)   06 58233114
8.00-14.00 Every Sunday

In Trastevere. One of Rome's Sunday morning highlights, the mercato Porta Portese is as much about people watching as about bargaining. Antiques, stalls with new, not so new and old carpets, prints, posters and paintings of uncertain vintage, Russian corner. Fascinating and very busy (with pickpockets).

Mercato Rionale

Via Sannio - **Roma** (RM)   06 36004399
9.00-13.00 Every day, Saturday 9.00-18.00

Metro A, San Giovanni. What fun this market is! Stand no.107, Massimo, sells handbags in perfect quality and style, also made to order. No.193, Betto, sells some furs (rabbit?), also look for stand no. 177, secondhand clothes from boiled wool jackets to used jeans.

Mercantico d'Abruzzo

Corso Marrucino - **Chieti** (CH)   085 7672513
9.00-19.00 4th Sunday of the month

Every kind of antique or bric-a-brac can be found, paintings and old prints, china and maiolica, table silver, old books, small furniture.

Il Trovarobe mercato

Porta Turistico - **Marina di Pescara** (PE)   06 9061288
Phone first

Near the tourist port of Marina di Pescara. Old and vintage cars and vintage race cars, carriages, calèches, cabriolet for sale but also for rent.

Mercatino di San Lorenzello

Centro storico del paese - **San Lorenzello** (BN)   0824 815134
9.00-19.00 Every last Saturday and Sunday

In the historical center. Small knickknacks, collectables like records and stamps, decorating objects, ceramics and minor furniture.

Mercato dell'usato

Via Pugliano - **Ercolano** (NA)   0824 815134
8.00-13.00 Every morning

A classical flea market, piles of used jeans and shirts, T-shirts and old sweaters, belts and military clothing at very low prices.

Fiera Antiquaria Napoletana

Viale Dorhn - **Napoli** (NA)   081 7612541
9.00-14.00 3rd Saturday and Sunday

Between Chiaia and Mergellina in the Villa Comunale. Very varied offer of bachelite telephones, old books, crystal chandeliers, church candlesticks, statues of plaster saints and pastoral scenes in oil. Also a fair offer of modern antiques from the 50's. There is a small bric-a-brac market on Friday in Via Santa Lucia and every Sunday at the Terme di Agnano.

Mercato settimanale Posillipo

Parco Virgiliano - **Napoli** (NA)
8.30-13.00 Thursday morning

Follow the Via Posillipo till the end to the Virgiliano park. A general market selling quantities of fake brandname clothing, silk shirts € 15,00-€ 20.00, suits and tailleurs, kid's clothing, household items, even fake perfumes by Crizia, Armeni and Versaci.

Mostra Mercato di Antiquariato e Modernariato

Piazza Libertini - **Lecce** (LE)   0832 308510
9.00-19.00 Last Sunday of the month

A mixture of old and nearly new, antiques and modern 50's furniture. Small collectables like comic books, playing cards and coins.

Mercatino dell' Antiquariato

Piazza Centrale - **Martina Franca** (TA)
9.00-13.00 Every 3rd Sunday

In the main square. Martina Franca is known for it's baroque center in a style known as 'barocco leccese'. Apart from the usual antiques and knickknacks there are lace-workers selling lace trimmed handkerchiefs and ribbons.

Mercatino dell'Antiquariato

Piazza Carlo Alberto - **Cagliari** (CA)   070 668815
18.00-24.00 2nd Sunday of the month

Every second Sunday except in July and August an antique market is held in Piazza Carlo Alberto, every Sunday a bric-a-brac market is organized in the Bastione di San Remy.

Amarcord

Via Mombasiglio, 59 - **Torino** (TO) 011 350657
14.00-19.00 Sat. 9.00-12.30

Bus 58, Via Gorizia or Bus 55 Via Tripoli. Their opening hours are rather flexible, better to phone first. At number 59 there is a small shop selling byoux, china and crystal from the Art Nouveau, Art Deco and 50's period. At number 61 a rather dusty warehouse sells odd pieces of china, sculptures and rather precious vintage evening bags from 1880 to 1950.

Arsenico & Breakfast

Via Gaudenzio Ferrari, 12/c - **Torino** (TO) 011 8172855
9.30-12.30/15.30-19.30 Sunday phone first

In the center, near Palazzo Nuovo and the Mole Antonelliana. Tram 16, 68, 13, 15, and 56. Vintage fashions from the USA & UK, leather, jeans, surplus military or street style with brand-names like Converse, Levi's, Miss Sixty, Freesoul, Alpha Industry, Dr. Martens. Large collection of classical pieces, smoking, cashmere knitwear, crocodile handbags at reasonable prices. They have clients of every age group and speak English and French.

Lo Zio d'America

Via Palazzo di Città, 14 - **Torino** (TO) 011 4361423
11.00-13.00/15.30-19.30

Close to Piazza Castello, trams 4, 12, 15, buses 57,58,63,68. Mostly 50's/60's clothes, bell-bottomed Levis, velvet jackets in Beatles style, gilets, leather jackets € 80,00. Small devoted clientele, friendly atmosphere, for the under 25. Small selection of original platform shoes and Clark's winkle-pickers straight from the 60's!

Nuovodinuovo

Via Guastalla, 6 - **Torino** (TO) 011 883606
10.00-13.00/15.00-19.30 Sat. 15.00-19.30

Near the University of Turin, between Corso San Maurizio and Corso Regina Margherita. This is quite an interesting address for those who manage to dress with flair in vintage and secondhand clothing. One pays per kilo, shirts, blouses and dresses € 35,00, Levi's and other jeans € 12,00, jackets and coats € 8,00, trousers € 25,00 per kilo. One can try everything on and new stock arrives every week.

Le Particolarità

Via Don Lorenzo Giordano, 23/27 - **Torino** (TO) 011 9214225
15.30-19.30 Closed Monday, Fri. & Sat. also 9.30-12.30

Autostrada A4, exit Brandizzo towards Leini-Caselle and Cirié or the Torino Tangenziale/ringroad to the Caselle airport and Cirié. A fascinating spot for collectors of military memorabilia. Military great coat € 15,00, bathrobes in basket-weave € 6,00, unused gasmasks anno 1938 € 18,00, moss green T-shirts. Also medals, buttons, pins, ribbons, trekking boots. They speak French.

Carnaby's

Via Pier della Francesca - **Milano** (MI) 02 33602092
9.00-12.30/15.00-19.30

Across from civic no. 40. Military surplus from the USA and Germany, piles of khaki shirts, dust coloured sweatshirts, cargo pants, bomber jackets in black leather. Reasonable prices, T-shirts € 4,50, leather trench coats € 30,00, cargo's € 15,00.

Cavalli e Nastri

Via Arena, 1 - **Milano** (MI)　　　　　　　　　02 89409452
10.30-19.30 Monday 15.30-19.30

In the center, Autobus 96, 97, on the corner of Via de Amicis. Ladylike dresses from the thirties to the seventies by french designers like Cardin, Courrèges, Chanel. Evening dresses € 90,00 and up, spectacles, scarves, hats, bijoux from the thirties € 22,50, tea & coffee sets, cutlery with bone handles, brushes, watches, buttons, hairpins, prints, boxes, shoes, remnants, tableclothes. There is another shop in Via Brera, 2.

Crazy Art

Via Lambrate, 14 (interno) - **Milano** (MI)　　　　02 2847003
9.00-12.300/15.00-19.30

Bus 55,62. Butcherblock tables, duck decoys, marble garden ornaments, ancient leather golf bags with wooden clubs plus a delightful kitsch department on the first floor. Fun to browse, their whole inventory is either for sale or for rent.

Franco Jacassi

Via Sacchi, 3 - **Milano** (MI)　　　　　　　　02 86462076
By appointment only

MM1 - Cairoli, MM2 Lanza. After collecting all the famous Italian 'sarte' or couturiers of the fifties and sixties like Biki, Sorelle Fontana, Gattinoni and the jackets and coats by Armani from the late seventies, Franco Jacassi now sells to museums and by auction. Also handbags by Roberto di Camerino, Gucci, etc. all in splendid condition as are the prices.

L'Officina delle fate

Piazza San Erasmo, 5 interno - **Milano** (MI)　　02 29060969
10.30-19.00 Closed Monday

MM3 Montenapoleone, tram 1,2. Evening clothes from the 40's to the 70's, and wedding gowns from € 50,00 up to € 1.000.00. Lots of accessories, cocktail hats, vintage shoes, byoux. Large asssortment of bridal accessories.

Mulino Docks Dora

Via Toffetti, 9 - **Milano** (MI)　　　　　　　02 56810393
10.30-19.30 Sunday 14.00-19.30

MM3 Rogoredo exit, Bus 95,84. By car from Corso Lodi take Via Marochetti to Piazza Mistral. Via Toffetti is the first on the left. Docks Dora is on the left corner of Via Boncompagni. Parking. Housed in an old mill, most of their merchandise comes from the Netherlands or the U.S. Jeans € 10,00, leather jackets € 25,00, hats, some in fur € 2,50, crimplene dresses straight from the sixties, T-shirts by OshKosh. In all 500mq of clothing to invent a new look. Corner with household linens sold per kilo at € 10,00. It's all fun.

Napoleone

Via degli Arcimboldi, 5 - **Milano** (MI)　　　　02 875223
10.00-13.00/15.30-19.00

From MM1 Duomo to Via Torino, 2nd street to the right, first left. Busy with young girls looking for American skirts and dresses from the 60's and 70's, all priced at € 19,00, or € 5,00 for the blouses and M. shirts. Also lots of (German) jeans, all cheap and cheerful, loads of clothes crammed into a very small shop, not bad at all.

Perché No/Cento Borse

Via Paris Bordone 11 - **Milano** (MI)　　　　　02 48005725
10.30-18.30 Only Mon., Wed. and Friday. Sat. 10.30-13.00

MM1 Amendola exit, towards Piazzale Brescia. No. 11 is behind the gate in a private street. Entrance in the court-yard on the right. Perché No was one of the very first in Milan to sell secondhand and vintage clothing. Large choice of dresses, tailleurs, cashmere sweaters and shoes, also household linens. The right address to rent or buy vintage handbags by Chanel, Gucci or Hermes.

Shabby Chic
Via B. Cellini, 21 - **Milano** (MI)   02 76018149
10.30-19.30 Monday 15.00-19.30

Tram 9,23,30. Near Viale Premuda, in front of Via Lincoln. A small shop, very neat, offering a savvy mixture of 60's and 70s American/Austrian/English styles, Harris tweed, Burberry's, kilts. Summer dresses, spotlessly ironed € 40,00 and up, sweaters € 15,00, polo Lacoste € 17,50, Tyrolean jackets with matching linen skirts € 60,00, leather bombers € 60,00. Mostly small sizes. They speak English and French and keep their clients informed of new arrivals by email.

Un te con le amiche
Via Visconti di Modrone, 33 - **Milano** (MI)   02 77331506
10.00-12.30/15.00-18.00 Saturday phone first

MM1, San Babila. A mixture of used, vintage, end of series, showroom samples, handbags, clothing, shoes by, Versace, Blumarine, Max Mara , Gucci, Etro, Furla, Fendi, Chanel etc. All sizes but more choice in 42/44. Also Hermès Kelly bags. They even offer a cup of tea!

Vintagespirit Multistore
Piazza Generale Cantore, 3 - **Milano** (MI)   02 8373814
10.00-13.00/15.30-19.30 Sabato 10.00-19.00

MM2, Porta Genova. This is the first multi-store of vintage clothing in Milan with 6 different shops: Elizabeth the First, etnic clothing. Miss Ghintig, Sartoria Italiana. A.N.G.E.L.O. with brandnames like Pucci, Y.St.L, Missoni, Ungaro, Pierre Cardin. Elite Vintage with pieces from the Pescetti store Genova, Letty & John, american byoux. Voss & Kompani, byoux from Scandinavia.

Il Bottegone
Via Petrarca, 2 - **Giussago** (PV)   0382 927244
9.00-12.00/14.00-19.00 Sun. 14.00-19.00 Monday closed

From Milan take the S.S. 35 dei Giovi, from Binasco turn left to Giussago, then turn right past the village in the direction of Certosa. A farmyard holding veritable treasures: old doors, beams, ladders, balconies in cast iron, ornamental gates and entrance doors, window shutters, stone balustrades. Inside rustic furniture, cupboards, side-boards, kitchen sinks. All to be restaurated. It's impossible not to find something interesting especially since their prices are very reasonable.

Ex New
Corso Torino, 97/99r - **Genova** (GE)   0382 927244
10.00-12.30/15.30-19.30

Autostrada A7, exit Genova Ovest towards the Fiera del Mare. Or take Bus 20,30,42 in Genova. They only sell vintage or 'gently worn' labels, mostly in small sizes, 42, 44 for W. Possible to find a snazzy mini dress at € 17,50 or Alta Moda tailleurs € 300,00. For men there are always some very elegant suits for sale sometimes brand new. Multi-lingual sales girls.

Maria Cristina Marotta
Corso Isonzo, 14 - **Ferrara** (FE)   3389895529
Phone first

Only clothing from the USA, little dresses by Cassini and Halston from the Jacky Kennedy era. Sigra. Marotta has a stand at the Montagnola market in Bologna every Friday and Saturday.

Senza Tempo
Via Fornace, 18 - **Fusignano** (RA)   0545 52800
10.00-13.00/15.30-19.30 Closed Thu. afternoon

Autostrada A14dir. exit Lugo Cotignola to Fusignano. Take the road to Alfonsine to the left before the center of Fusignano. A corner shop with vintage, old and not so old Burberry and Acquascutum raincoats € 75,00-€ 100,00, fringed suede jackets, poncho's of the 70's, nylon blouses from the 60's and USA skirts and Hawai shirts, polo's and bermudas. Prices are low.

A.N.G.E.L.O.

Corso Garibaldi, 59 - **Lugo** (RA)   0545 35200
10.30-19.30 Monday 15.00 - 19.30

Autostrada A24, exit Lugo Cottignola. Go to Lugo center and park in Piazza Garibaldi. Very well known selling point of vintage and second hand clothing. Possible to find unique dresses by Dior, Chanel, Gucci, Jacques Fath and Schiaperelli but also the more mundane every day wear of the fifties and sixties like nylon shirts with ruches or Brigitte Bardot Capri pants. They rent to cinema, theater, tv and disco. Fun place to visit for a dose of dejà-vu. They have a shop in the Vintage Palace in Milan.

D.A. Dress Agency

Via del Vantaggio, 1/b - **Roma** (RM)   06 3210898
10.30-12.00/16.30-19.00 Monday 16.00 - 19.30

Near the P.zza del Popolo. Parking Lungotevere. Luxurious and elegant clothing, maybe gently worn a couple of times before being taken to the Dress Agency to make room. One can find capacious handbags by Ferragamo at € 100,00, fashionable dresses by Prada or D&G at € 130,00, sunglasses by Chanel € 70,00, shoes by Ungaro € 55,00, sandals by Sergio Rossi and lots of trendy accessories to create an instantly updated deluxe look. There is another shop in Via Piana, 5.

Le Cugine

Via dei Vascellari, 19 - **Roma** (RM)   06 5894844
10.00-19.30

In the Trastevere area. A bric-a-brac store specializing in secondhand objects culled from the houses of Rome. It's a cheerful hodgepodge of 19th century birdcages, grandma's cups and saucers, dressers and lace handkerchiefs.

Omero & Cecilia

Via del Governo Vecchio, 110 - **Roma** (RM)   06 6833506
10.00-12.00/14.00-19.00 Sat. 10.00-12.00

Near Piazza Navona. Used Amercian jeans next to leather jackets. A black leather coat € 70,00, mini skirts and pants in leather € 40,00, suede jackets € 50,00. Lots of choice and all sizes, even some Burberry trench coats.

Pulp

Via del Boschetto, 140 - **Roma** (RM)   06 485511
10.00-13.00/16.00-19.00 Monday closed

Metro Republica, at the end of Via Nazionale, on the left. Accessories and dresses from Southern Italy, hippy trash from the 60's and 70's and pulp from the 80's. Fantasy print dresses for W € 16.00-€ 22,00, raincoats from the 70's € 40,00, leather and suede jackets from 60's-70's € 50,00. Sandals, bags, byoux. They speak English.

Roba da Matti

Via Massaciuccoli, 45 (Paral. VL.Libia) - **Roma** (RM)   06 86208006
10.00-13.00/16.00-19.30 Clothing, leatherwear

Between Via Nomentana and Via Salaria. Dresses, furs, lingerie sold here by theater and TV show girls or society ladies with overflowing cupboards. Though it has become more difficult it is still possible to find well made handbags and tailleurs for a fraction of their original price.

BRAND NAME INDEX

Photolithography by: Zincograf - Farigliano (CN) - Italy
Printed by: Milanostampa - A.G.G. Farigliano - CN